IMPROVISATIONS: METHODS AND METHODOLOGIES IN LIFESPAN WRITING RESEARCH

PERSPECTIVES ON WRITING
Series Editors: Rich Rice and J. Michael Rifenburg
Consulting Editor: Susan H. McLeod
Associate Editors: Johanna Phelps, Jonathan M. Marine, and Qingyang Sun

The Perspectives on Writing series addresses writing studies in a broad sense. Consistent with the wide ranging approaches characteristic of teaching and scholarship in writing across the curriculum, the series presents works that take divergent perspectives on working as a writer, teaching writing, administering writing programs, and studying writing in its various forms.

The WAC Clearinghouse and University Press of Colorado are collaborating so that these books will be widely available through free digital distribution and low-cost print editions. The publishers and the series editors are committed to the principle that knowledge should freely circulate and have embraced the use of technology to support open access to scholarly work.

Recent Books in the Series

Ashley J. Holmes and Elise Verzosa Hurley (Eds.), *Learning from the Mess: Method/ological Praxis in Rhetoric and Writing Studies* (2024)

Diane Kelly-Riley, Ti Macklin, and Carl Whithaus (Eds.), *Considering Students, Teachers, and Writing Assessment: Volumes 1 and 2* (2024)

Amy Cicchino and Troy Hicks (Eds.), *Better Practices: Exploring the Teaching of Writing in Online and Hybrid Spaces* (2024)

Genesea M. Carter and Aurora Matzke (Eds.), *Systems Shift: Creating and Navigating Change in Rhetoric and Composition Administration* (2023)

Michael J. Michaud, *A Writer Reforms (the Teaching of) Writing: Donald Murray and the Writing Process Movement, 1963–1987* (2023)

Michelle LaFrance and Melissa Nicolas (Eds.), *Institutional Ethnography as Writing Studies Practice* (2023)

Phoebe Jackson and Christopher Weaver (Eds.), *Rethinking Peer Review: Critical Reflections on a Pedagogical Practice* (2023)

Megan J. Kelly, Heather M. Falconer, Caleb L. González, and Jill Dahlman (Eds.), *Adapting the Past to Reimagine Possible Futures: Celebrating and Critiquing WAC at 50* (2023)

William J. Macauley, Jr. et al. (Eds.), *Threshold Conscripts: Rhetoric and Composition Teaching Assistantships* (2023)

Jennifer Grouling, *Adapting VALUEs: Tracing the Life of a Rubric through Institutional Ethnography* (2022)

IMPROVISATIONS: METHODS AND METHODOLOGIES IN LIFESPAN WRITING RESEARCH

Edited by Ryan J. Dippre and Talinn Phillips

The WAC Clearinghouse
wac.colostate.edu
Fort Collins, Colorado

University Press of Colorado
upcolorado.com
Denver, Colorado

The WAC Clearinghouse, Fort Collins, Colorado 80523

University Press of Colorado, Denver, Colorado 80202

© 2024 by Ryan J. Dippre and Talinn Phillips. This work is licensed under a Creative Commons Attribution-NonCommercial-NoDerivatives 4.0 International license.

ISBN 978-1-64215-228-9 (PDF) 978-1-64215-231-9 (ePub) 978-1-64642-685-0 (pbk.)

DOI 10.37514/PER-B.2024.2289

Library of Congress Cataloging-in-Publication Data

Names: Dippre, Ryan J., editor. | Phillips, Talinn, editor.
Title: Improvisations : methods and methodologies in lifespan writing research / edited by Ryan J. Dippre and Talinn Phillips.
Description: Fort Collins, Colorado : The WAC Clearinghouse ; Denver, Colorado : University Press of Colorado, 2024. | Series: Perspectives on writing | Includes bibliographical references.
Identifiers: LCCN 2024025396 (print) | LCCN 2024025397 (ebook) | ISBN 9781646426850 (paperback) | ISBN 9781642152289 (adobe pdf) | ISBN 9781642152319 (epub)
Subjects: LCSH: English language—Rhetoric—Study and teaching—Research—Methodolgy.
Classification: LCC PE1404 .I38 2024 (print) | LCC PE1404 (ebook) | DDC 808.06/692—dc23/eng/20240731
LC record available at https://lccn.loc.gov/2024025396
LC ebook record available at https://lccn.loc.gov/2024025397

Copyeditor: Caitlin Kahihikolo
Designer: Mike Palmquist
Cover Photo: Improvisation No. 30, by Kandinsky. RawPixel Image 3933132. Licensed.
Series Editors: Rich Rice and J. Michael Rifenburg
Consulting Editor: Susan H. McLeod
Associate Editors: Johanna Phelps, Jonathan M. Marine, and Qingyang Sun

The WAC Clearinghouse supports teachers of writing across the disciplines. Hosted by Colorado State University, it brings together scholarly journals and book series as well as resources for teachers who use writing in their courses. This book is available in digital formats for free download at wac.colostate.edu.

Founded in 1965, the University Press of Colorado is a nonprofit cooperative publishing enterprise supported, in part, by Adams State University, Colorado School of Mines, Colorado State University, Fort Lewis College, Metropolitan State University of Denver, University of Alaska Fairbanks, University of Colorado, University of Denver, University of Northern Colorado, University of Wyoming, Utah State University, and Western Colorado University. For more information, visit upcolorado.com.

Citation Information: Dippre, Ryan J. & Talinn Phillips (Eds.). (2024). *Improvisations: Methods and Methodologies in Lifespan Writing Research*. The WAC Clearinghouse; University Press of Colorado. https://doi.org/1010.37514/PER-B.2024.2289

Land Acknowledgment. The Colorado State University Land Acknowledgment can be found at landacknowledgment.colostate.edu.

CONTENTS

Acknowledgments vii

Introduction. Conducting Lifespan Writing Research: Challenges, Opportunities, and the State of a Radical Research Agenda 3
    Talinn Phillips and Ryan J. Dippre

PART 1. RIGOROUS CRAFTING + RADICAL IMPROVISATION: LWR IN ACTION 11

Chapter 1. Temporal Discourse Analysis as an Analytic for Lifespan Writing Research 15
    Catherine Compton-Lilly

Chapter 2. Writing Elementary School: The Cases of Gabby and Adam 29
    Catherine Compton-Lilly

Chapter 3. Methodologies for Lifespan Writing Research: Using Composite Narratives in Narrative Inquiry. 51
    Jennifer Sanders, Sarah Donovan, Joy Myers, and Danielle L. DeFauw

Chapter 4. Using Composite Narratives to Explore Writing Teachers' Development Across Their Careers. 67
    Danielle L. DeFauw, Joy Myers, Sarah Donovan, and Jennifer Sanders

Chapter 5. Interpreting Research with Participants: A Lifespan Writing Methodology 87
    Collie Fulford and Lauren Rosenberg

Chapter 6. Co-interpretation in Action 103
    Lauren Rosenberg, Collie Fulford, Gwen Porter McGowan, and Adrienne Long

Chapter 7. Studying Writing through the Lifespan with Grounded Theory 121
    Ryan J. Dippre

Chapter 8. Deepening and Keeping the Present: Grounded Theory in Action 137
    Ryan J. Dippre

Chapter 9. Improving Systematic Reviews of Longitudinal Writing Research: Definitions, Questions, and Procedures 153
    Teresa Jacques, Jonathan M. Marine, and Paul Rogers

Chapter 10. Implications of Longitudinal Writing Research Methods for Lifespan Perspectives on Writing Development: A Systematic Review 167
    Jonathan M. Marine, Paul Rogers, and Teresa Jacques

PART 2. A SELECTION OF "ANDS": IMAGINING METHODOLOGICAL FUTURES IN LIFESPAN WRITING RESEARCH 191

Chapter 11. An Autoethnographic Springboard to More Extensive Lifespan Writing Research 195
    Kathleen Shine Cain, Pamela B. Childers, and Leigh Ryan

Chapter 12. A Matter of Time and Memory: A Methodological Framework of Memory for Lifespan Writing Research 213
    Joe Cirio and Jeff Naftzinger

Chapter 13. Writing in Transitions across the Lifespan 231
    Soledad Montes and Karin Tusting

Chapter 14. Centering Positionality in Lifespan Writing Research through Institutional and Auto/Ethnographic Methodologies 249
    Erin Workman

Chapter 15. Wayfinding: The Development of an Approach to Lifespan Writing. 271
    Karen Lunsford, Jonathan Alexander, and Carl Whithaus

Chapter 16. How Might We Measure That? Considerations from Quantitative Research Approaches for Lifespan Writing Research. 287
    Matthew Carl Zajic and Apryl Lynn Poch

Chapter 17. Becoming Researcher-Poets: Poetic Inquiry as Method/ology for Writing (through the Lifespan) Research. 305
    Sandra L. Tarabochia

Chapter 18. Approaching Lifespan Writing Research from Indigenous, Decolonial Perspectives 325
    Bhushan Aryal

Chapter 19. Motivating Lifespan Writing Research Toward Education Policy. 339
    Jeremy Levine

Chapter 20. A Graduate School "Drop-Out"—After School 355
    Suellynn Duffey

Chapter 21. Radicality in the Short Term: Generating Structural Change. . 373
    Ryan J. Dippre and Talinn Phillips

Contributors 383

ACKNOWLEDGMENTS

Our deepest thanks to the leaders and participants of the 2023 Summer Seminar in Composition Research at Dartmouth College. We will forever associate this manuscript with Butterfield Hall. Also, thanks to Dr. Sarah Wyatt of Ohio University for setting aside her much more important work of launching plants into space (no, really) so that she could teach us about rhizomes. We also thank the UMaine English MA students in the Spring 2023 offering of English 570 for reading and discussing these chapters.

DEDICATION

To Lindsey and Daniel for their patience and support.

IMPROVISATIONS: METHODS AND METHODOLOGIES IN LIFESPAN WRITING RESEARCH

INTRODUCTION.
CONDUCTING LIFESPAN WRITING RESEARCH: CHALLENGES, OPPORTUNITIES, AND THE STATE OF A RADICAL RESEARCH AGENDA

Talinn Phillips
Ohio University

Ryan J. Dippre
University of Maine

While studies of writers over significant periods of time have long been of interest to researchers in writing studies, literacy, and education, thinking about writing as something happening throughout the entirety of a lifespan has been a recent, emerging research agenda. As Charles Bazerman has said in various venues, there is an "intuitive obviousness" to lifespan writing research (LWR) in that we recognize that people write in all kinds of contexts and ways which change over the course of one's life. Yet this obviousness also has distinct limits, some of which are tied to markers such as race, socioeconomic class, gender, age, and cultural context before we even consider the complications of work, hobbies, education, etc. We may all effectively be writers now, but we're hardly writing in all the same places, in the same ways, with the same tools, or for the same reasons. A fuller, more accurate picture of the ways in which writing and lives intersect potentially has profound implications for how societies create public education curricula, for how institutions and employers prepare people for new writing tasks, for how communities engage people in writing for their own and the public good, and perhaps, most profoundly, for how ordinary people understand themselves as writers. This diversity of both writing and life necessitates multiple ways of studying the writing people do as we move deeper into the 21st century.

In 2016, responding to Bazerman's call to look toward the entirety of the lifespan at the Dartmouth Summer Seminar in Composition Research, we began the *Writing through the Lifespan Collaboration*, an international assembly of writing, literacy, and education researchers interested in exploring what writing looks like from the cradle to the grave. In 2019, the Collaboration defined lifespan writing research as something that "examines acts of inscribed meaning-making, the products of it, and the multiple dimensions of human activity that relate to it in order to build accounts of whether and how writers and writing change throughout the duration and breadth of the lifespan" (Dippre & Phillips, 2020). This definition served as a focal point for our first edited collection, *Approaches to Lifespan Writing Research: Generating an Actionable Coherence* (Dippre & Phillips, 2020).

Since the conceptualization, development, and publication of *Approaches to Lifespan Writing Research* (Dippre & Phillips, 2020), a lot has changed, not the least of which has been a multi-year global pandemic. Throughout it, however, the work of studying writing through the lifespan has carried on, though not unchanged or unfazed. The Collaboration held two online conferences in 2020 and 2021, and the WAC Clearinghouse now has a dedicated book series, Lifespan Writing Research (https://wac.colostate.edu/books/lwr/).

We hope that this current volume will move the field forward in response to the needs that lifespan writing researchers have identified in recent years but also encourage—both in the methodologies shared in this book and the broader message we hope to convey in our editorial work—the continuation of an expansive, welcoming vision and implementation for studying writing through the lifespan. At this point in the trajectory of LWR, a sustained discussion of methodological approaches is one of the most powerful ways to expand that vision.

For while LWR has grown rapidly in the last ten years, we are also the first to acknowledge that this growth has not been what anyone would call "regular" or in many cases even "planned." There are too many people involved with too many constraints and aims for any rigid planning. We believe that creating room for all comers is essential to tackling something as ambitious and complex as LWR. Creating space also comes with some costs, though, including research that may appear rather diffuse in some key areas but extremely dense in others. The metaphor we find most apt for LWR's recent growth is *rhizomatic*. Soledad Montes and Karin Tusting's chapter in this volume brought this metaphor to our attention as a means of understanding transition. We find it to be similarly powerful for LWR. Though perhaps some research agendas are more like trees—a thick trunk of linear research with some related areas branching off—LWR is like a rhizome, spreading mostly underground and popping up in unexpected places.

Unlike a tree with one primary root burrowing deep into the soil, rhizomatic plants like irises have underground, horizontal stems with a shallow root system and nodes that are always shooting off in new directions to grow more plants. In consequence, there may not be a lot of visible rhyme or reason to where the next plant pops up. Is there space (instead of a wall or large rock)? Is there fertile soil? Then a node may grow in that direction, developing a new plant even in unexpected locations.

The growth of LWR has been similar, occurring where the researchers and nutrients are and where growth can occur unrestricted. The shape of LWR today is simply a reflection of who has been interested in LWR so far; today's shape doesn't prescribe its shape tomorrow or in a few years when the "soil" may change, or obstacles may be removed that allow new researchers and new directions to flourish.

This book is thus our effort to remove some obstacles to new researchers joining the work. We've made our central object of analysis and discussion in this text *methodologies*: the disciplined ways in which we engage with inquiry and how talented researchers improvise methodologies over time in order to account for writing through the lifespan. In this book, we'll talk about *methods*—that is, the particular tools that people use to collect and analyze records—but in the context of the logic of inquiry, or *methodologies*, that those tools are used with/in. *How shall we best study lifespan writing research? How must methodologies be adapted to account for lifespans of writing? How do we engage in rigorous methodological improvisation as projects, participants, and data possibilities change over time?* These are the essential questions that these chapters pursue.

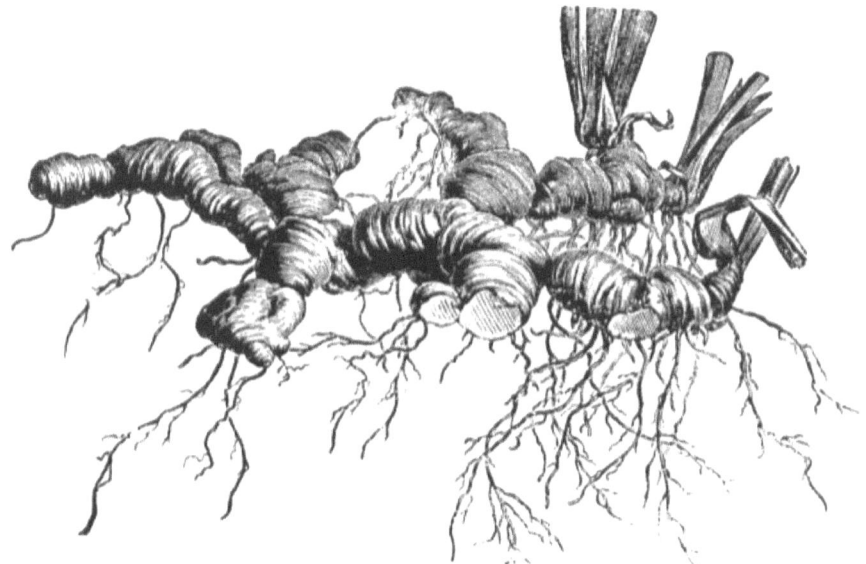

Figure 1. An illustration of an iris rhizome, showing horizontal growth.

In this volume, we attempt to carry the conversation we began in *Approaches to Lifespan Writing Research* further by not only examining methodologies for LWR, but also clarifying the details needed about those methodologies for future investigation, revision, and (we hope) multidisciplinary work on writing through the lifespan. We aim to show here that writing through the lifespan is, at its heart, a multidisciplinary, multimethodological endeavor, requiring all manner of approaches to studying writing, all of which must be highly adaptable as projects evolve over time.

This single volume, of course, cannot capture the incredible variety of approaches that LWR can and will take. While methodologies like the case study are well developed for LWR, others like ethnography or corpus analysis haven't taken off yet—not because they shouldn't but because the right researchers haven't been able to join the work yet. We hope that this volume will serve as a methodological introduction to a collection of LWR approaches that might remove obstacles for some novice researchers and create fertile ground for additional approaches that carry the conversation forward.

THE NEED TO EXPLORE METHODOLOGIES IN LWR

To say that we need to discuss methodologies is not all that radical of a claim. Over the past two decades, there have been both calls (Haswell, 2005) and attempts (Bazerman & Prior, 2004; Nickoson & Sheridan, 2012; Powell & Takayoshi, 2012) to talk methodologies in ways that are specific to writing research: the philosophical underpinnings, the particular methods, the ethics involved, and so on. Within Composition Studies at least, researchers learned early that they would need to chart their own paths in order to account for the complexity of writing as a research object. The field borrows freely from other disciplinary/methodological traditions, but rarely does so wholesale. Thus, as composition specialists who now simultaneously work in the wider field of writing studies, methodological innovation and improvisation is a comfortable space for the two of us. Yet to research lifespans and to do so in multiple cultural and national settings makes the subject of methodologies considerably more complex. Nevertheless, we argue that *methodological dialogue is at the very core of LWR because mutual methodological understanding and collaboration is essential to our radical aims* (Dippre & Phillips, 2023). We simply can't talk LWR without talking methodologies. And as a research agenda that is both emergent and radical, LWR needs to talk methodologies in the kinds of detailed, pragmatic ways that interested researchers can then take up and adapt. This volume is designed to offer researchers just that. However, we are not encouraging researchers to check their critical eye at the door: rather, we aim to present, in these pages, not just how we might *conduct* LWR in a particular way, but *why* we might do such a thing, what particular methodologies afford, what we take on when we work with certain methodologies, and how we might challenge the assumptions of some of these methodologies.

LWR is—and fundamentally has to be—a multidisciplinary endeavor: we need every tool that we can get our hands on if we want to understand how people engage in writing throughout their lives. To do this multidisciplinary work, it is certainly helpful to be aligned at the level of *method*. An ethnographer and a grounded theorist, for instance, might make useful sense of interviews, and therefore be able to pool resources, time, and attention. Such alignment can be helpful particularly now, when we have to do more with less time and money. However, we argue that such alignment is only one of many ways in which we need to bring multiple disciplines together to study writing through the lifespan. We need more than just shared transcripts, surveys, etc.: we need critical and frequent discussions about not just methods, but the broader logics of inquiry that shape our methods—the epistemological underpinnings, the realities of methods meeting materials, the ways in which we shape records into data and craft analyses from that data, and more.

Not only multidisciplinary and multimethodological, LWR is also inherently improvisational. Studying such diverse groups of people over long spans of time prevents "the method" from staying "the method" in some static sense. Instead, lifespan writing researchers evolve, adapt, and improvise their methods to meet their participants and situations as a matter of course. Ultimately, the authors of this collection create a collective argument that radical, rigorous improvisation is at the core of LWR. While improvisation sometimes connotes "slapdash" or lack of preparedness, true improvisation is a specialized ability that people develop over time with intensive practice. And so, we use that term *improvisation* in its most powerful sense—an intentional, deep engagement with openness and possibility and leveraging the available resources for the most powerful outcomes.

At the heart of improvisation is the idea of "yes, and . . . "—a commitment to taking anything that comes at you and forging it into something new and better. Improvisation requires quick thinking, embracing of a challenge, and continuous, successful, productive adaptation to one's situation. While improvisation artists always have agency in their situations, they are also clearly in contexts that they cannot fully control. Research improvisationists are thus not unprepared, inept researchers who didn't plan projects properly; they improvise because they recognize that *there are limits to the power of planning*. In LWR, those limits may include the complete collapse of a project if a researcher refuses to change course. Thus, the fact that lifespan writing researchers are pursuing a radical research agenda (Dippre & Phillips, 2023) places us in a context in which it's frequently essential to modify methods and plans. Lifespan writing researchers are (and are becoming) talented improvisation artists who skillfully use their expertise to adapt to new research situations. It's this becoming—this improvisation—that this collection ultimately explores and advocates.

Overview: Setting a Stage

We've developed this book with two main audiences in mind: experienced researchers who seek to develop more robust, "lifespan-ized" research projects as well as novice researchers who are just learning about research methodologies and who also have an interest in writing through the lifespan.

Part I, "Rigorous Crafting + Radical Improvisations: LWR Methods in Action," includes five pairs of chapters from authors whose first chapters offer a detailed overview of a particular methodological tradition—its history, essential features—with an emphasis on what this methodology affords lifespan writing researchers. That's the "rigorous crafting"—the how-to of developing a powerful project within a particular methodological tradition.

Then in the following chapter, each of those same researchers put those methodologies into action and share cutting-edge LWR projects. They pull back the curtain, show how the sausage gets made, or any other metaphor you like for the hot-mess reality of writing research in action. Our authors reveal what happened when their methods collided with actual writers and how clearly delineated methods were upended as writers, contexts, and writing changed over time. These collisions caused course corrections and, in many cases, exciting methodological improvisations that can now be employed to research lifespan writing more effectively. Thus, Part I of this volume provides clear, generative starting points for taking up *some* methodologies in LWR.

We'll note here that the methodologies in Part I are first and foremost those for which established lifespan writing researchers were willing to write a paired set of chapters. We don't see these methodologies as "the best" or even "better" than other possibilities for LWR. Part I certainly does include some well-known and wide-reaching methods—discourse analysis, grounded theory, narrative analysis—but is by no means exhaustive. More than just a convenience sample, though, the chapters in Part I offer a range of methodologies from different disciplines and with different aims highlighting the breadth of knowledge needed to study the whole of the lifespan. We introduce individual chapters in the Part I introduction.

In Part II, "A Selection of 'Ands': Imagining Methodological Futures in Lifespan Writing Research," our authors take a much wider view, identifying important considerations in methodological design and examining a range of methodological possibilities. The final chapters consider more carefully the social and policy implications of not just our research, but these very methods we employ. For as lifespan writing researchers, we are rapidly approaching a point where we can no longer wait: although we have much to learn about writing through the lifespan, we also have much to offer *now* to make writing and literacy education more inclusive and accessible, and it's time we start saying so.

Improvisations is, at best, a rough and approximate starting point for the next decade of lifespan writing research. We could not adequately capture, nor richly detail, the many and varied possibilities of lifespan writing research that exist. It is our hope that the chapters of this text provide readers with helpful, detailed starting points for their own journeys along the difficult and messy road of studying writing through the lifespan. But, furthermore, we hope that they encourage the kinds of rigorous, radical improvisations of the methods discussed throughout as detailed research plans give way to the rich, exciting, and unexpected lived experiences of studying writing throughout the lifespan.

REFERENCES

Bazerman, C. & Prior, P. (Eds.). (2004). *What writing does and how it does it: An introduction to analyzing texts and textual practices*. Routledge.

Bazerman, C., Applebee, A. N., Berninger, V. W., Brandt, D., Graham, S., Jeffery, J., Matsuda, P. K., Murphy, S., Rowe, D. W., Schleppegrell, M. & Wilcox, K. C. (2018). *The lifespan development of writing*. National Council of Teachers of English. https://wac.colostate.edu/books/ncte/lifespan-writing/.

Dippre, R. J. & Phillips, T. (Eds.). (2020). *Approaches to lifespan writing research: Generating an actionable coherence*. The WAC Clearinghouse; University Press of Colorado. https://doi.org/10.37514/PER-B.2020.1053.

Dippre, R. J. & Phillips, T. (2023). Radically longitudinal, radically contextual: The lifespan as a focus for longitudinal writing research. In A. K. Hea & J. Fishman (Eds.), *Telling stories: Perspectives on longitudinal writing research* (pp. 151–189). Utah State University Press.

Haswell, R. H. (2005). NCTE/CCCC's recent war on scholarship. *Written Communication*, 22(2), 198–223. https://doi.org/10.1177/0741088305275757.

Nickoson, L. & Sheridan, M. P. (2012). *Writing studies research in practice: Methods and methodologies*. Southern Illinois University Press.

Powell, K. M. & Takayoshi, P. (Eds.). (2012). *Practicing research in writing studies: Reflexive and ethically responsible research*. Hampton Press.

PART 1.

RIGOROUS CRAFTING + RADICAL IMPROVISATION: LWR IN ACTION

The authors in Part I first introduce us to a methodology that they've found useful for conducting their own LWR. In some cases, authors are introducing a well-known methodology to readers and describing what it offers to LWR in particular. In other cases, authors describe a new methodology that they've developed specifically to support lifespan writing research, along with that methodology's historic roots.

As established researchers who have been using the methodologies described here for years (and sometimes decades), these authors provide valuable methodological introductions that are solidly grounded in real-world research experience. Our intention is that by homing in on the affordances of methodologies for lifespan writing research, those who are unfamiliar with a particular methodological tool might use these chapters as primers as they plan their own research. Each author provides an overview of the methodology along with its origins (disciplinary, historical, etc.) and key turning points, making visible how the methodology can support lifespan writing research by offering examples from their own work.

These chapters also take us straight to the heart of improvisation as a lens for understanding lifespan writing research. Though they begin in recognizable strands of well-known methodologies, these authors also make clear the necessity of improvising new approaches in order to meet the moment of their particular projects. For no research plan survives first contact with reality. Not completely. Not all the way. Whenever we plan out a course of action in research, we find ourselves faced with the unexpected, the unanticipated, and we need to engage with these pleasant (or unpleasant, as the case may be) surprises in ways that allow our methodologies to move forward. Much of this complex intersection between plans and reality cannot be captured by merely a description of a methodology: one must see the methodology in action, as much as possible, to make sense of the continuous, deeply disciplined improvisations that bring a methodology to life. Toward that end, our authors each offer a companion or "application" chapter which brings the methodology to life. These companion chapters engage with research sites, participants, existing research, etc. to demonstrate the rich realities of their approaches to studying writing through the lifespan.

We begin in elementary school settings, moving through the lifespan to methodologies featuring older adults' writing. In Chapter 1, "Temporal

Discourse Analysis as an Analytic for Lifespan Writing Research," Catherine Compton-Lilly opens this section by introducing us to temporal discourse analysis (TDA), an analytical tool she developed to work in tandem with a range of research methodologies. TDA investigates change across time by examining participants' language choices and sense-making moments. Her chapter also highlights the improvisational work that infuses the methods and methodologies of this volume, noting that TDA is a tool she developed because, after years of data collection, she felt that her existing method was missing things. She developed TDA in order to analyze the relationships between her early and later data more rigorously and shares it with us here, using the cases of Adam and Gabby to illustrate TDA's uses. In her companion chapter, "Writing Elementary School: The Cases of Gabby and Adam," Compton-Lilly shows how TDA is able to "reveal the unique sense-making" that Gabby and Adam engaged in with schooling and literacy over the course of five years. By looking closely at the ongoing negotiations of activities, images, and texts over time, Compton-Lilly demonstrates how temporal discourse analysis can effectively trace the complex contours of children's acts of literacy over time.

Jennifer Sanders, Sarah Donovan, Joy Myers, and Danielle DeFauw then share in Chapter 3, "Methodologies for Lifespan Writing Research: Using Composite Narratives in Narrative Inquiry," how one of the latest innovations in narrative inquiry, composite narratives, can help lifespan writing researchers to synthesize the experiences of substantial numbers of participants in ways that are powerful to both researcher and participant. Describing its roots in narrative inquiry, Sanders et al. argue that composite narratives can help researchers identify patterns across larger participant pools without sacrificing the complexity and richness of qualitative methodologies. Composites also offer a way to share research findings in meaningful ways with audiences beyond the academy. In their companion chapter, "Using Composite Narratives to Explore Writing Teachers' Development Across Their Careers," the authors demonstrate the possibilities that composite narratives offer lifespan writing researchers. The authors share four composite narratives in their entirety, shedding important light on the trajectories of growth that teachers have regarding writing pedagogy throughout their careers which then also impact their students' writing experiences.

In Chapter 5, "Interpreting Research with Participants: A Lifespan Writing Methodology," Collie Fulford and Lauren Rosenberg describe a methodology of interpreting and writing research along with their adult participants. Drawing on a history of co-investigating and co-authoring within writing studies, they argue that "through acts of revisiting and dwelling with participants, we can center interpretive relationships" in our work. Given the imperative within much lifespan writing research to cultivate long-term relationships with participants,

Fulford and Rosenberg provide an invaluable framework for crafting ethical, productive, meaningful partnerships with the writers we research for and with. In "Co-interpretation in Action," the authors then put their approach to co-interpretation to work as they co-author with ongoing, long-term research participants Gwen Porter McGowan and Adrienne Long. This chapter takes us from the warm, feel-good idea of deepening our relationships to the nuts and bolts of how these two researchers have actually gone about composing together with their participant co-authors. As they put their co-interpreting principles into action, Fulford, Long, Rosenberg, and McGowan offer vital insight into how to move from a researcher-participant relationship towards equality, giving particular attention to the role that race has played in their relationships.

Ryan Dippre, in Chapter 7, "Studying Writing through the Lifespan with Grounded Theory," then introduces us to grounded theory as a methodology for lifespan writing research. Dippre traces grounded theory's roots from sociology, its incorporation into writing studies, and its particular affordances for lifespan writing research. His step-by-step approach to the mechanics of engaging in grounded theory research will be particularly helpful for researchers who are considering or developing a grounded theory project for the first time. In the next chapter, "Deepening and Keeping the Present: Grounded Theory in Action," Dippre explores the lifespan literate action development of Anna. Blending grounded theory with ethnomethodology and sociohistoric theory, Dippre identifies the process of *deepening* and *keeping* the present that Anna engages in through her writing—and, as a result, how that process contributes to her own agency in different aspects of her life.

We conclude with Teresa Jacques, Jonathan Marine, and Paul Rogers' methodology for a meta-analysis of longitudinal writing studies. Chapter 9, "Improving Systematic Reviews of Longitudinal Writing: Definitions, Questions, and Procedures," walks readers through the authors' decision-making process as they seek to understand the methodological choices in the field's longitudinal studies of writers. This chapter provides a rare opportunity to see the complexities of developing a meta-analysis which both the authors and editors hope will encourage more people to undertake these much-needed assessments of the state of writing studies' collective knowledge. Next the authors put their methodology to work on 54 longitudinal studies of writing in K-20 schooling dating back to 2000 in "Implications of Longitudinal Writing Research Methods for Lifespan Perspectives on Writing Development: Results of a Systematic Review." Here, we get to see the broader patterns that emerge when we look across longitudinal studies, rather than just within them.

These chapters create a two-way view of methodologies, offering us not just descriptions of how to study writing through the lifespan, but examples of how these studies can be brought to life. With these companion chapters, we hope that lifespan writing researchers will be encouraged to take up new studies of writers and writing at different points in the lifespan, informed by both the realities of their research settings and the methodological options presented here.

CHAPTER 1.

TEMPORAL DISCOURSE ANALYSIS AS AN ANALYTIC FOR LIFESPAN WRITING RESEARCH

Catherine Compton-Lilly
University of South Carolina

My attraction to Lifespan perspectives is related to the rich, contextualized ways in which readers and writers are positioned, described, and considered across time. I attend to literacy as operating within a "dynamic confluence of literate forms that are always changing in relation to social situations and purposes" (Dippre & Smith, 2020, p. 28). I am attracted to Lifespan perspectives that center learners and their lives. By recognizing the "whole child" (Noddings, 2005) as students move in and out of schools, operating in the present while drawing on past and carrying aspirations for the future, lifespan research centers people.

While this book and this chapter are ostensibly about being and becoming writers, writing is but one of a myriad of practices that produce and continually reproduce society through the "regular, ongoing work of participants from one minute to another" (Dippre & Smith, 2020, p. 29). Unlike retrospective interviews or life narratives, longitudinal research captures experiences in temporal proximity to events. Thus, longitudinal researchers are more likely to encounter the unfolding sense-making of participants. Lifespan researchers present fundamental challenges to linear, developmental models as they resist comparing individuals to established and assumedly universal trajectories of growth which have the potential to misrepresent what people can do and what they know. As Bazerman and his colleagues reported (2018), idealized norms can "mask, mischaracterize, or punish human variation" (p. 6). Lifespan writing researchers focus on unique, idiosyncratic and contextualized being and becoming across time. Thus, longitudinal qualitative research and lifespan approaches—particularly projects that involve rich and varied data sources that capture the textures and contexts of people's experiences—are particularly salient to people interested in equity and educational access. These data recognize and honor a vast range of individual experiences that reflect various social orientations, perceptions, behaviors, and the meanings that are made based on these experiences. In a significant way, these approaches reveal the longitudinal and life-long effects of bias, privilege, and opportunity.

DOI: https://doi.org/10.37514/PER-B.2024.2289.2.01

WHAT IS TEMPORAL DISCOURSE ANALYSIS, AND WHAT CAN IT DO?

The complex and creative process described above informed an analytic method that I call *temporal discourse analysis*. Specifically, *temporal discourse analysis* provides insights into how people make sense of their experiences across and within time. While this analytic method can be applied to discourses across long or short periods of time and data collected using a range of methodologies (e.g., case studies, ethnographies, classroom-based studies, narrative inquiries), it is particularly useful for scholars with an interest in lifespan writing research who may be interested in aspects of discourse that appear, re-appear, or change across time. Specifically, temporal discourse analysis is especially useful when dealing with large data sets that include similar and/or contrasting data across time. Temporal discourse analysis addresses research questions that ask: What has changed or is changing? What is the nature of becoming? And what changes might be important to educators as they work with children across time? Temporal discourse analysis is also useful when working with teams of scholars in that it provides a set of shared analytics that can be used to examine and make sense of data that have been collected by different people across time.

Temporal discourse analysis reveals three ways in which people draw upon time to convey meanings about themselves and their worlds: 1) how people locate themselves in time, 2) how people experience the pace of activities, and 3) how they make and convey meaning across time.

People use language to locate and present themselves in the present moment, relative to shared social histories, and within personal/familial histories that involve past, present, and future. People use temporal words (e.g., *yesterday, next week, a long time ago, last semester, next time, always*) to situate themselves and their activities relative to the present moment. These terms enable people to locate themselves, their understandings, and interpretations of what was, what is, and what could be.

People also reference the speed at which events occur. For example, references to the pace of schooling and timelines that operate in schools reveal lived experiences of time. Temporality operates through reading levels, writing rubrics, and benchmarks that correlate with children's ages and/or grade levels. As researchers, we might ask what it feels like to undertake activities relative to timelines and how temporal expectations are experienced by children. References to school bells, passing time between classes, and 45-minute class sessions point to the temporality of school.

Finally, repeated discourses and repeated stories reveal how people make sense of experiences across time. Repeated discourses can reveal not only what and how meanings circulate across time and among participants, but also indicate when and how discourses are sustained, shifted, and challenged. Tracking these discourses allows researchers to explore how people's understandings of their worlds may have expanded or been reimagined.

TEMPORAL DISCOURSE ANALYSIS: AN APPROACH TO LONGITUDINAL DATA ANALYSIS

By tracking discourses across time, I not only see slices of people's experiences but I also begin to witness their longitudinal sense-making. I am methodologically interested in the affordances of tracking how discourse practices emerge, are used, taken up, transformed, repurposed, and laminated, to meet new contextual demands across time. I argue that discourse serves as a marker—perhaps a proxy—of regular and ongoing work and meaning-making and, thus, serves as a viable and valuable tool for making sense of lifespan and longitudinal data.

While I see myself as a literacy scholar rather than a writing scholar, I appreciate and celebrate the affordances of writing as a longitudinal data source. First, written words can present snapshots of particular points in time. They can be read as the physical "lamination of practices" (Dippre & Smith, 2020, p. 31) and have a permanence not shared by spoken words and readings. When spoken words of participants are transcribed, they inevitably involve the researcher's transcription processes and stylistic preferences. Perhaps even more importantly, people's written words often serve as stimuli for talk about what was written. Participants can explain, rationalize, legitimize, or problematize what they have put on paper. Written products can be revisited across time. People can read what they wrote days, weeks, months, and years ago and tell us what makes sense and what has changed. People can identify strands of symmetry or challenge their past selves across time.

Written artifacts can also present challenges. For example, "social circumstances and social exigencies are less immediately visible in writing" (Bazerman et al., 2018, p. 26) than during observations of writers as they write, make their way to school, locate themselves in classrooms, and engage with other children. Thus, lifespan writing research must entail more than documents. Multiple data sources are essential, as contextual factors—"practices, people, artifacts, and environments operate in each moment of writing" (Dippre & Smith, 2020, p. 31). Contextual factors sometimes involve the re-inscription of hegemonic, mainstream, privileged, and dominant discourses. Thus, writing can be an important space for challenging hegemonic discourses and disseminating counter-narratives and non-dominant accounts.

By analyzing discourses across time, I glimpse into "how people and things are mobilized and paralyzed, facilitated and restricted, in different measure and in relation to institutions and systems with long histories" (Smith, 2020, p. 19). In short, temporal discourse analysis can reveal students' thoughts about being and becoming writers, and how they situate themselves in relation to school, community, home, and global spaces. Bazerman and colleagues (2018) highlight the need for lifespan writing researchers to intentionally focus on individual writers—their purposes, their efforts, and the challenges they face. By analyzing discourses and how writers present their thoughts, experiences, and practices across time, we can begin to jettison our assumptions and catalyze individual journeys as conveyed by their words—written and spoken—across time.

Lifespan writing research, with a focus on how people change and develop across time, requires analytic processes that attend to change and stasis. I have used temporal discourse to identify longitudinal patterns across data sets. Specifically, longitudinal research:

1. provides deep insights into people's experiences by considering not only the here-and-now, but also past experiences and future visions
2. invites researchers and participants to develop rich and trusting relationships
3. creates important opportunities for advocacy and collaboration
4. reveals the complexity of situations alongside the vulnerability of participants whose life situations are defined by limited resources

We cannot "overlook the cultural and linguistic differences, variations in circumstances, and social inequalities that characterize life as people experience it" (Bazerman et al., 2018, p. 12). In the examples below and in the following, power is revealed as we consider children from two very different immigrant families, from different parts of the world, with different languages, and with differential access to cultural and economic resources.

COMPTON-LILLY'S LONGITUDINAL BECOMING: THE ORIGINS OF TEMPORAL DISCOURSE ANALYSIS

This chapter revisits and extends a set of analytical processes that I have found useful for analyzing longitudinal data and, thus, lifespan writing research data. Specifically, I describe lessons that I learned as I extended a one-year dissertation study into a ten-year project (Compton-Lilly, 2003; 2007; 2012; 2017). Admittedly, my longitudinal methods were far from perfect, and the methods I came to use were often improvised through trial-and-error (e.g., Thomson & Holland, 2003).

When I began my dissertation study, I never dreamed I would follow the children into high school. Thus, as I collected data for this new longitudinal study, I treated each phase as a new study. While the data I collected was informed by what I had learned during earlier phases, I was neither intentional in how I collected my data nor how the study design could have facilitated longitudinal analysis of these data. Avowedly, I was a novice researcher with no background in longitudinal methods. My ignorance was exacerbated by an ongoing lack of transparent discussions about qualitative longitudinal research methods, which with few exceptions—including this current volume—continues today.

In my original study, my data analysis process involved four separate stages of coding interview data and field notes, which aligned with my four phases of data collection. During the first phase, data were coded across cases into grounded categories. As I analyzed data from Grade 5, I worried that students' stories were obfuscated by my cross-case analysis. Thus, during Phase 2 and again in phase 4, I coded and analyzed cases separately prior to identifying cross-case patterns. During Phase 3, I again used cross-case coding. Thus, I moved between identifying cross-case patterns and telling individual stories.

However, these analytics, while productive in allowing me to attend to both individual cases and cross-case patterns, did little to reveal longitudinal patterns. Comments from parents—who watched their children move through school—led me to consider the children's long-term experiences and trajectories. It became apparent that separate, sequential, and grounded codings of data obfuscated longitudinal patterns. Over time, I began to notice that data collected during early phases of the project gained significance when viewed in relation to data collected years later (e.g., Compton-Lilly, 2020). I began to hear repeated phrases and stories across time. However, writing about these longitudinal patterns required rereading huge stacks of data and using the search function on my word processor to locate words and phrases from interview transcripts collected years apart.

Based on these concerns and frustrations, my next longitudinal research study was intentionally designed to reveal longitudinal patterns across time. In that study, the research team collected parallel data sets, asking participants to complete the same or similar tasks, and answer the same or similar interview questions each year (Bazerman, 2018). We coded data using combinations of *a priori* codes—reflecting our initial research questions—and grounded codes which were periodically revised. Each case was coded longitudinally; the same codes were used for each year as we created one coded data set for each student. Thus, if I was interested in a particular child's literacy practices at school, I could download stacks of coded data for that child and read that data set for longitudinal patterns—repeated language or stories, changes across time, and reminiscences. In some cases, minor modifications were made in my code list to accommodate changes as the children grew older and technology changed.

The possibility of analyzing temporal discourses is not new. Gee's (e.g., 2004) discussion of discourse analysis consistently posed the possibility of attending to temporal language. Temporality is inherent in nexus analysis (Scollon & Scollon, 2007; Wohlwend, 2020) as researchers examine children's actions and analyze video footage, tracking what happens over time in classrooms and other spaces. What is different about temporal discourse analysis is the intentional focus on what people say and how they enact and display their understandings of their world over time. Temporal discourse analysis, while it can be used to analyze data from short-term studies, has a particular salience and applicability to longitudinal data sets.

Unlike other chapters in this volume, I do not present a full methodology. Instead, I describe an analytical process that can be used with a range of methodologies (e.g., case studies, ethnographies, classroom-based studies, narrative inquiries) when researchers are interested in temporality. While studies that use temporal discourse analysis will often be longitudinal, any research project that involves multiple data collection points and seeks to examine change may find these analytics useful.

APPLYING TEMPORAL DISCOURSE ANALYSIS TO MY DATA

In my past writing, I have identified five types of temporal discourses (Compton-Lilly 2014a; 2015) related to the educational experiences of my participants: 1) the language people use to situate themselves in ongoing time; 2) comments and practices related to long social histories; 3) references to the pace of schooling and the timelines that operate in schools; 4) repeated discourses across time that reveal shared ways of understanding the world, and 5) repeated stories that present changing or consistent meanings across time. The first two types of discourses listed above reveal how people locate themselves in time. The third type of discourse reveals how people experience the pace of activities. The fourth and fifth reveals how people make and convey meaning across time.

Together, I argue that attending to these temporal discourses allows researchers to explicitly focus on how participants situate themselves in time and how they use language to convey meaning. Below, I present an example of each type of temporal discourse from the study that I discuss in the following chapter.

The Language that People Use to Situate Themselves within Time

Across interviews with children, their parents, and their teachers, we often heard temporal language. This language revealed how participants situated themselves and others within time. Words, such as "always," "forward," and "was" convey temporality, situating the speakers in relation to events presented as past, present, recurring, or in the future. Teachers often used temporal language to report on children's learning or writing practices. For example, Maya's bilingual kindergarten teacher believed that her strong Spanish literacy skills would "help push her *forward* and keep pushing her *forward*." Felipe's second-grade teacher was concerned that when Felipe wrote stories "[the storyline] *always* has to be with those [video] games and playing with them."

Children and their parents routinely used temporal language. As a fourth grader, James commented on his mother's pronunciation of English words, saying, "*Once* my mom was reading the map, and she saw Houston, and she thought it said 'House-ten'." Maya's mother proudly reported, *"Peinso que sera multilingual cuando cresca"* (I think *she will be* multilingual when she grows up). Similarly, Adam's mother reported on the present with the future in mind, "I use the Arabic with him because *I don't want him to forget* . . . [For] the kids it's easy to forget their language so *I keep talking* to them just Arabic." By attending to temporal language, we glimpse how teachers, parents, and children position themselves and others within larger temporal and social contexts.

Language Related to the Pace of Schooling

Temporality also manifested in how participants spoke about schooling and the temporal expectations that defined school success. Temporal discourses were often related to the pace of learning. In some cases, participants reported being able to learn things quickly and easily. At age eight, Adam described speaking multiple languages as "easy" saying, "It took me like *only two days* to learn English." Adam claimed to know "five languages"—"English, Arabic, French, Spanish and a little bit Chinese." Similarly, Maya's kindergarten teacher reported, "she's *only been here a month and a half, maybe two now*, but it's like you can see every single sound represented and she's got spaces between her words."

In other cases, participants were concerned about children keeping pace with learning benchmarks. For example, by fourth grade, Maya's dual language teacher identified English vocabulary as a problem:

> Probably the one thing, understandably, that she's working on is the lack of vocabulary, and even then, she is doing so well in English. But [that's] compared to her Spanish, you know, I really see her *starting to catch up* in English . . . when you think about students being in the bilingual program, you are thinking about that great foundational basis in their native language [and] that it's *going to transfer*.

While this teacher reported that Maya's Spanish abilities exceeded her abilities in English, she noted that Maya was "starting to catch up" with English and predicted a promising future, explaining that her knowledge of Spanish was "going to transfer" and support her in reading and writing in Spanish.

THE LANGUAGE THAT PEOPLE USE TO LOCATE THEMSELVES IN LARGER SOCIAL HISTORIES

Historical and constructed meanings were apparent across the data set when participants described historical events that affected their understandings of school and literacy learning. When asked how he felt about the education his son, James, was getting in the United States, Mr. Li described his former teachers in China. He explained that these Chinese teachers used political slogans to teach English, including "China is a great country," and "Serve the people heart and soul." Mr. Li complained that these English phrases were useless, saying "Nobody [in the USA] says [things] this way." He described this instruction as "no good," saying, "I consider[ed] myself as a very good English student, but then when I saw my first [English] movie . . . I couldn't understand a thing [in] the whole movie." Mr. Li used this story—drawing on his experiences of historical practices in China—to explain and convey his support for the educational system in the United States.

REPEATED DISCOURSES ACROSS TIME

In some cases, similar discourses recurred across the data set. The most common example of repeated discourse in my current longitudinal study involved repeated talk about text reading levels:

> Elina (grade 2): I'm on level 14 for my reading.
>
> Carlos (grade 2): In English I'm level 20, and then [in] Spanish level 25.
>
> Felipe (grade 5): My teacher told me [my] grade in reading . . . I am close to "Z" which is the best grade or reading level.

Teachers also used textlevel discourses. For example, across the first four years of the study, Carlos' teachers routinely discussed his reading abilities in terms of text levels.

Grade 2 Teacher: I know he is reading at an advanced level. . . . He's reading at a level 20.

Grade 3 Teacher: He's done extremely well. He's not quite at a level 30, which is considered [the] end of 3rd grade, but he's like a 27 or something like that.

Grade 4 Teacher: I've done some assessments with him, and he's passed with flying colors [met the designated text level benchmark].

In some cases, discourses referencing the progress of children from immigrant families were repeatedly marked by references to the child's English learner status.

Grade 3 Teacher: [Felipe's] still an ESL kid.

Grade 4 Teacher: . . . especially for [Felipe] being an ELL student,

Grade 5 Teacher: [Felipe's] by far my strongest linguist-language learner reader.

Not only were discourses about text level and ELL status repeated across time, but they also circulated among children, their teachers, and sometimes family members. Tracking the same or similar discourses across time is one means of identifying how meanings are made, sustained, and sometimes disrupted as participants took up and sometimes challenged ways of discussing their experiences.

REPEATED STORIES ACROSS TIME

In some cases, participants told the same stories at different points of time. For example, in first grade, Gabby often spoke about going fishing with her father and her brothers. When asked what she wrote about at school, Gabby responded, "mostly going fishing" and described a fishing story that she had written at school. By the end of that year, Gabby's father had moved out of the home; Gabby reported that they used to fish "but not no more." A year later, she fondly recalled a fishing adventure with her dad, saying "I remember I caught a cod on [my brother's] fishing pole." In grade three, she again revisited this memory.

And I caught a huge carp, like this big. (Gabby spreads her hands apart to show the size) . . . My dad told me [that there was a fish on the line] because I was playing on the statue. There's a statue and me and my friend used to play on it when we went [fishing]. Well, me and Javon, my friend [were playing] and my dad and my uncle had to reel it [in] for me. . . . It was too [big].

As with many fishing stories, Gabby's account expanded across time, possibly because she was older and better able to articulate her thoughts or perhaps because this event, involving her estranged father, became increasingly salient after he left the household. Notably, the cod became a carp, the fishing party expanded to include her uncle and a friend, and a statue appeared. These morphings speak to how memories are negotiated, reworked, and rearranged as they become the stories people tell themselves and others.

LONGITUDINAL REFLEXIVITY AND METHODOLOGICAL COMPLICATIONS

When considering longitudinal and lifespan research, researcher reflexivity assumes particular significance. Revisiting findings, reworking claims, and complicating conclusions inherently involve reflexivity. While traditional statements of researcher reflexivity generally reference the significance of background, race, gender, age and other dimensions of self, there is much more that could be considered when thinking reflexively. Bourdieu argued that researchers must acknowledge their struggle for legitimation within academic fields, the scholarly capital they accumulate, and how capital operates within academic fields (Grenfell, 2011; Grenfell & Pahl, 2018). For example, my scholarly becoming was sometimes constrained by accepted methodological practices. For example, I conducted my dissertation as a short-term grounded theory study (Compton-Lilly, 2003). I have clear memories of repeatedly reading Strauss and Corbin's (1990) book to discern the correct method for conducting a grounded theory study. My focus was on doing things correctly. However, this quest for correctness was shattered by my longitudinal efforts and the need to accommodate longitudinal data and the long-term ethical commitments researchers make to participants (Compton-Lilly, 2014a; 2015).

Longitudinal trajectories do not unfold in empty spaces. Being/becoming always occurs within spaces populated by histories. Racism, colonization, inequity, and cruelty affect children's learning trajectories. While the details of our experiences differ, like my participants, I am operating in a post 9/11 world, post-Trump country, where Black Lives Matter, a pandemic has unfolded, and climate change is creating chaos in people's lives. Thus, my readings of my data are inseparable from the times in which I live, the field, participants' experiences, and my positionality, which invites me to read data in particular ways and launch particular ways of thinking, while discouraging other directions.

Finally, longitudinal relationships are often close and trusting, complicating claims of objectivity or distance. Participants in longitudinal educational studies often ask for advice related to schooling, educational opportunities, and children's college plans. In addition, participation in a research project can affect participants in unintentional ways. In my original longitudinal study, after eight years of participation, one of my former students asked me if I had selected him for the longitudinal study because he sometimes misbehaved in first grade. Behavior was neither the focus of the study nor among the criteria I used to recruit families. In short, participation in longitudinal projects can convey enduring unintended messages to participants.

As Thomson and Holland (2003) noted, "the structure of the research encouraged young people to present themselves as being involved in a progressive and developmental process of change" (p. 24). As they explain, this sometimes became a challenge for students whose long-term trajectories were less successful. As longitudinal and lifespan researchers, we must constantly ask ourselves what it might mean to young people when we repeatedly return to talk with them about literacy, if literacy learning is a site of personal challenge, failure, or distress. Are we playing a role in reifying that failure? Through longitudinal research, we learn that our interpretations are always provisional and that the next round of data collection has the potential to challenge past findings. The child who struggled in school can become successful. The religious and polite child can get in trouble. The struggling single mother can be promoted into management. However, to what degree are these possibilities visible, tangible, and viable for our participants?

A FEW LONGITUDINAL CONCLUSIONS

Not only does lifespan research provide insight into the lived experiences and insights of participants, but it also holds us accountable to participants and honors the complexity of literacy learning and practices. Lifespan writing research invokes a "special ethical responsibility to tend and care for the relationship with participants" (Smith, 2020, p. 24). This responsibility is necessary to ensure the continued participation of participants, but even more, it is deeply premised on the caring relationships that emerge alongside longitudinal relations with participants. These relationships are premised on listening to participants' accounts and the accounts of people around them. Considering the perspectives, intentions, interests, and experiences of participants is key to conducting thoughtful and responsive research. I maintain that temporal discourse analysis is a tool for listening closely (also see Fulford & Rosenberg, this volume).

Temporal discourse analysis reveals how people draw on time, use time, and make meaning across time as they convey understandings about themselves and their worlds. Specifically, we are allowed glimpses of how people locate themselves in time, how they experience time, and how they make and convey meaning across time. As Bazerman reported,

Longitudinal studies offer the possibility of understanding individuals following unique pathways leading to unique skills, orientations, and responses in situations rather than being normalized through cross-sectional groups of age, educational level, or other category, with individuals being characterized as typical or atypical. (2018, p. 328)

Discourse analysis is one tool for looking longitudinally at how people make sense of themselves, their worlds, and their becomings across time.

In short, temporal discourse analysis, rich description, and multiple data sources allow researchers to attend to change, trajectory, and becoming as fertile means for making sense of people's experiences. While many implications could be offered, I close by sharing three claims:

1. All research has the potential to become longitudinal and to explore lifespan eras. I would encourage lifespan writing researchers, when possible, to revisit former research sites and participants. Discover what has happened to people who were involved in past projects and be willing to challenge the findings and insights that seemed compelling at the time of the original study.
2. Lifespan writing researchers must continue to craft analytic procedures that allow them to analyze data collected across long periods of time. Simply coding events at each phase of a project will not reveal longitudinal patterns. Sophisticated methods for exploring change, documenting trajectories, and understanding processes of becoming are needed (Compton-Lilly, 2014b).
3. Understanding the cumulative effects of schooling and other aspects of people's lives across time require longitudinal methods. The effects of poverty, race, cultural and linguistic differences may become increasingly visible across long periods of time as participants describe and reflect on critical incidents, identify the accumulation of micro-aggressions (Compton-Lilly, 2020) and conceptualize alternative possibilities for literacy learning and school success.

Finally, I offer advice to novice scholars interested in using temporal discourse analysis to analyze data. I would encourage scholars to ask themselves two questions: First, are you asking research questions that involve discourses and/or change over time? If you are doing single interviews, you are only hearing participants' thoughts at one point in time; temporal discourse analysis requires multiple data points distributed across time in ways that allow change to become visible. For some research questions this will require long periods of time. For other research questions, shorter timespans will suffice. Second, have you designed your study to see change over time? For example, multiple interviews with very different foci might not reveal change in the same ways as interviews that entail similar or parallel data sources.

If temporal discourse analysis seems feasible, be prepared for a messy process. As you review transcribed files—which I always do in hard copy—note temporal language, watch for references to larger social histories, and note repeated discourses and stories. While you can aspire to code for temporal discourses, I have not found coding sufficient. The problem is that early data becomes increasingly salient as later data is reviewed. A passing comment in first grade becomes significant when repeated, extended, or challenged in third grade. Thus, rereading, revisiting, and reviewing of data is unavoidable. Getting started means digging in. As with all qualitative analysis, insights and surprises await. Enjoy the mess and cherish the opportunity to learn from people's lives and experiences.

RESOURCES FOR LEARNING MORE

Adam, B. (2013). *Time and social theory*. John Wiley & Sons.

Almond, P. & Apted, M. (1964–2021). *The Seven Up! documentary film series*, ITV/Granada Television.

Dyson, A. H., Taylor, D. & Compton-Lilly, C. (2021). Time in education: Intertwined dimensions and theoretical possibilities. In B. Kabuto (Ed.), *Great women scholars series*. Garn Press.

Feldstein, P. & Bloome, S.G. (2008). *The Oxford Project*. Welcome Books.

Thorne, B. (2009). The Seven Up! films: Connecting the personal and the sociological. *Ethnography, 10*(3), 327–340.

REFERENCES

Bazerman, C., Applebee, A. N., Berninger, V. W., Brandt, D., Graham, S., Jeffery, J., Matsuda, P. K., Murphy, S., Rowe, D. W., Schleppegrell, M. & Wilcox, K. C. (2018). *The lifespan development of writing*. National Council of Teachers of English. https://wac.colostate.edu/books/ncte/lifespan-writing/.

Compton-Lilly, C. (2003). *Reading families: The literate lives of urban children*. Teachers College Press.

Compton-Lilly, C. (2007). *Re-Reading families: The literate lives of urban children, four years later*. Teachers College Press.

Compton-Lilly, C. (2012). *Reading time: The literate lives of urban secondary students and their families*. Teachers College Press.

Compton-Lilly, C. (2014a). The development of writing habitus: A ten-year case study of a young writer. *Written Communication, 31*(4), 371–403. https://doi.org/10.4135/9781473945401.

Compton-Lilly, C. (2014b). Temporal discourse analysis. In P. Albers, T. Holbrook, A. Flint (Eds.), *New methods in literacy research* (pp. 40- 55). Routledge.

Compton-Lilly, C. (2015). Revisiting children and families: Temporal discourse analysis and the longitudinal construction of meaning. In J. Rowsell & J. Sefton-Greene (Eds.), *Learning and literacy over time: Longitudinal perspectives* (pp. 61–78). Routledge.

Compton-Lilly, C. (2017). *Reading students' lives: Literacy learning across time*. Routledge.

Compton-Lilly, C. (2020). Microaggressions and macroaggressions across time: The longitudinal construction of inequality in schools. *Urban Education, 55*(8–9), 1315–1349. https://doi.org/10.1177/0042085919893751.

Dippre, R. J. & Smith, A. (2020). Always already relocalized: The protean nature of context in lifespan writing research. In R. J. Dippre & T. Phillips (Eds.), *Approaches to lifespan writing research: Generating an actionable coherence* (pp. 27–38). The WAC Clearinghouse; University Press of Colorado. https://doi.org/10.37514/PER-B.2020.1053.2.02.

Gee, J. P. (2004). *An introduction to discourse analysis: Theory and method*. Routledge.

Grenfell, M. (2011). *Bourdieu: A theory of practice*. Continuum Press.

Grenfell, M. & Pahl, K. (2018). *Bourdieu, language-based ethnographies and reflexivity: Putting theory into practice*. Routledge.

Noddings, N. (2005). What does it mean to educate the whole child? *Educational Leadership, 63*(1), 3–11. https://doi.org/10.4135/9781452219295.n1.

Scollon, R. & Scollon, S. W. (2007). Nexus analysis: Refocusing ethnography on action. *Journal of Sociolinguistics, 11*(5), 608–625. https://doi.org/10.1111/j.1467-9841.2007.00342.x.

Smith, A. (2020). Across, through, and with: Ontological orientations for lifespan writing research. In R. J. Dippre & T. Phillips (Eds.), *Approaches to lifespan writing research: Generating an actionable coherence* (pp. 15–26). The WAC Clearinghouse; University Press of Colorado. https://doi.org/10.37514/PER-B.2020.1053.2.01.

Strauss, A. & Corbin, J. (1990). *Basics of qualitative research*. Sage.

Thomson, R. & Holland, J. (2003). Hindsight, foresight and insight: The challenges of longitudinal qualitative research. *International Journal of Social Research Methodology, 6*(3), 233–244. https://doi.org/10.1080/1364557032000091833.

Wohlwend, K. (2020). *Literacies that move and matter: Nexus analysis for contemporary childhoods*. Routledge.

CHAPTER 2.

WRITING ELEMENTARY SCHOOL: THE CASES OF GABBY AND ADAM

Catherine Compton-Lilly
University of South Carolina

As Dippre and Phillips (2020) explained, "When lifespan research is longitudinal and qualitative . . . it recursively, intentionally, and methodologically looks forward, backward, and across time as it works to understand the causes, triggers, and impacts on writing development in an individual life" (pp. 6–7). Lifespan approaches recognize the "complex relations of intervening variables, indirect influences, co-emerging life stories, and individuated pathways of development" (Smith, 2020, pp. 16–17) that other approaches can leave unexamined. I use temporal discourse analysis as a tool for making *some* sense of children's literacy becoming through writing.

In this chapter, I draw on two longitudinal cases studies with children from immigrant families. I explore patterns across time using the temporal discourse analysis techniques described in the previous methodological chapter. My goal is to reveal the unique sense-making journeys of Gabby and Adam—who were classmates in first grade—as they engaged in schooling and literacy learning across the first five years of a twelve-year study. Across time, Gabby moved from a notably progressive city to a conservative rural community. Gabby and Adam then attended different schools and graduated high school with different long-term goals. By focusing on two children with different becomings and life experiences, I cut "loose from our moorings of normalization into the great varieties of experience, the great varieties of trajectories, that look so different" (Bazerman, 2020, p. xii) and challenge reified models of literacy development.

As Gabby's and Adam's cases illustrate, writing and being a writer are in constant motion in relation to other ways of being and becoming literate; their becomings are "not tethered or isolated" (Smith, 2020, p. 18), but distributed across contexts—locations, genres, institutions, people, and times. Drawing on a lifespan perspective, I recognize writing as inclusive of everyday writing practices—making lists, sending text messages, posting on social networks—often relegated to the margins of scholarly discussions. For Gabby and Adam, writing contexts were sites of "ongoing change" as they moved through school, sometimes in contradiction to established, predictable, and "particular developmental

DOI: https://doi.org/10.37514/PER-B.2024.2289.2.02

trajectories" (Dippre & Smith, 2020, p. 27). Contexts involving people, texts, and institutions were not background; they were operative influences that textured what children thought and did and what and how they read and wrote.

Thus, I trace two students across curricular opportunities, classrooms, and home spaces as I consider their literate becomings and accompanying sensemaking (Smith, 2020). While a conventional analysis of qualitative data would aspire to a coherent narrative, attention to temporality complicates this possibility. In short, at any given moment particular dimensions of experience pose more or less influence and become more or less salient. Thus, researchers who aspire towards longitudinal accounts must remain aware that people's accounts of their experiences and activities are articulated, represented, and expressed at particular points in time and must be viewed as "temporary resting place(s)" (Murris, 2021, p. 230). Therefore, the words, images, and observations presented below are never considered enduring.

Fleeting meanings reflect recognitions from the past, including the past experiences of families and friends, the children's knowledge of larger social histories (Deleuze & Guattari, 1988), and their dreams for the future. Both envisionments of the future and tracings of the past are continually subject to revision, reiteration, and rejection, always located within textured contexts of experiences, texts, and people (Fenwick, 2010).

Not presenting a coherent account was difficult. In fact, scholars are trained to present coherent arguments that make particular claims. Writing this chapter entailed stepping back, resisting conclusions, and avoiding closure. I monitored my thinking, what I wrote, and the words I used to represent particular moments. As Fenwick and Landri (2012) argued, people craft provisional narratives that are made and remade across time. This "tentative and hesitant unfolding" (Coleman & Ringrose, 2013, p. 5) reflects becomings as eternally temporary and molten. Self is a jumbling of activities and meanings that produce multiple beings and eternal becomings, challenging traditional and contemporary conceptions of identity as developmental and predictable. As Fenwick (2010) noted, new possibilities for new *doings* constantly emerge in interaction with complex systems resulting in unpredictable outcomes.

I present a brief introduction to temporality as a salient dimension of the textured contexts within which people operate. I then briefly describe the methodology for the longitudinal study. Finally, I present the cases of Gabby and Adam with an eye to the discourses and practices that accompanied their being and becoming writers across time. I discuss a small subset of the writing tasks that the students completed across the first five years of the project in conjunction with other data. In a few cases, I briefly reference data collected after grade five to illustrate long-term emergences.

A BRIEF THEORETICAL FRAMING OF TEMPORALITY

I draw on the temporal theorizing of Barbara Adam (1989; 1990; 2000; 2001; 2003; 2004) to briefly focus on four claims: 1) time and meaning-making as multidimensional, complex, and intricately connected to people's experiences; 2) the past, present, and future as intertwined and inherently inseparable; 3) conceptions of time as culturally and socially negotiated; and 4) limiting, yet hegemonic, and overly-linear notions of time that can damage individual possibilities for becoming.

As I consider the becomings of children across time, I recognize time as multidimensional, complex, and intricately connected to experiences. As Adam (2004) reported, "time is embedded in the various technologies and economic relations" (p. 40) that constitute the spheres of people's lives, including society, home, nature, work, economics, and schooling. Importantly, time has multiple dimensions: tempo, timing, and temporality. Adam (2000) argued for an awareness of the complexity of time— "over and above clock and calendar time" (p. 138)—that honors the experiences and perspectives of people in sociocultural contexts. In Adam's (1989) words, time is "implicit in waiting, in planning, and in contemplating, and in guilt" (p. 468); time is both multidimensional and universal. Expanded notions of time highlight multiple and simultaneous realities that accompany social life. While Adam (1990) confronted the tendency of social science researchers to depict time as unidimensional, a lifespan approach insists that "personal experience, consciousness, existence, and context have to be taken as sources against which rational theories have to be checked" (Adam, 1989, p. 458).

Not only is time multidimensional and intrinsically connected to people's experiences, it is also inherently complex with past, present, and future as intertwined and inseparable. As Adam explained (2004), "life involves an unbroken chain of future-oriented discussions that bring the future into the present and allow it to fade into the past" (p. 54). Past, present, and future are always co-operative, co-mingled, and co-existing. For example, "aspects of past acts need to be selected from the vastness of the totality within which past and potential acts are embedded" (p. 36). This selection not only speaks to the inherent selectivity of accessing past experiences in the present, but also the tendency for people to strategically draw on experiences that produce coherent—sometimes causal—accounts of experiences and selves (Adam, 1990). Notably, Adam maintained that "the past is revocable and as hypothetical as the future" and "continuously recreated and reformulated into a different past from the standpoint of the emergent present" (1990, p. 39). This fluid and evolving notion of the past is challenged by the past as reified and preserved through artifacts, institutions, practices, stories, beliefs, and texts. A range of human actions—traditions, habits, goals, intentions, wishes, meanings, and values—operate and sustain hegemonic and historicized practices (Adam, 1990).

In short, culture, language, beliefs, and social practices affect how time is conceptualized and actualized within communities (Adam, 2004). The present is always defined in reference to "a particular event, system, biography or future" (Adam, 2004, p. 69) and "inseparable from our biography and biology, our context, beliefs, and values, our needs and our motives" (Adam, 1990, p. 7). Thus people, who operate within time, are "subject to conflicts that arise at the intersections of different temporal spheres" (p. 40).

Finally, discussions of time must recognize and question hegemonic, official, and overly linear notions of time that can damage individual becomings. Adam (2004) contrasted lived time with "machine time," which shifts the "experience and meaning of time towards invariability, quantity, and precise motion expressed by numbers" (p. 114). Adam (1990) explained that because schools have limited temporal resources, "they are structured to follow certain sequences and to happen at a specific rate, at a particular time, over a fixed period, and for a set number of times" (p. 105). In short, the daily timetable is designed to provide "all participants with a regular routine within which the carefully scheduled learning, teaching, examination, assessment, management, administration, cleaning, cooking, eating, and playing can proceed in an orderly and predictable manner" (p. 105). Furthermore, schools operate in alignment with age-based classes, achievement benchmarks, and temporal expectations that contradict organic learning and individualized becomings, creating stress and frustration for students and teachers (Adam, 2003). Perhaps most unsettling is the role that time plays in creating and maintaining inequitable learning opportunities (Adam, 2001). Adam (2001) argued that the task of educators is to "speak to the silences and thereby create the potential for changing social relations that reach deep into the very fabric of socio-economic inequalities" (Adam, 2001, p. 119).

A LONGITUDINAL METHODOLOGY

In the two longitudinal case studies below, I follow Gabby and Adam. Gabby's family originated in Mexico and has resided in the US for at least two generations; Adam's family came to the US from Morocco just before he started kindergarten. The larger study includes nine families who have immigrated to the United States from around the world and addressed a broad research question: *How do children in immigrant families become literate and construct literate identities?* Families were recruited through convenience sampling. I intentionally chose Gabby and Adam as they were among the students that I worked with most closely across the study. They were in the same first-grade class. Gabby and Adam have participated in the project for 13 years and graduated from high school in June 2021; I focus on data from the first five years of the study.

My analysis draws on interviews with Gabby and Adam, their mothers, siblings, and teachers. Data include observations at home and school, artifacts created by the children (e.g., writing samples, self-portraits, maps, photographs) and conversations about those artifacts. During the first year of the study, I visited the children at home and school five times. During years two through eight, I visited three times. Starting in year nine when I moved to a different state, I visited twice annually. Data targeted spaces the families had occupied across time (i.e., home/neighborhood/school, native country/USA). Each year, members of the research team invited the children to complete the same or similar tasks. For example, we asked children to draw self-portraits to explore identities across time. Semi-structured interviews focused on school experiences, interests, literacy achievement, and literacy engagements.

Across the study, I coded interviews and field notes using *a priori* codes reflecting my research foci (e.g., child identity, home literacy practices, school literacy practices). Interviews and field notes were subsequently subjected to a grounded analysis resulting in additional codes (e.g., pop culture, technology). Artifacts were reviewed in relation to the emerging code set. In many cases, patterns suggested by interviews and observations were echoed in artifacts. At other times, artifacts complicated emerging themes.

As described in the previous chapter, coding was only partially helpful in identifying longitudinal patterns. To attend to change, consistency, and nuance across time, I attended to five types of temporal discourse: 1) the language participants used to situate themselves in time, 2.) references to the pace of schooling and school timelines, 3) comments and practices reflecting social histories, 4) repeated discourses, and 5) repeated stories involving changing or consistent meaning-making. Each case presents a different approach to school and literacy learning as the children moved through their respective becomings. As I linked these discourses and identified temporal patterns across the data set, I identified *through-lines*—repeated references to similar ideas, discoursal motifs, and imagery that recurred across the data set. Importantly these through-lines were *not* straight, incremental, or mono-directional. They were curvaceous and multi-directional through-lines that looped back on themselves. These through-lines sometimes ended and re-generated at later points in time. The through-lines are not real and do not have boundaries that separate them from other through-lines. They are not empirically established truths. Instead, through-lines are reflections of my sense-making, which serve my purpose of putting ideas on paper. Below, I present what must be conceptualized as points in time when Gabby and members of her family described or engaged in activities that informed my sense-making of moments alongside my account of the Gabby's longitudinal becomings.

GABBY'S BECOMINGS

In this section, I explore through-lines and repeated motifs that marked Gabby's becomings across five years. Notably, I consider Gabby's interests at particular moments, while recognizing these as resting places for sense-making within ever-emerging through-lines of becomings. Admittedly, I was limited by what Gabby and her mother shared. Gabby's longitudinal becomings are a million times richer, deeper, and more complex than this sampling and even my full thirteen-year data set suggests. Regardless, I present this glimpse of becomings to explore how Gabby's experiences, preferences, identities, and interests resonated and served as more or less salient to her contextualized becomings across time.

In Table 2.1, I present three through-lines that emerged, recurred, and were revisited across multiple interviews with participants. In Figure 2.1, I identify drawings and writing samples that intersect with and across these through-lines. Each time these through-lines appeared in the data set, they were treated and described in different and consistent ways. Sometimes they gained momentum and became increasingly salient. At other times, their vibrancy waned. Some things seemed forgotten, only to re-emerge during future interviews. Other things took on new forms. However, at no point were these through-lines linear or causal. Early experiences did not lead to particular outcomes; instead through-lines curved, changed direction, and sometimes circled back. Through-lines spoke to temporality and inextricable networks of connections, links, evasions, and repellings that informed Gabby's becomings. Specifically, I explore through-lines related to clothing and adornment, animals, and LEGOs and *Minecraft*.

Table 2.1. Gabby's Through-lines

Through-lines	Artifacts	Writing Samples
Through-lines Related to Clothing and Adornment	Butterfly chair, "pink" and "fringy" girl clothes, earrings, short hair, hair dye, oversized sweatpants and sweatshirts	Grade 1: Dog poop
		Grade 2: House by the river
		Grade 3: My block
Through-lines Related to Animals	Pets, animal books, lion jigsaw puzzle, lion tapestry, animal video games	Grade 4: Me
		Grade 5a: Declawing Cats
Through-lines Related to LEGOs and *Minecraft*	LEGOs, *Minecraft* videos, pink LEGO pieces.	Grade 5b: House by the river

Writing Elementary School

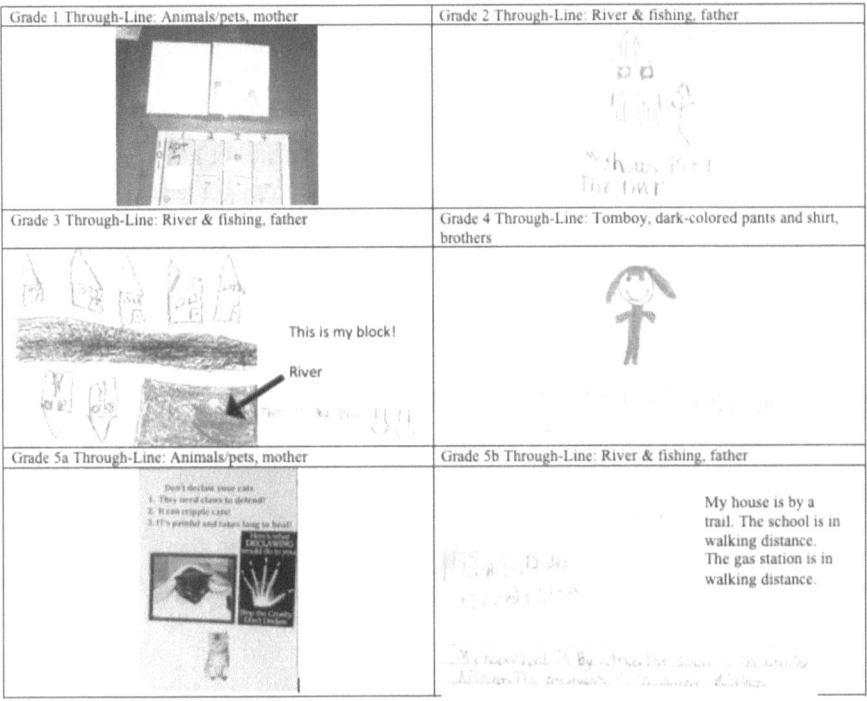

Figure 2.1. Gabby's Writing Samples

THROUGH-LINES RELATED TO CLOTHING AND ADORNMENT

Across the five-year study, a through-line involving clothing and adornment often surfaced with Gabby and her mother. During the first year of interviews, Gabby's mother shared a photograph of Gabby sitting in a chair that resembled a large pink butterfly. As I viewed the picture, I turned to Gabby, saying "I didn't know you had a butterfly chair." Her mother explained, "[That] was when I could get her to wear pink. Now I can't. . . . We don't do girl clothes at all." Across Gabby's interviews references to "pink" invoked cultural models of femininity and girlhood. However, pink highlighted ways of being that Gabby adamantly rejected, especially when embellishing clothing. The entire time I have known Gabby, she has worn over-sized and dark-colored sweatshirts, T-shirts, and sweatpants borrowed from her older brothers. With the exception of one drawing in grade one when Gabby depicted herself wearing a red shirt and pink pants, Gabby always depicted herself wearing dark-colored shirts and pants (e.g., Figure 2.1, grades 2 & 4). Her writing typically provided few personal details. Furthermore, Gabby did not like to write and often complained when asked to write during interviews.

Across the interviews, Ms. Rodriguez often commented on Gabby's attire, identifying possible signs that Gabby might be becoming more feminine. In second grade, her mother believed that she was "slowly coming out of it [being a 'tomboy']" saying, "the other day she asked me to pierce her ears." Gabby's mother then moderated her comment saying, "But I still can't get her to put [on] the girl clothes . . . if anything looks remotely girly, fringy, she's not going for it." By grade four, Ms. Rodriguez noted that Gabby wanted "to dye her hair;" across the next two years Gabby's hair went from a bright red, to orange, to blue. Blonde or pink were never color candidates. That same year, Gabby surprised us when she begged for a curling iron; yet, when asked to choose between the curling iron and LEGO, Gabby chose the LEGO. Gabby's mother lamented, "She has no, like girly attentions" and then admitted, "I was a tomboy for many years."

As I trace through-lines, marked by recurring discourses, I observe constant negotiation. At age six, Gabby teased her older brother, saying "You play with dollies" and proudly reported, "I play with Transformers." Her words highlighted toughness: "I'm a tomboy. I like to stick around with my brothers." A year later, Gabby's mother remarked on her propensity for action, predicting that Gabby would grow up to be a fire fighter, "I can see something like fire fighter something [like] that . . . she'd get into it and the adrenaline would just go." Similarly, as reported in the previous chapter, Gabby loved fishing with her father and brothers. Doing things—especially activities associated with her brothers—attracted Gabby.

Importantly, Gabby's through-lines involved people. The shirts that Gabby wore were not *like* her brothers' shirts; they *were* her brothers'. Thus, Gabby engaged with people as she negotiated possibilities and produced through-lines accompanied by sometimes fleeting becomings. For example, Ms. Rodriguez connected Gabby's tomboy stance to her own memories of being a tomboy and her recollection of growing out of that phase. While Gabby's mother watched for—perhaps hoped for—a transition from tomboy to young lady, Gabby made her own way. Her through-line was not linear; it was a multifaceted, tangential, and curvaceous series of false starts and new directions (Adam, 2004; Dippre & Smith, 2020), alongside her emerging sense of self, her memories of the past, and possibilities for future becomings. The stories her mother told, her brothers' sweatshirts, and the smiling preschooler in the butterfly chair inform this through-line, which I, as a researcher, marvel at but never fully understand.

The influence of her three older brothers could explain Gabby's tomboy stance. As her third grade teacher reported, "She puts up a good front on being a tough girl. She'll come in and talk about her brothers picking on her and doing things to her and beating her up and she's like, 'That doesn't hurt.' She's like, 'I can take it.'" However, Gabby's interest in activity is not limited to being tough and wearing her brother's shirts. Across time, Gabby has consistently engaged in discourses that compelled me, as a researcher, to identify a through-line related to gender representation. However, this through-line was complicated by significant spaces of affiliation shared by Gabby and her mother.

THROUGH-LINES RELATED TO ANIMALS

When visiting Gabby, it was common to encounter a menagerie of pets (e.g., dogs, birds, rats, snakes, hamsters, lizards, cats and litters of kittens). Ms. Rodriguez was an ardent animal lover and often adopted unwanted pets from friends and acquaintances; Gabby was her primary accomplice. In first grade, Gabby and her mother made and hung a sign next the apartment building's mailboxes (Figure 2.2).

> TO ALL TENETS w/ Canine Pets
>
> Pick up your pet's feces
>
> **DISCARD** in the TRASH
>
> Thank you
>
> Management

Figure 2.2. Gabby's Note

Gabby's favorite activity was playing with her dog. When attending a first-grade reading intervention at school, Gabby enjoyed "fun books" that featured "lions, tigers, wolves, dogs . . . and how tigers can catch wild pigs."

In second grade, Gabby reported, "I like learning about animals and stuff . . . that's the only thing." Her favorite school library books featured color illustrations of "wild wolves" and "big cats." When asked to photograph things at home, she photographed a partially complete jigsaw puzzle and a tapestry that hung in the living room. Both pictured close-up images of a male lion.

By grade three, Gabby's favorite video game involved taking care of animals. She explained, "You gotta keep them healthy. You have to feed them and groom them, like you can give them a bath and stuff like that." In fourth grade, Gabby continued to prefer books about animals, admitting that she "read [only] some of the pages or looked at the pictures." In fifth grade, Gabby choose to write about declawing cats. She used a computer to write and illustrate the text presented in Figure 2.1 (grade 5a).

This through-line of animals involved home and school writing, picture puzzles, video games, and books. I witnessed connections—not only with animals—but also with her mother, who shared her animal affinity. Thus, while Gabby's tomboy nature often involved her brothers and invoked her mother's concern, her animal through-line complicated and supported this tomboy stance. "Big cats" and "wild wolves" spoke to rough and tough activity, while feeding and caring for pets spoke to nurturing and her mother.

THROUGH-LINES RELATED TO LEGO AND *MINECRAFT*

Perhaps more than any other, Gabby's play with LEGO and *Minecraft* highlighted the complex, nonlinear, and unpredictable vibrancies that characterized her through-lines. Through-lines involving physical and digital building revealed moments of sense-making across gender, activity, and animals. Gabby's interest in LEGO first appeared during grade three. Her mother reported, "LEGOs is her biggest thing right now . . . that's just kind of [started] in the last couple of weeks." Gabby explained, "I can make like a cat, dog, I made a bunny, I made an office, [stuff] like that too." Ms. Rodriguez added, "She's extremely talented." Among her most impressive creations was her LEGO version of an owl from the *Clash of the Titans* movie.

Our conversation turned to the high cost of LEGO and Ms. Rodriguez explained that while a friend had given them a used set of LEGOs, she wanted to buy more, but it was "thirty-two bucks for one of those buckets" and then "they have like this tiny box of Mario [LEGOs for] fifty bucks. And I'm like, no way." Cost surfaced again when Gabby became "obsessed" with *Minecraft* during grade four. *Minecraft* is a video game that could be described as a digital version of LEGO. *Minecraft* involves players building 3D worlds. However, as Gabby lamented, *Minecraft* requires the purchase of an app that is downloaded onto an Android or iOS device. Even if Gabby's family could have afforded the program, purchasing a device to host the game was prohibitive. Thus, Gabby's engagement with *Minecraft* was limited to what she could do on her mother's cell phone—watching videos of other people playing the game on YouTube. However, this did not curb Gabby's enthusiasm.

> I'm obsessed with *Minecraft, Minecraft, Minecraft, Minecraft, Minecraft!* . . . Yeah. It's like they have people, you can build houses, you can build things that [are] pressure proof. Like you can open a door just by standing on a plate that is used by red stone. There are like little block people and they have a thing where you can put your armor on. There's leather armor, diamond armor and there is iron armor.

Gabby's interest in *Minecraft* continued through middle school alongside her continuing enthusiasm for LEGO.

When I visited the family, I would often bring Gabby books related to *Minecraft* or sets of LEGO. When Gabby was in sixth grade, I brought her a set of

LEGO that could be used to make a farm with animals. Gabby was excited and immediately poured the LEGO onto the floor. As she dug through the pieces, she pulled out the pink LEGO pieces that, according to the instructions, could be used to make a pig. She placed them in a pile, commenting "I'm leaving all the pink [LEGO] . . . This is going to go bye-bye. . . . I don't want these." I replied, "Whatever you don't want you can just trash." While Gabby decided not to discard the pink LEGO, she made it clear that they would be used sparingly. Her love of LEGO was complicated by the pinkness of the pieces to the degree that even the possibility of making a pig was over-ridden by the objectionable nature of pink.

By exploring discourses related to gender, animals, and LEGO across time, I witnessed the continual emergence, negotiation, intersection, and repellation of through-lines that marked Gabby's becomings. These through-lines were textured and contextualized by the events and practices of her experiences. They were expressed in what Gabby said, did, and wrote and in the recurring motifs, words and representations of her writing samples. Consistencies were suggested and plateaus formed, but moments of sense-making were always tentative and eternally emerging, fading, evaporating, re-emerging, and/or strengthening. There was no clear linear path among or across the through-lines. No coherent narrative emerged (Dippre & Smith, 2020). There were false starts, increasing saliencies, and unpredictable stops. While encountered in the present, through-lines are always informed by past meanings—butterfly chairs, litters of kittens, LEGO, and family members—alongside future possibilities (Adam, 2004).

ADAM'S BECOMINGS

As for Gabby, temporal discourse analysis revealed through-lines that accompanied Adam's becomings that were richer, deeper, and more complex than the data below suggests. I present this glimpse of through-lines to attend to strands of becomings that Adam referenced across time. While Gabby's through-lines rarely involved reading and writing, and she often deflected our questions about literacy, Adam highlighted texts and literacy practices; texts appeared in the pictures he drew and the photographs he took. Across the five years, Adam's texts included books, video games, comics, a letter from President Obama, websites, and wall-hangings.

In Table 2.2, I present three recurring through-lines across Adam's interviews. As Adam treated topics across time, some gained momentum, while others waned and seemed forgotten only to re-emerge. Like Gabby's becomings, Adam's through-lines were curvaceous and reiterative; they looped back and propelled forward and were neither linear nor causal. Early experiences did not predict later outcomes. Adam's data spoke to the complexity of being human and networks that surrounded, constituted, and informed his becomings. Specifically, I explore Adam's through-lines related to accomplishment, superheroes and video games, and Morocco and Adam's Muslim faith. Figure 2.3 presents a sampling of Adam's writing and drawing during elementary school.

Table 2.2. Adam's Through-lines

Through-lines	Artifacts	Writing Samples (Figure 2.3)
Through-lines Related to Accomplishment	Long chapter books, one million words, complicated books, reading levels, Harry Potter book, soccer uniform, sports medals, first grade self-portrait	Grade 1: Self-Portrait and Eid

Grade 2a: Self-Portrait, Narina and Basketball

Grade 2b: Moroccan Beach

Grade 3: Moroccan Mosque

Grade 4: Moroccan Beach

Grade 5: Moroccan Castle |
| Through-lines Related to Superheroes and Video Games | Superhero movies, video games, laptop, mother's cell phone, comics, mythology-themed books, educational videos, Netflix | |
| Through-lines Related to Morocco and Adam's Muslim Faith | First grade self-portrait, drawing of the mosque, slaughtered sheep, the ninety-nine names of Allah, Moroccan fabrics, Adam's map of his school, Arabic news broadcasts, letter and photo from President Obama | |

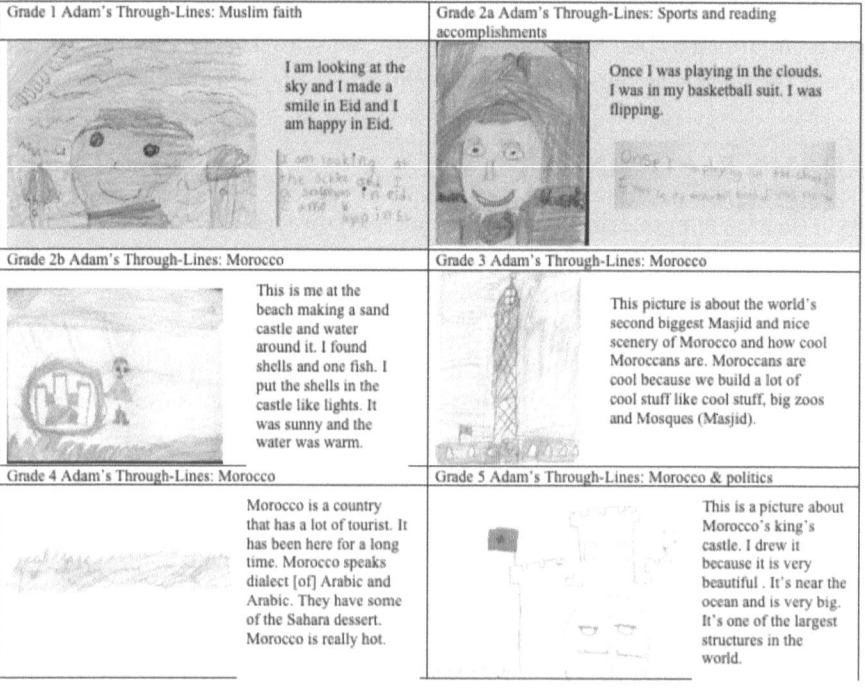

Figure 2.3. Adam's Through-line Writing Samples

THROUGH-LINES RELATED TO ACCOMPLISHMENT

When asked why Adam considered himself a good reader, he routinely voiced discourses that referenced books:

> Adam (grade 3): [I am a good reader] because I am in eighth grade reading [level]. . . . Because I read long chapter books.
>
> Adam (grade 4): Yeah [I am a good reader]. One time, I had to read one million words.
>
> Adam (grade 4): I read a lot. And I am starting to read like a bunch of chapter books.
>
> Adam (grade 5): [I am a good reader] because I read a really complicated book.

Across these accounts, discoursal through-lines highlighted the qualities of the books Adam had read, which he described as "long chapter books," "really complicated books," and books with "one million words." These textual qualities convey meanings about both the books and about Adam. In Adam's second grade self-portrait (Figure 2.3, grade 2a), Adam's face is flagged on both sides by the word "Narnia", referencing a book series that he admitted was beyond his second-grade reading ability. Adam claimed to read "a lot" and a "bunch" of books. Claims of proficiency extended to writing with Adam describing himself as a good writer because "I type a lot."

Adam often presented texts and avid reading as evidence of competence. As his third-grade teacher explained, Adam "would run [and get] or [pretend to] read a really hard book that he couldn't really read. So, it was that kind of insecurity, that sometimes he just needed to be [seen as] smart." His sixth-grade teacher agreed, describing him as "a very proud individual." Regardless, Adam's teachers confirmed his claims of being a skilled reader, describing his "greatest success" as reading (grade one teacher), noting that he had "progressed in reading and math and writing" (grade three teacher), and stating "he's above grade level" (grade five teacher). In short, Adam worked to convey messages of competence to his classmates and teachers presenting a through-line of discourses and artifacts to present himself as a skilled reader at school and during our interviews.

Like Gabby's connections to her father, mother, and brothers, Adam's textual through-lines connected to family members. Adam's attraction to long books and reading levels echoed comments from his older sister, Laila. When Adam was in second grade, Laila proudly described herself as a good reader, "because I finished a book that has 380 pages in like four days." Two years later, Adam claimed that he was "winning" a competition with his sister, explaining "it's a Harry Potter book. Yeah, I am better than her. I am already at page one hundred something." For Adam and his sister, long books, reading a lot, and reading quickly were markers of reading ability.

In addition to Adam's literacy accomplishments, Adam often voiced discourses of achievement in relation to sports and artistic abilities. In fact, Adam sometimes shifted our discussions of his reading prowess to his accomplishments in sports, especially soccer. For example, in grade three, Adam claimed "I don't like writing" explaining, "It is just something I don't like and it gets my hand tired." Adam then redirected the conversation with the *non sequitur* "I *also* play soccer" and enthusiastically described his community soccer team as a "*real* flag team." The following year when asked if he read more than the other kids in his class, Adam responded, "Yeah" and again redirected our conversation saying, "I'm probably the best swimmer in my family. I'm faster than Laila." When asked in grade two to take photographs of favorite possessions, Adam photographed the medals he had won for basketball and running (also see Figure 2.3, grade 2a), saying "I really like my medals."

Adam's competitive tendencies were evident when he reflected on his self-portrait commenting "I messed up. . . . I can do better." He then compared himself to his cousin, who could "draw a picture almost like it's a camera took a picture." That same year, Adam and I revisited a self-portrait that Adam had drawn two years earlier. Adam laughed, commenting "That's more like a bad drawing."

Across the interviews, Adam engaged with discourses and markers of accomplishment. Significantly, Adam's sister, his father, his cousin, his teachers, and I were all part of the textured context that framed Adam's through-line of accomplishment. Adam used things (e.g., books, medals) as evidence of ability, he compared himself to the textual doings of his sister, father, and cousin. Thus, things, people, discourses, and activities intermix, defying linear trajectories and definitive predictions (Adam, 2000; 2004). Books were part of Adam's through-line of accomplishment, conveying meanings to his teachers, family, himself, and me. Adam's focus on competence and accomplishment may have links to his early fascination with superheroes, as described below.

THROUGH-LINES RELATED TO SUPERHEROES AND TECHNOLOGY

Across the five years, Adam's through-lines sometimes took new directions. For example, in early elementary school Adam was enthusiastic about superheroes and video games. Adam's mother shared pictures of Adam as a smiling kindergartener wearing a Superman shirt. Two years later, Adam identified "The Amazing Spiderman" as his favorite movie and reported that he liked "Batman and Thor and Captain Incredible, too." He was watching the Avengers movie on his laptop, which he also used to play the video games that were popular with his classmates.

Thus, I was surprised when in grade four Adam reported that he rarely used technology and cleverly reported, "I use my brain." Across grades four and five, Adam increasingly reported little interest in—and perhaps a rejection of—technology.

> Adam (grade 4): You know I am not really a laptop person. I'm not an electronic person. I really don't use the computer. I am more of an outdoor person.
>
> Adam (grade 5): Yeah, there's games on it [his mom's cell phone], but I don't really play games on it. I just use it [as a phone].
>
> Adam (grade 5): But even if it [his computer] was working, I still wouldn't use it that much.

By grade five, Adam only used his laptop for school assignments.

Adam's through-line of superheroes led to hard-copy "comics [graphic novels]" including the *Amulet Series* (Kbuishi & Caffoe, 2008-present). Through these texts was a partial re-emergence of Adam's earlier interest in superheroes. For example, Adam excitedly explained that the protagonist in the Amulet series was "a stone keeper . . . it's like a hero except like she's controlled by a stone." He then clarified, "it's a girl and there is a generation of stone keepers and she's not like technically a hero but like she does save people because she has powers." Adam's description of the Amulet series inspired me to ask if the Amulet comics included mythological characters from the books he had been reading a year earlier. Adam responded, "no" but then noted that he was "waiting for a book that's coming in [the] Percy Jackson [series]," which features characters from Greek mythology.

Across this through-line of superheroes and technology, there are circulating and sometimes recursive vacillations among superheroes, mythological characters, comics, books, video games, movies, and technological devices. By fifth grade, the movies and video games that Adam enjoyed in earlier years were replaced by *Amulets* comics, featuring a hero who is "not like technically a hero" and books with mythological characters. At various points in time, Adam assumed "temporary resting place(s)" (Murris, 2021, p. 230), yet his through-line continued to emerge and re-emerge with tendrils reaching forward and backward and in different directions across past, present, and future (Dippre & Smith, 2020; Adam, 2004).

By grade six, Adam reported, "Well, I used to want to watch like science videos . . . and like educational videos [on my computer] to like help me in school." Adam then pointed to his laptop saying, "I don't use this. I'm more, I'm still an outdoor person." Across these through-lines, Adam used discourses and activities to make various claims: wearing his Spiderman shirt (kindergarten), "I am not really a laptop person" (grade four), and "I'm still an outdoor person" (grade six). However, affinities continued to emerge and re-emerge. For example, in sixth grade Adam continued to watch a few superhero shows on Netflix and competed with a friend to see who could be the first to watch the entire Green Arrow superhero series. This competition harkens back to both his interest in superheroes and competitions with his sister. As I continued to follow Adam across time, a through-line related to Morocco and his Muslim faith expanded in new directions highlighting history, Middle-Eastern politics, and environmental issues.

THROUGH-LINES RELATED TO MOROCCO AND ADAM'S MUSLIM FAITH

Returning to Adam's six-year-old self-portrait (Figure 2.3, grade 1)—which he later described as a "bad drawing"—we see Adam's smiling face surrounded by the sun and birds. When asked about the drawing, Adam explained, "I was looking in the sky and dreaming that I was in Morocco that there was eleven birds and two trees and I loved my grandma that died and right now she is with Allah and I made a big smile on Eid [*Day of Celebration*] and that's all." Adam's self-portrait and his talk highlighted joyous memories of sunny days in Morocco and a past Eid Celebration. Significantly, this first grade drawing brought together Morocco and Adam's Muslim faith through connections to his grandmother's passing.

Adam's Muslim faith was a recurring motif that assumed different forms and led in multiple directions. In third grade, when asked to draw a picture of Morocco, Adam drew the image presented in Figure 2.2 (grade three) explaining, "[It's] the world's second biggest mosque and nice scenery of Morocco and how cool Moroccans are. Moroccans are cool because we build a lot of cool stuff like big zoos and mosques." The Mosque and Morocco are connected, as are "nice scenery" and "big zoos." Discourses of Adam's pride in reading big books and winning medals are evident in Adam's pride in being Moroccan (Figure 2.3, grades 2b, 3, 4 & 5).

Significantly, the Mosque was the primary social space for Adam and his family. When Adam was in second grade, he participated in an Eid a-Adha celebration with his uncle in which the men slaughtered a sheep. Adam was excited and recounted the gory details of the slaughter to Rohany, a Muslim research team member. He reported, "We said *Bismillah* (In the name of Allah) and cut the sheep's throat quickly with a sharp knife. My uncle cut out the stomach and took the inside organs out." Adam reported, "I pulled down the sheep's skin." As he concluded, he proudly proclaimed, "Now, I'm a man." Through-lines of faith and Morocco involved family members, people at the Mosque, and the meanings that accompanied Eid, the sheep's slaughter and becoming a man. This through-line cut across the Mosque and family (also see Figure 2.3, grade 1).

Home—Adam's family's small apartment—also reflected his Muslim faith and Moroccan heritage. The furnishing featured Moroccan fabrics and a Moroccan melody alerted family members when it was time to pray. In third grade, Adam reported on his first experience of fasting for a full day during Ramadan: "It's just like you eat before four o'clock, morning, and you just fast the whole day. And then when it's like, eight o'clock [at night], you eat." When asked to photograph some of his favorite things at home, he photographed the television set, his laptop, money that he had saved, and a large panel of Arabic text that hung in his living room. Adam explained, "It's the ninety-nine names of God." While Adam knew what the text represented, he admitted that he could not read the words, saying "I never memorized them." Regardless, this text held meaning. Adam's home space was distinctly different from school spaces, where Adam was one of very few Muslim students.

When asked in fifth grade to draw a map of his school, Adam identified the cardinal directions on his drawing. Adam explained that knowing these directions was essential in order to direct his prayers towards Mecca. He explained,

> My teacher told me where North is and I just figured out the rest. So that is North, East, Southeast, West (Adam pointed to the directions on his map as he spoke). When asked if he prayed during school, Adam responded "No," explaining, "I would but it is not like the right times because when we have the first prayer, it is during school. I have that during math and sometimes during the test, so I can't.

Adam's mother was sitting nearby as we spoke. She understood Adam's reluctance, saying, "I know, the kids like at this age . . . even [in] the home [I have to remind him to] 'Go pray, go pray.' So of course in school, he can forget. Maybe when he grows up." Here, we witness the complexities of prayer at school. Adam was clearly aware of when and in what direction he should be praying; he noted, "I would feel more comfortable in doing it [if everyone were praying at school]." Prayer and faith contributed to a through-line of family, peers, teachers, and the physical spaces that simultaneously propelled and repelled Adam toward and away from prayer.

Starting in grade three, Adam's connections to Morocco and Islam emerged in an unpredicted direction. In short, Adam was becoming increasingly politically aware as he drew on historical events, conversations with family members, and interactions at the Mosque with Muslims from around the world. In addition, Adam was watching Arabic cable television news with his mother "to see what's happening, like in Morocco [and] Syria." Adam explained "Libya is free, but Syria is not. They having a war right now." He contrasted the political systems in Morocco and the United States, saying "Our [Moroccan] King is very good. He gives like poor people like houses. . . . We have a king and in every city he has a castle. And then [for] every castle he has guards. So he does not have to get scared. Like there's 500 guards all over his castle" (Figure 2.3, grade 5).

In fifth grade, Adam attended a "rally for Palestine" at the state capital saying, "'cause all that stuff is happening, it's really sad [so] we were downtown at [the] Capital, and they were doing a protest." Adam was concerned about the historical annexation of Palestinian territory by Israel, although as Adam noted, Palestinians had been living on the land for "more than like 2000 years." He worried that so many Palestinians had been killed recently, saying "they don't have the right to kill a few million [people]."

Later during that same interview, Adam's interest in politics surfaced. He was excited about a signed letter and photograph that he had received from President Obama after his class had written letters to the President. Adam's letter addressed bullying. When I photographed the letter for our data set, Adam suggested, "you should [also] take a picture of his [Obama's] picture." Adam enthusiastically pointed to the letter adding, "And that's his signature." While at the time these texts seemed to be a novelty, across time Adam's political interests gained traction and emerged in various directions as Adam moved through middle and high school. For example, in eighth-grade, Adam was highly critical of President Trump and wrote a powerful argumentative essay about the war in Syria. In later years, Adam proposed Muslim-oriented and environmentally-conscious businesses and made critical comparisons between the media attention paid to the burning of Notre Dame Cathedral and the burning of Mosques.

Across time, I observed a through-line related to Morocco and Islam. This through-line incorporated multiple directions—religious practices, current events, politics, and affinity with the local Muslim community. Moroccan accomplishments like the building of great Mosques reverberate with Adam's pride in being an accomplished reader and writer. Not only do we observe emergences and connections, but I also observed connections across through-lines (Adam, 2000; 2004). This focus on political interests emerged alongside the fading of superheroes and video games as well as technology being reserved for academic purposes. However, these trends were neither stable nor consistent. There were ruptures, redirections, and reiterations that trouble singular and linear developmental claims (Dippre & Smith, 2020; Smith, 2020).

DISCUSSION AND CONCLUSIONS

Despite sitting in the same first grade classroom, Gabby's and Adam's becomings took very different directions and involved unique through-lines contextualized by textured interactions with people, practices, and events. Temporal discourse analysis allowed me to attend to how Gabby and Adam situated themselves in time and revealed patterns across time as they spoke, wrote, drew, and acted. These through-lines involved temporal words, references to social histories, and repeated and/or revised words and stories. Significantly, across these cases we see becomings with both limitless possibilities and differential limits. Adam's through-lines were packed with texts and competitive doings—activities that resonated with school and operated as capital within academic spaces. In contrast, Gabby's through-lines were connected to family, pets, and physical activities. Academic interests and investment were over-shadowed by the vibrancy of Gabby's makings, buildings, and doings. While both becomings were packed with possibilities, as an observer, I witnessed differing resonances with schools and teachers.

Importantly, this analysis required a particular confluence of data, analytics, and my own positionality relative to participants' stories and their becomings. Specifically, the longitudinal nature of the data set and a research design that highlighted stasis and change over time created a context in which through-lines might be both visible and salient. However, it was through my analysis—temporal discourse analysis—that I intentionally and explicitly attended to what emerged, changed, and was revisited across time. The through-lines presented above required me to assume observational, tentative, and flexible positionings. These through-lines did not align with expected trajectories and were not framed by models of causality. In many ways, they defied contemporary discourses about what education is and should be. I am less interested in whether Gabby or Adam met standards or benchmarks and much more interested in who they were and who they continue to become.

I am inspired by Dippre's and Phillips's (2020) metaphor of murmuration as described by Bazerman (2020). They explain that the "order that emerges and coordinates motion in a flock forms not because any of the birds have a spatial sense of the whole or a plan for coordinated movement. The order emerges because each is attuned to the movement of a few and its close neighbors" (p. xii). As with the other authors who have contributed to this volume, I place my trust in this power of "murmuration" (Dippre & Phillips, 2020). I recognize that it operated within textured contexts and across the literacy, writing, and life experiences of Gabby and Adam as they moved from grade one through grade five. It also operated across and through the methodological and theoretical murmuration of methodologies, ideas, patterns, researcher positionalities, and insights from fellow contributors to this volume.

Children and researchers do not operate as individuals in separate spaces; instead, we participate in emerging becomings of writing flows, practices, venues, and ventures that bring us together and move us apart. As Bazerman (2020) reminded us, "writing evolves, textual worlds evolve, the social worlds that writing is a part of evolve, people evolve as writers, and our research to understand this emergent world itself evolves" (p. xiii). We contribute not only to a self-organizing assemblage of thought and sense-making, but also to phenomena of "patterned fluid beauty" (Bazerman, 2020, xii). This is what draws us to this scholarship and to the colleagues whose work we find inspiring.

So, what does this mean for researchers with an interest in lifespan writing research? While books could be written on the subject, I humbly offer the following:

1. Listen closely, and when possible, use multiple forms of data (drawings, writing, spoken words) that provide multiple ways for participants to convey their sense-makings.
2. Stay flexible and honor the tentativeness of all data, recognizing data as located within being and within longer chains of becomings.
3. Jettison limiting and prescriptive notions of what people, including yourself as a researcher, should be at particular points in becomings.
4. Relish differences, unique becomings, and emerging possibilities.

Bazerman and his colleagues (2018) described the "interwoven effects of history, people, linguistic resources and material contexts" (p. 26) and recognized that "individual writing development will always bear the marks of larger arrangements by which the powers of writing are being harnessed as economic, political, and cultural assets" (p. 27). Like Bazerman and his colleagues (2018), I worry that "socially diminished environments of examination by distant examiners [in schools] may become influential social contexts for writing development, constraining more local and more engaging writing activities" (pp. 22–23). This may be particularly true for Gabby, whose through-lines were not consistently recognized or celebrated at school.

In closing, I note the failure of linear accounts to make sense of Gabby's and Adam's directions, redirections, and lost and resumed through-lines that were apparent across time. As Deleuze and Guattari (1988) argued, becomings are always rhizomatic, moving in unpredictable and unintentional directions; they are underground and emerging, non-hierarchical, and continually (re)forming, and ever-emerging. The past—Gabby's mother's experience of being a tomboy and Adam's memories of beaches in Morocco—were woven into the present and operated with possible futures in view. There is no "smooth continuous manifold" (Barad, 2013, p. 18) for longitudinal researchers to identify, name, or explain. Becomings simply *are*.

REFERENCES

Adam, B. (2000). The temporal gaze: the challenge for social theory in the context of GM food. *The British Journal of Sociology*, *51*(1), 125–142. https://doi.org/10.1080/000713100358462.

Adam, B. (2003). Reflexive modernization temporalized. *Theory, Culture & Society*, *20*(2), 59–78. https://doi.org/10.1177/0263276403020002004.

Adam B. (2004). *Time*. Polity Press.

Adam, B. (2008). The timescapes challenge: Engagement with the invisible temporal. In R. Edwards (Ed.), *Researching lives through time: Time, generation, and life stories*. Timescapes Working Paper Series no. 1. University of Leeds.

Barad, K. (2013). Ma(r)king time: Material entanglements and re-memberings: Cutting together-apart. In P. Carlile, D. Nicolini, A. Langley & H. Tsoukas (Eds.), *How matter matters: Objects, artifacts, and materiality in organization studies* (pp. 16–31). Oxford University Press.

Bazerman, C., Applebee, A. N., Berninger, V. W., Brandt, D., Graham, S., Jeffery, J., Matsuda, P. K., Murphy, S., Rowe, D. W., Schleppegrell, M. & Wilcox, K. C. (2018). *The lifespan development of writing*. National Council of Teachers of English. https://wac.colostate.edu/books/ncte/lifespan-writing/.

Bazerman, C. (2020). Preface. In R. J. Dippre & T. Phillips (Eds.), *Approaches to lifespan writing research: Generating an actionable coherence* (pp. 15–26). The WAC Clearinghouse; University Press of Colorado. https://doi.org/10.37514/PER-B.2020.1053.1.1.

Coleman, R. & Ringrose, J. (2013). Introduction. In J. Ringrose (Ed.), *Deleuze and research methodologies* (pp. 1–22). Edinburgh University Press.

Deleuze, G. & Guattari, F. (1988). *A thousand plateaus: Capitalism and schizophrenia*. University of Minnesota Press.

Dippre, R. J. & Phillips, T. (2020). Introduction: Generating murmurations for an actionable coherence. In R. J. Dippre & T. Phillips (Eds.), *Approaches to lifespan writing research: Generating an actionable coherence* (pp. 3–12). The WAC Clearinghouse; University Press of Colorado. https://doi.org/10.37514/PER-B.2020.1053.1.3.

Fenwick, T. (2010). Re-thinking the "thing": Sociomaterial approaches to understanding and researching learning in work. *Journal of Workplace Learning*, *2*(1/2), pp. 104–116. https://doi.org/10.1108/13665621011012898.

Fenwick, T. & Landri, P. (2012). Materialities, textures and pedagogies: Socio-material assemblages in education. *Pedagogy, Culture & Society*, *20*(1), 1–7. https://doi.org/10.1080/14681366.2012.649421.

Kbuishi, K. & Caffoe, J. (2008 – present). *Amulet Series*. Scholastic.

Murris, K. (Ed.). (2021). *Navigating the postqualitative, new materialist and critical posthumanist terrain across disciplines: An introductory guide.* Routledge.

Smith, A. (2020). Across, through, and with: Ontological orientations for lifespan writing research. In R. J. Dippre & T. Phillips (Eds.), *Approaches to lifespan writing research: Generating an actionable coherence* (pp. 15–26). The WAC Clearinghouse; University Press of Colorado. https://doi.org/10.37514/PER-B.2020.1053.2.01.

CHAPTER 3.

METHODOLOGIES FOR LIFESPAN WRITING RESEARCH: USING COMPOSITE NARRATIVES IN NARRATIVE INQUIRY

Jennifer Sanders
Oklahoma State University

Sarah Donovan
Oklahoma State University

Joy Myers
James Madison University

Danielle L. DeFauw
University of Michigan, Dearborn

In this chapter, we focus on the narrative inquiry method of creating composite narratives that embrace storied accounts and focus on the places, actions, and agents of a group's experiences. Composite narratives draw on the power of shared experiences by combining multiple stories into one narrative that highlights patterns and themes of experience, provides anonymity to participants, and conveys findings in narrative modes that foster understanding. Our interest in this method stems from a study that we (four teacher education researchers) conducted to understand how in-service K-12 teachers grow as writing educators across their career span. While this project did not investigate writing itself, an important part of writing teacher development involves their experiences as writers, and writing teachers' pedagogical orientations shape the way others are taught writing. Moreover, we see composite narratives as a useful method for lifespan writing research because composites draw from the genre of creative nonfiction to reveal patterns of participants' shared experiences.

In our own research, we used narrative inquiry (Clandinin, 2013) and composite narratives to represent 19 teachers' experiences of writing pedagogy development across their lifespan. The full composite narratives are presented in the next chapter, and a condensed version was originally published in *Literacy Practice and Research* (Donovan et al., 2023). Exploring the teachers' lifespan of writing pedagogy development (Bazerman, 2018; Dippre & Phillips, 2020) through composite narratives afforded us an opportunity to detail the teachers' shared experiences evident in their varied yet similar trajectories of learning how to implement writing pedagogy with K-12 students. In this chapter, we explore the history of narrative inquiry and composites, discuss the affordances of composites for lifespan writing research, and share our processes for creating composite narratives so researchers can apply the methods according to their needs.

AN OVERVIEW OF NARRATIVE METHODOLOGY AND ITS HISTORY

Narrative inquiry methodology grew out of the premise that lived experience and narrative are valid and valuable ways of knowing (Clandinin, 2013). Interdisciplinary research in educational psychology and neuroscience reveals that the human brain is activated complexly when telling stories; also, the emotional connections and experiential thinking that take place in storytelling are vital for long-term learning and knowledge development (Immordino-Yang & Knecht, 2020). Therefore, narrative is a generative tool for understanding human experience and developing new knowledge, and for these same purposes, it's an equally powerful research methodology that draws on people's physiological affinity for stories.

Narrative methodologies focus on how human beings live their lives through story and construct their lived experiences through the telling and retelling of critical events (Webster & Mertova, 2007). Narrative inquiry has broad, interdisciplinary origins across fields such as education, literature, psychology, healthcare, and history (Clandinin & Connelly, 2000) and may draw upon the following method(s): narrating or storytelling as a mode of understanding and generating data; narratives or the textual narrative data that are examined; and/or narrative analysis that focuses on setting (place and time), people, and actions or events (Riessman, 2008).

Although stories themselves date back to the beginnings of oral literacy, the narrative turn in social science research occurred as a response to an emphasis in the early 1900s on scientific generalizations derived from quantifiable data (Lagemann, 1996). Following the early and widespread uptake of behaviorist learning theories such as Thorndike's operant conditioning, there have been frequent and aggressive returns to measuring teaching and learning throughout the history of education, as exemplified by the current "science of reading" era inundating the US (Goodwin & Jiménez, 2020).

In the 1980s, Bruner's (1986) articulation of narrative as an epistemological stance and the development of narrative analysis methods counteracted positivist and post-positivist researchers' insistence on "truth and proof" (p. 12). Bruner (1986) asserted that there were two primary modes of thought—narrative and argument—and theorized that they were very different "ways of ordering experience" and "constructing reality" (p. 11). Arguments move toward universal truth and proof statements, whereas narratives seek to situate the details of experience "in time and place" in a way that illustrates the "likely particular connections" between events (Bruner, 1986, p. 12–13). Polkinghorne (1988) added the distinction between two kinds of narrative inquiry products—descriptive narratives that detailed sequences of significant events in people's lives and explanatory narratives that highlighted causal connections between events. Lyotard (1984) described narrative's usefulness as a research tool and distinguished between meta-narratives (or grand narratives) that operate in generalizations and micro-narratives that are grounded in differences and diversity. These interdisciplinary works were influential in the development of narrative inquiry.

Clandinin and Connelly (2000) built on this interdisciplinary scholarship and expanded it through their own decades of work with narrative inquiry and methodology in their landmark book, *Narrative Inquiry*. Drawing upon Dewey's (1934, 1938) work with experience, they aimed to develop a research methodology that would resist researchers' tendencies toward identifying "manageable," measurable, and "miniscule realities" by highlighting people's lived experiences and how they are composed in narrative events (Clandinin & Connelly, 2000, p. xxii). Clandinin and Connelly's (2000) book, along with scholars such as Riessman (2008) and Schaafsma and Vinz (2011), provide a multifaceted methodology of narrative inquiry that returns the researcher's gaze to people's experiences. The goal of narrative inquiry is understanding *how* those experiences happen, *how* growth and change take place, and *how* temporality and context influence experience (Clandinin & Connelly, 2000).

Several theoretical concepts help researchers attend to questions of how experiences take place and guide data collection and analysis in narrative inquiries. The concept of *story*—a temporally and spatially sequenced telling of events that includes a problem, conflict, or disruptor that leads to a change—is central to understanding an experience, although there is variation among scholars (and across cultures) about the essential structural components of a story (Riessman, 2008). Related to temporality and the sequencing of events, *continuity* is another important narrative inquiry concept; continuity refers to how experiences are linked and the ways past and future experiences are connected as part of a narrative unity (Clandinin & Connelly, 2000). Regarding narrative plot structures, nuclear *episodes* of "specific autobiographical events which have been . . . reinterpreted over time to assume a privileged status in the story," and *thematic lines* of "recurrent content clusters in stories" provide additional analytic concepts (Plummer, 2007, pp. 399–400). Within a narrative perspective, then, life stories include a point of view or lens that necessarily shape the tone of the episodes and thus construct its meaning and significance. These and other narrative elements such as *social interaction* and *situation* (Schaafsma & Vinz, 2011) are employed by educational researchers to create complex, contextualized narratives of teaching and learning that (re)present accounts in a way that the initial narrator, the researcher-narrator, and the reader "can imagine or 'feel' as right" (Bruner, 1986, p. 52).

Beyond the goal of understanding how experiences take place, "narratives do political work" (Riessman, 2008, p. 8). For individuals, narratives may provide connection, persuade, argue, or entertain, among other purposes, but for groups, narratives can serve as a means of advocacy and activism (The Center for Story-based Strategy, n.d.). Riessman (2008) states, "Stories can mobilize others into action for progressive social change" (p. 9), and this mobilization is enacted in present-day activist organizations such as The Center for Story-based Strategy. The political affordances of narrative can also be seen in related methodologies such as oral history and ethnographic case study. For example, Dyke et al.'s (2022) oral history of the 2018 teacher strikes in Oklahoma and Heath's (1983) landmark ethnographic case study of socio-cultural literacy development do political work to expose oppressive social systems and equity issues.

While narrative, oral history, and ethnographic methodologies use similar narrative methods, they also differ in important ways. Although oral histories capture individual people's lived experiences through story, the narratives are typically presented in the participant's original words, without interpretation, revision, or reconstruction by the researcher and/or considered raw data for further study (Ritchie, 2015). On the other hand, although the data of ethnographic case studies are often storied to varying degrees, they are not necessarily presented in narrative form and typically do not systematically employ narrative analysis in the ways that a study using narrative inquiry as a methodology would.

As mentioned, narrative inquiry studies include a variety of data collection, analysis, and representation methods that draw upon narrative theory and narrative elements to understand human experience through and with story. Narrative can serve simultaneously—or separately—in the following roles: the methodology, informed by an epistemological and theoretical perspective and the researcher's questions; a data collection method to gather stories through narrative interview protocols or written accounts; a data analysis method using some of the narrative elements and concepts discussed above to interpret the data; and/or a data representation method that might convey storied themes of experiences, significant narrative elements of the experiences, or full or partial stories as findings. There are many possible permutations of these methods with any given application.

Scholars from many disciplines contributed to the development and acceptance of narrative inquiry methodologies that include diverse approaches to storying people's lived experiences holistically, structurally, episodically, or thematically (Riessman, 2008). Composite narratives grew out of this complex and interdisciplinary history of narrative inquiry.

COMPOSITE NARRATIVE METHODS: ORIGINS AND AFFORDANCES

The composite narrative is a method of data representation that involves synthesizing multiple stories into one narrative to convey both the patterns of experience across individuals as well as the particularities of those experiences (Willis, 2019). There are many approaches to narrative analysis and data representation (Riessman, 2008), including the layering of narratives with methods such as *tandem tellings* in which two or three people story the same experience from different perspectives, demonstrating that one narrator's account is not more or less true than another's (Schaafsma & Vinz, 2011). Rather than focusing on one participant's story, as is often seen in traditional narrative inquiry (Clandinin & Connelly, 2000), or chaining individual stories or cameos together in a manner common to oral history analysis (e.g., Brandt, 2001), composite narratives provide a way to synthesize multiple stories or interviews into one narrative that represents patterns of shared experience. The researcher attends to the patterns so that each participant's story resonates in the composite synthesis.

Composite narratives represent specific aspects of the research findings (they are not all-encompassing) in an analytic-interpretive act that moves beyond a simple retelling:

> It is interpretation by the researcher in several important ways: through her knowledge of the literature regarding the phenomenon under enquiry, through listening and hearing the stories told by the informants, and through her own reflexivity during the process. (Wertz et al., 2011, p. 2)

This interpretive work is supported by the researcher's experience with the content and context of the study; therefore, insider perspectives are viewed as an asset, not a hindrance (Willis, 2019). The end product, the composite narrative, presents empirical, interpretive findings that maintain a narrative structure and sense of a narrative whole.

THE EVOLUTION OF COMPOSITE NARRATIVES

Composite narratives, as a research method, developed recently, with most publications occurring within the last quarter-century (Johnston et al., 2021). Much of the early composite narrative antecedents came from feminist post-structural scholarship in social sciences (Brook, 2004). For example, Haug (1987), an early pioneer of composite narratives in the form of *collective memory work*, helped participants and researchers fill memory gaps as they recalled their lived experiences as women. Haug's (2000) approach differs from other composite narrative methods because it involves a group of participants collectively revising one member's personal account or scene from a memory into a complete narrative that includes a co-constructed theme and interpretive elements. Building on Haug's work, Davies et al. (1997) and Davies and Gannon (2006) employed a form of collaborative dialogue and writing they called *collective biography*. Used as a data generation/collection approach rather than a data representation method, collective biographies involve memory work and a recursive composing process of individual storytelling with group feedback to elicit details, followed by writing, sharing, and revising the personal narrative. These collaboratively developed but individually written biographies are then studied as data for the focal topic.

The *essence statement* in phenomenological research (e.g., Moustakas, 1994) can be considered another antecedent genre to composite narratives. To present study findings, phenomenologists have historically composed essence statements, a synthesis of several participants' experiences distilled down to the experience's structurally essential elements and textures. Todres and Galvin (2008) stated that, traditionally, phenomenological essence statements have a more summative nature "that can over-sterilize or even deaden the aliveness of the shown phenomena" (p. 569). Thus, they developed a more "embodied interpretation" method that evokes emotional connection and elicits "concrete, lifeworld descriptions of the experience" (p. 578). As with our own study detailed in the next chapter, Todres' (2007) goal was not to be exhaustive with a particular composite narrative but to tell a story that allows readers personal insight into a storied experience's themes.

To convey detailed experiences, composite narratives have been used in education (Miller et al., 2020), medicine (Creese et al., 2021), and social work (Hordyk et al., 2014). Lambert (2003) employed composite narratives to describe four kinds of principals that correspond with her grounded theory model of school leadership: each composite narrated one quadrant of her leadership model. In Lambert's findings, composite narratives provided anonymity for the schools and principals exemplifying low leadership capacity, but they also showed the patterns of behavior, characterization, and context across cases. Johnston et al. (2021) also used composites with grounded theory and found they can represent "multiple facets of theory construction through a singular narrative point-of-view" with potentially higher transferability due to their relational and memorable qualities (p. 1). These researchers demonstrate how composites can "reflect the complex theoretical categories, properties, and dimensions of a grounded theory," and posit their usefulness in a range of methodologies (Johnston et al., 2021, p. 3). Because of the interdisciplinary origins and affordances of composite narratives, they are well suited to several research methodologies and problems.

Affordances of Composite Narratives

A main advantage of composite narratives is their ability to forward participants' voices through incorporation of their own language while masking identities in sensitive situations. For example, Willis (2019) studied 14 United Kingdom politicians' decision making. She used composites to provide anonymity while conveying how the politicians, as a group, navigated their complex work contexts. Anonymity was key in the politicians' abilities to share their experiences openly.

A second affordance of composites is that experimentation with form is encouraged, which allows for countless ways to represent multiple voices (Clandinin & Connelly, 2000). Researchers can incorporate direct quotes or text from participants in narratives from any literary point of view. Researchers can create multiple, layered narratives for one person's composite like Richmond et al. (2011): they created three narratives for each preservice teacher participant, narrating their identities as educators through "stories they told about themselves to others and to themselves in first-person narratives, stories others told about them to them in second-person narratives, and stories others told about them to others in third-person narratives" (p. 1894). Flexibility of form enables the researcher to present findings in ways that align with the research purpose, question, and theoretical perspective.

Third, composites provide an avenue for pushing back against Western and "scientific" hegemony in research through narrative inquiry methods (Tierney, 2018). Supporting a variety of data representation structures that are responsive to both participants and diverse research frameworks is one way composites counter a narrowed research paradigm: the length and structure of the composite can range from a brief "cameo" (McAlpine et al., 2014) up to full chapter-length composites (Lambert, 2003). Privileging participants' voices in research products is another counter-hegemonic affordance. Researchers may also integrate their own stories into those of their participants to create a co-storied, polyvocal composite, such as Vintz (1996) does in her research of teachers' early career experiences. Forwarding participants' own voices, engaging them as co-researchers, prioritizing their own storied interpretations of their experiences, and publishing scholarship that challenges the measurement culture with humanizing and contextualized data are critical affordances of narrative inquiry.

A fourth benefit of composites is that they represent patterns across experiences without reducing data to categories. Composites allow the reader to retain the sense of the big idea or theme while hearing multiple people's stories. Johnston et al. (2021) argue this affordance supports readers' understanding of the experience and enables findings to transfer from research to real life. Through the process of coming together and compiling, the composite narrative can resonate with all participants (Brook, 2004).

A fifth affordance of composite narratives is the researcher's ability to synthesize data across large participant samples into relatively brief representations. For example, Bosanquet et al. (2017) created five composites to represent the various early-career academics' experiences across 522 participants. Their brief, composite narratives layer participants' voices via direct quotes along with researcher-created portions to characterize the trajectories they observed. Altogether, these affordances make composites a flexible method for presenting qualitative, narrative findings that synthesize multiple participant voices and shared experiences, sometimes across large data sets, with anonymity and detail.

AFFORDANCES OF COMPOSITE NARRATIVES FOR LIFESPAN WRITING RESEARCH

Although the field of lifespan writing research, like composite narratives, is early in its development, and its repertoire of characteristics, methodologies, and methods is yet to be compiled (Bazerman, 2020), its main defining feature is its longitudinal examination of writing development and writing lives (Dippre & Phillips, 2020). We argue that composite narratives allow researchers to harness agentive representations across many participants and/or across a lifespan study. "Narratives are inherently and explicitly agentive, demonstrating individuals' hopes and intentions as they attempt to navigate their present and future" (McAlpine et al., 2014, p. 955).

Through our experience as researchers, we propose that these two relatively young approaches, composites and lifespan writing research, can be productively paired for research focused on (a) expansive data collected during lifespan writing research, (b) developmental trends of writers and writing teachers, and (c) stories that capture the intricate tapestries of living as writers across contexts.

Understanding lifespan writing development is imperative for writers and teachers of writing because the complex journey of writing evolves across writers' learning trajectories and experiences. As teachers of writing develop their pedagogical understanding of how to write and how to teach writing, their insight directly impacts the quality of instruction from which writers develop. Because writers' experiences and trajectories vary, align, and intersect, composites provide many affordances for lifespan writing research.

First, researchers need methods for analyzing and presenting the vast data required for effective longitudinal research. Illustrating her findings based on the reading and writing life histories of 80 Americans born across a hundred-year timespan, Brandt (2001) presents brief, partial biographies and character sketches, organized thematically. Without these narratives, her findings risk being fragmented and decontextualized. While Brandt composed several short biographies to illustrate common themes of experience, composites synthesize by integrating common experiences into one or more composites that capture themes and convey a narrative arc. With or without direct quotes from participants, composite narratives offer an approach for representing the writing or literacy lifespan data of multiple people across a long timeframe.

Second, because variability exists across writers' and writing teachers' experiences, particularly in large studies, composites are useful in storying the patterns. Researchers investigating the developmental trends of writers and their teachers must be able to present their findings in a way that helps stakeholders understand "the varied pathways to competence and expertise in writing" (Bazerman, 2018, p. 327). Such knowledge "can help educators provide support to writers at every stage from early childhood through adulthood, and further it can help people self-monitor and guide their own development" (Bazerman, 2018, p. 327). Developmental trends are complex and dependent upon individuals' opportunities to learn and to transfer their understanding from past to present to future contexts (Brandt, 2001) and they are also influenced by learning opportunities in and outside of the classroom. As Bazerman et al. (2018) highlight, lifespan writing research is riddled with challenges; however, those challenges can be overcome through intentional, longitudinal research designed to understand how writing teachers' development intersects with their students' writing development. Composite narratives provide a valuable method for synthesizing shared experiences and highlighting developmental trends.

Third, composite narratives make findings accessible to a wider readership (Wertz et al., 2011). Stories can be transferred more easily into existing conceptions and situations of practice (Willis, 2019). In the same way that individuals connect with one another's stories, participants' experiences and feelings represented in composite narratives are relatable for other individuals. Thus, each composite is at once singular and multi-voiced. In lifespan research, composite narratives offer relevant scenes with explanation, reflection, and a re-seeing of the past along with a reimagining of the future, which is unique to the temporal and spatial nature of narrative.

Creating Composite Narratives

Composite narratives are a relatively modern analysis method. The works of Wertz et al. (2011), Willis (2019), and Johnston et al. (2021) are foundational in articulating procedures for composing composites. Composite narratives may be written from first-, second-, or third-person perspectives. Wertz et al. (2011) describe their approach to writing first person composites, stipulating that the composite be written with the pronoun "I" to create an "increased sense of contact" (p. 3). This approach conveys the composite person or storyteller as "someone who typifies the general experience within a living and situated context" (Wertz et al., 2011, p. 3). Other researchers prefer to create third-person narratives using "he/him" or "she/her" pronouns (or non-binary pronouns, as appropriate)). A third-person composite may include verbatim quotes from multiple participants who make up one composite, and specific details in the narrative are included because they exemplify patterns across participants (Willis, 2019).

A narrative study that employs composites might have a range of participants from as few as two to five who comprise one composite to as many as dozens represented in multiple composites. Participants are typically represented in one composite narrative, with participants grouped by shared experiences, attributes, critical events, narrative threads, or story themes related to the research question. Researchers assess the fit of each participant's salient experiences with its group members' experiences to solidify the final composite groupings. The final composite should have resonance for all participants represented in that composite group.

Compiling practices from resources listed later in this chapter and our own study, we provide the following additional procedures for composing composite narratives:

1. The research questions, focal findings, units of narrative analysis employed, and the narrative elements (e.g., story grammar, temporality, sociality, physicality, continuity, nuclear episodes, thematic lines) foregrounded in that analysis will determine the shape and content of the composite narrative (Brook, 2004)
2. The quotes used in the composite are data taken directly from the represented group's participants. Even if written in third person, the composite text draws heavily from participants' own words. Johnston et al.

(2021) recommend keeping an audit trail of the raw data excerpts used to develop the composite
3. Other details (e.g., setting, people, actions, events) are taken directly from one or more of the original data sources from the group's participants
4. Researchers must not impose judgment or assume motivations; thus, any statements to these effects must come directly from the group's data (Willis, 2019). For example, in our composites included in the next chapter, the feelings Sam expressed came from one of the "Sam" participant's raw data: "Sam often pushes back when things do not go the way he thinks they should go. Sometimes this is well received, other times it is not."
5. The composite's length will depend on the story itself and on the constraints of the publication venue. Willis' (2019) composite narratives were 500–600 words. Our final composites are 800–900 words. In book-length publications, one composite may be a chapter
6. Composites offer a unique opportunity for member checking. Researchers can share the composites with participants, gather their feedback via focus group discussions or written response, and revise the composites to reflect any missing or misinterpreted nuances of their experiences

These steps help researchers create composite narratives clearly grounded in the data and participants' own storying of their experiences while also representing the shared experiences through narrative arcs that may resonate with or reflect readers' experiences. Even with clear guidelines for compiling composites, researchers may experience challenges in composing them and may encounter limitations of the method.

LIMITATIONS OF COMPOSITE NARRATIVES

One limitation of a composite narrative is reliance on researchers to create the composites (Willis, 2019). Because we, as researchers and narrative composers, must select what to include in each narrative, we also inevitably decide what to exclude (Schaafsma, 1993) and important details in individual stories are left out in the process of constructing composites. The readability, resonance, and representation afforded by composites come at the expense of some specific details of each person's story. This limitation speaks to the importance of collaborative data analysis and narrative composing, in addition to member checking.

A second limitation of composites is the problem of what to do with a single outlier experience or perhaps two experiences that are divergent from others. If one participant's story is quite different from the others and does not fit into any of the other composite groups' experiences, a researcher will have to decide what to do with the divergent story. It might be omitted from the findings or addressed in a discussion or limitation section.

Another limitation might be "a danger of privileging narrative, relying too much on accounts provided by individuals, and not seeing the wider context or structure" (Willis, 2019, p. 478), but this concern for understanding the wider context may also be an epistemological question of what counts as knowledge and knowing. In our study, we could have taken an ethnographic approach, observing each teacher's place and practice to situate their story, but this would risk negating the participants' lived and told story. We relied on the teachers' reflections on and storying of the critical events, people, and places in their development as writing teachers, and we were clear about how these stories were generated and how the composites were constructed. But we were only able to provide context and representation of structures at work insofar as the teachers narrated those contexts or structures themselves, which may result in limited contextualization. Ultimately, a researcher chooses a methodology and data representation methods based on the research purpose and questions as well as the kinds of knowledge valued in each particular inquiry.

GETTING STARTED WITH COMPOSITE NARRATIVES

Throughout our journey to better understand narrative inquiry and composite narratives, we found the following resources useful: AERA's Narrative Research Special Interest Group; *Narrative Inquiry* (Clandinin & Caine, 2013); "Constructing Composite Narratives" (Johnston et al., 2021); and "The Use of Composite Narratives to Present Interview Findings" (Willis, 2019). Additional resources can be found in the reference list.

Researchers who are ready to try out composite narratives for the first time might consider conducting a self-study (Myers et al., 2022) or collaborative autoethnography (Hernandez et al., 2017) with a group of colleagues. The participant-researchers could interview one another and/or write personal narratives about the experience under investigation, analyze the data for narrative elements, and collaboratively construct one composite narrative to represent thematic lines and critical elements of the group's experiences. We found that it was easier to shape a composite narrative that represents one's own experiences when it was developed in collaboration with other researchers.

We conclude that composite narratives can assist scholars in understanding of how writers and writing teachers develop throughout the lifespan and understanding the experiential trajectories that impact writing development. This social science method enables scholars to continue the narrative turn toward relational, humanizing, and contextualized forms of research.

REFERENCES

Bazerman, C. (2018). Lifespan longitudinal studies of writing development: A heuristic for an impossible dream. In C. Bazerman, A. N. Applebee, V. W. Berninger, D. Brandt, S. Graham, J. V. Jeffery, P. K. Matsuda, S. Murphy, D. W. Rowe, M. Schleppegrell & K. C. Wilcox (Eds.), *The lifespan development of writing* (pp. 326–365). National Council of Teachers of English.

Bazerman, C. (2020). Preface. In R. J. Dippre & T. Phillips (Eds.), *Approaches to lifespan writing research: Generating an actionable coherence* (pp. xi–xiii). The WAC Clearinghouse; University Press of Colorado. https://doi.org/10.37514/PER-B.2020.1053.1.1.

Bazerman, C., Applebee, A. N., Berninger, V. W., Brandt, D., Graham, S., Jeffery, J. V., Matsuda, P. K., Murphy, S., Rowe, D. W., Schleppegrell, M. & Wilcox, K. C. (2018). *The lifespan development of writing*. National Council of Teachers of English. https://wac.colostate.edu/books/ncte/lifespan-writing/.

Bosanquet, A., Mailey, A., Matthews, K. E. & Lodge, J. M. (2017). Redefining 'early career' in academia: A collective narrative approach. *Higher Education Research & Development, 36*(5), 890–902. https://doi.org/10.1080/07294360.2016.1263934.

Brandt, D. (2001). *Literacy in American lives*. Cambridge University Press.

Brook, B. (2004). *Slipping through the cracks: Constructing a composite narrative of postgraduate researchers.* https://www.aare.edu.au/data/publications/2004/bro04970.pdf.

Bruner, J. (1986). *Actual minds, possible worlds*. Harvard University Press.

Clandinin, D. J. (2013). *Engaging in narrative inquiry*. Left Coast Press, Inc.

Clandinin, D. J. & Caine, V. (2013). Narrative inquiry. In A. A. Trainor & E. Graue (Eds.), *Reviewing qualitative research in the social sciences* (pp. 178–191). Routledge.

Clandinin, D. J. & Connelly, F. M. (2000). *Narrative inquiry: Experience and story in qualitative research*. Jossey-Bass.

Creese, J., Byrne, J. P., Conway, E., Barrett, E., Prihodova, L. & Humphries, N. (2021). We all really need to just take a breath": Composite narratives of hospital doctors' well-being during the COVID-19 Pandemic. *International Journal of Environmental Research and Public Health, 18,* 1–18. https://doi.org/10.3390/ijerph18042051.

Davies, B., Dormer, S., Honan, E., McAllister, N., O'Reilly, R., Rocco, S. & Walker, A. (1997). Ruptures in the skin of silence: A collective biography. *Hecate—A Women's Studies Interdisciplinary Journal, 23*(1), 62–79.

Davies, B. & Gannon, S. (Eds.). (2006). *Doing collective biography*. Open University Press.

Dewey, J. (1934). *Art as experience*. Capricorn Books.

Dewey, J. (1938). *Experience and education*. Collier Books.

Dippre, R. J. & Phillips, T. (Eds.). (2020). *Approaches to lifespan writing research: Generating an actionable coherence*. The WAC Clearinghouse; University Press of Colorado. https://doi.org/10.37514/PER-B.2020.1053.

Donovan, S., Sanders, J., DeFauw, D. & Myers, J. K. (2023). K-12 writing teachers' careerspan development: Participatory pedagogical content knowledge of writing. *Literacy Practice and Research, 48*(2), 4. https://digitalcommons.fiu.edu/lpr/vol48/iss2/4.

Dyke, E., Anderson, H., Brown, A., El Sabbagh, J., Fernandez, H., Goodwin, S., Lowther, J., Price, S., Ruby, M., Self, K., Williams, D., Williams, J. & Worth, A. (2022). Beyond defeat: Understanding educators' experiences in the 2018 Oklahoma walkouts. *Critical Education, 13*(2), pp. 77–95. https://doi.org/10.14288/ce.v13i2.186610.

Goodwin, A. P. & Jiménez, R. T. (Eds.). (2020). The science of reading: Supports, critiques, and questions. *Reading Research Quarterly, 55*(S1), S7–S16. https://doi.org/10.1002/rrq.360.

Haug, F. (1987). Female sexualization: A collective work of memory. (E. Carter, Trans.). Verso.

Haug, F. (2000). *Memory-work as a method of social science research, a detailed rendering of memory work method.* http://www.friggahaug.inkrit.de/documents/memorywork-researchguidei7.pdf.

Heath, S. B. (1983). *Ways with words.* Cambridge University Press.

Hernandez, K. A. C., Chang, H. & Ngunjiri, F. W. (2017). Collaborative autoethnography as multivocal, relational, and democratic research: Opportunities, challenges, and aspirations. *Auto/Biography Studies, 32*(2), 251–254.

Hordyk, S. R., Soltane, S. B. & Hanley, J. (2014). Sometimes you have to go under water to come up: A poetic, critical realist approach to documenting the voices of homeless immigrant women. *Qualitative Social Work, 13*(2), 203–220. https://doi.org/10.1177%2F1473325013491448.

Immordino-Yang, M. H. & Knecht, D. R. (2020). Building meaning builds teens' brains. *Educational Leadership, 77*(8), 36–43.

Johnston, O., Wildy, H. & Shand, J. (2021). Student voices that resonate–Constructing composite narratives that represent students' classroom experiences. *Qualitative Research*, 1–17. https://doi.org/10.1177%2F14687941211016158.

Lagemann, E. C. (1996). *Contested terrain: A history of education research in the United States, 1890–1990.* Spencer Foundation.

Lambert, L. (2003). *Leadership capacity for lasting school improvement.* ASCD.

Lyotard, J. F. (1984). *The postmodern condition: A report on knowledge* (Vol. 10). University of Minnesota Press.

McAlpine, L., Amundsen, C. & Turner, G. (2014). Identity-trajectory: Reframing early career academic experience. *British Educational Research Journal, 40*(6), 952–969. https://doi.org/10.1002/berj.3123.

Miller, R., Liu, K. & Ball, A. F. (2020). Critical counter-narrative as transformative methodology for educational equity. *Review of Research in Education, 44*, 269–300. https://doi.org/10.3102%2F0091732X20908501.

Moustakas, C. (1994). *Phenomenological research methods.* Sage.

Myers, J., DeFauw, D., Sanders, J. & Donovan, S. (2022). Using collaborative self-study to examine writing teacher educators' career continuums. *Studying Teacher Education, 19*(1), 44–62. https://doi.org/10.1080/17425964.2022.2057941.

Plummer, K. (2007). The call of life stories in ethnographic research. In P. Atkinson, A. Coffey, S. Delamont, J. Lofland & L. Lofland (Eds.), *Handbook of ethnography* (pp. 395–406). Sage.

Polkinghorne, D. E. (1988). *Narrative knowing and the human sciences*. Suny Press.

Richmond, G., Juzwik, M. M. & Steele, M. D. (2011). Trajectories of teacher identity development across institutional contexts: Constructing a narrative approach. *Teachers College Record, 113*(9), 1863–1905. https://doi.org/10.1177/016146811 111300907.

Riessman, C. K. (2008). *Narrative methods for the human sciences*. Sage.

Ritchie, D. A. (2015). *Doing oral history* (3rd ed). Oxford University Press.

Schaafsma, D. (1993). *Eating on the street: Teaching literacy in a multicultural society*. University of Pittsburgh Press.

Schaafsma, D. & Vinz, R. (2011). *Narrative inquiry: Approaches to language and literacy research*. Teachers College Press.

The Center for Story-based Strategy. (n.d.). *Theory of change*. https://static1.squarespace.com/static/59b848d980bd5ee35b495f6e/t/59d91e6029f187b71a7bcceb/1507401313613/css_theory_of_change_final.pdf.

Tierney, R. J. (2018). Toward a model of global meaning making. *Journal of Literacy Research, 50*(4), 397–422. https://doi.org/10.1177/1086296X18803.

Todres, L. (2007). *Embodied enquiry: Phenomenological touchstones for research, psychotherapy and spirituality*. Palgrave Macmillan.

Todres, L. & Galvin, K. T. (2008). Embodied interpretation: A novel way of evocatively re-presenting meanings in phenomenological research. *Qualitative Research, 8*(5), 568–583. https://doi.org/10.1177/146879410809.

Vintz, R. (1996). *Composing a teaching life*. Portsmouth.

Webster, L. & Mertova, P. (2007). *Using narrative inquiry as a research method: An introduction to using critical event narrative analysis in research on learning and teaching*. Routledge.

Wertz, M. S., Nosek, M., McNiesh, S. & Marlow, E. (2011). The composite first person narrative: Texture, structure, and meaning in writing phenomenological descriptions. *International Journal of Qualitative Studies on Health and Well-Being, 6*(2), 1–10. https://doi.org/10.3402/qhw.v6i2.5882.

Willis, R. (2019). The use of composite narratives to present interview findings. *Qualitative Research, 19*(4), 471–480. https://doi.org/10.1177/1468794118787711.

CHAPTER 4.

USING COMPOSITE NARRATIVES TO EXPLORE WRITING TEACHERS' DEVELOPMENT ACROSS THEIR CAREERS

Danielle L. DeFauw
University of Michigan, Dearborn

Joy Myers
James Madison University

Sarah Donovan
Oklahoma State University

Jennifer Sanders
Oklahoma State University

This chapter details our (four teacher educators') narrative inquiry study designed to investigate the following question: What is the developmental growth trajectory of writing pedagogy and content knowledge for K-12 in-service teachers? Interested in lifespan writing research, we aimed to understand writing teachers' development of pedagogical content knowledge of writing (PCKW), which encompasses writing teachers' understandings of what discipline-specific content to teach and how to teach it. Effective writing teachers have a profound impact on students' lifespan writing development (Murphy & Smith, 2018). Teachers enrich students' writing development through their instruction, influence, and identity as a writer, teacher-writer, and/or teacher of writing. We describe the steps we took to explore K-12 writing teachers' trajectories using an empirically and aesthetically powerful and flexible method: composite narratives, hereafter identified as composites. This narrative inquiry method permitted an exploration of shared experiences that highlighted K-12 writing teachers' development of PCKW.[1]

---

1   Note: Portions of this chapter were originally published by Donovan et al. (2023) in *Literacy Practice and Research*, and are reprinted here with permission.

DOI: https://doi.org/10.37514/PER-B.2024.2289.2.04

THEORETICAL FRAMEWORK

When teachers apply pedagogical content knowledge (PCK) in their instruction, they thread together pertinent content and effective pedagogy to meet students' learning needs (Shulman, 1986; 1987); extending this research, Shulman and Shulman (2004) evolved the notion of PCK from an individualistic to a community focus. As teachers gain contextualized experience with PCK within communities, they acquire a growing sense of pedagogical content knowing (PCKg) defined as "*a teacher's integrated understanding of four components of pedagogy, subject matter content, student characteristics, and the environmental context of learning*" (Cochran et al., 1993, p. 266, italics in original). PCK or PCKg of writing addresses "the control of two crafts, teaching and writing" (Graves, 1983, p. 56). Along with Parr et al. (2007), Houghton et al. (2006) were some of the early scholars to write about pedagogical content knowledge of writing as "the special language of writing" and "how to enact that language" in the practice of teaching (p. 12). Writing teachers need a deep understanding of this pedagogical content knowledge of writing (PCKW) to support students' writing development (Parr et al., 2007).

K-12 Writing Teachers' Development

As writing teacher educators, we want preservice and in-service teachers to develop strong teacher-writer or writer-teacher identities to support their students' writing development (Cremin & Oliver, 2017). Unfortunately, most K-12 teachers are never required to take a writing methods course (Morgan & Pytash, 2014) even though scholars advocate for required writing methods courses in undergraduate and graduate teacher preparation programs (National Commission on Writing, 2003; Sanders et al., 2020). Graham (2019) states many teachers do not teach writing well due to a lack of systemic structures designed to provide them with thorough preparation and ongoing learning opportunities to develop high-quality writing instruction across their careers.

Additional support for writing teachers may include both formal and informal learning opportunities. Formally, engaging with professional organizations such as the National Writing Project assists teachers in developing voice, ownership, and agency in their professional lives (Whitney, 2009). Informally, some teachers choose self-selected professional development (PD) that influences their instructional practices (Limbrick et al., 2010). Engaging in PD across a career span is necessary because just as students develop their writing skills year to year, teachers must also continue to develop their PCKW. Learning to write and learning how to teach writing take time (Schmidt, 1998). Every new context "makes new demands and requires new learning," and writers and writing teachers will need "time to develop" and become familiar with the new expectations (Bazerman et al., 2018, p. 43). Because teachers are resilient, they work to formally and informally gain the experiences they need to develop as writing teachers. Understanding the various avenues teachers may take to develop PCKW is important for facilitating teachers' growth intentionally, thus our focus on exploring the developmental growth trajectory of PCKW for K-12 in-service teachers.

METHODOLOGY

Using composites (Willis, 2019), we drew upon teachers' stories of their professional learning experiences to understand the key components, critical events, significant actors, and transformational actions that led to their learning. As writing teacher educators, we believe story is a way of knowing and a method for conducting humanizing and humanized research; therefore, we used a narrative inquiry methodology (Clandinin & Connelly, 2000) that provided the "methodological flexibility . . . to meet the challenge of understanding writing through the lifespan," namely K-12 writing teachers' careers as they develop PCKW (Dippre & Phillips, 2020, p. 247).

In order to explore writing teachers' developmental processes, we synthesized 19 teachers' growth stories in four composites, presented in the findings. The data analysis and representation method are detailed in the previous chapter. Here, we briefly overview the methods and focus on the findings.

Participants and Data Collection

We invited 41 teachers, nominated by their colleagues as exemplary writing teachers (which we intentionally left open to the nominator's interpretation of what constituted exemplary), to participate in the study. Twenty-seven teachers responded with interest, and 19 met our criteria as current K-12 classroom writing teachers. The 19 participants—four males and 15 females—taught four to 36 years, across ten states of the US, with teaching placements in nine high schools, three middle schools, and four elementary schools. We did not collect additional demographic data. Additionally, although the teachers permitted us to use their names, we chose to use pseudonyms to provide anonymity, a decision explained in the findings.

These 19 teachers consented and were interviewed in February–March 2021. We used the initial, semi-structured interviews to elicit stories about the teachers' experiences of learning to teach writing from their preservice education through their current practices. Our goal for the interviews was "to ensure that the narratives we collected had a biographical arc" that conveyed "developmental trajectories" (Knappick, 2020, p. 73). Donovan et al. (2023) detail the interview questions. The interviews were transcribed verbatim for analysis. Additionally, we asked participants to complete a qualitative reading-response activity in which teachers read, responded to, and ranked our four composite narratives according to details with which they resonated most.

Data Analysis

As researchers in different locations across the US, we met for two hours weekly via Zoom to share analytic insights, develop analytic memos about the significant narrative elements of teachers' experiences, and discuss and debate emerging findings. Our shared value of narrative ethics guided our analysis. In research that elicits narrative, Adams (2008) asserts it would be wrong to categorize or de-personalize accounts in presenting the data: "We must not approach stories with a prescription or typology for analysis; an evaluation of narrative must remain contingent on the stories, authors, and audiences as they interact" (p. 179). We kept this goal central as we transcribed and analyzed interviews.

Initially, each interview was open coded first by the interviewer and then by a second researcher (Corbin & Strauss, 2014) applying four "commonplaces of narrative" to explore the teachers' stories across their careers: temporality (time aspects), sociality (characters/actors), physicality (places), and continuity (chains of events) (Connelly & Clandinin, 2006). In open coding, we used line-by-line micro analysis, coding for actions, actors, places, milestones, changes in thinking or practice, and any experiential moment that seemed important to each teacher's learning-teaching journey.

As a group, we continued to open code the interviews and wrote analytic memos to develop an intimate knowledge of the narratives and triangulated emerging conclusions. We discussed any discrepancies in our individual understandings of the data and how we defined narrative elements. Once we reached agreement, we charted in a data table each teacher's narrative elements, including settings, protagonists, antagonists, characteristics, and critical events. We maintained a sense of the whole by memoing the narrative elements of teachers' experiences. As we analyzed our memos, patterns emerged across teachers that resulted in us grouping teachers with similar trajectories. We grappled with how to represent each teacher's trajectory. Like Brandt (2001), we did not see individuals as the unit of analysis; rather, we focused on critical events and actors to identify the forces at work in their teaching trajectories. We created a matrix to chart each teacher's major influential experiences, critical events, protagonists, and antagonists. We turned to composite narratives to represent the shared and divergent dimensions of the teachers' experiences (Willis, 2019).

To create the composites, we grouped the open codes (using Dedoose) by the major experiences and influences in the teachers' trajectories. Each composite included four to five teachers who had similar timelines, social conditions that influenced their trajectories, actors or agents of change, and/or physical spaces that contributed to growth events. We created smaller matrices of critical events, attributes, and relevant quotations for each composite narrative group to keep our composites grounded in the teachers' stories.

Our aim was not to distinguish between individuals but to investigate how teachers came to and continue to become "exemplary" writing teachers. Thus, we found composites presented a compelling way to study the 19 individual stories and maintain cohesiveness through teachers' shared narrative arcs. Each of us wrote a first draft of a composite in third person voice to story four to five teachers' shared critical elements and themes to synthesize their teaching experiences. We added quotations from interview transcripts representative of the teachers' shared narrative experiences or attributes. Then we each read, revised, and edited the composites so that they represented our collective understanding. Composite narratives provided us with a generative and useful approach for exploring our research inquiry.

Because the composites highlighted the teachers' shared experiences in narrative format and provided a prime opportunity to conduct member-checking, we added another data collection step. Rather than conducting a second interview as initially anticipated, we asked teachers to complete an open-ended survey that acted as a reader-response activity. Eleven of the 19 teachers we interviewed completed this activity. We believe teachers' Fall 2021 workload while returning to the classroom during the COVID-19 pandemic factored into the 58 percent response rate.

We first wrote the composites without verbatim language that teachers would easily identify as "theirs," because we wanted them to focus on the overall story, trajectory, and critical events. In the activity, teachers read each composite, without any direct quotes, and responded to questions about their personal resonance with each character's experiences. Teachers included phrases or details that illustrated their connections or differences. Then, they ranked the composites from one (most identified with) to four (least identified with) and provided explanations for their rankings. We charted the teachers' activity results in a data table to further explore their developmental growth trajectory of PCKW.

FINDINGS

The following composites of Alex, Melanie, Peyton, and Sam represent the 19 teachers' experiences as they iteratively learned to be effective writing teachers.

Each composite synthesizes four to five teachers' critical events sequenced across their career trajectories that shaped their writing-teacher development. All narrative details stemmed from one or more of the teachers represented in that composite, and direct quotes were included within the following findings to integrate the participants' voices, feelings, impressions, and tensions.

ALEX

Alex didn't necessarily plan to become a teacher, even though teaching in some form runs in the family. For undergrad, she studied communications where she did a lot of writing but spent a few years in the business world before finding her way to teaching. She moved to a new state where there was a teacher shortage and saw that she could get a provisional certificate while teaching, and so she did it. However, she would move a few more times before finding a school that was a good fit. She stated, "It was so hard, and I didn't feel supported or even know what I was doing. And I felt I was becoming somebody else . . . but at this school, I make sense here."

At first, Alex adopted writing practices she saw happening in her department—the five-paragraph essay and the traits-based rubric: "At that point in my career teaching writing, I feel it was very prescriptive. . . . I now view it as pretty formulaic and not authentic. It was guided by prompts that were not created by me, were not created for my specific students." When she was assigned the AP (Advanced Placement) literature course the second year, her colleague urged her to take advantage of the district's PD stipend to attend the local AP summer institute, where she learned some strategies for literary analysis. She stated, "The district sent me to a one-day training, which gave me a framework and a language for actually talking about writing with my students. . . . My training in college didn't prepare me for this." This intensive PD offered Alex much needed resources to support her students in critical reading and analytic writing, but she had also begun following educators on social media and had ideas of integrating peer feedback and blogging. Alex's principal noticed her creative take on the district's ideas and the student engagement that followed, so she was invited to do some teacher training in the district. The more she worked with colleagues, the better she understood that the focus of writing needed to be on the students and on supporting their individual progression.

So, in the subsequent years, Alex began self-PD, reading books and continuing to follow social media for the latest idea. She stated, "I'm self-taught. And I read everything. So, I bought every book that my budget would allow. . . . Some of my mentors are actually from books. . . . I just go find what I need." While some colleagues began to attend national and local conferences, she just didn't have a lot of time for that given her growing family and side jobs. Throughout her teaching career, Alex would occasionally teach a class at the local college or run a community writing workshop. This engagement with different learning spaces and post-high school students offered Alex perspective on what writers in different stages of their lives may need from and experience through writing.

Last year, Alex found a new model for high school curriculum that offered an alternative to AP scope and sequence. This approach was more of a balance of reading and writing experiences that centered student choice and process over "covering" a set series of tasks. Alex proposed to her principal to buy her department a book so they could, together, begin to make shifts in their program. She stated, "One of the most revolutionary things for my life as a writing teacher I have seen is taking a skills-based approach and not necessarily a product-based approach. . . . I have seen more authentic writing for my students. . . . We are able to talk more about their writing lives and where they start out in the year and then where they end up." She is so happy to have the support of her principal but would likely do it on her own anyway.

After a number of years in teaching, Alex, in some ways, feels like she is just finding her stride, understanding how the five-paragraph essay structure and Six Traits offer a framework that makes sense if the focus of writing is on the product and skills. From her teacher training, Alex was missing knowledge of how to develop writers' identities and a capacity to make choices that writers need to make in school but also beyond. She is excited to navigate this book study and program shift with her department and students, but she continues to keep an eye out for other resources centered around her local school community. "We're trying to cultivate a life of writing here, we're trying to cultivate you as a writer and everyone can be a writer . . . as a daily practice that also includes conversation, that includes making mistakes, that includes making edits and changes and revisions. That you're not in trouble for having to make edits. That's part of the messy, beautiful process of writing."

Melanie

Melanie remembers positive experiences as a writer in her elementary and secondary school years, including an influential English teacher who encouraged her to keep writing. She chose English education as her college major because she enjoyed reading and writing and felt confident in those areas. Melanie has taught in the same school for nine years. She is one of the more experienced teachers at the school and has taken on some of the curriculum leadership work. "I'm one of the only teachers who's still here from when I started," she says. "So, I have my hand in a little bit in every curriculum." The AP Literature students,

12th graders, are her favorite group to teach because they are equally as motivated as she is to engage in the reading and writing assignments. She also teaches 11th grade Language Arts and Literature and a "below level/remedial" Language Arts class.

Thinking back to her teacher preparation program, Melanie had a writing methods course, but the content is barely memorable. Most of her classes were literature classes focused on literature analysis. Instead, her student-teaching mentor and her colleague mentor have been her most influential writing teachers and helped Melanie work through pedagogical problems as they arose. She still uses many writing lesson ideas she learned from her mentors. "A mentor taught me a way of writing research papers using index cards for source cards. You would write one quote on one side, and then by the time you're done reading all your sources, you have all these little index cards with different ideas. And then, it was just a matter of sorting them into categories, and your research paper came to life from that." Having little memorable preparation in writing instruction led to a fair amount of struggle during her first few years of teaching. "I had to teach them and go back and teach myself analytical writing. Because they would write the most vague analysis, and I knew when I read it that something was wrong, but I had to go back and teach myself, why is that wrong? Why is that not quite hitting right?" Not only did she have to re-teach herself the ins and outs of academic, analytic, and argumentative writing, but she also had to figure out how to teach it to students at a variety of skill levels in an engaging manner.

Her instructional scope and sequence are fairly pre-determined with the literature anthology and novels that are part of the AP curriculum or the British literature historically taught. Most assignments are based on genres or skills that are on the AP exam and the kinds of literature-based analytic writing or argumentative writing that students are tested on, but she wants to begin including more creative nonfiction and fiction writing assignments. Melanie doesn't usually write on her own time for personal enjoyment, but when students are given an essay assignment, she writes to the prompt with them and models her thinking for students. She also demonstrates choices in sentence structure and teaches sentence style as a focal point in her grammar instruction.

She believes it is important for students to be familiar with the academic essay structure, which often takes a five-paragraph essay form. "When I first started teaching writing, I said I was never going to teach the five-paragraph essay, ever, and that lasted—not very long—because I realized that students needed that simple structure." Templates or structures like outlining the main idea and three details of a nonfiction essay, or including a claim/assertion, warrant, evidence, and examples for argument, are mainstays of her writing instruction and help students who struggle to get their ideas on paper. There have been significant moments of reflection on her practice that have led to strategic changes in her instruction, including a move to help students be more independent writers who are less reliant on her as writers. Her instruction has evolved to include more explicit teaching of writing devices such as hooking the reader with a particular opener or backing up a claim as well as an explicit understanding of how to draw conclusions that answer the questions of "so what?" and "why?.." Now, she gets excited about seeing students' aha-moments and writing breakthroughs and seeing their confidence grow as writers and skilled grammar users. She enjoys seeing them start to take on ownership of their revisions and help their peers problem solve in their writing. "What I love about asking them questions and offering them advice is that they will get to the point where they will offer up their own solutions. And . . . they just puzzle it out on their own." She believes students need to be able to write clear and compelling arguments using an academic essay structure for their success in college and participation as active citizens.

Advanced PD isn't accessible in her rural school community, with no nearby university or National Writing Project site. National Board Certification is accessible, however, and she is in the midst of that reflective process. She is also beginning to engage in process-oriented PD by reading books like Penny Kittle and Kelly Gallagher's *180 Days* with colleagues and implementing conferencing and other approaches. Melanie plans to keep teaching for the foreseeable future. She loves being in the classroom; her students make each day interesting. Without them, what would she have to talk about with her friends and family?

Peyton

Peyton identifies with the teachers as writers, teacher-writer, and/or writer-teacher philosophy inherent in teacher writing groups such as the National Writing Project and TeachWrite. She found writing communities to be supportive, not only for her writer identity, but also for her lived experiences. She stated, "The writing group that we write with on a weekly basis . . . that's probably been the most significant, for me as a writer, that's impacting how I instruct as a teacher, as a writing teacher."

She would love to attend more writing sessions if time and opportunity would permit, but each session attended has added to her writerly experiences. She trusts serendipity to open writing opportunities, in-person or virtually, but did she discover the opportunities because she always loved writing or because she taught writing? Which identity centers her professionally and/or personally? She stated, "You don't say, 'I'm a teacher who writes,' or 'I'm a teacher writer'; you're a teacher and you're a writer."

Childhood writing experiences such as school projects, writing festivals, or entering and maybe winning writing contests provided a strong foundation from which her writer identity stems. Peyton stated, "I think, for me, as someone who has always written since I was little, I still have books from when I was in elementary school, and I'll show them to my kids." Peyton has always enjoyed writing, aside from moments when a teacher, elementary through higher education, may not have given her the grades or feedback she felt she deserved. Still, she persevered, holding true to her voice as teacher-as-writer/teacher-writer/writer-teacher. She gravitated toward writing and loved reading and learning about published authors.

As she learned to be a teacher, she would have enjoyed a writing methods course in her undergraduate or graduate teacher preparation program, but such opportunities were not made available. Still, because of her love for writing, she felt confident teaching writing. She modeled her messy writing process to be transparent and to show her students that the reciprocal writing process is hard work for everyone. She emphasized revision throughout the writing process. She stated, "I think you have to be a writer to be a writing teacher."

She helped her students write about topics that mattered to them within genres she had to teach. She loved conferencing with her students, learning about the stories and topics that were important to them as individuals. She aimed to make writing as authentic as possible, ensuring the purpose and audience of her students' writing expanded beyond the four walls of her classroom. She encouraged students to submit their writing to contests, magazines, the school's publications, the local newspaper, or any authentic publication opportunity. She stated, "I'm trying to become a published author. I have a couple of manuscripts I'm working on. They've been rejected a bunch of times, and I tell my students that I'm willing to take risks. I want you too as well." Supporting her students in seeking publication was rewarding, albeit the feedback process was a challenge she struggled to balance. Yet, still, she persevered.

In some seasons of life, she can focus more on who she is as a writer, while in other seasons, especially when the grading load is daunting, she focuses on her role as teacher. But when she teaches, she cannot help but model her writer identity, which informs how she teaches writing and impacts how her students view her as a writer. She stated, "I want to publish a novel and be able to give a shout out to my students, like in the acknowledgments or something, because I don't think I would have continued to push myself if it weren't for those students who got excited for me." She would love to spend her time writing instead of providing feedback to her students, but she lives inspired by her students' writing, which motivates her to continue to write. She wants to nourish her students' writing identities to help her students understand the importance of not only writing, but most importantly, the choice and need to identify as writers. She knows she teaches writing well because she knows what it means to live a writer's life.

Peyton dreams of publishing her own work. She embraces her writer identity within her genres of choice, for the purposes she chooses, for the audiences she seeks to influence, even if the audience is only herself. She awaits news of an acceptance for the piece she submitted recently, a piece she is confident will influence her audience. For now, living a writer's life is rewarding, even if she hasn't succeeded in publishing, yet. Still, she blogs, she journals, she reflects, and she writes, because not writing leaves a hole within the center of who she is, personally and professionally. And so, she writes.

Sam

Sam has been teaching for quite a while. Growing up, Sam thought about being a writer since that is truly what provided sanity and an escape from the hardships of life, but Sam ended up pursuing teaching.

There is a fire inside of Sam. It pushes Sam to be persistent and prevents him from taking no for an answer. Sam often pushes back when things do not go the way he thinks they should go. Sometimes this is well received; other times it is not. Over the years, Sam's confidence and voice have grown stronger and although he is now nearing the end of a teaching career, Sam has yet to give up and settle. It is, at times, exhausting. He shared, "I see retirement in four or five years, but that's okay because that's not going to stop me. So, between now and then, I will continue to be uncompromising. I don't intend to ever lessen my expectations. I don't ever intend to compromise on what to expect from kids."

Although Sam felt like he did not always fit in with his colleagues, he stayed strong in his belief that he must continue to teach in a way that benefits students. The role of choice in Sam's teaching has always been key. Sam shared his experience with choice as a student saying, "The fact that we could write about whatever we wanted to really ignited a sense of love of writing. I always appreciated words, but that ignited a huge sense of writing for me." Sam wants to develop students' love of writing, so they feel like he did about writing growing up. Sam values the writing process but knows that the product shows evidence to his students that they are, in fact, writers. That is why Sam encourages his students to enter writing contests, and over the years, his students have done quite well.

About mid-career, a principal suggested Sam present the information from a PD he led at a state literacy conference. Sam put in a proposal and it was accepted, much to his surprise. Sam loved talking to teachers about teaching almost as much as he loved teaching students. This started a pattern of presenting at state and eventually national conferences. However, Sam's colleagues didn't understand—why go to the extra trouble of presenting? Why can't he just be happy doing what they were doing? He shared, "I think I've been true to my style of teaching to the best of my knowledge, but I think there's always that pressure early on to do what all the other teachers are doing."

Over the years, Sam has hosted numerous student teachers. He sees that he learns as much from them as they learn from him. In particular, his understanding and use of technology have grown exponentially from working with student teachers. For example, Sam stated, "using Google Classroom where their document I can enter at any moment, and we can talk through their piece. It has allowed such collaboration between student and teacher." Sam embeds various technology tools into his teaching in authentic ways, allowing his students to experience the various purposes of writing that he hopes are not only school based but also personal.

Due to a long career, Sam is at the top of the pay scale and has no intention of leaving the district. Although he did not choose to earn another degree, Sam kept moving forward in terms of professional growth, finding mentors while attending conferences and through networking on social media. In addition, Sam never considered moving into higher education or becoming a principal, although many have described him as a natural leader. Sam recently began writing professionally and has published a few articles in academic journals. He shared, "About five years ago, I started writing myself, at first just for myself, but then, about writing pedagogy and then, people started to read it slowly, but surely, and so, that's been a lot of fun to do that now." This work has been well received, and it compels Sam to engage in continued inquiry. Plus, he loves sharing what he knows about teaching with other educators. When attending conferences, Sam makes sure to connect with other teachers. That is how he met the co-author of the first book he is now writing. Sam truly values the interdependence of both scholar and teacher identities.

READER-RESPONSE ACTIVITY: CONNECTING TO THE COMPOSITES

As writing teacher educator researchers, we were curious if the composites we created would resonate with the teachers whose narratives were embedded in them, so we asked the teachers to order the composites from one to four, most identified to least identified with, respectively, and provide a written explanation of their rankings. Per Table 4.1, of the 11 teachers who completed the reader-response activity, the following is evident: (a) 45 percent ranked the research-team-identified composite as most strongly resonating with their own experiences (five teachers);

(b) 37 percent chose the research-team-identified composite as the second most relatable composite (four teachers); and (c) 18 percent ranked the research-team-identified composite as the third most relatable composite (two teachers). Because some teachers connected more strongly with a different composite than the one in which we represented their story, we chose to use pseudonyms to convey our analytic agency and rendering of the final composites.

The reader-response activity provided an opportunity for us, as researchers, to see if the composites we created truly were a synthesis of the teachers' individual experiences. Since nine teachers resonated strongly with the research-team-identified composite as first or second, we felt confident that our composites accurately represented the teachers' experiences and provided a valuable member-checking method. If, for example, none, or very few, of the teachers had identified themselves in a composite, as a research team we would have revised the composite to better represent the teachers' experiences. Overall, the reader-response activity allowed the teachers the opportunity to affirm whether or not the composites' data reflected their views, feelings, and experiences with teaching writing, thus, improving the findings' accuracy and credibility.

Table 4.1. Research-Team and Teacher Composite Identification

Teacher (Pseudonym)	Research-Team-Identified Composite	Self-identified Composite Ranking
Alexandra	Alex	Melanie, Alex, Sam, Peyton
Ester	Melanie	Melanie, Sam, Alex, Peyton
Katie	Melanie	Melanie, Alex, Sam, Peyton
Ann	Melanie	Sam, Melanie, Alex, Peyton
Doris	Peyton	Peyton, Sam, Alex, Melanie
Heather	Peyton	Sam, Alex, Peyton, Melanie
Jolynne	Peyton	Sam, Peyton, Alex, Melanie
Samantha	Peyton	Sam, Alex, Peyton, Melanie
Chelsey	Sam	Alex, Sam, Peyton, Melanie
Drew	Sam	Sam, Peyton, Alex, Melanie
Michael	Sam	Sam, Peyton, Alex, Melanie

Several teachers saw themselves strongly represented in two or more composites, indicating that these narratives collectively, rather than individually or typologically, describe writing teachers' trajectories. To illustrate, Jolynne stated:

> There were aspects of each teacher that felt like me (almost like each one was a "that's me"), except for the last . . . I'm

really a combination of . . . three. I have moved the furthest from Melanie's approach, which seems solidly traditional and geared toward an outcome of placement rather than individual student growth.

Connecting with two of the four composites, Doris stated that, like Peyton, she enjoys "writing in community . . . conferencing with [her] scholars and reading their writing." Doris shares Sam's passion for teaching, choice to advocate for students, and connection with social media. Heather stated, "I feel like Peyton and Melanie are more structured in their teaching whereas I felt more connected to Sam and Alex who seemed a bit more led by passion." Ann stated, "Sam and Melanie both reminded me of beliefs and practices I have as an educator." This phenomenon of finding oneself in multiple composites shows that these PD pathways are not discrete or exclusive of one another. While the composites were assessed as resonating and representative by the teachers, most felt their experiences were broader than one composite, indicating that the composites provide insights as separate narratives and as a collective account, an anthology of sorts, of writing teacher development. We anticipate future research with additional participants will reveal new and complementary composite experiences.

DISCUSSION

Learning to write and learning how to teach writing are journeys that require "well-practiced and deeply understood capacities working together . . . that can vary in their realization and developmental trajectories from one individual to another" (Bazerman et al., 2018, p. 16). To support K-12 in-service teachers through their individual developmental growth trajectory of PCKW, this study's findings highlight three key ideas that warrant further discussion: (a) PD requires an intersection with people and events that bring about changes, (b) PCKW empowers teachers to move away from scripted curricula and toward writing engagements that foster student choice and voice for authentic audiences, and (c) teacher identities are networked across activities in mutually nurturing ways for teachers and students.

Our data showed teachers are resilient, willing to work with available opportunities; however, especially when teachers are not provided necessary preparation, stakeholders need to facilitate networking opportunities, access to PD (Graham, 2019), and participation in writing communities (Whitney, 2009). To support K-12 teachers' PCKW development, teacher educators, teachers, and administrators must intentionally facilitate positive-change events for writing teachers across their careers. As writing teachers develop their teaching repertoire, their views toward writing instruction evolve, impacting their PCKW development. Bazerman et al. (2018) describe teachers' development as a process of reorganizing or realigning one's experiences and knowledge in a way that results in an action, change effort, and/or a new relationship with writing, not simply a measurable achievement. Because "writing trajectories are complex and ultimately highly individual," teachers need opportunities for positive-change events to impact their identities as writers and their self-efficacy for teaching writing (Bazerman, 2019, p. 327).

These positive-change events must extend to teacher preparation programming. Graham (2019) stated colleges need to "become a reliable and trusted partner in improving writing instruction in the future" (p. 298). We argue teacher education programs must empower preservice and in-service teachers to teach writing strategies and processes while they also develop as writers. For better or worse, ideally better, students' writing trajectories are intimately connected to teachers' writing trajectories (Murphy & Smith, 2018). Teachers need to nurture a writerly teacher identity beyond their initial teacher preparation programs and into their career trajectories to enrich their students' writing development.

Our findings also suggest that as teachers experience positive-change events, grow their teaching repertoire, and claim a writer identity, they are empowered to move away from prescriptive curricula. As Murphy and Smith (2018) identify, "[T]eachers play a critical role as the key architects in designing or remodeling curriculum for their students" (p. 228). As teachers gain PCKW, they move toward writing curricula and engagements that foster student choice and voice for authentic audiences. This study illustrates that as teachers and students engage with authentic writing curricula with conferencing, feedback, and support as a classroom writing community, teachers and students reciprocally develop their writer identities.

Writerly identities need to be supported within classrooms across teachers' career spans, which in turn supports teachers' and students' lifespan writing development. For example, although Alex was not taught how to develop writers' identities in her teacher preparation program, she read books to learn how to teach "the messy, beautiful process of writing" that requires her students to make mistakes, revise, edit, and converse about writing as writers. Melanie's teachers supported her writer identity as a child and her mentors supported her identity as a writing teacher who empowers students to take ownership of their writing. Peyton always loved writing and identifies as a teacher-writer, an identity she uses to support her students' active engagement with authentic writing opportunities. Sam rekindled his love for writing as he taught his students to live as writers. Inspired by his students, Sam's writing evolved into writing for teachers. Thus, across their career spans and through their PCKW, these teachers impacted their own and, at least, the initial stages of their students' lifespan writing development.

Our data also showcase how teachers' writer identities—teacher-writers, writer-teachers, teacher-scholars—are networked across contexts. Contexts for writers' lives include myriad elements such as place, histories, development, genres, culture, experiences, and relationships (Bazerman, 2019). Ivanič (2006) argued, "People's identities are networked across the activities in which they participate" (p. 26); thus, varied experiences across teachers' careers need to be orchestrated to develop their writer identities related to their "own beliefs and practices" (Locke, 2017, p. 135). Through such social contexts, teachers as writers and teachers of writing experience positive-change events that help them continually evolve and re-construct their teaching repertoires to impact their own and their students' writing development (Dippre, 2019). "Writing and teaching are . . . intertwined, essential ways to construct meaning in life" (Schmidt, 1998, p. xi). Our data support the notion that teachers' beliefs and practices connect with their teacher identities across their career span, but those identities are strongly influenced by and developed through networking opportunities and critical life events; therefore, time in the field must include intersections with people and positive-change events that influence writing teachers' and students' developmental change.

IMPLICATIONS

Using Composites as Researchers

We aimed to understand 19 writing teachers' shared narrative arcs across their developmental growth trajectories. Because nine teachers ranked the research-identified composite as first or second in the reader-response activity, we felt the data speak to the commonalities across teachers' experiences and/or PD needs, even though trajectories were different.

Based on our analysis of the reader-response activity data, we contemplated revising the composites because some teachers focused on narrow details as their reason(s) for not connecting with the research-team-identified composite. For example, Ann did not connect with Melanie's composite due to specific details such as rural education and National Board certification, even though the research team used her data to craft, in part, Melanie's composite. We felt inherent tension in deciding whether or not we should remove such distracting details that inhibited some teachers from identifying with a composite as a whole. Ultimately, we decided to not edit the composites for this study.

We believe composites highlight the varied trajectories teachers experience. Teachers connected with multiple composites, even though their data were used to support the crafting of one composite. Certainly, we did not expect every teacher to connect with each composite, but Samantha resonated with three composites. Like Alex, she engaged in self-selected PD on her own. She connected most with Sam's personality and years of experience. Like Peyton, she desired high-quality feedback but felt she did not receive the feedback she always needed.

Overall, we believe the composites are useful for researchers in understanding writing teachers' trajectories, but these four composites are not exhaustive. Because understanding writing through the lifespan is riddled with challenges (Dippre & Phillips, 2020), future research needs to highlight other composites of writing teachers' trajectories. Such a collection of composites will provide a growing data set from which lifespan writing researchers, especially, may explore writing trajectories. For teacher educators of writing, such composites provide myriad opportunities as well.

Using Composites as Teacher Educators

Specific to supporting K-12 writing teachers' growth trajectory of PCKW, teacher educators may use the composites to explore case studies within required writing methods courses. As teacher educators, we look forward to using the composites with our K-12 preservice and in-service teachers. Exploring these trajectories will provide case study data to discuss steps teacher educators need to facilitate and/or K-12 teachers need to complete across their career spans to develop their PCKW. As participants shared, improving their PCKW later impacted their students' writing (e.g., motivation, choice, revision).

Teacher educators also may replicate the positive-change events evident in PD opportunities that this study's participants experienced. Professional development, such as participating in non-profit organizations (e.g., National Writing Project, TeachWrite), served as positive-change events for some of the teachers in this study, especially in developing their teacher-writer or writing-teacher identities. The teachers also noted the importance of (and sometimes critically questioned) PD they received through AP programs or 6+1 Traits workshops. Professional development must not only focus on the content but also on how to assess and tailor instruction to meet students' needs (Bazerman et al., 2018). Thus, through the composites, teacher educators may gain an understanding of the positive-change events they may orchestrate to connect K-12 teachers within shared networks of PD.

Participants also mentioned the role of mentors in initiating positive-change events in their writing teacher growth trajectory. Whether teachers sought or were assigned mentors, they noted mentors' beneficial feedback, encouragement, and guidance. These critical encounters occurred along their career paths, from their student teaching experiences through their early career phases. For example, Alex completed PD her mentor suggested and implemented the five-paragraph essay and the traits-based rubric. Alex also committed to self-PD, reading authors she identified as her mentors. Melanie's mentors—from student teaching and her first years of teaching—supported her through pedagogical challenges related to writing. Sam is committed to mentoring new teachers. Facilitating positive mentor/mentee relationships and understanding how mentors may support teachers' PCKW are pertinent to writing teachers' development.

Using the composites, we created a writing teacher development model that highlights teacher-training experiences that support teachers' participatory PCKW development of process pedagogies to support student writing communities. "We define participatory PCKW as the process of actively, agentively, and iteratively seeking and engaging in critical experiences to learn and grow as writers and teachers of writing in ways that tackle self-determined problems of practice" (Donovan et al., 2023, p. 18). Teachers' PCK and effectiveness to teach writing impact student achievement (Murphy & Smith, 2018), and we found through these composites that the more positive-change events teacher educators and other stakeholders facilitate for preservice, student, and in-service teachers, the more K-12 writing teachers benefit, which we believe benefits their students as well.

In closing, composite narrative methods supported our analysis of the developmental growth trajectory of 19 in-service writing teachers' development of PCKW across their career trajectories. The composites highlight the shared experiences and narrative arcs teachers described in their interviews and reader-response activities. However, these four composites are not the end of the story, and lifespan writing research will benefit from collecting additional composites to understand and support teachers' and students' writing trajectories.

Composites offer a context-rich method for presenting experiential narrative data. When dealing with large data sets such as one person's writing lifespan or several writers' development over time, composite narratives are one valuable tool for synthesizing those data into a format that can be published or presented. Overall, composite narratives provided us with an invaluable tool for understanding writing teachers' writerly and pedagogical trajectories across their lifespan.

REFERENCES

Adams, T. E. (2008). A review of narrative ethics. *Qualitative Inquiry, 14*(2), 175–194. https://doi.org/10.1177/1077800407304417.

Bazerman, C. (2019). Lives of writing. *Writing & Pedagogy, 10*(3), 327–331. https://doi.org/10.1558/wap.37066.

Bazerman, C., Applebee, A. N., Berninger, V. W., Brandt, D., Graham, S., Jeffery, J. V., Matsuda, P. K., Murphy, S., Rowe, D. W., Schleppegrell, M. & Wilcox, K. C. (2018). *The lifespan development of writing.* National Council of Teachers of English. https://wac.colostate.edu/books/ncte/lifespan-writing/.

Brandt, D. (2001). *Literacy in American lives.* Cambridge University Press.

Clandinin, D. J. & Connelly, F. M. (2000). *Narrative inquiry: Experience and story in qualitative research.* Jossey-Bass.

Cochran, K. F., DeRuiter, J. A. & King, R. A. (1993). Pedagogical content knowing: An integrative model for teacher preparation. *Journal of Teacher Education, 44*(4), 263–272.

Connelly, F. M. & Clandinin, D. J. (2006). Narrative inquiry. In J. L. Green, G. Camilli & P. Elmore (Eds.), *Handbook of complementary methods in education research* (3rd ed., pp. 477–487). Lawrence Erlbaum.

Corbin, J. & Strauss, A. (2014). *Basics of qualitative research: Techniques and procedures for developing grounded theory* (4th ed.). Sage.

Cremin, T. & Oliver, L. (2017). Teachers as writers: A systematic review. *Research Papers in Education, 32*(3), 269–295. http://dx.doi.org/10.1080/02671522.2016.1187664.

Dippre, R. J. (2019). *Talk, tools, and texts: A logic-in-use for studying lifespan literate action development.* The WAC Clearinghouse; University Press of Colorado. https://doi.org/10.37514/PRA-B.2019.0384.

Dippre, R. J. & Phillips, T. (2020). Conclusion as prolegomena: From points of convergence to murmurations across sites, researchers, and methods. In R. J. Dippre & T. Phillips (Eds.), *Approaches to lifespan writing research: Generating an actionable coherence* (pp. 247–254). The WAC Clearinghouse; University Press of Colorado. https://doi.org/10.37514/PER-B.2020.1053.

Donovan, S., Sanders, J., DeFauw, D. & Myers, J. K. (2023). K-12 writing teachers' careerspan development: Participatory pedagogical content knowledge of writing. *Literacy Practice and Research, 48*(2), 4. https://digitalcommons.fiu.edu/lpr/vol48/iss2/4.

Graham, S. (2019). Changing how writing is taught. *Review of Research in Education, 43*(1), 277–303. http://dx.doi.org/10.3102/0091732X18821125.

Graves, D. H. (1983). *Writing: Teachers & children at work.* Heinemann.

Houghton, N., Heenan, B., Huntwork, D., Meyer, E. & John, M. S. (2006). *The benefits to new teachers of the National Writing Project's new teacher initiative.* Inverness Research Associates. https://inverness-research.org/reports/2006-03-nwp-nti/2006-03-Rpt-NWP-NTI_2BenefitsToNewTeachers.pdf.

Ivanič, R. (2006). Language learning and identification. In R. Kiely, P. Rea-Dickens, H. Woodfield & G. Clibbon (Eds.), *Language, culture and identity in applied linguistics* (pp. 7–29). Equinox.

Knappick, M. (2020). Making sense of a person's literate life: Literacy narratives in a 100-year-study on literacy development. In R. J. Dippre & T. Phillips (Eds.), *Approaches to lifespan writing research: Generating an actionable coherence* (pp. 67–80). The WAC Clearinghouse; University Press of Colorado. https://doi.org/10.37514/PER-B.2020.1053.2.04.

Limbrick, L., Buchanan, P., Goodwin, M. & Schwarcz, H. (2010). Doing things differently: The outcomes of teachers researching their own practices in teaching writing. *Canadian Journal of Education, 33*(4), 897–924.

Locke, T. (2017). Developing a whole-school culture of writing. In T. Cremin & T. Locke (Eds.), *Writer identity and the teaching and learning of writing* (pp. 132–148). Routledge. http://dx.doi.org/10.4324/9781315669373.

Morgan, D. N. & Pytash, K. E. (2014). Preparing preservice teachers to become teachers of writing: A 20-year review of the research literature. *English Education, 47*(1), 6–37.

Murphy, S. & Smith, M. A. (2018). The faraway stick cannot kill the nearby snake. In C. Bazerman, A. N. Applebee, V. W. Berninger, D. Brandt, S. Graham, J. V. Jeffery, P. K. Matsuda, S. Murphy, D. W. Rowe, M. Schleppegrell & K. C. Wilcox (Eds.), *The lifespan development of writing* (pp. 210–243). National Council of Teachers of English.

National Commission on Writing. (2003). The neglected "R": The need for a writing revolution. https://files.eric.ed.gov/fulltext/ED475856.pdf.

Parr, J. M., Glasswell, K. & Aikman, M. (2007). Supporting teacher learning and information and informed practice in writing through assessment tools for teaching and learning. *Asia Pacific Journal of Teacher Education, 35*(1), 69–87. https://doi.org/10.1080/13598660601111281.

Sanders, J., Myers, J., Ikpeze, C., Scales, R., Tracy, K., Yoder, K. K., Smetana, L. & Grisham, D. (2020). A curriculum model for K-12 writing teacher education. *Research in the Teaching of English, 54*(4), 392–417.

Schmidt, J. Z. (1998). *Women/ writing/ teaching*. State University of New York Press.

Shulman, L. S. (1986). Those who understand: Knowledge growth in teaching. *Educational Researcher, 15*(2), 4–14. https://doi.org/10.2307/1175860.

Shulman, L. S. (1987). Knowledge and teaching: Foundations of the new reform. *Harvard Educational Review, 57*(1), 1–22.

Shulman, L. S. & Shulman, J. H. (2004). How and what teachers learn: A shifting perspective. *Journal of Curriculum Studies, 36*(2), 257–271. https://doi.org/10.1177/0022057409189001-202.

Whitney, A. (2009). Writer, teacher, person: Tensions between personal and professional writing in a National Writing Project summer institute. *English Education, 41*(3), 236–259.

Willis, R. (2019). The use of composite narratives to present interview findings. *Qualitative Research, 19*(4), 471–480. https://doi.org/10.1177/1468794118787711.

CHAPTER 5.

INTERPRETING RESEARCH WITH PARTICIPANTS: A LIFESPAN WRITING METHODOLOGY

Collie Fulford
University at Buffalo SUNY

Lauren Rosenberg
The University of Texas at El Paso

The methodology we share across these two chapters is rooted in our ongoing relationships with participants. It is through our research interactions, in combination with what we gain from other scholars committed to continually interrogating and revising their research practices, that we approach our writing research. We are two literacy researchers in rhetoric and writing studies who practice close-up investigations of ordinary adults' writing practices in disciplinary (Collie) and non-disciplinary (Lauren) settings. We choose to study adult learners because they have had opportunities to separate from compulsory education. Whatever connections to literacy education they pursue are ones they seek for purposes other than getting a high school diploma with its promise of entry into the workforce. Whether the participants in our studies come to us through their engagement with higher education as nontraditional students (Fulford, 2022), or whether they have come to literacy education for their purposes on their own terms (Rosenberg, 2015), the participants we engage with are adults who have had many life experiences aside from attending school. We learn from their multi-layered perspectives as parents, workers, and members of various communities; in addition, they offer us knowledge as adults who have had degrees of distance from mainstream academic pathways. Although we begin this chapter by introducing ourselves as researchers who study adult learners, we also flip this positioning: We conduct qualitative case studies and interviews with adults who are experts in—and on—their own lives and who have made very conscious decisions regarding their writing pathways. As researchers, we learn from them the reasons that writing matters—and continues to matter in new ways—across the lifespan.

In this chapter, we demonstrate that involving participants in collaborative meaning making is an established research practice that is well suited to lifespan writing studies conducted with adult participants and adult co-researchers. Collaborative interpretation is especially apt for interview-based studies. This is demonstrated in works spanning from at least the 1980s to the present. Berkenkotter, Huckin, and Ackerman (1988); Berry, Hawisher, and Selfe (2012); Halbritter and Lindquist (2012); Micciche and Carr (2011); Prior (2018); Roozen and Erickson (2017); and Selfe and Hawisher (2004) are representative of interview-based studies that involve participants as interpreters of their own literate experiences. In addition to co-investigative research, we review longitudinal writing studies that have helped to shape our understanding of writers continuing to develop across their educational trajectories, such as Herrington and Curtis's *Persons in Process* (2000) and Compton-Lilly's (2003) series of books that began with *Reading Families*. After reviewing some of the prominent scholarship that attends to participant and researcher interactions, we turn to our own methodology for lifespan writing research, which we articulate as an approach to conducting the studies themselves rather than a set of methods that can be put into action. We aim to offer adaptable models that others can take up and our frank assessments of the concerns, limitations, and possibilities of such approaches. We identify several practices we use for interpreting or reinterpreting texts, interview transcripts, and findings with participants. We conclude by providing a set of guiding principles for lifespan writing researchers.

ROOTS OF OUR PARTICIPANT-LED METHODOLOGY

Our methodology has emerged from our work using narrative inquiry, poetic inquiry, case study and interviews (Fine, 2018; Seidman, 2019), and feminist principles for ethical interactions with participants (Kirsch & Ritchie, 1995; Royster, 1996; Royster & Kirsch, 2012; Tarabochia, 2021). The resulting methodology that we articulate here is a fusion of those we were trained in and those we have developed throughout our careers. As we refine our methods, we continue to learn from the actual encounters we have with participants and our reflections on those encounters as they deepen and change. We encourage new researchers to search for their own place among and with the methodologies that inform them, to modify rather than accept methods wholesale. Because the work we do is participant focused, the sites and individuals have to influence the methods, a position we emphasize throughout this work.

Before delving into our histories, we pause to parse out the distinctions between methodology and method as we employ the terms in our work. When we speak of a methodology, we are connecting the theories that guide us with the principles we embrace as practitioners of lifespan studies. This leads us to design a particular pathway into the project that shifts to meet our goals of foregrounding co-interpretive practices. To achieve this, we concentrate on yielding and watching, reflecting and revising, fine-tuning and testing our objectives to see how they appear in relation to the values we claim to uphold. When we speak of methods, we are making plans. How are we going to do it? How will our interview process change to suit the methodology? What roles will participants have in analysis and revision? The methods develop from the methodology, and then we consider them in a kind of back-and-forth as we continually check ourselves (are we doing what we said we would do?).

We begin with our own history. Both of us were trained as researchers in Composition and Rhetoric at the University of Massachusetts-Amherst where we studied qualitative research methods with Anne Herrington in the early 2000s. Anne and Marcia Curtis's book, *Persons in Process: Four Stories of Writing and Personal Development in College* (2000), had recently been published. In addition to studying the methods and methodologies of numerous qualitative researchers in the field, Anne had us practice discourse analysis in class using some of the data she and Marcia had analyzed in their study. As part of learning how to become qualitative researchers, we were taught to "linger" with participants' texts, a term that Jacqueline Jones Royster and Gesa E. Kirsch (2012) would reflect on years later as a key element of "strategic contemplation" (*Feminist Rhetorical Practices*). We were energized by Anne's enthusiasm over raw data as something that could be interpreted individually and collaboratively. We continue to admire *Persons in Process* for its close up, careful attention to participants' lived experiences as they intersect with their academic lives. Looking back on the development of Herrington and Curtis's longitudinal project, we note that they never intended for it to become longitudinal: "We did not plan to follow these students' experiences any further than their first year. [W]e felt we had more than enough information to work from and more than enough of a challenge to determine how to proceed" (p. 9); yet, they found that their sustained interest in participants' ongoing development as writers and as people, especially in response to questions from audience members who listened to them present their findings at a conference, propelled the two researchers to extend their study: "We did not have an answer, but we did have a new resolve to pursue the telling of Nam's, Lawrence's, and Rachel's stories and make them the center of this book. . . . We had stumbled—or been pushed—instead into what could be called a "longitudinal" study of four students. . . ." (p. 11).

We linger on our recollections of being trained by Anne to highlight our own receptivity to the notion of research participants as "persons in process." Throughout our subsequent careers, we have continued to be interested in relationships with participants as co-interpreters of our studies and co-creators of knowledge. (See Fulford, 2022; Rosenberg, 2020; Rosenberg, 2023; Wymer, Fulford, Baskerville & Washington, 2012; Wymer & Fulford, 2019.)

Interpreting research with participants in lifespan literacy studies is an extension of established interview practices that honor participants' perspectives on their own lived experiences. Seidman's discussion of phenomenological interviewing, for instance, guides researchers to develop protocols that invite participants not only to describe but also to reflect on the meanings of their own experiences (2019). In this way, the subjective points of view of both researcher and researched contribute to the meanings made from the latter's histories. A tradition exists within writing studies for involving students in the interpretation of their own literacy experiences. Some of this has resulted in co-authorship, which can be a conventional academic practice for acknowledging contributions. This approach may be particularly relevant for graduate students whose professional identities and academic aspirations tangibly benefit from such arrangements. Early instances of this approach are reported in an article by Berkenkotter, Huckin, and Ackerman (1988) and a chapter by the same team (1991). Ackerman was covertly (at the time) the case study participant "Nate" whose experiences navigating new literacies during his initial years of a Ph.D. program are the subject of both publications. Ackerman took part in analyzing his own textual productions and experiences, but his complete relationship to the case was not disclosed until 1995 in a postscript to a subsequent publication (Ackerman, 1995). In contrast, a collaborative essay between Micciche and Carr (2011) while Carr was still a graduate student illustrates frank explanation of the co-authorship relationship:

> In an effort to construct a multivoiced account of the need for graduate writing instruction and the difference it makes, the essay includes commentary by Allison Carr, who enrolled in my spring 2008 course when she was a master's student. . . . Allison's remarks, which consist of writing completed during the course and some written a year later, appear in text boxes throughout the essay. Her writing is sometimes in direct dialogue with my ideas and other times operates as an open-ended reflection on issues relevant to graduate student writers. (pp. 480–81)

In the years between Ackerman's and Carr's co-authoring with their respective faculty investigators, it has become expected for researchers to disclose participants' degrees of involvement in interpreting their own cases. However, the CCCC Guidelines for the Ethical Conduct of Research in Composition Studies (2015) acknowledge that there is considerable disciplinary and institutional variation in how we define the terms co-author and co-researcher: "In some cases, participants . . . should be considered co-researchers and/or co-authors. Determining who should be a co-researcher and/or co-author depends on disciplinary convention, institutional regulation, and local expectations." The guidelines further note that the status of participants may change during a study or be designated as collaborative from the start.

CENTERING INTERPRETIVE RELATIONSHIPS

Our own approach to longitudinal writing studies, while influenced by the work of scholars invested in exploring longitudinal, latitudinal, and heterogenous development of writing, is inspired by a feminist activist ethos. We cannot position ourselves as researchers without acknowledging the principles of Royster and Kirsch (2012) and the many femtors who guide our research ethics and stand alongside participants in their own studies (Glenn, 2018; Kerschbaum, 2014; Kirsch & Ritchie, 1995; Moss, 2003; Ratcliffe, 2005; and Royster, 1996). We call attention to recent contributions by feminist educational researcher Michelle Fine (2017), who writes about the responsibility of critical qualitative researchers: "[W]e are obligated to animate the histories, structures, policies, ideologies, and practices that have spawned [participants'] social exclusion, and perhaps have fomented their deep commitments to justice. 'Voices' alone will not suffice" (p. 12).

We recognize Fine's commitment to participants as essential to an ethical research methodology. Our work is not merely to document stories and shifts in writing development throughout our qualitative longitudinal studies. We have a greater responsibility to participants and our field than simply sharing models and their implications for further studies of writing development. Fine's ethos inspires us to attend deeply not only to our processes but also to the ends that our research achieves. We are always asking: how does this research serve the people and communities that it is about? We work towards social change, interpreting with participants and individually in our analyses with the goal of making education more equitable. Our commitment to writing research looks toward the possibilities that writing (our own and our participants') offers for challenging oppressions and intervening in unjust social, racial, and class systems. The most significant goal is to circulate and synthesize the material we collect for Freirean praxis, that is, to actively seek changes to benefit the lives of participants. This is also what we offer to future researchers. Part of our interpretation of the writing practices of our participants (whether the analysis is done by the researcher alone or collaboratively with those who are researched) is tending to the relationships fostered within and outside of the research relationship, while together we do the work of interpreting their writing development.

Participants' interpretive relationships to research projects about them can vary considerably, as can the ways we name and mark their roles and contributions. When making such determinations, it is important to consider the nature of participants' actions within each project, the extent of their responsibilities, and their desires for visibility or anonymity, among other factors. What follows are a few categories of participants' active interpretive roles with our caveat that researchers are continually seeking meaningful, ethical, and accurate ways to acknowledge participants' collaborative positions in our projects.

CO-RESEARCHERS / PARTICIPANT CO-RESEARCHERS / COLLABORATORS

Roozen and Erickson (2017) indicate that when they engage with the people in their studies, the prevalent term "participant" does not capture the nature of the close reading and collaborative discussion about what texts and literacy experiences mean. Following Ivanič (1998), they identify the five individuals in their study as "participant-co-researchers," or often simply "co-researchers." These contributors are referred to by pseudonym and are not listed as co-authors, but they are repeatedly acknowledged as interpreters of their own texts and lives. Halbritter and Lindquist (2012) use both "participant" and "collaborator" when describing participants who contribute to data collection and self-narration in their studies of outsider literacy narratives. They realized that "to collect such stories, we would need to do more than ask our students simply to tell them: we would need to go find these stories—together, researchers and students" (p.173). In their variation on Seidman's interview sequencing, Halbritter and Lindquist engage collaborators in generating their own videotaped data, then co-creating documentaries of their literacy experiences.

PROXIMAL PARTICIPANT CO-RESEARCHERS

Investigators whose academic statuses or other identities are different from their participants can greatly benefit from listening to and learning from co-researchers who have closer life proximity to participants. For example, methods described in *The Meaningful Writing Project* (2016) include a practice that Collie uses when conducting research about student writers, that is to invite co-investigators from among or close to the population being studied. Eodice, Geller, and Lerner engage first-year seminar students, writing center peer consultants, and graduate students in data collection and analysis in their multi-institutional study of undergraduate seniors' most meaningful academic writing experiences. The authors justify this near-peer approach: "We could think of no better way to capture the perspective of undergraduates–and to value those perspectives–than to have undergraduates play a key role as co-researchers, particularly as interviewers" (p. 10). Student researchers are credited by being named in an addendum to the book.

The line between participant co-researcher and proximal participant co-researcher can become blurry as activities and relationships change. For instance, in Collie's research about and with adult student writers at a historically Black university, two participants requested that they shift into the role of co-investigators in subsequent projects (Fulford, 2022). These co-investigators' perspectives from both sides of the researcher-researched divide provided unusually rich interpretive contributions because of their sustained investment in the project and its implications for their communities. Collie came to regard them as partners whom she could consult even after their formal involvement in studies ended. These co-researchers leveraged the findings and the research process as advocates for the adult student population at their university.

Co-authors / Participant-Co-authors

Micciche and Carr's (2011) essay is an example of co-authorship in which Carr's literacy experiences as a graduate student and her reflections on them are foregrounded and formatted somewhat differently from Micciche's, the faculty author. Selfe and Hawisher (2004) also mark student co-authors' contributions. They choose the term "co-authorship" with case study participants because "we . . . came to the realization that the project we had undertaken was no longer our own. It belonged, as well, to the people we interviewed and surveyed—their words and their stories were continual reminders that they had claimed the intellectual ground of the project as their own" (p. 13). Although most participants reflected positively about becoming named authors, Selfe and Hawisher acknowledge that some wanted to preserve their anonymity and some questioned whether their actions merited co-authorship. Selfe and Hawisher are forthcoming that this method, especially with a large study, is "fraught with difficulties" (p. 23). Yet instead of shying away from its ambiguities, these researchers found ways in a subsequent multi-year study (Berry, Hawisher & Selfe 2012) to invite deeper co-participation, to engage their students in the narration and meaning making in even richer ways that enabled more ownership of the text. To signify co-authorship in both books, case study participants who contributed are listed as co-authors on their respective chapters. Block quotations from the student co-authors are formatted as we are accustomed to seeing quotations from participants.

Participant-Authors

In *The Desire for Literacy* (Rosenberg, 2015), Lauren studied the emerging writing practices of four adult learners who had the opportunity to pursue literacy only when they reached older adulthood. As the participants composed more, and when their writing became the center of discussions between them and Lauren, she began to refer to them as "the participant authors in my study" (p. 107), to emphasize that the participants *were* authors, an identity that resisted the subjectivity of the nonliterate Other. She observed that in their writing, the participant authors "tend not to self-censor, avoid, or look towards positive representations of their experiences. . . . Articulating an accurate representation of self is most valuable for these people who previously have not had the privilege of self-representation through writing" (p. 107). By calling the participants "authors" or "participant authors" when she wanted to call attention to their writing or to their civic intervention through writing, Lauren was able to shift the representation of the adult learners in her study. They were participating with her by sharing their interview remarks and writing samples and they were also participating as the authors of their writing. Those comments, and the texts they produced, were the subject of their research conversations as well as the core of Lauren's analysis. She explained, "In this way, subaltern voices can be acknowledged as those of authors rather than subordinated others," as researcher and researched "engage in mutual contemplation of their experiences and their writing" (p. 147). The acknowledgement of participant/author/participant-authors' changing roles follows the CCCC (2015) guideline for indicating shifts within the write up of research.

When we trouble the terms participant "co-author," "co-researcher," "co-interpreter," or "participant-author," and when we talk about interpreting experiences, transcripts, and materials with participants, we draw from various established and emerging methodologies. Researchers new to these practices can refer to a spectrum of participant involvement in interpretation as they design—and redesign—lifespan writing research. We have access to layers of co-authorship when we are open to changes to our studies. We encourage others to lean into the messiness, toward participants becoming co-authors in narration, meaning making, and the uses of findings.

TRAJECTORIES AND TEMPORALITIES

This review of different categories of participants in interpreting roles illustrates some of the range of possibilities for working with research participants across the boundary of researcher-researched. In all of these styles of research interaction, we value the efforts researchers are making toward more substantial engagement with participants as interpreters of data. We also acknowledge the limitations of traditional research relationships. When we argue that we learn from and with participants, we mean that we are committed to finding new ways to deepen those methods of learning together.

Within writing studies, one lens that we find helpful is Paul Prior's (2018) "trajectories of semiotic becoming," which carries Jay Lemke's science education research on life scales into a lifespan development of writing framework. Noting that moments of learning, including shared moments, are significant to our sense of being, Prior describes semiotic becoming as occurring "not inside domains, but across the many moments of a life. Becoming happens in spaces that are never pure or settled, where discourses and knowledge are necessarily heterogeneous, and where multiple semiotic resources are so deeply entangled that distinct modes simply don't make sense" (par. 6). This notion of becoming, of crossing domains of experience, is central to our understanding of lifespan writing. In our methodology of interpreting experiences with participants, we presume that participants are always crossing domains of experience, and that they are often aware of those crossings, although they may not have been asked to examine the interrelationships among experience, identity, and ways of knowing.

Roozen and Erickson (2017) build upon Prior's work by looking into the writing trajectories of various age and discipline-concentrated students, noting the crisscrossing influences that drive their academic and life pathways. By examining case studies across areas of expertise, identities, and age as they share interviews and multimedia artifacts, the authors add to the body of scholarship on lifespan development of writing as occurring longitudinally and latitudinally in a complex fabric of experience.

Among the authors included in this volume, we value the contributions of our colleagues theorizing new methodologies for lifespan research, especially Compton-Lilly's (2017) in which she extends her previous studies of a group of students' literacy learning from childhood through adulthood. In *Reading Students' Lives* (2017), Compton-Lilly builds a case for centering time as a significant element of educational research. She zeroes in on the temporality of literacy development, arguing that literacy learning is constrained by the "temporal benchmarks" of schooling (pp. 119–120), at the same time that learning pathways are multiple and intersecting, and often benefit from their ongoingness. Learning trajectories can be problematic when they are *un*changing (for example, when educational research measures student success by performance on achievement tests over grade levels), as well as challenging when the multiplicity of a learners' trajectories (home and family influences, competing ways of meaning making, and the effects of microaggressions) are under-recognized or ignored. She notes in conclusion the importance of timescale analysis, which "calls attention to events and the construction of meaning across multiple timescales as historical pasts, lived pasts, and ongoing experiences converge as children construct and reconstruct meanings related to self, literacy, and schooling" (p. 119).

While Compton-Lilly's research focuses on children and their families negotiating the school system through childhood and into adulthood, our longitudinal research centers different populations of adult learners when they negotiate the meanings of education in their lives. Drawing upon the contributions of Compton-Lilly, Prior, Roozen and Erickson, and others, we note the intersecting trajectories of adult participants' many identities and social roles. Reflecting on her case studies of students' temporal pathways, Compton-Lilly recognized, "In each case, ways of seeing the world came together, collided, sedimented and conflicted across time as people drew on the past within a lived present that was constantly being reconstructed relative to possible futures" (p. 120). This work on trajectories of learning previews the methods we use for co-interpretation. When we work with participants, we are drawn into their ways of knowing and being and becoming. Our relationships with them are about the mutuality of being together in a moment of co-constructing knowledge.

DWELLING WITH PARTICIPANTS: WHAT THIS OFFERS LIFESPAN WRITING RESEARCH

A methodology of interpreting with participants offers lifespan writing studies a fluid and organic means of reconsidering research interactions. By this, we mean that the process of engaging with participants in discussions of their writing can change from the original project design, and that it does change, based on conversations with participants about how they understand their texts and transcripts. Our methodology of dwelling together responds to shifts in both participants' and researchers' life conditions. It also varies depending on the moment of the interaction. Both of us have longitudinal relationships with participants that involve periodic revisits to check in about the research. Each moment is distinct. Each time we approach the research situation, we (researchers and participants) come to it with slightly different perspectives. Events in our lives, reflection, self-analysis, changing conditions in the world around us and in our communities—all these factors influence the research moment. It is from that understanding that we engage and listen to the stories and analysis participants share. The relationships we form through these co-interpretive methods advance our findings. The depth of engagement we can achieve throughout relationships, revisiting, and dwelling with participants is a form of validity that we cannot approach through traditional research methods. We are able to learn things that we cannot with more bounded designs and roles.

Our methodology particularly lends itself to longitudinal work because it references research done previously while re-examining themes and throughlines in the analysis when they emerge. We see this revisiting with participants as a form of member checking in action. While conventional member checking can be as perfunctory as offering participants drafts and transcripts to review for accuracy, we're talking about truly checking in with participants in collaboration. When this works well, there are two minds focused on the material. Lifespan Writing Research as a subfield may create more consequential research because participants will have other uses for our findings and may bring them to other publics. Another benefit of gaining insider knowledge from participants is that it can reveal holistic and multiple perspectives that mitigate the limited cultural and personal knowledge of solo researchers. This helps us address the risk of speaking for participants (Kirsch and Ritchie, 1995, p. 8). With this approach, meaning making belongs both to the researcher and the researched, potentially amplifying the value of the project for all involved. As participant/co-researchers have their own insights and make their own discoveries, they may find uses for the findings and realizations that differ from scholarly end products. What we have learned from participants' insights is even more than what we have learned from published scholarship.

We also are aware of contradictions and other limitations that arise with this methodology, some of which involve dealing with disciplinary and institutional conventions. As researchers who work primarily with case studies that involve interviews and writing samples as data, our primary interpretations are with the people who participate in our research as we relate to their transcripts and texts. One of the concerns we have as we conduct these studies is with navigating our institutional review boards (IRB). Longitudinal writing studies sometimes exceed the limitations of the IRB. At times, we have found that the IRB has become perfunctory for us as our research takes us in directions that involve collaborating with participants in ways we couldn't have predicted when we drafted the protocol. We discuss this subject in detail in the next chapter.

We conclude this chapter by framing some of the ways that our work pays attention to the overlapping roles and responsibilities of researchers, research participants, collaborators, co-constructors of knowledge, and our growing understanding of what's important for the subfield of Lifespan Writing Research. Our common objective is to study relationships between everyday non-school practices and more formal academic practices so that we can better understand the many factors that contribute to how adult learners develop as writers and the power that their writing has in their lives. Rooted in our studies with adults in various learning settings, we peer into a few examples from our interview-based qualitative case studies to look at how our research designs are influenced by interactions with participants. We ask these central questions:

- How do participants' experiences, material needs, and interpretation of the study affect our research plans?

- In what ways does the reshaping of research in response to participants inform our practices as lifespan writing researchers?

GUIDING PRINCIPLES FOR INTERPRETING RESEARCH WITH PARTICIPANTS

We offer a set of guiding principles for lifespan researchers that summarize the writing we have done in this chapter. In the next chapter, we demonstrate how these principles apply in our own projects.

1. **Researchers and participants are both experts.** We want to emphasize that participants are experts in their own lives. Our knowledge as researchers is shaped by their expertise. Differences of being and ways of interpreting the world influence our research. For instance, our understanding of racial difference is shaped by participants' willingness to explain their experiences. Researchers can develop a deliberate, self-conscious listening practice by yielding their position to the narratives expressed by participants.

2. **Researchers and participants can dwell together in interpretation and writing.** For us to engage our studies responsibly, with respect for the many interlocking perspectives that shape participants' subjectivity, we interpret experiences together with our participants, sometimes co-writing. It is important to develop informal methods and to inhabit spaces of inquiry where we share the research in ways that matter both to participants and researchers. We show them that their words are being taken seriously, and they influence our interpretations and the ways we write about them.

3. **Research design is best when it is flexible.** Taking participants' interpretations seriously means being open to reconfiguration as we document necessary procedural changes. We invite organic developments and expect changes because our projects continue to be shaped by our co-interpretation with participants whose roles in the research can change across time. Even tautly planned projects are at their best when they are intentionally designed to shift in response to organic developments and unexpected results. Altering an IRB-approved procedure in response to participant-led insights and directions may feel risky and cumbersome, but the larger risk is in missing the opportunity to reshape the study.

For researchers who see the value in co-inquiry but who are not yet experienced in the practice, we recommend setting the stage starting with research design and initial interactions with participants. For instance, we suggest drafting semi-structured interview protocols that ask participants to reflect on and thus make their own meanings about their lives, literacies, and written artifacts. During interviews, a researcher may experiment with yielding to where a participant takes them, showing openness to pathways in the discourse that may exceed their design. Member checking is another place to frame as an open practice in which the conversation is about building relationships, not just fact checking. Those being supervised by a faculty advisor may want to discuss further ways to open the research design to participant feedback.

In our next chapter, readers will become acquainted with how we enact these principles in multiple moments during our studies when we put our co-interpretive methodology into action. We believe that the approaches we have promoted in this chapter, which we are actively using in our own qualitative studies of writing, can offer lifespan researchers organic, flexible, participant-centered means of engaging with research. Through ongoing interaction with participants, and by inviting them—not just once, but across time and phases of our studies—to contribute to the work, we demonstrate our commitment to their writing lives.

REFERENCES

Ackerman, J. (1995). Postscript: The tactics of Nate. In C. Berkenkotter & T. N. Huckin (Eds.), *Genre knowledge and disciplinary communication* (pp. 145–50). Lawrence Erlbaum Associates.

Berkenkotter, C., Huckin, T. N. & Ackerman, J. (1988). Conventions, conversations, and the writer: Case study of a student in a rhetoric Ph.D. program. *Research in the Teaching of English 22*(1), 9–44.

Berkenkotter, C., Huckin, T. & Ackerman, J. (1991). Social context and socially constructed texts: The initiation of a graduate student into a writing research community. In C. Bazerman and J. Paradis (Eds.), *Textual dynamics of the professions: Historical and contemporary studies of writing in professional communities.* (pp. 191–215). University of Wisconsin Press. https://wac.colostate.edu/books/landmarks/textual-dynamics.

Berry, P. W., Hawisher, G. E. & Selfe, C. L. (2012). *Transnational literate lives in digital times.* The Computers and Composition Digital Press; Utah State University Press. https://ccdigitalpress.org/book/transnational/.

Conference on College Composition and Communication. (2015). Guidelines for the ethical conduct of research in composition studies. National Council of Teachers of English. https://cccc.ncte.org/cccc/resources/positions/ethicalconduct.

Compton-Lilly, C. (2017). *Reading students' lives: Literacy learning across time.* Routledge.

Compton-Lilly, C. (2003). *Reading families: The literate lives of urban children.* Teachers College Press.

Eodice, M., Lerner, N. & Geller, A. E. (2016). *The meaningful writing project.* Utah State University Press.

Fine, M. (2018). *Just research in contentious times: Widening the methodological imagination*. Teachers College Press.

Fulford, C. (2022). Rethinking research in English with nontraditional adult students. *Pedagogy: Critical Approaches to Teaching Literature, Language, Composition, and Culture 22*(1), 79–98. https://doi.org/10.1215/15314200-9385488.

Glenn, C. (2018). *Rhetorical feminism and this thing called hope*. Southern Illinois University Press.

Halbritter, B. & Lindquist, J. (2012). Time, lives, and videotape: Operationalizing discovery in scenes of literacy sponsorship. *College English, 75*(2), 171–198. http://www.jstor.org/stable/24238138.

Herrington, A. J. & Curtis, M. (2000). *Persons in process: Four stories of writing and personal development in college*. National Council of Teachers of English.

Ivanič, R. (1998). *Writing and identity: The discoursal construction of identity in academic writing*. John Benjamins.

Kerschbaum, S. L. (2014). *Toward a new rhetoric of difference*. National Council of Teachers of English.

Kirsch, G. & Ritchie, J. S. (1995). Beyond the personal: Theorizing a politics of location in composition research. *College Composition and Communication 46*(1), 7–29. https://doi.org/10.2307/358867.

Micciche, L. R. & Carr, A. D. (2011). Toward graduate-level writing instruction. *College Composition and Communication, 62*(3), 477–501. https://www.jstor.org/stable/27917909.

Moss, B. J. (2003). *A community text arises: A literate text and a literacy tradition in African-American churches*. Hampton Press.

Prior, P. A. (2018). How do moments add up to lives: Trajectories of semiotic becoming vs. tales of school learning in four modes. In R. Wysocki & M. P. Sheridan (Eds.), *Making future matters*. The Computers and Composition Digital Press; Utah State University Press. http://ccdigitalpress.org/book/makingfuturematters/index.html.

Ratcliffe, K. (2005). *Rhetorical listening: Identification, gender, whiteness*. Southern Illinois University Press.

Rosenberg, L. (2015). *The desire for literacy: Writing in the lives of adult learners*. National Council of Teachers of English.

Rosenberg, L. (2020). "Revisiting participants after publication: Continuing writing partnerships." In T. Phillips & R. J. Dippre (Eds.), *Approaches to lifespan writing research: Generating an actionable coherence* (pp. 97–110). The WAC Clearinghouse; University Press of Colorado. https://doi.org/10.37514/PER-B.2020.1053.2.06.

Rosenberg, L. (2023). Following participants as leaders in long research. In A. K. Hea & J. Fishman (Eds.), *Telling stories: Perspectives on longitudinal writing research*. Utah State University Press.

Roozen, K. & Erickson, J. (2017). *Expanding literate landscapes: Persons, practices, and sociohistoric perspectives of disciplinary development*. The Computers and Composition Digital Press; Utah State University Press. http://ccdigitalpress.org/expanding/.

Royster, J. J. (1996). When the first voice you hear is not your own. *College Composition and Communication 47*(1), 29–40. https://doi.org/10.2307/358272.

Royster, J. J. & Kirsch, G. E. (2012). *Feminist rhetorical practices: New horizons for rhetoric, composition, and literacy studies.* Southern Illinois University Press.

Seidman, I. (2019). *Interviewing as qualitative research: A guide for researchers in education and the social sciences* (5th ed.). Teachers College Press.

Selfe, C. L. & Hawisher, G. E. (2004). *Literate lives in the information age: Narratives of literacy from the United States.* Lawrence Erlbaum Associates.

Tarabochia, S. L. (2021). From resilience to resistance: Repurposing faculty writers' survival strategies. *Peitho, 23(3).*

Wymer, K. & Fulford, C. (2019). Students as co-producers of queer pedagogy. *Journal of Effective Teaching in Higher Education, 2*(1), 45–59. https://doi.org/10.36021/jethe.v2i1.29.

Wymer, K., Fulford, C., Baskerville, N. & Washington. M. (2012). Necessity and the unexpected: SoTL student-faculty collaboration in writing program research. *International Journal for the Scholarship of Teaching and Learning 6*(1). https://doi.org/10.20429/ijsotl.2012.060120.

CHAPTER 6.
CO-INTERPRETATION IN ACTION

Lauren Rosenberg with Gwen Porter McGowan
The University of Texas at El Paso

Collie Fulford with Adrienne Long
University at Buffalo SUNY

In the previous chapter, we rationalized our approach to engaging with participants from our position as feminist qualitative researchers who work across institutional, racial, age-related, and other boundaries with the goal of making writing research more just. We turn now to our individual research projects to demonstrate a methodology of interpreting and writing with participants who have become research partners. Throughout this chapter, we ask readers to pay attention to the process we create along with, and in response to, Adrienne and Gwen as we are guided by them as co-interpreters. We learn with them how to become more ethical researchers and how to shape our practices from these three principles:

1. Researchers and participants are both experts.
2. Researchers and participants can dwell together in interpretation and writing.
3. Research design is best when it is flexible.

The three principles guide us during the co-interpretative process that we discuss throughout this chapter. Because our studies have become longitudinal, and because they sprawl in unexpected directions, we emphasize the importance of tending to research relationships. We sustain our work by checking in, sharing drafts and listening to feedback, showing curiosity about our participants' lives beyond the limits of the traditional researcher-researched interaction, swapping stories and photos, even strategizing about ways to be a caregiver. These very personal, ordinary exchanges can only occur when there is genuine respect and trust. The respect and trust soften boundaries and permit us to take risks together; they hold us in a space of ongoing productivity. The co-interpretive activities described in this chapter depend on already established relationships. However, this does not mean that researchers need to know participants for ten years before they can work together. Our point is that we always try to be real and open and considerate of participants' needs as well as our own.

DOI: https://doi.org/10.37514/PER-B.2024.2289.2.06

When participants put so much trust in us, it changes what and how we produce. We strongly believe that sustaining research relationships is even more valuable than obtaining a work product. The product may come and is likely to be different from what we imagined at the planning stage. We have to be open to research design and the product shifting in response to the people who are involved. We are always asking how this research serves the people and communities that it is about.

In this chapter, we illustrate each of the three principles in action as we look closely at relationships with two longtime research participants whom we introduce in the following section. In addition to considering their involvement in multiple living and learning contexts, we acknowledge that Adrienne and Gwen have come to our research through unconventional educational pathways, something that defines them as people and research analysts. We describe the processes we engage with them, then conclude by speculating about the future of our collaborative work because, even as we write this, our longitudinal research continues. This is co-interpretation in action with these participants in this moment.

Adrienne and Gwen's involvement in research shows that co-interpretation is more than a member check on a researcher's analysis. It asserts participants' expertise about their own lives and texts. They have opportunities for narrating experiences, selecting examples and stories, rationalizing those selections, defining their actions, and theorizing their situations. Some of those responsibilities are conventionally associated with the researcher role but less often ascribed to participants. It takes conscious effort for researchers to release some of the control and to share responsibility for thinking about the research itself alongside participants. Yet the quality of work that co-interpretation enables justifies such a joint approach.

The principles we articulated in the previous chapter are elaborated with examples from our ongoing studies. Although we organize this chapter by principle, we also note the fluidity and simultaneity of the concepts we are constructing. We encourage readers to layer and combine research practices; similarly, we hope that researchers will view these principles as adaptable and co-informing. Even though we do not name it distinctly as a principle, we believe that co-interpretive research should always serve participants, partners, and their communities. We rely on our research and writing partners to remind us of those interests and needs and to steer our work in mutually beneficial directions.

ONE: RECOGNIZING PARTICIPANTS AS EXPERTS

As ethical researchers, it is important for us to put aside the sense that we come to research relationships as the specialists. To truly respect participants, we need to yield our view of academic knowing to their perspectives. The first principle takes into account all our ways of knowing. That's how we co-create new knowledge that we can bring back to our respective communities.

Lauren: From Shirley to Gwen

Lauren began conducting literacy case studies with a group of adult learners in 2005. One of the original participants in those studies, Chief, has been involved in Lauren's research until the present. His participation has included formal and informal interviews, sharing writing samples, and fortunately, the willingness to stay in touch. Lauren has published a monograph and articles about her work with Chief (2015; 2018; 2020; Rosenberg & Kerschbaum, 2021). This work (2018; 2023), including a chapter for a previous collection in Lifespan Studies (2020), demonstrates how, across time, Lauren's research on the writing practices of adults who have become more literate later in life has become longitudinal. She reflects on the development of her relationships with participants, which initially were for the purpose of academic research but later morphed into the warm social interactions one might enjoy with close friends or family.

A few months after her book was published, Lauren met Chief's wife Shirley for the first time. She writes in "'Still Learning,'"

> During that visit to Chief's house, I was introduced to the vibrant Shirley, whom I had only heard described before by Chief. Relaxing on the sofa after an early morning stint volunteering at the local food pantry, Shirley was effusive about her lifelong love of reading. Her passion for literate activity includes the personal and the practical. For example, as a home care nurse's aide for most of her career, Shirley engaged in the daily practices she needed to provide care for her clients, which included managing their household and bank accounts, paying bills, driving the car, and even having power of attorney. . . .
>
> While I listened to her describe her literacy habits that day in their living room, I wondered whether it was Shirley's practical intelligence combined with her enthusiasm for writing and reading that made literacy education so desirable to Chief. I recalled a discussion I had had with him during our earlier interviews, in which we discussed a pattern I'd heard talk of at the literacy center where we had met: that it is common

> in traditional marriages for women to be more literate than their male partners and that a change in one partner's writing development can cause a significant disruption. When I reminded Chief of this conversation, Shirley exclaimed that this was not the case for them. Conditions in their lives improved as Chief acquired more literacy. Afterwards, I could not stop thinking about Chief and Shirley together, the way she reclined on the sofa telling her story while I spoke with Chief about the book. (pp. 20–21)

Since then, Shirley has become a participant in Lauren's research. The passage above draws from an article on the entwined trajectory of Chief and Shirley's literate lives (Rosenberg, 2018) that explores Shirley's uses of writing in contexts such as work, community, and church. Lauren also considers how Shirley's engagement with writing and reading influences her husband's choices about his literate activities. Shirley and Lauren stay in touch regularly. Sometimes it is over a draft of an article that Lauren wants Shirley to member-check or simply have in its final form (Shirley always reads promptly and sends a comment), or it might be a holiday card or letter. The personal correspondence always expresses love from Shirley and Chief and a reminder that Lauren has become someone close to them. Their ongoing conversations around Shirley's writing led Lauren to broach the subject of writing together. Shirley said yes immediately, which brings us to the present moment when they are figuring out what it means to be co-authors.

There's something else important to address before turning to the content of co-authoring with Shirley. The shift from participant to author acknowledges Shirley's authority. As a participant, Shirley was protected by a pseudonym. The research she engaged in with Lauren underwent human subjects review and was IRB approved at three institutions where Lauren worked and conducted research. Even in the role of participant, confidentiality slipped when Shirley got a Facebook account and began commenting on Lauren's posts. While Facebook Messenger is one of the primary platforms they use to communicate personally, Shirley's public postings on Lauren's wall demonstrate slippage of IRB protection. In this case, it is the participant's choice to break confidentiality when she writes on social media, sometimes referencing visits they have had or mentioning her husband by name.

We believe that it would be unethical to refer to Shirley as an author by pseudonym unless that was her choice. It is also important for her to represent herself as an author who is an expert on her experiences. Therefore, in this chapter, we refer to Gwen by her actual name as a way to indicate the shift to author.

We compose without disguise because our collaborators are not vulnerable and do not call for protection of their identity. Their visibility is important; they should receive credit within this work and future work that stems from it with acknowledgement of their recognizable, identifiable names, as is reflected in the credits for this chapter.

COLLIE: ADRIENNE AS PARTICIPANT, ACTIVIST, RESEARCHER, AND ADULT STUDENT

"You have to meet Adrienne," a staff member at transfer services told Collie. He recommended Collie meet a forthright new transfer student whom he thought would be interested in her research. Fall 2019 was Adrienne Long's first semester back in college since 1997. She had intermittently attended three different colleges in the 1990s before she "put things on hold" to raise her two children. Once they were in college, it was Adrienne's turn. In the intervening 22 years, Adrienne's professional life had included work as a learning consultant within a large company's career center and corporate sales and marketing for a trucking company. When Collie met her, Adrienne was holding two jobs, nanny and retail associate, and taking four classes toward a degree in psychology. Despite the considerable know-how from her years of employment and family life, and her firm desire to complete her degree, Adrienne's reentry to the university was difficult. She felt disorientation as she tried to restart her academic life in a system that did not recognize her experiential knowledge gained from learning outside of the academy.

Of the thirty participants who eventually joined Collie's study, Adrienne's involvement was unique. Collie and Adrienne developed a lasting and flexible relationship that contributed to the research. They shared an investment in adult students within higher education, and that investment manifested in different projects they each initiated and involved the other in.

For Adrienne and Collie, 2019–2021 were years marked by intensive change. Adrienne completed her studies by attending school full time, year-round, while founding the Adult Learners Student Organization ("ALSO, because we are *also* students") to lift up other students like herself. Meanwhile, she continued as an essential worker through the COVID-19 pandemic. That Adrienne was never Collie's student probably contributes to the ease with which they slid between positions that blur research roles, institutional hierarchies, and their personal lives. Before Adrienne joined the study of adult students' writing lives as a participant, she and Collie already regarded each other as co-conspirators in the mission of educational equity for adult students. Adrienne invited Collie to attend planning meetings of her nascent student organization and Collie invited

Adrienne to join her studies first as a participant and later as a researcher. The boundaries between Collie's research and Adrienne's activism became extremely porous. They wove in and out of each other's projects, amplifying and endorsing each other's work as equals. Collie came to regard ALSO almost as an advisory board for the research, while Adrienne treated Collie as a de facto faculty advisor to the student organization.

The most significant deepening of Adrienne's and Collie's partnership occurred during the summer of 2021 when Adrienne joined a research team that Collie co-led as part of Duke University's Story+ project. The "HBCU Counterstories" project included analysis of transcripts from a previous study about adult students' reasons for leaving and returning to college. The team also compiled media about adult students, HBCUs, and the intersections of these research topics. Long after the summer ended, Adrienne continued independently investigating using both new skills and prior expertise. She seamlessly folded research about adult students into her advocacy work. She created a Facebook group where she curated more media about adult HBCU students. She made a video about their research to share with one of Collie's classes. In these ways, Adrienne evolved from participant to co-researcher on Collie's studies. Adrienne has since independently initiated related projects, including forming a documentary team to produce media about the experiences of adult students.

Considerations about Race in Research Partnerships

We cannot write this chapter without acknowledging the presence of race and the ways that our whiteness has shaped and informed our projects with Gwen and Adrienne. As two white women researchers involved in long term collaborations with Black women participants, we are in precarious positions because of the history of white racial domination and our own complicity within that apparatus; we try not to avoid responsibility. Our subject positions intersect with other identities, most obviously, our roles as mid-career academic researchers. Adrienne and Gwen, whom we respect and learn from on many levels, do not come from positions of academic authority. Working across racial differences is work we take on together by acknowledging our differences and using them as opportunities to self-reflect and act mindfully. We all want to be involved in this research and to learn and grow from it. Since our desire to collaborate on research and writing is mutual, we continue to make the effort to sustain these important relationships. Though we work toward maintaining open and honest communication with Adrienne and Gwen, it is also important for us to critically interrogate our own positions and actions throughout this work. We resist succumbing to white fragility and instead try to be truthful with ourselves as responsible researchers and writers.

In the introduction to *Race, Rhetoric, and Research Methods,* co-authors Alexandria Lockett, Iris Ruiz, James Chase Sanchez, and Christopher Carter (2021) ask, "[For example,] what motivates a White researcher to study 'people of color' without disclosing what's at stake for them to be writing about difference, race, equity, diversity, etc.? What kinds of risks are White researchers willing to take in their work that match the intensity of the life/death urgency of eradicating racial, gender, and economic inequality?" (p. 24). We take their questions seriously. Both of us have devoted our academic careers to working against appropriating the experiences of other people by taking steps in our analysis of data, writing, and revision to challenge our assumptions about representation. (See Fulford, 2022; Rosenberg, 2015; Wymer & Fulford, 2019; Wymer, Fulford, Baskerville & Washington, 2012.) We present our research participants' stories so that they speak for themselves rather than be spoken for by us. As researcher-writers, we mediate the telling. However, we do so by continually checking ourselves in the process (and asking for participants to check as well when they read drafts of our writing) to catch our assumptions and biases, and to be sure that we are honest when we claim the goal of writing without appropriation of experience. Because of the relative power of our positions as white mid-career academics, we are aware of the damage we might do when writing about race and equity. However, we try to use our privilege productively as a means to center our participants' lives and the stories they wish to tell.

Lockett, Ruiz, Sanchez, and Carter (2021) call out white researchers who "fail to be critical of their own privileged position because they are often given the space and opportunity to perform research and publish findings on individuals who occupy linguistic minority space" (2021, p. 25). These authors make recommendations for researchers in rhetoric and composition that we find important: "RCWS researchers should concede the limitations of their cultural knowledge as an outsider, recognizing that their vantage point will not be as rich as those intimately tied to the traditions of literacy and rhetorical prowess under discussion" (p. 26).

One way that we do this is to listen for the lessons about race that our research partners choose to tell us. Here is one example: Lauren and Gwen are sitting on Gwen's back deck. Gwen is reminiscing about some of the inappropriate remarks her white neighbors have made over the years. Gwen recalls moving into the home that she and Chief own in a middle-class suburban neighborhood. When they were newcomers, the neighbors, who were mostly white, made remarks like: We don't want to see any drugs coming into the neighborhood. Gwen told them, "I don't want to see any drugs coming into the neighborhood either." She follows up: "And, do you know, there was a bust at a house down the street where there were all white folks dealing drugs." And here they had told Gwen:

We don't want to see any drugs coming into the neighborhood. The story ends, and they sit with it together, Gwen in her memory of the neighborhood dynamics, and Lauren listening. Lauren hears Gwen teaching her: This is the way it is with white folks in the neighborhood making assumptions about drugs and crime and then unapologetically telling Chief and Gwen a cautionary un-welcome-to-the-neighborhood. Lauren listens without response because she knows that her friend is telling her what racism feels like so that she will learn from Gwen's cultural expertise. In this instance, Gwen tells her story purposefully to make a point about how racism manifests in ordinary life. By narrating her experience on these terms, she gives Lauren a new perspective for understanding their writing and research conversation. This is co-interpretation in action.

In a related example, Collie shares with student researchers the task of comparing interview audio recordings to commercially prepared transcripts and making corrections for accuracy. Most participants in her studies are Black. Research on court reporting has demonstrated the prevalence of radical inaccuracy in the transcription and interpretation of Black people's speech, with dire consequences for them in the legal system (Jones, Kalbfeld, Hancock & Clark, 2019). Black and white student researchers read about this and take extra care correcting transcripts. Through her work with Adrienne, Collie now recognizes that this task is not just about ensuring fidelity to participants' words. After Adrienne had reviewed several recordings, she pointed out how the record of Collie's interactions with one Black participant indicated their distance, and thus the likely incompleteness of the participant's narrative. "She called you *Ma'am*," Adrienne said, and then she walked Collie through places in the transcript where, had this student been interviewed by Adrienne instead of Collie, she probably would have been more forthcoming. Adrienne noted Collie's rank—and more significantly her race—as obstacles to this participant's responses.

Representations of life, education, and writing experiences that Black participants share with Collie will differ from what they would share with one another. She knows that her whiteness occludes full knowing and trustworthiness. Collie can only partially redress this problem. Adrienne's authority about racial difference helps Collie accept that her cultural limitations, racial positioning, and institutional power can be acknowledged and mitigated but never erased.

TWO: RESEARCHERS AND PARTICIPANTS CAN DWELL TOGETHER IN INTERPRETATION AND WRITING

Dwelling with participants in the present, and revisiting interview transcripts and conversations, sets up the conditions through which we construct processes of co-authorship and ongoing co-interpretation. In this section, we focus on two aspects of dwelling together and how those experiences and the strategies we developed deepened our meaning making. The story that follows of dwelling as writing together illustrates our becoming more fluent with possibilities for co-interpretation. We invite researchers to explore other opportunities for dwelling that can give greater impact to their co-interpretive research.

What do we mean when we claim that we write together? Since we are defining this process alongside our participants, we can be loose: Writing together can mean what our collaborators decide, and then we, the researchers, can learn from them. This doesn't require that we necessarily accept what they propose wholesale, but it does mean that we remain open to their ways of seeing. For Lauren and Gwen, dwelling together occurs frequently on Zoom. Because they reside thousands of miles apart, the virtual setting offers a gathering place they wouldn't have otherwise. Lauren sees Gwen and Chief one or two times a year when she travels east to visit family and friends. On those occasions, they sometimes work and sometimes visit only. Both activities are important. During a face-to-face visit earlier in the year, Lauren and Gwen discussed what it might be like to write together, but they didn't come up with a conclusive answer. They're figuring it out as they go. One thing they agreed on was that they would meet regularly on Zoom to "write together." The Zoom room became one dwelling space, but so are the other platforms where they interact such as email and Facebook Messenger, the Google doc where Lauren writes notes in comment boxes while Gwen speaks, and occasionally, letters or the phone. Each of these sites becomes a dwelling place.

Lauren and Gwen intended to write together for a long time. When they met after not seeing each other during the pandemic, Lauren gave Gwen a copy of the transcript from an interview they had recorded two years earlier. Because of pandemic lockdowns and personal limitations, they hadn't had an opportunity to interpret that part of the research. Their ongoing collaboration depended on them using numerous technologies, some of which were new for Gwen, but she was eager to experiment. So, Gwen held the paper transcript in one hand while Lauren shuttled across screens. Through this back-and-forth, Lauren developed a process of writing onto the transcript in comment boxes, essentially creating a meta commentary that was a blend of the two women's dialogue and Lauren's other thoughts in response to the conversation they were having about the transcript. They called this activity *writing together*, the writing being a process of talking with simultaneous notetaking within their dwelling space. This was the process they created for that occasion, aware that in the future they may write together differently.

Experimenting in this way, Lauren and Gwen moved through the written text of their former conversation and remarked on topics that had emerged already.

When they got to the subject of the food pantry where Gwen volunteers, Gwen interrupted the script when she said, "Guess what? On January 15, we lost Ronn Johnson, the head of the pantry." She continued to describe the loss while simultaneously reading aloud from Johnson's obituary: "Ronn spent 'forty-plus years working to make the city of Springfield, especially the community surrounding Mason Square, a better place'" (Henderson's, 2022). Gwen read from the obituary, then asked, "The big question is, what's going to happen to the center?" She described to Lauren how she found out about Johnson's passing: "We hadn't seen him in two weeks. Someone called my brother. They said Ronn Johnson just died. It was just, the shock. [People said,] 'What's going to happen to MLK [Community Center]? Who's going to take over MLK?'"

Clearly, the passing of a leader in her community was a subject of great interest and one that Gwen wanted to write about. After their video call that day, Gwen took the initiative to send Johnson's obituary over email. It was her first time sending a PDF attachment. At their next virtual meeting a couple weeks later, Gwen and Lauren combed through the article together, and while Gwen read and mused aloud, they transitioned from interpreting to writing together on a subject Gwen had chosen. The conversation was steered by Gwen, illustrating part of the principle of dwelling together. They spent weeks reading, interpreting, and writing in response to the event of Johnson's passing and its effects on the community.

When Lauren asked Gwen why she believed they should read Johnson's obituary as part of their writing process. Gwen said,

> I wanted you to see what kind of man he was, how giving, how concerned he was about the Mason Square community, such as the MLK Community Center, which is in the heart of Mason Square. There at the community center, there is so much going on.... [For example,] children whose parents are working use the MLK center as a place of learning, have access to computers, and to the internet.... Here's a man who worked at Mass Mutual. He was a director, a director of community responsibility at Mass Mutual. But he took it further. He took it out into the community. After he finished working at Mass Mutual, he decided to come to work at Martin Luther King Jr. Family Services.

The work of the MLK center, and the way Gwen locates herself as a long-term volunteer in its food pantry, are significant to her sense of herself as a person, and now, as a writer inhabiting a space of inquiry with Lauren. Although the writing process appears to be one of simply talking, reading, commenting, and sharing stories, Lauren contends that this practice *is* their writing together because it is the process that Gwen has chosen.

THREE: RESEARCH DESIGN IS BEST WHEN IT IS FLEXIBLE

Because we make it a priority to yield to participants to make their perspectives prominent, we put ourselves in a position where we're always trying to figure out how their interests and insights prompt us to reconfigure our research design and the boundaries between us. We were taught to design tight studies before putting them into action, but we have learned from working longitudinally and collaboratively that openness to redesign based on our experiences dwelling with participants is equally important. In this section, Collie and Adrienne respond to a situation that altered their research.

Reopening

Collie had not planned to interview Adrienne a fourth time for the Writing Lives study. In fact, she had thought she was finished with that stage of the research in May 2020. There was a numerical tidiness that made her feel that she had done enough. It was the end of the school year, the end of her fellowship. As per her protocol: She had thirty participants. Six of them provided case studies. She had three interviews per case. Folders of writing samples were piled up for further analysis. But a year after the data collection phase was presumably over, Adrienne sent an email to the university's chancellor, forwarding it to Collie. Her subject line read: "IMPORTANT: The catastrophic effect on adult learners with the recent class schedule changes." Adrienne wanted Collie to know that the university had quietly and suddenly reversed their position about continuing remote instruction as the pandemic wore on. Over the summer, without advising sessions or advance notification, the university changed students' schedules predominantly to in-person classes. This was, as Adrienne's subject line indicated, catastrophic for students whose coursework had to accommodate myriad other adult responsibilities. She wrote to Collie, "I plan to continue to fight this as far as I can and hopefully something will get worked out for all of us."

Adrienne and Collie corresponded about the situation further, not as researchers, but because of their shared concern for adult students. Collie couldn't put this writing out of her mind. She felt that the email to the chancellor merited another interview even though she had thought the data collection period was over. It was a dramatic instance of Adrienne's characteristic way of sticking up for herself and others through writing, and there had been results. Adrienne agreed to another interview about this text. However, the fall of 2021 was complicated. Both Adrienne and Collie were in their respective final semesters at NCCU with many life situations to manage amidst the stress, grief, and uncertainty of the grueling pandemic. It was months before they could both fit in a fourth interview. Adrienne had sent the email to the chancellor in June, and it was the week after her December graduation that she and Collie revisited this piece and the whole situation around it. It was important to wait for the right time in their lives and continue the study rather than stick to the original protocol.

They took their time. At first, they spoke unscripted. They had a lot to share even though they had been together just a few days prior at Adrienne's graduation party. The interview was two hours, the longest of the four meetings with Adrienne. Collie had prepared a semi-structured protocol for discussing the email. She also had selected excerpts of Adrienne's past three interviews. They dwelled on each of these before looking together at recent correspondence. Across the prior interviews, Collie had noticed Adrienne writing for self-advocacy and activism, and she wanted to discuss this analysis with Adrienne. Eventually, the two narrowed their focus specifically to the email with the chancellor. They lingered on the subject line so they could examine strategy and context. "Talk to me about that subject line, Adrienne." And she started with the first word, "IMPORTANT":

> I was desperate. It was very strategic in my head like, "I have to capture his attention. This is more than just an email from anybody, this is important. You need to stop, drop and roll. Read this, even if it's spam. You see the word IMPORTANT in that subject? You need to know this is coming from somebody important, and this is important." That was my immediate feeling. And that's why I did that. It takes a lot of guts to write somebody at that level [a chancellor], especially when you're a student.

Then Collie and Adrienne worked through the body of the email itself, paragraph by paragraph, re-examining the text. Collie read it aloud. She asked Adrienne, "What do you notice when you hear that first paragraph again?" And after reading aloud the second paragraph, she asked the same. In this way, bit by bit, Adrienne provided detailed reflective verbal annotation on a text she had written six months prior. This unpredicted expansion of the research added dimension to Collie's understanding of Adrienne's sophisticated rhetorical moves and her beliefs about this kind of activist communication.

To this fourth interview, Adrienne and Collie brought complementary expertise as they dwelled together during an unexpected shift in their co-investigation.

Adrienne understood the high stakes situation and her own decisions in addressing it. She could explain her strategy for producing this text and trace its lineage. She could also point to her other writings for different audiences that contributed to the power of the email. As a writing researcher, Collie marked this text as having another kind of significance, that of an exemplar for the theme of advocacy that was emerging in their joint interpretations due to the malleable research design. If Collie and Adrienne had ended their research after the third interview, Collie would have had something of scholarly value to say about Adrienne's writing, yet this fourth interview was motivated by an opportunity to co-interpret Adrienne's response to a high-stakes situation. Following up enabled Collie to learn much more about what propelled Adrienne to write on behalf of other people and in difficult circumstances.

Revisiting

In "Revisiting Participants After Publication" (2020), a chapter from an earlier collection of lifespan writing research, Lauren developed a theory of revisiting as a dynamic interaction between writing partners. She argues in that chapter that,

> revisiting participants and reflecting with them after publication can be viewed as an important part of the research process that has not been considered in writing studies and that can offer a valuable lens for lifespan research. Through revisiting, researchers and participants can work toward undercutting a one-way knowledge-making tradition that privileges the researcher's findings at the moment of publication as final, limiting possibilities for partnership. Participants' responses to the published text contain possibilities for expanding the way they continue to interpret their stories. We can challenge the conventions of research when we foreground the insights of participants as they continue to reflect on and analyze their experiences. (2020, p. 99)

Revisiting Gwen and Adrienne gave us opportunities to question our assumptions about what constitutes a finished study. Revisiting grants a kind of permission to open work that has presumably been closed and to follow new lines of inquiry and analysis. For this process to succeed, however, it must be participant driven. Revisiting depends on the researcher yielding to the interpretations made by participants. We learn to listen afresh because of new concerns and insights that they bring to the researcher-researched relationship. Our experiences with Gwen and Adrienne illustrate how research and writing relationships gain meaning through ongoing negotiation when we dwell together and when we redesign our studies. Revisiting makes room for the surprises that can emerge when we encounter participants again and find out what has been on their minds during a period (however long) when we were not involved in research together. Their current thinking, including reflections on previous research interactions, can shape how we make sense of the project and the ways we view our findings. These findings can take us to unexpected places where participants' experiential knowledge exceeds and reshapes disciplinary knowledge. We can learn more by consciously disrupting a traditional empirical research process as we question the value of that process and how it serves the objectives of our project. With an open process, we can ask ourselves midstream, what are the best methods *now* for understanding what the participants are trying to express?

Rethinking IRBs

We chose Gwen and Adrienne as participants, and later, we decided mutually to become collaborators because of their wish for further investment in our research. For all of us, working together offers more possibilities for developing ideas across minds and making meaning in more complex ways. The introductions to our collaborators in the first part of this chapter illustrate the value of rethinking boundaries so that we can become even more connected with the participants with whom we collaborate.

We witnessed this in section one of this chapter in the example of Gwen's shift from the pseudonymous Shirley to using her real name as a co-author. The confidentiality stipulated by the IRB, which was important for protecting her and her peers when they were vulnerable as subjects of a study, became an unnecessary constraint that interfered with Gwen's autonomy to express herself as an author. In fact, Lauren consulted with the IRB office that oversaw the research to talk about her concerns with ethical treatment of participants, and it was the IRB officer who explained that our research can sometimes exceed the IRB strictures. Negotiating the shift in naming with Gwen became a matter of recognizing her authority as a writer who was not vulnerable and who wanted to transition into a different role from the one that she had previously inhabited. IRBs, disciplinary expectations, and our own consciences remind us continuously of the importance of maintaining good boundaries. Yet, these prevailing attitudes about what constitutes responsible research behavior can be restraining, essentially curtailing possibility and the potential for taking worthwhile risks.

While we honor the ethics that guide human subjects' interactions, we also respond to the leads we get from partners like Gwen and Adrienne when they have new uses for the research that are meaningful to them. The ethics we are most bound to are therefore relational to specific participants and co-researchers even more than to the abstract ethics of IRB protocols. If we kept our boundaries rigid and opaque, we would not be able to transition into the kinds of trusting collaborations that we describe.

DOING JUSTICE WITH PARTICIPANTS AS RESEARCH PARTNERS

Throughout the composition of both our chapters in this volume, our assumption has been that readers interested in our approach will be involved in qualitative projects and that they may be attracted to the idea that such projects can spill out across time, life course, relationships with other participants, and around the twists of an academic career. However, it is not essential that readers are—or aspire to be—conducting longitudinal studies. While that is the approach to literacy work that is most compelling to us, here we are more interested in offering possibilities for how researchers can engage with participants in meaningful ways. We hope that readers will be left contemplating the quality of their connections, their willingness to revise a study design or protocol, and how that flexibility can make them better practitioners. We grow as scholars based on what we learn from the people with whom we interact. Relating to participants is a significant part of learning to be a qualitative researcher.

Our work should do more than contribute to scholarly knowledge about writing. The research process should be beneficial to participants, and dissemination of results should benefit people like them. We can consult with participants about what would be valuable to them and their communities.

We believe that co-interpretation can also be a useful methodology for lifespan researchers working within a shorter time frame. For instance, we can imagine researchers setting up a sequence of interviews that occur over a period of a few months, during which participants are invited to give feedback on the data collected, not simply to member-check or approve documents, but to contribute to the analysis. Part of the research process could include revising the data collection methods as we have discussed in Principle 3.

Often, our task is to follow the path of our studies, a path that necessarily changes course as a result of co-interpretation. We have shown this throughout the chapter when we look at the decisions our research partners make as they select the relevant topics and steer the conversations. We remain committed to confronting our biases about race and writing as they surface in various forms. We will seek our trusted partners' guidance about what matters in the work ahead both in terms of co-interpretation and in navigating our subjectivities.

At the moment, Collie is writing a book about adult students as researchers and writers that features Adrienne as a central participant and advisor. She plans to ask Adrienne to read occasional excerpts to make sure Adrienne is represented in the ways she wants to be. It's also important that the book be legible to readers who are not rhetoric and composition scholars. Other students, like those who participated in Collie's study, should be able to read the work and recognize themselves, so Adrienne's perspective on style, representation, and facts will all be valuable. That said, Collie knows that the book is her responsibility, not Adrienne's.

Lauren and Gwen continue to meet. Their last encounter while this chapter was being composed was in person at Gwen and Chief's home, but it was not a visit devoted to research. Chief's health had been declining drastically, and in recent months, many of Lauren and Gwen's conversations landed on the subject of being caregivers to ailing husbands. Lauren was also a caregiver to her partner who passed away a couple of years ago. While their writing together matters greatly to Gwen and Lauren, the friendship matters too, in different ways than the research. Sometimes the two women spend their hour online talking about negotiating paperwork for different agencies on their husbands' behalf. Sometimes they focus on what they are doing to take care of their own health. At other times, the conversation stays centered on writing, and their stories spill out.

For us as two qualitative writing researchers committed to longitudinal case studies that do justice to our participants' perspectives, this chapter has given us a chance to share some of the experiences and principles that are most important to us as we continue to follow the twists and turns of our research trajectories. We have confirmed in these pages that research isn't ever done, even after publication. Findings are always provisional and open to revision, as are research processes. Developing partnerships with participants enables us to produce research that is *for* and *with*, not just *about*. That's an ethical stance that both of us will continue unfolding in our current and new projects. Co-interpretation emphasizes the *with*, and there are many different practices for doing so that we can develop with future research participants and partners.

REFERENCES

Fulford, C. (2022). Rethinking research in English with nontraditional adult students. *Pedagogy: Critical Approaches to Teaching Literature, Language, Composition, and Culture, 22*(1), 79–98. https://doi.org/10.1215/15314200-9385488.

Henderson's Funeral Home and Cremation Services, Inc. (2022). Ronn Johnson (January 07, 1959–January 15, 2022). www.hendersonsfh.com/obituaries/print?o_id=7828953.

Jones, T., Kalbfeld, J. R., Hancock, R. & Clark, R. (2019). Testifying while black: An experimental study of court reporter accuracy in transcription of African American English. *Language, 95*(2), 216–252. https://doi.org/10.1353/lan.2019.0042.

Lockett, A. L., Ruiz, I. D., Sanchez, J. C. & Carter, C. (2021). *Race, rhetoric, and research methods*. The WAC Clearinghouse; University Press of Colorado. https://doi.org/10.37514/PER-B.2021.1206.

Rosenberg, L. (2015). *The desire for literacy: Writing in the lives of adult learners*. The National Council of Teachers of English; Conference on College Composition and Communication.

Rosenberg, L. (2018). "Still learning": One couple's literacy development in older adulthood. *Literacy in Composition Studies, 6*(2), 18–35. https://doi.org/10.21623/1.6.2.3.

Rosenberg, L. (2020). Revisiting participants after publication: Continuing writing partnerships. In R. J. Dippre & T. Phillips (Eds.), *Approaches to lifespan writing research: Generating an actionable coherence* (pp. 97–110). The WAC Clearinghouse; University Press of Colorado. https://doi.org/10.37514/PER-B.2020.1053.2.06.

Rosenberg, L. (2023). Following participants as leaders in long research. In J. Fishman & A. K. Hea (Eds.), *Telling stories: Perspectives on longitudinal writing research*. Utah State University Press.

Rosenberg, L. & Kerschbaum, S. L. (2021). Entanglements of literacy studies and disability studies. *College English, 83*(4), 267–288. https://doi.org/10.58680/ce202131193.

Wymer, K. & Fulford, C. (2019). "Students as co-producers of queer pedagogy." *Journal of Effective Teaching in Higher Education, 2*(1), 45–59. https://doi.org/10.36021/jethe.v2i1.29.

Wymer, K., Fulford, C., Baskerville, N. & Washington, M. (2019). "Necessity and the unexpected: SoTL student-faculty collaboration in writing program research." *International Journal for the Scholarship of Teaching and Learning, 6*(1). https://doi.org/10.20429/ijsotl.2012.060120.

CHAPTER 7.

STUDYING WRITING THROUGH THE LIFESPAN WITH GROUNDED THEORY

Ryan J. Dippre
University of Maine

By almost any measure, grounded theory (GT) has been a massive success as a methodology since its inception in the 1960s. Three common texts referenced by grounded theorists—Glaser and Strauss' (1967) *The Discovery of Grounded Theory*; Corbin and Strauss' (2014) *The Basics of Qualitative Research*; and Kathy Charmaz' (2014) *Constructing Grounded Theory*—have nearly three hundred thousand citations combined, according to Google Scholar. GT has become, in most ways we can measure, a highly influential, frequently applied approach to making sense of qualitative and quantitative data. Indeed, GT's very success limits what we can generalize about it: in the half century since its inception, grounded theory has certainly taken on a life of its own, with new generations (Morse, 2009), approaches (Charmaz, 2014), and theoretical underpinnings (Clarke, 2005) shaping how and why people take up this methodology. In this chapter, I outline the key components of GT, make the case for how this can be used to study writing through the lifespan, and articulate a process that lifespan writing researchers can use to get to work through text-based interviews.

DISCOVERING GROUNDED THEORY

Because of the range of GT's uses today, it is easy to forget that grounded theory's discovery happened in the field of sociology and was a response to specific methodological issues in the field of sociology during the 1960s. U.S. sociology in 1960s appears to have been a period of some tumult. Quantitative methods were continuing a development begun decades before, and quantitative researchers were clashing with qualitative researchers in ways that challenged not just methods but the aims and purposes of sociology (Charmaz, 2014). As would be exemplified in Leo Coser's 1975 address excoriating micro approaches, the very notion of what counts as sociology was, at times, in question.

DOI: https://doi.org/10.37514/PER-B.2024.2289.2.07

The lone paragraph above is insufficient to capture the depth and complexity of the decade, but it does highlight the clash between qualitative and quantitative, micro and macro sociology. This clash is at the heart of the development of grounded theory: two people (Barney Glaser and Anselm Strauss) with different training, at different points in their careers, found a way to engage in qualitative research that would be sensible to journal reviewers and editors in a discipline that, in the words of Charmaz (2014), "marched toward defining research in quantitative terms" (p. 6) at that time.

Glaser and Strauss met at the University of California, San Francisco, where they conducted studies on death and dying in hospitals (Glaser & Strauss, 1965; 1979). Strauss arrived at UCSF with a well-established career, having earned his Ph.D. at the University of Chicago. Glaser, on the other hand, was a recent Ph.D. from Columbia, where he trained under Paul Lazarsfeld and Robert Merton. The two worked together on *Awareness of Dying* and its associated articles in what Gynnild and Martin (2011) refer to as a "peer-to-peer mentoring relationship" (p. 3). After the success of that study, Glaser and Strauss realized that, while trying to generate sociological theory about dying in hospitals, they had stumbled upon a new approach to studying qualitative data. They then produced *The Discovery of Grounded Theory*, which brought grounded theory forward as a qualitative methodology to sociologists.

The differences of Glaser and Strauss's training and inclinations shaped the assumptions underpinning GT's invention. Influenced as he was by the interactionist focus at the Chicago school, Strauss brought a focus on the attentions of those under study; how they made sense of the world around them, how they created that sense through collaborative work, etc. Glaser, on the other hand, was from Columbia, having trained under Paul Lazarsfeld and Robert Merton. He came to see grounded theory as a method that "aggregates incidents like surveys aggregate people" (1998, p. 31) in order to find meaningful patterns in data.

In Glaser's work with him, Lazarsfeld "did not perceive any research method as wholly quantitative or wholly qualitative. He showed constantly how all research contained both elements" (1998, p. 29). This bridging of qualitative and quantitative methods served as a spark for Glaser's later work with Strauss. Glaser also drew on the work of Merton, under whom he studied the construction of logical theory (Glaser, 1998). For Merton (again, in Glaser's experience), "substantive concepts had to be related by theoretical codes to generate theory of the middle range" (p. 30). Glaser's work in grounded theory allowed for a construction of theory that bridged qualitative and quantitative work (Lazarsfeld's influence) to generate more abstract theory from interlinked concepts (Merton's influence) but also—and this is where Glaser sees his contribution as moving beyond Lazarsfeld and Merton—beginning the work of theory by abstracting from data collected, not from the logical deduction of social action.

Glaser and Strauss' work to bring their backgrounds together led to a method that successfully navigated the tensions of the era. It allowed for the continued study of social action through qualitative means but did so in a way that could address methodological concerns of the growing number of quantitatively-oriented researchers at the time. GT managed to navigate the qualitative-quantitative, macro-micro battles that were taking place across the discipline successfully and escaped from that raucous period in a position to grow exponentially over the course of the next several decades.

WHAT HAS BEEN DISCOVERED?

The above section usefully characterizes the time period that saw GT's initial discovery. But . . . *what* was discovered? What *is* GT? What does it do? How does it do it?

To begin with, grounded theory is a way to generate explanations *of* data, *from* data. That is, it does not *test* hypotheses on data, but rather allows theory to be generated from the concurrent collection and analysis of data. What exactly is meant by theory is another matter (see Charmaz, 2014), but we can refer to "theory" for the moment as a sense-maker for a set of data. Grounded theorists try to make sense of a set of data that they collect by generating a theory that organizes data in meaningful patterns. A good example of this kind of theorizing in writing studies might be Deborah Brandt's (2001) sponsors of literacy. The notion of sponsorship helps her trace out meaningful patterns in the literacy histories of her research participants.

The way that grounded theorists generate theory is through the act of *constant comparison*. Under the banner of "all is data," grounded theorists collect information in a range of ways—observation, interview, document and artifact collection—and, as they collect it, engage in *coding*, affixing descriptive labels to bits of data that abstracts the social action at work in a meaningful way. The coding process is ongoing and recursive.

Two tools help the researcher through this process of collecting and analyzing data. The first tool is the *memo*: researchers write notes of varying length and detail to themselves as they try to understand how their codes fit together to make sense of their data. The memo is where the coded data begins to fit together (or not) into a developing theory. The second tool is *theoretical sampling*: the researcher lets the emerging theory of what's happening with the social action guide their data collection and analysis. Eventually, the theory that the researcher generates is built up sufficiently to *saturate* the data. Saturation means that the theory now explains the phenomenon of interest at a particular research site, and more data only provides additional examples of the theory at work.

These basic components make up a methodology of grounded theory. Through the use of these components together, the researcher engages in a logic of inquiry that leads from the words, actions, and objects of the people at a selected research site to an abstracted theory that explains the data in a way that, generally speaking, resonates with both the people at the research site and the interests of the researcher's discipline. In GT parlance, theory *emerges* from the ground of a research site; it is not *forced* onto a set of data.

As I mention above, GT has proliferated considerably in the past half century. We can effectively differentiate from what Glaser (1992; 1998) calls *classic grounded theory* (CGT), Corbin & Strauss' (2014) approach to GT, Charmaz's constructivist grounded theory, Clarke's postmodern approach to situation analysis, and a slew of other approaches that make up what Morse (2009) frames as *second generation* grounded theory. Each of these approaches varies in one way or another from the others, but all have the same core of components and an aligned logic of inquiry at their hearts.

GT AND LWR

Lifespan writing research, as defined in Dippre and Phillips (2020), "examines acts of inscribed meaning-making, the products of it, and the multiple dimensions of human activity that relate to it." The goal of this examination is to "build accounts of whether and how writers and writing change through the duration and breadth of the lifespan" (p. 6). This definition attends to writing (of course), but it also turns attention to the actions *surrounding* writing. This is important for understanding how we might operationalize grounded theory for lifespan writing research. Because of GT's sociological roots, we need to call our attention not just to words but to *social action*. Through GT, we can understand how particular actions are recognized by the writer and those around the writer *as* writing, or some activity related to it, and how that shapes future social actions.

GT's power comes from its ability to carefully attend to how social action becomes understood, framed, and bound within a particular context. As you'll see below (in the "Trio of Death" section), the theory is rendered from the codes and categories at a particular research site. These codes and categories bound the claims of the theory and provide the starting points for future applications of that theory, whether that be with further grounded theory analysis or a take-up of the theory for teaching, learning, or design purposes. The open-endedness of the theorizing, in other words, creates productive conditions for future uptake.

This open-endedness is of particular importance in lifespan writing research. One of the great difficulties in understanding writing through the lifespan is the incredible diversity of writing that individuals encounter throughout their lives. By generating focused theories in one part of the lifespan that can serve as a sensitizing lens for further studies in other parts of the lifespan, we can identify patterns of social action with and around writing that resonate with one another.

Below, I propose a "second generation" approach to grounded theory (Morse, 2009), one that builds on the foundational work of Glaser and Strauss (1967) and the later work of Charmaz (2014) to create a pathway toward meaningful theory generation. To be clear, this is not the *only* way to go about applying grounded theory to lifespan writing research. What I articulate here, though, is a way of using GT that has proven useful to me in my own work (i.e., Dippre, 2021) and pairs productively with the broader issue of understanding writing through the lifespan.

GETTING TO WORK: TEXT-BASED INTERVIEWS, GT, AND LWR

In the above section, I traced out some of the theoretical roots and historical happenstance that influenced the development of GT. In this section, and the subsections that follow, I will show how to put that knowledge to work to generate and act on a sensitizing lens that will allow researchers to generate some theoretical claims about writing through the lifespan. As I mention above, I'll be working across text-based interviews from one interview participant at a time to generate our insights, and letting the theory emerge from the lived reality of those participants' writing lives.

Specifying a Sensitizing Framework

A sensitizing framework is something I organize on my way into a study, as a way of making sense of what it is that interests me, how I plan to mobilize the components of grounded theory, and how that mobilization connects to the foundations of the methodology. Once I've established each of those three, I'll find a way to create some orienting questions that I'll use as I craft my research site. Each of these components—identifying interests, mobilizing the components, connecting to GT foundations, and creating orienting questions—are needed to have a GT study that follows a logic of inquiry, rather than a set of collected methods with various degrees of compatibility.

To begin with, what is it that interests me about a potential research site? Why am I intending to collect data there? No doubt my motivations, like all of our motivations, are multiple, but for whatever reasons I have, I've chosen *this particular* site for study. Once I have a sense of what interests me, I can start to build connections between that interest—and, in particular the theoretical and philosophical underpinnings of those interests—and the historical development of grounded theory. I identified several theoretical starting points for building connections earlier in this chapter: the Chicago school, the second Chicago school, Lazarsfeld, and Merton. These are the schools of thought through which the first iteration of GT developed in the 1960s. Later schools of thought, which Morse (2009) refers to as the second generation of grounded theory, brought in other approaches, such as constructivism (Charmaz, 2014) and postmodernism (Clarke, 2005).

The list of options I present in the above paragraph probably sound like a bit of a mess. It seems like we can start just about anywhere, and link GT to just about any theoretical framework. As true as such a statement might feel, though, it's not actually the truth. At some point, the work one has to do to resolve incongruities between the foundations of GT and one's own theoretical assumptions becomes too much work to be worth the effort, and the result might not even be reasonably referred to as a "grounded theory." What I'm looking to do is to work up some basic connections with some of the underlying theoretical assumptions that are implicit in GT so that I can figure out how I can best mobilize the components I mention above toward a study of my interests.

Researchers can start this work by making explicit some of their own theoretical assumptions. For instance, you might imagine, if you're working through a Vygotskian lens, that our understanding of the world is mediated by language, and that this language is shared, but not wholly shared. This has some connections with the Chicago school through Strauss (and, by extension, Hughes and Blumer). These assumptions can lead you to a particular understanding of the components of GT and how you might make use of them (more on this below). Before you get into those components, though, you need to start by articulating the assumptions that you have, and identifying links (and disconnects) from the foundations of GT.

Once I've got a sense of my interests in the site, some records I might need, and the connections between my interests and the underpinnings of GT articulated, I can think about the components of grounded theory, as specified above. For instance, how might I collect data? I will be conducting text-based interviews, sure, but that only covers part of the question. How will I create a record from my interviews? How will I study texts? How will I link texts and interviews? How will I transcribe interviews? Answering these questions can help me identify equipment I need, scheduling issues, and other practical concerns that I may want to think through.

When these questions are answered, I can begin to craft a specified and useful sensitizing framework. It's crucial that I make sense of the sensitizing framework correctly, here, to maintain a GT approach to collecting and studying data: I am not looking to apply a theory, such as heterogeneous symbolic engineering (Bazerman, 1999), to a particular research site. Rather, I'm figuring out how to mobilize my interests and theoretical understandings without losing sight of what's going on "on the ground" of a particular research site. I can do this with some generative questions that (1) start me on the process of record collection and (2) shove into the background, temporarily, my theories and assumptions, so that I can more effectively pay attention to what is going on at a particular research site.

There are many ways we can frame questions, of course. In my own experience, I've benefited best from a series of questions I modeled after the work of Green, Skukauskaite, and Baker (2012) and their work on interactional ethnography. Looking across my interests, the theoretical connections to GT's foundation, and the way I intend to make use of tools to pursue those interests, I identify a particular phenomenon of interest, broadly construed in the language that might relate to the research site (in my Part II text, this would be the interviews with my research participant). I avoid technical language for these questions. So, instead of asking "what counts as literate action?" I would ask "what counts as *writing*?" and explore a research site from there.

Here are the questions I start with, which you can also find in Dippre (2021):

1. What counts as X?
2. When?
3. Where?
4. Under what circumstances?
5. With what social and historical antecedents and consequences?

These are not questions I ask in interviews, but rather the questions behind the questions that I ask. So, if I want to know what counts as writing, I won't ask a participant "what counts as writing to you?" Instead, I might ask "what kinds of writing do you do?" From this question (and its follow-ups), I can begin to generate a sense of what counts as writing.

These kinds of questions are informed by my interests (the phenomenology of literate action) because they ask people about what they're experiencing and can serve as a starting point for pursuing observations of the kinds of experiences people have with literate action. They are also connected to the underpinnings of GT in several ways. First, they allow me to identify incidents and treat them, as Glaser does, like survey data—points that can accumulate over time as the records I gather are dimensionalized into data. Since I'm working from the point of view of the participants, I can eventually engage in mid-range theorizing (connecting to Merton) that keeps the experiences of the participants as its frame (and thus the boundary of the theory). Finally, although the questions do not explicitly do this, they allow me to see the decisions about "what counts as X" as fundamentally social in nature (this becomes important as I build out the sensitizing framework for my study in the next chapter).

THE TRIO OF DEATH: RECORDS / CODING / MEMOING

I cannot, in good conscience, take credit for this title. Back when I could charitably be called an athlete, one period of football practice was given to three drills, done back-to-back-to-back, that my teammate, Josh, referred to as "the Trio of Death." Then, it described the hopelessness I generally felt just before the drills finished. Now, it describes the hopelessness I generally feel after seemingly ceaseless movement among collecting records, coding data, and memoing about my coding.

So, why do I put myself through this Trio of Death? For me, it all goes back to the word "ground" in grounded theory. The work of generating a theory doesn't leave the ground very far, even when I'm engaged in what amounts to, in the end, rather abstract work. I can remain engaged with a research site, try to understand the lived reality of the people at the site, and—through that work—end up rendering a theory that reflects meaningfully (for researcher and participant) on the lived experience of literate action. There is no *forcing* of the data. I'm not at a site to explore, say, sponsors of literacy: I'm trying to understand the writing I see through the words, actions, and artifacts of people engaged in the writing. If the theory that develops connects to, extends, or revises sponsors of literacy in some way, that's an exciting breakthrough not just for an eventual reader of my work, but for me, in the process of my daily work with writers and their writing. The Trio of Death is almost as grueling as it sounds (although you don't actually die, so you've got that going for you), but you end up with theories about writing that, in the end, you can use to help writers write.

Unlike the college drills, the Trio of Death here is simultaneous; you're always going back and forth among collecting records, coding data, and writing memos. Note that I don't discuss collecting *data*—which is a common enough phrase in GT—but rather collecting *records*. Records are the things we make data out of—in our case, interviews, transcripts, notes from interviews, and the written texts that research participants share with us. I draw from Richard Haswell's (2012) definition of *datum* to describe records: they are once-occurring historical artifacts that the researcher cannot change. When we are out looking for sources of information, records are what we collect.

Collecting records. As we collect records, we begin the process of making these into *data*. I fracture (Farkas & Haas, 2012), I pulverize (Brandt, 2016) the records into something that I can begin to code. This can happen in a variety of ways, of course. I might transcribe a recorded interview and segment the interviewee's responses into message units (Bloome et al., 2004) or topical chains (Geisler & Swarts, 2019). I might cut up a written text into paragraphs and code each paragraph. Or maybe each sentence in a paragraph. On the other hand, I might take extensive notes of a writer writing, and then code my notes. Whatever I choose (again, on the basis of what I worked out in developing my sensitizing framework), this act of pulverizing is a logic of inquiry in action, taking my records and *turning them into* data that can be analyzed.

The decisions about how to pulverize my records are shaped by the records I encounter. I can cut up a transcribed interview in one way, the notes from that interview in another way, and a shared text in a third way. What matters is not that the unit of analysis remain unchanged from one record to the next, but that any shifts emerge from the logic of inquiry that follows from my sensitizing framework. Since I'm starting with "what counts as X" and trying to get at the phenomenological experience of whatever X is, I can do this work by attending to the message units (Bloome et al., 2004) of speech that my participants engage in during interviews. The segments for analysis are bound by the intentions (as I can understand them) of the participants.

I can connect those meaning units to particular chunks of text in the text-based interview by letting the meaning units I see at work in the interviews bound the segments of the text I analyze. So, if an interviewee discusses the introduction to an academic article, I could use their sense of the introduction as expressed in the meaning unit to identify the starting and stopping points of those chunks of text.

Writing memos. Rendering data from records involves a great deal of decision-making. So, even before I actually begin coding (and, in fact, *while* I am coding—more on this in a moment), I am making decisions, and decisions that I need to keep track of. I can do this with memos: notes to myself of various length that track my decision-making before, during, and after coding. The memo is where theory is generated, in the end.

There are numerous resources—in particular, Charmaz (2014) and Glaser (2014)—that explain how to write memos in greater detail. What is crucial to me as someone engaging in GT is that each memo I write contains (1) the date and (2) exactly what I need to get a thought out of my head at the moment. Sometimes it's a sentence. Sometimes it's a few pages. But, whatever I decide, I'm using the memo to keep a record of my thinking. The memos I write to myself as I develop my sensitizing lens and start the work of collecting records and transforming data all will be helpful to me as I eventually work up and bound my theory.

One final note on memos: because GT is fundamentally recursive, I may find myself returning to earlier decisions and making different ones. I may decide that bounding interviews by meaning units leaves me with data that is too finely or coarsely grained for me to usefully generate theory, and I have to re-organize and re-code by a bigger unit (such as an "incident" (Charmaz, 2014) or a smaller unit (such as a word). This move into a different unit of analysis is no cause for concern, and having a record of my initial decision *and* my subsequent decisions about bounding will be good to have on hand.

Coding. I don't quite code *as* I bound my data, but not that much time separates the two (and, as I mentioned, I'm collecting some records even as I'm coding data constructed from other records). It really depends on my data, in the end—if I'm coding interview notes, then I can sit down after the interview and start coding immediately. If I need to transcribe an interview before I code, that's a time-intensive task and naps are important. The fundamentally recursive nature of coding allows me to move back and forth across my data.

The beginning of my coding will be *open* (Glaser, 1992) or *initial* (Charmaz, 2014) coding. In this phase of coding, I'll be reading through the data I've constructed unit by unit, describing the social action I see happening in a few words in the margin. I'll keep a record, as I go along, of what the codes seem to mean to me. I may find some codes recur. I may find that a code comes along that actually describes both the unit I'm looking at *and* a previous one—this is the kind of thing I would write a memo about, as it will shape my second stage of coding.

Let's contextualize this in the specific context of text-based interviews. I establish my sensitizing lens, identify my initial questions, and conduct my first text-based interview. After the interview, I engage in open coding, creating and defining codes that emerge for me. I'm also memoing to keep track of the codes and their relationships to one another. After coding the transcript, I probably have a decent idea (through memo writing) of a few codes that seem like they can be useful. I can use those codes to develop my next set of questions for my next interview with this participant in (you guessed it!) a memo.

After my next interview, I'll again be open coding, although some codes from the first interview will no doubt recur—particularly those that shaped my interview questions. I might get more fine-grained codes that relate to the codes I established after my first interview. I might, at this point, be ready for a second stage of coding, which is sometimes called *focused* (Charmaz, 2014) or *selective* (Glaser & Strauss, 1967) coding. At this stage of coding, I am bringing my codes together in some way: trying to see the relationships among codes, perhaps creating broader codes that subsume the codes I found in my first interview, focusing my attention on codes that seem central to my emerging understanding of this writer's literate life, etc.

BEYOND THE TRIO: CORE CATEGORIES, SATURATION, LITERATURE REVIEW

In this section, I have moved beyond the Trio of Death: I've shifted from the gloom of never-ending collection / coding / memoing to the sense that maybe, just maybe, I won't be lost forever in a sea of memos. At this point, I begin rendering a theory. Rather than allowing the coding to run free, as it has been with open coding, I'm now narrowing down my selective coding to a particular category that will serve as the centerpiece for my theory. In these steps, I work my way from identifying that category and fully building out a theory to saturation, and the subsequent literature review.

Articulating a Core Category

As I engage in selective coding, I'll find particular codes pulling at my attention. They seem to provide insight in aspects of my data that seem crucial. I probably have a few codes that stand out in this way. But not all of these codes can be explained in a single paper. Perhaps, if I have a big enough data set, they can't even be explained in an entire dissertation. So these will have to be worked up one at a time, developing a core category from selective codes and dimensionalizing it through *theoretical sampling*, or further data collection that is shaped by the demands of my emerging theory.

By *category*, I am referring to the sense-maker of an emergent theory, a concept that is at the center of my emerging understanding of the literate action of the person I'm working with. Again, this the core of *this particular research project*. I'm homing in on something meaningful in the literate action of the writer(s) I'm studying to generate a publication. For instance, in my study of a writer's notebook practices over two decades (Dippre, 2021), I found *adapting/adopting* to be the emergent core category for making sense of how his notebook writing practice changed over time. The acts of adapting and adopting helped me pull together the various other codes I was working with in the transcripts and texts.

As I develop my core category, I'll need some additional theoretical sampling. While I'm still coding, though, I'm beyond the Trio of Death now. The sense of being adrift in a sea of codes and memos has given way to the excitement of having an emerging theory. The momentum has begun to build, and the theoretical sampling allows me to see what I need for the theory to cross the finish line.

Saturation

Eventually, my theoretical sampling gives way to saturation: no matter how much more data I collect, all I do is find more instances of my core category at work. This is not to say that I have created a comprehensive theory of literate action, of course, but rather that, in terms of data that directly falls under the theory I have articulated, I am explaining everything that I can. Once I've achieved saturation, I can turn to the literature, and start to work out the consequences of my theory on what we know about lifespan writing research.

Connecting to the Literature

At this point, I have a grounded theory that explains the social action I am tracing in a series of text-based interviews. Because of my sensitizing framework, my understandings of writing and how it happens have been caught up in the process of theory generation. But I have not yet done the work of connecting this theory explicitly to what we know about writing in general and writing through the lifespan in particular. Now that I *have* the theory, I can turn my attention toward the literature, and see what my findings resonate with, how I might craft a space for my project in the field in a way that will be both meaningful for my emerging theory and beneficial for lifespan writing research. At present, there are some volumes that I can turn to if I am looking for particular themes in lifespan writing research. I might draw on Bazerman et al. (2018) to generate some connections with their eight principles (p. 20–51) and see how my theory enriches or problematizes particular principles, or even how it identifies particular relationships across two or more principles.

Drawing on Dippre and Phillips (2020), I might turn to the definition of lifespan writing research (p. 6) and generate some potential revisions, enrichments, or problems with aspects of that definition. I could also turn to the end of that collection, either Dippre and Phillips' conclusion (p. 247) or Brandt's epilogue (p. 255) and build from those. Dippre and Phillips suggest *lines of inquiry*—"a rigorous investigation of a concept or set of concepts that can be traced through the lifespan and scaled from a case study to a large data set" (p. 253). Perhaps there is a line of inquiry that my theory can contribute to—Dippre and Phillips offer some suggestions, but I could also identify a new one. In her epilogue, Brandt closes the collection by identifying four questions of immediate import for lifespan writing research. Those questions may be addressed, in part, by my theory, and I can build my literature connections out from there.

Finally, I can move from these broader structures offered from earlier volumes to the particular choices, questions, and conclusions offered by other lifespan writing researchers. In Chapter 8, I draw in particular on Dippre (2019), so I'll spare you the details here, but many other approaches (e.g., Brandt, 2018; Bowen, 2020) offer productive starting points for bringing together a theory with a larger discussion. Using particular chapters or articles as a starting point for bringing a theory into contact with the field can help you craft a focused link that (1) respects the boundaries of your theory and (2) provides a targeted, meaningful contribution to the ongoing conversation of lifespan writing research.

CONCLUSION

Perhaps the greatest asset that GT has for lifespan writing research is its flexibility and durability. It is flexible, in that it can—and has—been used in a range of ways and to good effect in a variety of different fields. It is also durable, in that its various incarnations stand up well to a wide range of data, of settings, and of research questions. With GT—and, particularly, with second-generation GT oriented to text-based interviews—lifespan writing researchers can have a method that works well across different kinds of records, and that has a successful track record.

But, thanks to its open-ended nature, grounded theory is durable in another sense. As Fulford and Rosenberg demonstrate in their chapters, lifespan writing researchers may not know how their studies will unfold or how long they will take. By constantly attending to what is *on the ground*, what is in the records under study, grounded theory remains open-ended. Additional interviews, texts, surveys, etc. can be usefully integrated into ongoing work toward a particular grounded theory. If lifespan writing research is serious about not just multi-site but multi-*generational* research studies (and I hope we are!), then grounded theory provides a flexible, durable procedure for generating meaningful theory that can handle the perpetual open-endedness of such a project.

Finally, I encourage readers to see this chapter not as some kind of demand for orthodoxy, but rather a useful process for getting to useful insights about writers writing through the lifespan. Interested researchers can follow this process for text-based interviews, or they can look at other approaches, cited above, to use grounded theory in different ways. In Chapter 8, I use the process I describe here to generate a grounded theory about one writer's literate action throughout her life. In that example, you can see how I make particular choices while conducting a grounded theory study, which might help you firm up how you intend to go about the work of lifespan writing research through grounded theory.

REFERENCES

Bazerman, C. (1999). *The languages of Edison's light*. MIT Press.

Bazerman, C., Applebee, A. N., Berninger, V. W., Brandt, D., Graham, S., Jeffery, J., Matsuda, P. K., Murphy, S., Rowe, D. W., Schleppegrell, M. & Wilcox, K. C. (2018). *The lifespan development of writing*. National Council of Teachers of English. https://wac.colostate.edu/books/ncte/lifespan-writing/.

Bloome, D., Carter, S. P., Christian, B. M., Otto, S. & Shuart-Faris, N. (2004). *Discourse analysis and the study of classroom language and literacy events: A microethnographic perspective*. Routledge.

Bowen, L. M. (2020). Literacy tours and material matters: Principles for studying the literate lives of older adults. In R. J. Dippre & T. Phillips (Eds *Approaches to lifespan writing research: Generating an actionable coherence* (pp. 111–126). The WAC Clearinghouse; University Press of Colorado. https://doi.org/10.37514/PER-B.2020.1053.2.07.

Brandt, D. (2001). *Literacy in American lives*. Cambridge University Press. https://doi.org/10.1017/ cbo9780511810237.

Brandt, D. (2016). Studying writing sociologically. Paper and Workshop on the 50th Anniversary of the Dartmouth Research Institute. Hanover, NH. August 1–8.

Brandt, D. (2018). Writing development and life-course development: The case of working adults. In C. Bazerman, A. N. Applebee, V. W. Berninger, D. Brandt, S. Graham, J. V. Jeffery, P. K. Matsuda, S. Murphy, D. W. Rowe, M. Schleppegrell & K. C. Wilcox (Eds.), *The lifespan development of writing* (pp. 244–271). National Council of Teachers of English.

Brandt, D. (2020). Epilogue. In R. J. Dippre & T. Phillips (Eds.), *Approaches to lifespan writing research: Generating an actionable coherence* (pp. 255–249). The WAC Clearinghouse; University Press of Colorado. https://doi.org/10.37514/PER-B.2020.1053.3.2.

Charmaz, K. (2014). *Constructing Grounded Theory*. Thousand Oaks: Sage.

Clarke, Adele E. (2005). *Situational Analysis: Grounded Theory after the Postmodern Turn*. Thousand Oaks: Sage.

Corbin, J. & Strauss, A. (2014). *Basics of qualitative research: Techniques and procedures for developing grounded theory* (4th ed.). Sage.

Coser, L. A. (1975). Presidential Address: Two methods in search of a substance. *American Sociological Review*, 40(6), 691–700. https://doi.org/10.2307/2094174.

Dippre, R. J. (2019). *Talk, tools, and texts: A logic-in-use for studying lifespan literate action development*. The WAC Clearinghouse; University Press of Colorado. https://doi.org/10.37514/PRA-B.2019.0384.

Dippre, R. J. & Phillips, T. (Eds.). (2020). *Approaches to lifespan writing research: Generating an actionable coherence*. The WAC Clearinghouse; University Press of Colorado. https://doi.org/10.37514/PER-B.2020.1053.

Dippre, R. J. (2021). Haikus, lists, submarine maintenance, and *Star Trek*: Tracing the rambling paths of writing development. In K. Blewett, C. Donahue & C. Monroe (Eds.), *The expanding universe of writing studies: Higher education writing research* (pp. 381–397). Peter Lang.

Farkas, K. L. & Haas, C. (2012). A grounded theory approach for studying writing and literacy. In K. Powell & P. Takayoshi (Eds.), *Practicing research in writing studies: Reflexive and ethically responsible research* (pp. 81–95). Hampton Press.

Geisler, C. & Swarts, J. (2019). *Coding streams of language*. The WAC Clearinghouse; University Press of Colorado. https://doi.org/10.37514/PRA-B.2019.0230.

Glaser, B. (1992). *The basics of grounded theory analysis: Emergence vs. forcing*. Sociology Press.

Glaser, B. (1998). *Doing grounded theory: Issues and discussions*. Sociology Press.

Glaser, B. (2014). *Memoing: A vital grounded theory procedure*. Sociology Press.

Glaser, B. & Strauss, A. (1967). *The discovery of grounded theory: Strategies of qualitative research*. Transaction Publishers.

Glaser, B. & Strauss, A. L. (1965). Temporal aspects of dying as a non-scheduled status passage. *American Journal of Sociology, 71*(1), 48–59.

Glaser, B. & Strauss, A. L. (1979). *Awareness of dying*. Transaction Publishers.

Green, J. L., Skukauskaite, A. & Baker, W. D. (2012). Ethnography as epistemology. In J. Arthur, M. Waring, R. Coe & L. V. Hedges (Eds.), *Research methods and methodologies in education* (pp. 309–321). Sage.

Gynnild, A. & Martin, V.B. (2011). Introduction: Mentoring a method. In A. Gynnild & B. V. Martin (Eds.), *Grounded theory: The philosophy, method, and work of Barney Glaser* (pp. 1–12). BrownWalker Press.

Haswell, R.H. (2012). Quantitative methods in composition studies: An introduction to their functionality. In K. Powell & P. Takayoshi (Eds.) *Writing studies research in practice: Methods and methodologies* (pp. 185–196). Hampton Press.

Morse, J.M. (2009). *Developing grounded theory: The second generation*. Routledge.

CHAPTER 8.
DEEPENING AND KEEPING THE PRESENT: GROUNDED THEORY IN ACTION

Ryan J. Dippre
University of Maine

> And I asked myself about the present:
> How wide it was, how deep it was,
> How much was mine to keep.
>
> – Kurt Vonnegut

In Chapter 7, I provided an overview of grounded theory (GT) and closed with some guidelines that lifespan writing researchers can use to make GT useful to lifespan-related questions about writing. In this chapter, I show those guidelines in action, and I use them to make sense of how one writer transformed her writing practice across contexts throughout her life. In doing so, I aim to (1) provide a useful example for future writing researchers interested in using GT to study writing through the lifespan and (2) generate some findings that future GT-driven lifespan writing research can build on. In particular, I focus on how writers come to circulate agency back to themselves, from one moment to the next, through literate action.

LIFESPAN LITERATE ACTION AND AGENCY

One of the emerging interests in my work has been how human agency shapes literate action throughout the lifespan. My understanding of agency emerges from Bazerman's (2013) uptake of Merton but makes a bit of a sharp turn through ethnomethodology. Merton's agentive vision of structured choice-making among alternatives is framed by Bazerman as follows:

> . . . the social facts people perceive provide the field upon which they conceive, shape, and choose actions. In so acting they advance their own perception of the socially structured world, reinforcing that vision within the externalized world for others to interpret and respond to (p. 108).

This vision of agency—as making choices among perceived alternatives—is at the heart of my interest in how agency is taken up by writers when they perform literate action throughout the lifespan. But I'm also interested in how the perceptions they have that lead to such choice-making is constructed *just-here, just-now*, with *just-these-tools* (Garfinkel, 2002). How do people work together via interaction to establish certain social facts, take them for granted, and *then* act off of them? How do we create social conditions in which we have more (or less) capacity to act?

In exploring these questions (Dippre 2018, Dippre 2019), I refer to agency as *circulating*, as moving through talk, tools, and texts and back to individuated actors in particular circumstances. By tracing how agency circulates to and through people and objects, I can understand how literate action develops in writers over time. Because of its open-ended nature (which I describe in further detail in Chapter 4), grounded theory is a useful approach to tracing such agentive work. GT allows me to follow agency as it circulates, allowing me to code across interviews, artifacts, and observations according to a coherent logic-in-use.

In *Talk, Tools, and Texts*, I identify *circulating agency* as a rich concept, something that can serve as the basis for an eventual theory of the middle range about lifespan literate action development.[1] Circulating agency as a concept helps us pay attention to the way agency is circulated back to humans through objects. But, rather than offering explanation or understanding enough to make theoretical claims, it poses issues that researchers will need to explore in order to understand how agency circulates through the successive performance of literate action through the lifespan. In particular, by the end of *Talk, Tools, and Texts*, we still have not figured out the mechanisms through which agency is circulated. I move this notion of agency forward in this chapter by studying the writing of Anna (a pseudonym) through the sensitizing framework of what I call *autochthonously grounded theory*.[2] I aim to generate theory that emerges from the just-here, just-now, with-just-these-tools work of writers trying to keep literate acts going. The scope of the eventual theory moves beyond particular locales, but the

---

1   A note on the word "theory" so that the reader isn't confused. Grounded theory does, indeed, generate theory: explanations of sets of data that help us understand what is happening. And my earlier work (Dippre 2019) is also interested in theory. Both grounded theory and the theory I hope to build in my future work is usefully characterized as "middle range" theory, in that both attempt to go beyond the scope of the immediate research site without creating all-encompassing grand theories. However, the theory I hope to generate in the future would be accumulations of several grounded theories of the kind that you are reading about here. So the theory that emerges from my work with Anna will eventually contribute (with other, smaller theories) to a larger, but still middle-range theory.

2   Thanks to Kelly Hartwell, August Adent, and Elizabeth Zavodny for their early work with me as I shaped up "AGT."

initial work of the theory is keenly aware of the particular circumstances of the particular literate acts (and their products) being studied.

AUTOCHTHONOUSLY GROUNDED THEORY: A SENSITIZING LENS

As I have noted elsewhere (Dippre, 2019), I find it valuable when trying to understand writing through the lifespan to attend to the *lived reality*, the moment-to-moment work of making writing happen. The lived reality is the one constant we can always turn to, whatever part of the lifespan we might be studying. The lived reality, and the totality of the literate experience that individuals engage in from one moment to the next, is not something that can be directly accessed. I cannot step into the shoes of a writer and experience their life. In my work, I draw on interviews, observations, and written documents to approximate an understanding of that lived reality. I code across these artifacts to frame three aspects of literate action:

1. **Ongoing, joint action:** how social order is practiced for another first time
2. **The individuated actor:** how the challenge of each passing moment is faced in the production of writing (or work done for writing)
3. **The scenic reduction of uncertainty:** how the talk, tools, and texts brought to bear on a particular writing task are used to produce order, reduce uncertainty, and keep the act of reading and writing going

I am not looking to mark instances of these frames. That is, I do not want to read through transcripts and note "ongoing, joint action" in the margin. Rather, I examine artifacts and code by looking through these frames. I want the particular ways in which these three aspects of literate action are taken up by particular actors to be rendered through my coding.

In looking through these frames, I am looking at the autochthonous properties of how literate action was produced in a given moment: just-here, just-now, with just-these-people-and-talk-and-tools (see Garfinkel, 2002). I refer to this attention to the immediate, local production of social order as *autochthonously grounded theory* for this reason. Also, no one else in our field is weird enough to see the word *autochthonous* and say "wow, what a great name for a methodology," so I don't have to worry that I stole the title from someone else accidentally.

Autochthonously grounded theory will help me to trace the literate action that my research participant, Anna, recounts in her retrospective, text-based interviews. In order to set these frames—and thus this approach—into motion as a sensitizing framework (see Chapter 7), I've identified a few questions to help me identify the records I would like to turn into data through coding:

- What counts as writing to Anna?
- What of this writing is meaningful to Anna?
- When does/did she do it?
- Why?
- Under what circumstances?
- With what social and historical antecedents and consequences?

Note what these questions do: they help me zero in on (1) particular acts of writing by Anna and (2) the important elements that lead up to and follow from those acts of writing. So, by thinking through these questions, I can both pay attention to and see the impacts of the autochthonous properties of Anna's literate action.

INTERVIEWING ANNA AND COLLECTING RECORDS

Anna and I met soon after I moved to Maine. A middle-aged, cisgender woman from the Midwestern United States, Anna is a professor at a public university in Maine. She writes as part of her job on a regular basis, both for publication and for institutional purposes. Anna demonstrated an interest in my work on writing through the lifespan during one of our conversations, and I invited her to meet with me and discuss her writing life. She agreed, and we met multiple times across the span of four months.

I began our work together with a literacy history interview, taking handwritten notes about what she said. Once the interview was finished, I coded the interview, wrote some memos to myself, and generated some questions and guiding themes for our next interview. I emailed Anna these questions and themes as a way of setting up our next meeting. I repeated this process after each interview. Our interviews together touched on a range of topics: her upbringing, her history as a student, her family (she is married, with two children), her career, and of course her writing.

THE TRIO OF DEATH

The constant movement among interviewing, coding, and memoing certainly earned its name during my work with Anna. I struggled—as those engaged in grounded theory often do—to have the abductive breakthrough I was hoping to have, and identify a core category. But I was able to identify some insights into Anna's literate life that—I hoped—would shed light on whether and how she circulated agency through literate action.

For instance, Anna frequently—if unevenly—engaged in journal writing throughout her life. She was given a lavender journal at age seven, which she filled with stickers, drawings, and writing over the course of a few years. When she was 14, she began filling journals in just a few months. Her journal writing did not continue at that pace throughout her life—the various demands outside of writing took her attention—but her earliest bouts with journaling served as an important starting point for what would become a more complex, reader-oriented performance of sustained literate action over time.

Anna's earliest attempts at journaling seemed to her (in retrospect) to have an audience in mind. Notably, Anna lied in her journals at various times. There was no reason for her to do so, in Anna's mind, so the lying must have been done with an audience in mind. As she continued to journal, though, her sense of audience became more complex. The journaling first became a space for her to write to herself—a place to generate a stronger sense of self, to make sense of herself *to* herself, it seemed. Anna mentioned the journals as a way of "defining myself as introspective" while also giving her space to develop "different ways to think about myself."

The identity work that Anna is engaged in throughout her journaling is evident, and I caught it in my coding frequently. I noted "Identity Building" as a code, something that she seemed to be doing both at the time and in her current, retrospective understanding of it. I also coded for "meaning-making writing," which I defined as "Writing that has helped Anna make sense of herself." Anna's identity-building (what I call identity (re)construction [Dippre, 2019]) is fascinating, of course, and it could have been a direction for the project to move in. Since this is a GT study, I had to follow the compelling data where it led, even if that led me away from agency, which I thought would be particularly visible here.

However, there was not yet anywhere particularly compelling to go with the data—or, at least, I did not see it in my notes at the time. The journals—and Anna's discussion of them—were strategic in that they made visible Anna's emerging understanding of how her identity was developed over time, but I saw little of the small, social-fact-constructing moves that would help me peg that to the production of social order. The visibility of ongoing, joint action (the first frame) was low, making a focus on identity rather difficult.

I was able to notice, in my coding, attention to how she built relationships with others through writing. She was able to engage in what I labeled as "space making" through writing: that is, she created opportunities to think to herself, to keep herself at arm's length, to communicate (when she wanted to) through writing. Mentions of space making also happened around acts of what I coded as "enjoying,"[3] or discussions of positive experiences with writing. So Anna seemed

---

3   Not all of my initial codes are gold.

to be crafting social interactions with and through writing, which also seemed to lead to her enjoying it further. I started to get a sense that this might impact how she circulated agency to herself in various social encounters, and that I might be moving toward a breakthrough.

Just as I started to get that sense, though, I was reminded why I labeled this process the "Trio of Death." I noted a code that I referred to as "powering through," which I defined as "continuing on something despite uncertainty and/or unhappiness." Anna, at several points in our meetings, identified some uncertainty or unhappiness in her life and just tried to, in my words, power through it. Although this ended well much of the time—for instance, she confesses to not understanding much about graduate school when she was accepted, but "powered through" and ended up with a Ph.D.—I was not sure how that resonated with agency, and it seemed to knock me off of my selective coding. Could the creation of an artifact cataloguing unhappiness or uncertainty then be circulated back to one's self, only to have nothing change, and still count as agency? I was not sure.

RENDERING CODES AND A TENTATIVE CORE CATEGORY

Other attempts at moving toward a core category were similar failures. Or, at least, that's how I felt while I was enduring the difficulties of the Trio of Death. But the attempts, while themselves unsuccessful, ended up leading me to a core category in an unexpected way. I was working on a presentation on grounded theory for Talinn Phillips' methods course, and my notes and coding were on the table next to me while I was putting together a PowerPoint presentation. Like many presenters, I had initially developed an eight-hour presentation for what was supposed to be a fifteen-minute talk, and I was trying to winnow down what I had to say.

I had been tinkering with a PowerPoint slide that was particularly troublesome, and I sat back and let my mind wander for a moment. Or, rather, my mind wandered of its own accord, whether I wanted to or not. Whatever the reason, I glanced to my left, and saw my latest attempt at selective coding. I thought to myself "huh, Anna's really messing around with time through her writing." Then I shook myself, turned back to the PowerPoint, and kept working.

For about a minute, anyway, until I realized what had happened: *time* was at the heart of the agency in the writing that Anna was doing. It was about pausing time, living in the important moments in her life, filling them out with as much detail as she could muster, so that she could then turn to use that detail to inform what she did later on. To reference the Vonnegut quote at the start of this chapter, she was mining the depths of the present as a means of enriching her life, or her understanding of her life. By freezing a moment, enriching it, and elaborating on it through her writing (particularly her journaling, although this extended also to letter writing to friends and family), Anna was able to not only understand particular moments in her life in more nuanced ways, but that nuance could be drawn upon in future literate acts in ways that allowed Anna to circulate agency back to herself.

This abductive insight was crucial to helping me understand the work that Anna's writing did for her, and how it bolstered her sense of agency not only in the production of writing but, much like Frank (Dippre, 2018), in her recurring interactions with friends and family. Anna would—in a code I developed—"endow value" on a particular moment through her writing, with both the value-endowing and the subsequent use of that value being agentive acts. She saw it as "preserving something" in a way that "lends you more control." By giving "a moment that's passed something of value" through writing, she could make use of that value at a later production of literate (or other social) action.

Keeping in mind Deborah Brandt's (2021) focus on *action* via coding, I referred to Anna's act as "deepening." "Deepening," here, is a way to keep my focus on the work that Anna is doing to mine the depths of a moment, to "endow value" and "preserve something" through her act of writing. This seemed to be a useful way to describe my core category for the moment, but I also sensed it was lacking in some way. Anna did, indeed, deepen the present through her writing, but she also *made use of* that writing later on, and the word "deepening" did not capture that very well. The term worked for the moment, though, as I sought to round out my sense of what it might, indeed, mean to deepen a moment for Anna.

I roped in a few other codes to align with deepening, though I was unsure at this point how they all related to one another. Much like with "deepening," I focused on the act of writing, rather than what Anna would come to do with that writing. I identified the following codes as relating to the work of deepening:

- Space making: Creating opportunities to think via writing
- Connecting: Writing to make connections with others visible (to herself or to others)
- Endowing value: Deliberately making a moment more meaningful by writing about it
- Gaining control: Using writing to transform an experience into something of greater value

I dropped "Gaining control," as the distinction between that and "Endowing value" was without a difference. That left "space making," "connecting," and "endowing value" as codes related to "deepening."

These three selective codes served as intensifiers of an act of deepening the present. For instance, Anna mentioned a feeling of control that writing helped her get over an unhappy relationship she was in during her college years. The writing endowed value not to the relationship but to her unhappiness, and gave her the space from the relationship she needed to sort it out. The presence of both codes in this particular writing experience made for a more intense act of deepening. In this framing, then, all three codes could be present at once in a discussion of Anna's acts of deepening the present.

RETURNING TO RECORDS AND CONSTRUCTING FURTHER DATA

A selective coding of my notes from the interviews confirmed, for me, two things. First, that the core category I had identified seemed to be a recurring phenomenon in the records. Second, it confirmed that the phenomenon was happening *frequently enough* that the records were useful to analyze through the core category. At this point, though, the confirmation was more of a hunch. I could point to the number of lines that the deepening addressed through one code or another (65 / 233), but that is only a starting point. And, besides, I still had the other, currently unaddressed half of the equation to worry about: what Anna did *after* she deepened the moment. I would have to return to the bigger set of my records and construct more data to sort this out.

I turned, then, to my interview recordings. I organized them into meaning units (that is, units of analysis bound by the intentionality that Anna seemed to be working to convey) in order to better get a sense of how saturated my data was with the core category. This process gave me a greater number of more nuanced units to attend to, which I could use to apply my coding a bit more carefully. The smaller units would also allow me to extend the "deepening" category into what Anna does subsequently, as her acts of deepening become, through writing, available to her to use.

A problem that emerged from me at this stage of coding was the separation between the deepening of the present and its consequences. Anna was able to articulate with precision some specific acts of deepening the present—a letter to her mother, or child, or some journaling to herself about a particular moment. Her articulation of how she was able to draw on those moments, however, proved more general. The strategic research materials of her discussions of deepening the present, in other words, was not matched with equally strategic research materials in the consequences of those acts of deepening the present.

Toward this end, then I turned to *theoretical* sampling, which allowed me to draw on my emerging theory to direct additional data collection. This came about in an additional look through interview material that I had set aside. While reviewing some of my earlier codes, I noticed that some of the meaning units I had coded as "identity building" had a connection to some of the acts of deepening the present that I had identified, and that those message units had more information for me about the consequences of these moments of deepening. I had sort of pushed these units to the side, since they were related to identity and thus perhaps useful in a future, different core category.

But with those meaning units at my disposal, two things happened. First, I gained information that I needed to round out the theory. Second, I was able to develop a theory that had greater coverage of the available meaning units. The finding increased both my coverage and the power of my emerging grounded theory.

My rounded-out grounded theory turned out to be a two-step process. First, Anna would *deepen* the present through writing with different degrees of intensity depending on the three variables (space making / endowing value / connecting). Then, once the present had been deepened, Anna would *keep* the present in a future moment, also with different degrees of intensity based on a new subset of codes. By processing a moment through deepening / keeping, Anna was able to circulate agency through her writing and back to herself in a range of times and places. In the next section, I trace the acts of deepening and keeping that she engages in to highlight the role of this core category in Anna's life.

A note, before we move on. The chapter to this point has focused on my own work to generate theory. This is a deliberate choice, in keeping with the aims of this volume. In the next section, however, I turn from my methodological choice-making to Anna's work as a writer throughout her life. I try to demonstrate how Anna circulates agency to herself, in part, through the manipulation of time. The findings from my work with Anna are both confirmation of the usefulness of an autochthonously grounded theory approach and a genuine insight that later, more expansive work may build from as we continue to learn more about writing through the lifespan.

ANALYSIS THROUGH A CORE CATEGORY

Table 8.1 provides a visual of the theory. Deepening and keeping are symmetrical in that, just as deepening contains three intensifiers, so does keeping. In fact, as I demonstrate below, the intensity of the deepening has, at least for Anna, resonated with the intensity of the keeping. That is, intensity at one end of the process leads to intensity at the other end. To be sure, however, the intensifiers of the two stages of the process do not line up with one another. There's no predictive value in what, for instance, space making will intensify in the "keeping" side of the process. Below, I trace out several prominent acts of deepening and keeping, as well as how they impact the literate action that Anna performs. The particular literate acts I have chosen to emphasize are from different parts of her life but are often in response to rather significant life events. Several examples I reference focus on the writing that Anna did to and about her mother throughout her illness and passing several years ago.

Table 8.1. A Theory of Deepening / Keeping

Deepening		Keeping
Space making	leads to	Sharing
Value endowing		Transforming
Connecting		Professionalizing

Step 1: Deepening the Present. The first step of this complex series of literate acts for Anna is to recognize, in her interactions with others and the world, the important nature of a particular moment. This may be something she identifies ahead of time, or something she recognizes after the fact. A long vacation with her mother, for example, was a moment that seemed, even before it began, to be important and worth chronicling to her. Other moments in her life had their importance signaled after the fact—for instance, writing about an experience of a track meet after it happened. Anna did not *know* that the experience would be worth recording before it happened but was moved to after the fact.

Anna's act of deepening a moment—that is, of mining the depths of a personal experience—happens with and through writing, although the extent of that writing can vary widely. For instance, Anna might do something as brief as a short entry in a journal—or, in one case, saving a piece of someone else's writing (her mother's) to deepen her experience of understanding her mother's life (see Figure 8.1). Anna's writing (as well as her engagement with her mother's writing) allowed her to not only understand herself better, but those she cares about. In Figure 8.1, we see the literate action of another as a mechanism for Anna to understand (along with other artifacts and writings) her mother's illness through her mother's eyes.

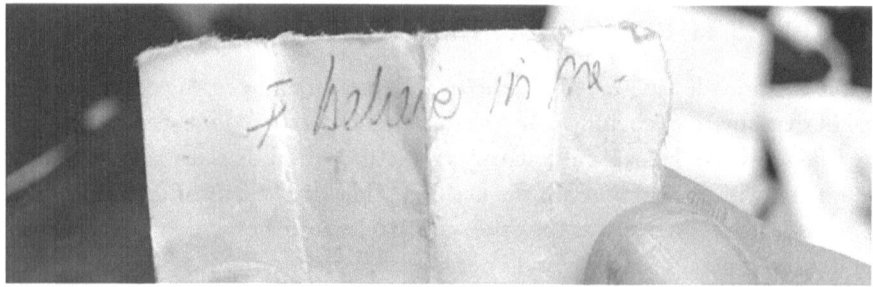

Figure 8.1. Anna's Mother's Writing

But Anna could do more—and did do more—than just record small notes (or hang on to the notes of others) here and there. She could also engage in *space making*, creating opportunities for her to think with and through her writing. These structured opportunities to write—at the time of our work together, it was in the early morning—would let her explore the space of a past moment, what that moment meant to her, and how she might better understand the experience.

Anna could also do this writing as a means of *connecting* with others, to make her relationship(s) with them more visible. This could be something that she writes to herself, but that is oriented to making sense of connections she has to others. She seems to work, in some of her journals, to make sense of her relationships among herself and her sister and mother. Other times, this connecting work is articulated with *an intention of sharing* with others (though, to be clear, she has not yet done so at the "deepening" stage). For instance, Anna has a collection of letters that she has written to her daughter on her birthday, so that her daughter can, later in life, have a sense of her life through her mother's eyes (as well as their relationship). The letters, she says, highlight something "that's intersubjective" about their lives, and that also "conveys who she is at that time." Anna also writes letters to other friends and family.

Finally, Anna can intensify her act of deepening by adding value to a moment, by speculating, exploring, or otherwise challenging the seeming mundaneness of a given act by linking it to broader themes, more complex histories, or perhaps more current events. This, as the reader may suspect, can coincide with acts of connecting, but it can also stand apart: it may be something that Anna experiences in the act of her writing, but that she is using to make sense of things to herself, rather than to others (or her connections with others). These acts of endowing meaning, as she says in one interview, are a way "to preserve something" in a way that "lends you more control." This act of controlled preservation "lends a moment that's passed something of value" that she can take up and use again. Once that moment has value, Anna has a number of ways of using that value to circulate agency to herself in future activities.

Step 2: Keeping the Present. Once the present has been *deepened* through writing by Anna, that moment has transformed into a tool, a potential way to make sure that, in a future, related moment, Anna will be able to circulate agency back to herself in order to pursue particular goals. *Keeping*, unlike *deepening*, is less concerned with an enriching of the past and more with the accomplishment of social action in the present. When Anna engages in acts of *keeping*, she is pulling these past movements forward in time—and, in doing so, creating conditions in which she can act through various talk, tools, and texts.

Anna's work on *keeping* is often tied to her journal writing, a practice she began when she was a teenager. This journal writing has been a regular presence in her life, although her journal writing seems to increase at some points and decrease at others. For instance, when she was in high school and college, "journal-writing remained really important" to her, and she "would—especially in the summer months—[she] would fill up a journal in maybe two or three months." Much like my other research participants who engage in journal writing (see, for instance, Dippre, 2021), Anna's journal writing has moved from physical journals to computer entries.

Anna's act of keeping can be a simple one: she can simply draw on her past writing to help her act in a current moment in a straightforward way, such as by confirming certain events in the past during an act of writing ("writing" here broadly construed—this could be a journal entry, an email, a letter, etc.). But Anna can also intensify this act of keeping in several ways. She might choose to *share* writing with others. As Anna points out, "I'm not as private as some people would be with this private writing." This writing can be something that she intended to share (and thus was written for a particular audience) or writing that seems, to her, to be worth sharing. Such sharing circulates agency back to Anna because it becomes a shared resource between her and another that helps her with the goal of a particular interaction or set of interactions.

The act of keeping can also be intensified by *transforming* through the originally deepened moment. The work of particular journal entries, letters, etc.—by the act of deepening a moment—come to show Anna a new sense of who she is.[4] In other words, her writing has transformed her into a different person, one who acts in certain ways and does certain things, and so these pieces of writing become an anchoring point for those new actions. Her writing to and about her mother during her illness, for instance, "created another dynamic" in the relationship she had with her, transforming not only that relationship but, through that transformation, her sense of who she was when she was engaging with and around others.

The reader might note that Anna seems capable of stacking these intensifiers. She can share her writing and, in that act of sharing, highlight a transformed self. So her actions and the materials around her (in this case, the writing) work together to intensify an act of keeping. The third intensifier, *professionalizing*, can also be either stacked or stand on its own. One of the interesting insights in Anna's writing was the cross-pollination of her personal and professional writing. Anna saw her professional writing not as entirely separate from her personal writing—and, over the years, she came to see the two as more deeply intertwined acts of "artistry." Anna was thus able to draw on those past moments of her

---

4 Note the connection here to identity (re)construction (Dippre, 2019). This may serve as a valuable starting point for putting agency circulation into conversation with this concept in the future.

personal experiences to generate text (chapters, talks, etc.) that could put her in a position to continue on her professional pathway. She could make "something happen through writing" in many lifeworlds that could be professionalized into something generative for her career.

We can see, in this articulation of the autochthonously grounded theory, a pattern of Anna's work with and through writing to deepen and then, later on, keep a moment through the performance of literate action. To paraphrase Glaser (1998), through deepening and keeping, Anna's attention to moments *processes out* in ongoing, moment-to-moment, material work of literate action. As this happens, Anna is able to circulate agency to herself in new and varied ways, for individual, social, and professional purposes.

SATURATION

The core category of *deepening/keeping* seems to have sufficiently saturated my available data. The theory provides sufficient power to help me understand how Anna's literate life has developed in at least one sense. Furthermore, it has helped me to understand how Anna accumulates and works with agency (again, in at least one sense). I expect and hope to work with Anna in the future, to understand more of the complexity of her literate life. Deepening/keeping will serve as a useful sensitizing framework when I turn to that work in the future.

FROM CONCEPT TO THEORY

At this point, I am comfortable identifying *deepening/keeping* as a theory in a small-t, grounded theory sense of the word: something that provides some explanation of how writers can manipulate one moment to circulate agency back to themselves in a future moment. As I hoped it would, the theory adds some dimensionality to the robust concept of *circulating agency,* and it gives us a mechanism to attend to (time), a lens to look at the mechanism (a particular moment) and a series of questions (articulated below) to explore in future studies.

But, do we have enough information, now, to raise *circulating agency* from a concept to a more comprehensive theory? One that, though wider in scope than deepening/keeping, still serves as a middle range theory? No. We're not there. Not yet. What I can see through my interviews with Anna is how she was able to use writing to *deepen* the present, how she was able to enrich a moment through writing, capture more of it, and *keep* it meaningful to her in multiple ways throughout her life. The act of deepening the present became a way for her to carry a moment of action, through reflection, into the future: both her thinking (that is, about a particular moment—say, an interaction with her mother) and her actual practice of literate action (the writing that does the work of deepening the moment) become tools for her to circulate agency back to herself in future situations.

All of this helps me understand how Anna (and other writers) might create conditions for agency in the future by deepening a moment through writing. It has certainly sharpened the image of agency circulation that my earlier work (Dippre, 2019) began to trace. But the image of circulating agency, though sharper, remains quite blurry. Anna is able to deepen a moment through writing, sure. But why? How might deepening one moment interact with other deepened moments? What are the consequences of this writing both one moment at a time and collectively for Anna's development of literate action and the overall rich complexity of her life?

These outstanding questions lead me to conclude that a theory of the scope I hope to build has not yet emerged. Progress continues, to be sure, and the connection between lifelong literate agency and the articulation of a particular moment is worth looking further into. We now know, thanks to Anna's willingness to work with me, how time can be manipulated through writing, and how that manipulation can become a tool for increased agency in future moments. We may not yet have arrived at a theory with the broad (but still middle-range) scope I'm looking for, but we're far closer than in 2019. And, crucially, what we have is usable for future research.

WHERE WE GO FROM HERE?: LIFESPAN LITERATE ACTION, AGENCY, AND FUTURE DIRECTIONS

My work with Anna demonstrates just how much there is we can learn about how writers manipulate time through writing. How can moments be frozen, enriched, and explored through writing in ways that support (or suppress) agency in future moments? What we see with Anna is likely just the tip of the iceberg. She was able to zero in on particular moments of her life and flesh them out through writing, learning more about the important moments in her life both during and after the production of literate action she engaged in. Studying with writers doing other kinds of writing—and perhaps deepening moments that are important to them (or not) in other ways—might help us see the many possibilities of messing with time that are available.

Future research might also take on a study of lower-stakes acts of deepening the present. What might the relationship be between Anna engaging in thoughtful writing about moments with her mother and someone, say, taking thorough notes at an orientation? Emotionally, these two moments are quite different. But practically, in terms of how people circulate agency back to themselves, what might we learn by putting these side by side? How might we get a better sense of the multifaceted nature of what it means to deepen a moment in ways that promote future agency? Additional work through autochthonously grounded theory with multiple writers, generating codes, categories, and insights one writer at a time, can help us to explore these questions further.

We also need to consider how the ongoing work of writers to (re)construct their identities (Dippre, 2019) each next first time they perform literate action relates (or doesn't) to the agency that they circulate to themselves. How does identity (re)construction support or restrict agency, and vice versa? In what ways do we transform our sense(s) of who we are (or who we pretend to be) in order to circulate agency back to ourselves? How might we forego agency in order to (re)construct a particular identity or identities in a moment?

Finally, the ethnomethodological and sociohistoric threads that shape this study offer potential links for setting the future work I have outlined above to other approaches to study literate action (Bazerman, 2013), literate activity (Prior, 1998), and literate practices (Roozen & Erickson, 2017). Following these threads can help us to identify the limits of autochthonously grounded theory—what gets missed in this particular process of data construction and analysis, and how it might be further buttressed by additional theoretical complication. With the suggestions I make above, the rich image of theory can be sharpened into a coherent theory, one that not only helps us to understand the role of agency in the production of literate action, but that also helps us to productively interfere with student writing as teachers of writing through our crafting of assignments, curricula, and feedback.

REFERENCES

Bazerman, C. (2013). *A theory of literate action: Literate action*. The WAC Clearinghouse; University Press of Colorado. https://doi.org/10.37514/PER-B.2013.4791.

Brandt, D. (2021). Studying writing sociologically. In K. Blewett, C. Donahue & C. Monroe (Eds.), *The expanding universe of writing studies: Higher education writing research* (pp. 261–270). Peter Lang.

Dippre, R. J. (2018). Faith, squirrels, and artwork: The expansive agency of textual coordination in the literate action of older writers. *Literacy in Composition Studies*, 6(2), 76–93. https://doi.org/10.21623/1.6.2.6.

Dippre, R. J. (2019). *Talk, tools, and texts: A logic-in-use for studying lifespan literate action development*. The WAC Clearinghouse; University Press of Colorado. https://doi.org/10.37514/PRA-B.2019.0384.

Dippre, R. J. (2021). Haikus, lists, submarine maintenance, and *Star Trek*: Tracing the rambling paths of writing development. In K. Blewett, C. Donahue & C. Monroe (Eds.), *The expanding universe of writing studies: Higher education writing research* (pp. 383–399). Peter Lang.

Garfinkel, H. (2002). *Ethnomethodology's program: Working out Durkheim's aphorism*. Rowman & Littlefield Publishers.

Glaser, B. (1998). *Doing grounded theory: Issues and discussions*. Sociology Press.

Prior, P. (1998). *Writing/disciplinarity: A sociohistoric account of literate activity in the academy*. Routledge.

Roozen, K. R. & Erickson, J. (2017). *Expanding literate landscapes: Persons, practices, and sociohistoric perspectives of disciplinary development*. The Computers and Composition Digital Press; Utah State University Press.

Vonnegut, K. (1994). *Slaughterhouse-Five: A Novel*. Modern Library.

CHAPTER 9.

IMPROVING SYSTEMATIC REVIEWS OF LONGITUDINAL WRITING RESEARCH: DEFINITIONS, QUESTIONS, AND PROCEDURES

Teresa Jacques
University of Porto

Jonathan M. Marine
George Mason University

Paul Rogers
University of California, Santa Barbara

This chapter describes the theoretical background and methods used to conduct a systematic review of longitudinal writing studies (readers can find the results of the systematic review in the following chapter).[1] As longitudinal writing research involves a wide spectrum of different types of methods and methodologies, we conducted a systematic review of this broad area of work in order to bring together what's been learned from longitudinal writing research, to add our own contribution to that research base, and to provide a model of transparent, replicable methods for future research reviews. This review builds on the critical questions and varying definitions of what constitutes longitudinal writing research, as discussed in previous work (see Bazerman, 2018; Rogers, 2009; Tierney & Sheehy, 2005), which we used to shape our efforts to select and critically review longitudinal writing research from 2000–2020.

Within the framework of a larger inquiry into what we have learned about writing development from longitudinal studies of writing around the world and how that might be relevant to those interested in lifespan perspectives on writing development, in this chapter we provide a model for other researchers by telling the story of *how* we conducted a review of longitudinal writing research focused on methods of data collection and data analysis.

---

1   The first author is supported by a doctoral grant from the Portuguese Foundation for Science and Technology (grant 2020.05024.BD). We have no conflicts of interest to disclose.

THEORETICAL FRAMEWORK

Longitudinal studies have long been used to study writing development. From the earliest longitudinal studies of writing (see Gage, 1973; Loban, 1963; Rentel & King, 1983) to those most recently published (Aldossary, 2021; Duan & Shi, 2021; Guo et al., 2021), these inquiries have proven particularly impactful for studying writing development as they highlight change over time and across contexts for all kinds of writers. According to Bazerman (2018), most longitudinal studies share several common features including the periodic and repeated collection of data from a specific group of people across a long enough time sequence to surface meaningful comparisons. In addition, longitudinal research typically includes an intentional periodicity (i.e., recurrent activities) in the application of measurement tools (like scales, surveys, or interviews) and in the ways in which data are collected. Longitudinal studies are particularly useful for studying writing since they can help to find patterns, surface meaningful correlations, and predict future outcomes amongst the many variables associated with writing development, including family and social activities (e.g., the amount of time parents write or read with their children), school-based interventions (e.g., curriculum, instruction, etc.) and personal factors (e.g., self-efficacy or socio-economic status), all of which can impact writing practices and learning to write. Further, because almost all pedagogical writing research involves a focus on learning and improvement, longitudinal writing research can be extremely valuable for those interested in learning and instruction, as measuring that growth inevitably means looking at changes that take place over time.

Ultimately, what makes this work so valuable (and worth the tremendous effort and investment of time and resources that longitudinal studies require) is that results of longitudinal research can provide insights into the ways in which writing development can be supported by revealing what development is and when and how it happens. The long-term view of writing development associated with longitudinal research can help clarify what is developmentally appropriate for specific individuals or groups within the same community, for writers at various ages and grade levels, and by comparing differences in outcomes for those who have different access to resources. Longitudinal writing research is also useful in tracking personal writing trajectories, the ways in which writers deal with learning opportunities and challenges, and changes in writer's identities.

By collecting situational data (socio economic status, cultural context, instructional level, etc.), growth in writing within the individual's ecosystem and context can be seen. Further, this research can surface information related to the interactions between the intra-individual and the inter-individual variables in writing development, which is critical because so much writing research is predicated on such a wide spectrum of interrelated variables which can be difficult to differentiate from one another. Knowledge gleaned from longitudinal writing research can thus influence decision making related to writing development at the policy, curricular, and instructional levels.

The complex network of factors which can affect any one person's writing development are complicated by the general social, developmental, and familial milieu which varies so widely across languages, cultures, and contexts. In this regard, longitudinal writing research holds particular promise in looking at growth and development during important transitions, such as from preschool to kindergarten, from elementary to middle school or secondary school, from high school to college, from undergraduate studies to graduate-level work, and from graduate studies to the highest levels of professional life and beyond. Longitudinal research helps illuminate the uneven, nonlinear, and multidimensional aspects of writing development (Rogers, 2009) including the spurts of growth, disruptions, redirections, and regressions of writing skills that can occur (Haswell, 1991). For these reasons, writing researchers have long made calls for more and better quality longitudinal studies of writing (see Bazerman, 2018, p. 327; Emig, 1971, p. 95). Yet, due to the many complicating factors associated with writing development, Bazerman (2018) has called the pursuit of true lifespan longitudinal studies "the impossible dream."

In spite of these difficulties, longitudinal writing research has contributed to the field's understanding of different aspects of the long, individual, and complex writing trajectories found across the full arc of human development (Bazerman, 2018; Rogers, 2009). Lifespan longitudinal research, while currently out of reach, would involve studying all dimensions potentially relevant to writing development beginning with the very earliest developments of print literacy in young children before school, accounting for the multiple and varied contexts of schooling, and extending to all aspects of an individual's literate life.

The cognitive complexity and social aspects of writing make defining writing development a difficult task as writing development is always dependent on context (Rogers, 2009), and the term "development" itself is rooted in cultural and social practices (Matusov, 2007). Further writing development is related to other aspects of development at both the microgenetic (small changes in knowledge, attitudes, skills, and behaviors associated with writing, like motivation, or learning a grammatical rule) and ontogenetic levels (i.e., related developmental changes related to the whole person such as one's identity (Ivanič, 1998) or occupation. Since human development is an extremely complex process (Hickel, 2020; Sagar & Najam, 1998), writing development is therefore equally complex and difficult to precisely define.

Longitudinal studies, however, have helped us to better understand the complexity of child development by following children from birth, and/or through to adulthood (Faden et al., 2004), and by following a particular individual across time. Following child growth over time, particularly in their context of development, helps identify trends, indicators of causal relationships, and individual differences in development (Shulruf et al., 2007) which hold immense potential value for researchers, teachers, and learners across other disciplines. Since human development results from the individuals' ongoing interactions with the various contexts they are in (Zeanah et al., 1997), any developmental outcome, whether social, physical, behavioral, or psychological, represents a uniquely complex and idiosyncratic trajectory. Further, since the various contextual elements within an individual are interrelated it is especially difficult to precisely pinpoint when, where, how, and why different developmental influences occur and shape growth trajectories (Shulruf et al., 2007).

DISTINGUISHING WRITING DEVELOPMENT FROM WRITING CURRICULUM

In research, distinguishing between what counts as writing development and the influence of curriculum is difficult since trajectories of writing growth are intertwined with all other aspects of our life (Moffett, 1968; 1992), especially within literacy instruction and formal schooling. Given the importance of curriculum in learning to write, we might ask why it is important to separate in research the influences of curriculum from development. This turns out to be a critical question because if researchers investigate the results of a particular intervention that is focused on one or more specific elements of writing and then test to see if students indeed grew in those ways, we have to question whether or not that learning is permanent; that is, will it *transfer* to other contexts of other writing experiences across time and throughout development?

So, while a study may show positive results of an intervention, say, in a pre-post-test design, our argument is that conceptions of writing development must extend beyond particular curricular interventions (e.g., beyond a single course of instruction) in ways that can be compared over time within and between individuals and groups to see what in fact is developing and how that development is proceeding beyond a particular classroom experience. Researchers therefore must account for the powerful influence of curriculum on development. As Bazerman (2018) noted, "research should have its eye not just on the immediate success of a lesson or the short-term improvement of scores through a particular curriculum, intervention, or practice—for such studies do not look beyond the current standards or curricula to see whether the learned curriculum best serves the long-term development of writers" (p. 377–378).

One way to separate what we might think of as normative writing development from writing curriculum is by systematically identifying, selecting, and appraising a body of longitudinal studies of writing development across the entire lifespan drawn from a diverse series of populations (people of varied backgrounds and experience) (Bazerman, 2018). Longitudinal writing research of this kind would examine meaning-making, writing products and the various dimensions that influence if and how writers and writing change throughout the lifespan (Dippre & Phillips, 2020a; Writing through the Lifespan Collaboration, 2019). Ideally, therefore, lifespan longitudinal writing research would involve a wide range of methods and methodologies, theoretical frameworks, and populations and samples (Dippre & Phillips, 2020b).

THE CURRENT REVIEW

Since systematic reviews call for the researchers to make a set of decisions, in this chapter we explain how we conducted a systematic review of longitudinal writing studies. In this review we set out to provide an updated perspective on the current methods being used to conduct longitudinal studies of writing since the turn of the century (beginning in 2000). Why did we decide to conduct a systematic review and not a narrative review? To answer that question first we need to clarify the difference between the two. A narrative review summarizes available literature without adhering to a set of formal guidelines and they are generally written when the topic or questions are best suited to a narrative, for example when reviewing research perspectives (Gregory & Denniss, 2018). On the other hand, a systematic review uses a well-defined set of steps to remove the risk of bias as much as possible. This adherence to strict guidelines is what qualifies a systematic review as "evidence-based" (Gregory & Denniss, 2018).

We approached this study with a sense of the value and importance of longitudinal research methods for the study of writing and, although we had identified some partial narrative accounts of longitudinal writing research (for example, Rogers, 2009 narrative review of longitudinal studies in higher education in North America), we saw a clear need to identify the state of the art in longitudinal writing research and to ground our understanding of the landscape of longitudinal writing research landscape empirically. Given these goals, it was clear we needed to conduct a systematic review. In conducting our review, we also decided that we wanted to provide other researchers with information and tools that would assist them in carrying out their own systematic reviews, which in our view would be of great benefit to the field.

We further wanted to support researchers in designing and carrying out longitudinal studies, especially in ways that contribute to conceptions of lifespan writing research as outlined by Bazerman et al. (2018) and Dippre & Phillips (2020b). In particular, we wanted to learn:

1. General study characteristics
2. The quality of studies
3. Study settings
4. Methodologies
5. Methods of data collection and analysis
6. Longitudinal characteristics
7. Participant characteristics
8. Educational context
9. Funding Sources

THE PROCESS: FROM THE INITIAL SEARCH TO THE RESEARCH SYNTHESIS: DECIDING TO CONDUCT A SYSTEMATIC REVIEW

At the forefront of the many concerns about longitudinal writing research are charges that what constitutes 'longitudinal' research varies widely (Rogers, 2009). While a great deal of work has been done on longitudinal writing research over the preceding two decades, the data collection and analysis methods, objects of study, and research questions remain disparate. In response to this potential incongruity, along with the sheer volume of research and scholarship in this area since the year 2000, we decided to conduct a systematic review in order to see if we could identify the state of the art in longitudinal writing research (identify, select, and critically appraise relevant research), while at the same time we wanted to be extremely clear and transparent about the methods we used to carry out that systematic review in the hopes of supporting the efforts of future writing researchers in carrying out similar reviews.

Our goal was to build and analyze the longitudinal writing research base in a replicable, aggregable, and data-driven manner. We wanted to understand the state of the art in longitudinal writing research and to fully map the research program as it was being carried out around the world. We further wanted to see the degree to which results from these studies might contribute to the theoretical frameworks associated with lifespan approaches to writing development. In our view, longitudinal research provides the most promising approach to building the knowledge base to empirically support a vision of lifespan writing development.

Steps in the Systematic Review

We started the process by conducting a search of the literature to identify the corpus of longitudinal studies used in writing research since the year 2000, following Alexander's (2020) recommendations, which meant reviewing handbooks, narrative reviews, and empirical articles. This first step identified the full corpus of potentially longitudinal writing research. For a full description of the literature search, see the preferred reporting items for systematic reviews and meta-analysis (PRISMA) flow diagram (Panic et al., 2013; see https://osf.io/tjyu2/?view_only=72272c4f124b4b00bbd41667798edc76).

To identify these studies we carried out a thorough database search in November 2020 in the following databases: Google scholar, Linguistics and Language Behaviour abstracts, Elsevier, communication abstracts, APA psycinfo, Psychology and Behavioural sciences, JSTOR, Education database, Education Research Complete, Teacher Reference Center, Social Science database, Science Direct, Anthropology Online, Sociological Abstracts, and ProQuest. The search string included the keywords "writing" and "longitudinal", to prevent the exclusion of relevant articles at this early stage. We focused on research from 2000–2020 in order to identify the most current trends in longitudinal writing research. The search yielded a total of 594 records across 14 databases.

Creating and Completing a Matrix with all Longitudinal Studies of Writing

Out of these 594 records, we narrowed the corpus down to 290 records by screening out duplicates, studies conducted before 2000, and those not strictly related to longitudinal research on writing. All remaining records were tagged according to nine non-exclusive categories (i.e., a study could receive multiple category tags): adult learners, L2, K-12, pedagogical studies (studies focused on teachers and teaching more than learning, students, or writing), higher ed, naturalistic, WID (writing in the disciplines), cognitive, and methodological (studies that were focused on research methods rather than actual writing development).

Discussing with Other Researchers

At this point in the process, we met with two senior scholars who are considered experts in longitudinal writing research: Charles Bazerman and Rui Alves. This conversation guided our research design and general thinking as we began our data analysis. We were encouraged to continue considering longitudinal writing research in the broader context of lifespan growth but were advised to avoid searching for an overarching narrative, as the maturity of the field would not warrant generalizations at the lifespan level. Rather we were encouraged to identify the smaller stories within the lifespan; in particular, we were counseled to focus on L1 learners in the K-20 context (leaving out for now, L2, preschool, workplace, and adult learning).

We were also prompted to use a low inference, binary definition for what counts as a longitudinal study (which for us was a really important question: "what counts as a longitudinal study?") by applying the following simple criteria: Does the study have two points of measurement? Additionally, we were strongly encouraged to avoid conflating the effects or impact of curriculum and targeted instructional interventions with writing development. Finally, we were advised to separate L1 and L2 studies as discrete areas of research for now, but to retain the goal of comparing results from both areas for future work. These considerations shaped our understanding of and approach to designing our analysis of this systematic review.

Methodological Focus of the Systematic Review

At this point we began developing inclusion and exclusion criteria. As we were advised, we began with L1 longitudinal studies in order to identify a baseline of writing development. We also decided to only include studies from the schooling years (kindergarten through university) because research indicates this is the period when the bulk of writing development occurs. Following this decision, all records labeled preschool, workplace, adult learners, as well as pedagogical and methodologically focused works were removed from the corpus to include only works of L1 writing research from kindergarten to university. This cut the final dataset to 111 studies.

Screening for the Systematic Synthesis: Inclusion and Exclusion Criteria. In developing our inclusion and exclusion criteria we began with a quality assessment screening that included two items: first, the study needed to have been published in a peer-reviewed journal, book, or book chapter. The second quality measure was methodological rigor, which meant that to be included, a study needed to be empirically grounded and conceptually focused with qualitative or quantitative data appropriate to the study's claims.

Next we created a set of exclusion criteria which aligned with our research goals. First, we only included studies in which writing was the central focus. This became an important and somewhat difficult distinction at times, as writing is frequently used in other studies related broadly to literacy, such as reading and especially emergent literacy, but it is not necessarily *the central focus* of those studies. As Berninger (2010) noted, "Few longitudinal studies of writing exist . . . moreover, comparatively little research has focused on writing alone. The research on writing that does exist is often focused on writing–reading relationships" (p. 281). Therefore, in our coding of quantitative longitudinal studies of writing we only included studies in which writing growth, development, change or learning was the core dependent variable, or in which writing was the primary independent variable and the dependent variable was a construct centrally related to writing, such as self-regulation or motivation. We only included qualitative studies in which the primary object of study was writing development, growth, learning, or change over time. Secondly, we only included studies that included at least two points of measurement so as to ensure that all studies were in fact longitudinal studies of writing.

Third, outcomes from the studies needed to be distinct from curricular intervention as to distinguish development from curriculum. For example, we screened out a study in which the intervention was supporting undergraduate students in better using APA style because the study set out to strictly measure improvement in the usage of APA style rather than a more general writing development construct such as knowledge of conventions or another item that would not simply be measuring precisely what was taught. We excluded a variety of studies across grade levels which presented similarly narrow conceptions of development based on measures limited to the constructs presented in the curriculum.

Fourth, quantitative studies needed to specify the measures collected (qualitative studies were excluded if writing and/or writing development was not clearly the central object of the study). The fifth criteria asked if a study included participants in the schooling years (K-university): kindergarten, elementary school, middle school, high school/secondary school, university (undergraduate or graduate). Finally, we added studies that *only* included L1; so, if a study was of both L1 and L2 writers it was excluded.

Screening and Agreement Between Judges. A screening procedure took place for the 111 articles following the PRISMA guidelines (Moher et al., 2009) and the screening guide explained above. All 111 abstracts were screened using Rayyan, an online tool for systematic reviews (Ouzzani et al., 2016). All three authors read all 111 titles and abstracts and decided to include or exclude for all 111 records based on the screening guide. The initial agreement was calculated by conducting an interclass correlation (ICC). This analysis showed an ICC of .75 which indicated moderate to good reliability (Bobak et al., 2018). Of the 111 initial articles, 42 required further screening; i.e., there was some disagreement among the reviewers. Whenever a disagreement occurred, the study was discussed to reach a consensus decision to include or exclude. In the end, 53 studies were selected as eligible for the review.

Complementary Searches. To ensure we included every possible study we could find, at this time we also conducted an additional "hand-search" of possible eligible records. To do this, the 2nd and 3rd author checked every reference list of the 53 studies selected in Rayyan and read full texts when the title and abstract didn't provide enough information. The complementary search found 13 more eligible studies to add to the first 53. The final dataset included 66 articles. All selected articles were added to a reference management software, Zotero, as recommended in Cooper (2010) for ease of use in writing up the results of the review.

Coding Eligible Studies. After deciding on the final set of 66 studies, we created a coding guide to extract information from the studies. Our coding guide was constructed with our research questions and goals in mind and according to the recommendations on creating a coding guide as found in Cooper (2010). At this step, we designed each coding category to be as low-inference as possible, to avoid any bias in the data entry (Cooper, 2010). Low-inference coding happens when we only need to locate the information in the research report and transfer it to the coding sheet (see Cooper, 2010). However, some high-inference categories were unavoidable as they provided critical information related to our research questions.

The high inference categories were methods of data collection and data analysis, which on the surface might appear counterintuitive. However, in practice, many of these studies used a battery of different measures to collect a wide range of different types of data, all of which were analyzed in different ways. Reducing a study which collected nine different forms of data to a single code required capturing more detail. To address the complex and inferential nature of these coding categories, we also collected the stated methods of data collection and analysis within each article in order to review as a group later.

Based on our aims, we coded nine categories of data: 1) General characteristics of the study; 2) Quality assessment; 3) Study settings; 4) Methodology; 5) Methods of Data Collection and Analysis; 6) Longitudinal Characteristics; 7) Participants' characteristics; 8) Grade level and 9) Funding Sources (We coded for funding, even though it isn't strictly related to writing development, in order to better understand the landscape within and conditions under which longitudinal research on writing is carried out, as longitudinal writing research can be costly given that it takes place over long periods of time and can require a great deal of resources.)

The 66 studies were coded by the first and second authors to ensure any potential bias was eliminated from the coding. Any disagreements were resolved by the 3rd author. During the coding we eliminated ten more articles since we realized that they did not meet the inclusion criteria when the full texts were read. The final corpus for our systematic review included 56 references.

CONCLUSION

In our systematic review of methods and methodology used in longitudinal studies of L1 writing development, our goal was to provide a comprehensive review of the methods and methodology being used to study writing development across the lifespan since the turn of the century. We further aimed to help inform future research designs and to draw attention to current trends.

We conducted this review to support researchers in designing and carrying out longitudinal studies. With that in mind we: 1) Framed a critical question worthy of review and posed an unanswered but answerable critical question (Alexander, 2020, p. 7); 2) Searched the databases according to our goals; 3) Created a matrix with all the studies found; 4) Divided our goals into three different reviews; 5) Decided to conduct a review of methods and methodology first; 6) Decided on inclusion and exclusion criteria; 7) Screened for eligible reports in Rayyan; 8) Conducted a complementary search; 9) Created a coding guide; 10) Entered the information on every study in the coding guide; 11) Wrote the systematic review following the PRISMA guidelines. The screening guide and coding sheet are available on the Open Science Framework, an online platform that promotes open, centralized access to research elements (Foster & Deardorff, 2017), which promotes open science practices, so that the editable files can be accessed by anyone who wants to use them. To access our coding sheet and screening guide visit https://osf.io/tjyu2/?view_only=72272c4f124b4b00bbd41667798edc76.

The Research Goals as the Driving Force

To conduct this review, we followed the PRISMA guidelines and Cooper (2010) to report a comprehensive and objective systematic review. However, we adapted some aspects of our review to align with our research objectives which were focused exclusively on research methods and methodology. These modifications included adding a general matrix of all the current longitudinal studies of writing as part of our initial identification of studies; modifying the quality assessment to not privilege certain methods over other methods; and adding crucial high inference items to the coding sheet, which precluded us from calculating ICC for reliability in the coding of articles as we felt we would lose vital information related to our understanding of longitudinal writing research methods.

The study reported on here is the first part of a larger project of synthesizing what has been learned about writing development through international longitudinal studies of writing from preschool through adult life. We encourage others to conduct their systematic analysis according to the PRISMA guidelines. Cooper (2010) and Alexander (2020), however, recommended that researchers always consider what guidelines should be followed according to the goals they set for their reviews.

We hope many other researchers, especially those at early stages, will consider conducting their own systematic reviews. To those who take up the charge, we encourage you to collaborate; that is, create a research team, and consult often with senior scholars and other colleagues at all levels of your work. Additionally, we strongly recommend that researchers conducting systematic reviews take advantage of the outstanding tools that have been developed including, but not limited to Rayann, PRISMA, and Zotero. Finally, we encourage those conducting such reviews to "go where the action is;" that is, to investigate the most pressing and impactful issues related to writing as together we pursue achieving the impossible dream.

REFERENCES

Aldossary, S. K. (2021). The impact of collaborative writing on EFL learners' writing development: A longitudinal classroom-based study in Saudi Arabia. *Arab World English Journal, 12*(3), 174–185. https://doi.org/10.24093/awej/vol12no3.12.

Alexander, P. A. (2020). Methodological guidance paper: The art and science of quality systematic reviews. *Review of Educational Research, 90*(1), 6–23. https://doi.org/10.3102/0034654319854352.

Bazerman, C. (2018). Lifespan longitudinal studies of writing development: A heuristic for an impossible dream. In C. Bazerman, A. N. Applebee, V. W. Berninger, D. Brandt, S. Graham, J. V. Jeffery, P. K. Matsuda, S. Murphy, D. W. Rowe, M. Schleppegrell & K. C. Wilcox (Eds.), *The lifespan development of writing* (pp. 326–365). The WAC Clearinghouse; University Press of Colorado. https://wac.colostate.edu/books/ncte/lifespan-writing/.

Bobak, C. A., Barr, P. J. & O'Malley, A. J. (2018). Estimation of an inter-rater intraclass correlation coefficient that overcomes common assumption violations in the assessment of health measurement scales. *BMC Medical Research Methodology, 18*(1), 93. https://doi.org/10.1186/s12874-018-0550-6.

Cooper, H. M. (2010). *Research synthesis and meta-analysis: A step-by-step approach* (4th ed.). Sage.

Cooper, H., Hedges, L. V. & Valentine, J. C. (Eds.). (2009). *The handbook of research synthesis and meta-analysis*. Russell Sage Foundation. http://www.jstor.org/stable/10.7758/9781610441384.

Dippre, R. J. & Phillips, T. (2020a). Conclusion as prolegomena: From points of convergence to murmurations across sites, researchers, and methods. In R. J. Dippre & T. Phillips (Eds.), *Approaches to lifespan writing research: Generating an actionable coherence* (pp. 249–256). The WAC Clearinghouse; University Press of Colorado. https://doi.org/10.37514/PER-B.2020.1053.3.1.

Dippre, R. J. & Phillips, T. (2020b). Introduction. Generating murmurations for an actionable coherence. In R. J. Dippre & T. Phillips (Eds.), *Approaches to lifespan* writing research: Generating an actionable coherence (pp. 3–11). The WAC Clearinghouse; University Press of Colorado. https://doi.org/10.37514/PER-B.2020.1053.1.3.

Duan, S. & Shi, Z. (2021). A longitudinal study of formulaic sequence use in second language writing: Complex dynamic systems perspective. *Language Teaching Research*. https://doi.org/10.1177/13621688211002942.

Emig, J. (1971). *The composing processes of twelfth graders*. National Council of Teachers of English.

Faden, V. B., Day, N. L., Windle, M., Windle, R., Grube, J. W., Molina, B. S., Pelham, W. E., Jr, Gnagy, E. M., Wilson, T. K., Jackson, K. M. & Sher, K. J. (2004). Collecting longitudinal data through childhood, adolescence, and young adulthood: Methodological challenges. *Alcoholism, Clinical and Experimental Research, 28*(2), 330–340. https://doi.org/10.1097/01.alc.0000113411.33088.fe.

Foster, E. D. & Deardorff, A. (2017). Open Science Framework (OSF). *Journal of the Medical Library Association, 105*(2). https://doi.org/10.5195/JMLA.2017.88.

Gage, T. E. (1973). *The impact of the non-graded, multi-selective English curriculum on high school students* [Doctoral dissertation, University of California, Berkeley].

Gregory, A. T. & Denniss, A. R. (2018). An introduction to writing narrative and systematic reviews—Tasks, tips and traps for aspiring authors. *Heart, Lung and Circulation, 27*(7), 893–898. https://doi.org/10.1016/j.hlc.2018.03.027.

Guo, Y., Puranik, C., Kelcey, B., Sun, J., Dinnesen, M. S. & Breit-Smith, A. (2021). The role of home literacy practices in kindergarten children's early writing development: A one-year longitudinal study. *Early Education and Development, 32*(2), 209–227. https://doi.org/10.1080/10409289.2020.1746618.

Haswell, R. H. (1991). *Gaining ground in college writing: Tales of development and interpretation*. Southern Methodist University Press.

Hickel, J. (2020). The sustainable development index: Measuring the ecological efficiency of human development in the anthropocene. *Ecological Economics, 167*, 106331. https://doi.org/10.1016/j.ecolecon.2019.05.011.

Ivanič, R. (1998). *Writing and identity: The discoursal construction of identity in academic writing*. John Benjamins. https://doi.org/10.1075/swll.5.

Kokaliari, E. D., Brainerd, M. & Roy, A. (2012). A longitudinal study of assessing APA writing competence at a BSW program. *Journal of Teaching in Social Work, 32*(5), 566–577.

Loban, W. D. (1963). *The language of elementary school children*. National Council of Teachers of English.

Matusov, E., DePalma, R. & Drye, S. (2007). Whose development? Salvaging the concept of development within a sociocultural approach to education. *Educational Theory, 57*(4), 403–421.

Moffett, J. (1968). *Teaching the universe of discourse*. Houghton Mifflin.

Moffett, J. (1992). *Detecting growth in language*. Boynton/Cook.

Ouzzani, M., Hammady, H., Fedorowicz, Z. & Elmagarmid, A. (2016). Rayyan: A web and mobile app for systematic reviews. *Systematic Reviews, 5*(1), 210. https://doi.org/10.1186/s13643-016-0384-4.

Panic, N., Leoncini, E., de Belvis, G., Ricciardi, W. & Boccia, S. (2013). Evaluation of the endorsement of the preferred reporting items for systematic reviews and meta-analysis (PRISMA) statement on the quality of published systematic review and meta-analyses. *PLoS ONE, 8*(12), e83138. https://doi.org/10.1371/journal.pone.0083138.

Rentel, V. & King, M. (1983). A longitudinal study of coherence in children's written narrative. Research Foundation.

Rogers, P. (2009). The contributions of North American longitudinal studies of writing in higher education to our understanding of writing development. In C. Bazerman, R. Krut, K. Lunsford, S. McLeod, S. Null, P. Rogers & A. Stansell (Eds.), *Traditions of writing research* (pp. 337–389). Routledge.

Sagar, A. D. & Najam, A. (1998). The human development index: A critical review. *Ecological Economics, 25*(3), 249–264. https://doi.org/10.1016/S0921-8009(97)00168-7.

Shulruf, B., Morton, S., Goodyear-Smith, F., O'Loughlin, C. & Dixon, R. (2007). Designing multidisciplinary longitudinal studies of human development: Analyzing past research to inform methodology. *Evaluation & the Health Professions, 30*(3), 207–228. https://doi.org/10.1177/0163278707304030.

Tierney, R. J. & Sheehy, M. (2005). What longitudinal studies say about literacy development/What literacy development says about longitudinal studies. In J. Flood, D. Lapp, R. Squire & M. Jensen (Eds.), *Methods of research on teaching the English language arts* (pp. 79–124). Lawrence Erlbaum.

Zeanah, C. H., Boris, N. W. & Larrieu, J. A. (1997). Infant development and developmental risk: A review of the past 10 years. *Journal of the American Academy of Child & Adolescent Psychiatry, 36*(2), 165–178. https://doi.org/10.1097/00004583-199702000-00007.

CHAPTER 10.

IMPLICATIONS OF LONGITUDINAL WRITING RESEARCH METHODS FOR LIFESPAN PERSPECTIVES ON WRITING DEVELOPMENT: A SYSTEMATIC REVIEW

Jonathan M. Marine
George Mason University

Paul Rogers
University of California, Santa Barbara

Teresa Jacques
University of Porto

Like all research methods, longitudinal research methods are linked to epistemologies, axiologies, and ideologies which help shape and undergird lines of inquiry and the particulars of individual research studies. Longitudinal research methods are common across many disciplines including psychology, biology, economics, education, neurology, gerontology, and other subfields in the health sciences (Hedeker & Gibbons, 2006; Fitzmaurice et al., 2012). Longitudinal research serves two primary purposes, "to describe patterns of change and to establish the direction and magnitude of causal relationships" (Lewis-Beck et al., 2004). Typically, longitudinal studies use ongoing, recurrent measures to follow individuals over prolonged periods of time or across ages frequently "without any external influences being applied" (Caruana et al., 2015). While cross-sectional methods attempt to analyze several variables at a given point in time in order to examine differences *between* cases, longitudinal studies instead foreground the influence of time on the variables being measured in order to examine changes *within* cases (Lewis-Beck et al., 2004). Given the importance of understanding the relationships among and between the many variables and factors associated with acquiring writing abilities and how those abilities change over time, longitudinal methods are especially useful in studying writing development.

Longitudinal writing research methods can be broadly categorized as either qualitative, quantitative or mixed methods in nature (Hartley & Chesworth, 2000). Writing research benefits from work in all of these methodological categories because, broadly speaking, qualitative research methods allow researchers to explore new phenomena in order to generate hypotheses while quantitative research allows researchers to investigate causality and correlation in order to test hypotheses (Sullivan & Sergeant, 2011). Quantitative studies use positivist paradigms as their basis while investigating a single or limited set of related variables while qualitative research uses a more phenomenological paradigm (Firestone, 1987) and attends to the multiple variables associated with context. This distinction between quantitative and qualitative research methods plays an important role in our review, and in the section below we further elaborate on the importance of these distinctions.

QUALITATIVE LONGITUDINAL WRITING RESEARCH

Qualitative longitudinal writing research includes many different types of methods of research and research designs. From single-subject interview-based studies that follow a student throughout their entire school career (e.g., Svensson, 2018), to text-based studies that attempt to gauge how college students' literate lives beyond the academy shape their writing in the classroom (e.g., Roozen, 2008), to grounded theory-based accounts of how extracurricular writing helps to support students' development of voice through writing (e.g., Chen, 2017), qualitative studies of longitudinal writing all share the common concern of trying to understand how writers develop over time by attending closely to a wide range of complex contexts and situations.

QUANTITATIVE LONGITUDINAL WRITING RESEARCH

Typically experimental or correlational in nature, quantitative methods usually aim to combine a wide array of measures (textual, spoken, or otherwise) into a few key points of data collection in order to try and gauge how one variable (e.g., particular language abilities or skills) might track or correlate with another (e.g., literacy and vocabulary, spelling and reading comprehension, phonemic reading and written expression, etc.). From quasi-experimental studies that investigate what elements of neuropsychological development contribute to writing development in first graders (Hooper et al., 2010), to studies which seek to trace correlations between reading and writing motivation across multiple cohorts of primary school students (Hamilton et al., 2013), to studies which attempt to describe the strategies used in undergraduate writing (Torrance et al., 2000), to studies which seek to account for extracurricular factors that might influence children's writing development from ages 4 to 7 (Dunsmuir & Blatchford, 2004), quantitative studies of longitudinal writing all share the common goal of trying to capture in what ways and to what degree the varying factors which influence writing development relate to, predict, and correlate with one another.

MIXED METHODS LONGITUDINAL WRITING RESEARCH

An important alternative research design is mixed methods research, which includes both quantitative and qualitative research used in a single study (Doyle et al., 2009). Mixed methods research can deepen the information retrieved from a study, ultimately leading to more informed findings; however, mixed methods can be time-consuming (Almalki, 2016; Greene et al., 1989). From studies which attempt to investigate changes in the nature and amount of preschoolers' parental writing support (Skibbe et al., 2013), to single-subject studies which attempt to examine the development of figurative competence in narrative writing from elementary school through high school and beyond (Svensson, 2018), longitudinal mixed methods studies of writing draw on both qualitative and quantitative methods in combination with one another in order to quantify the phenomena under investigation while also accounting for the contexts in which the phenomena occurs.

Putting the systematic review methodology into action, in the section below, we present the results of our longitudinal review in order to illuminate the methodological characteristics and trends of longitudinal writing research during the past 21 years. Although at this current juncture, these studies address shorter time sequences than the lifespan model ultimately demands, these smaller stories are important for continuing the pursuit of what Bazerman (2018) called, "the impossible dream" of an empirically grounded lifespan view of writing development.

RESULTS

In this section, we present the results of our systematic review of L1, international, longitudinal, studies of writing since the year 2000 across the following categories:

- Longitudinal Writing Research Design
- Educational and Study Settings

- Longitudinal and Participant Characteristics
- Methods of Data Collection and Analysis
- Publication of Longitudinal Writing Research
- Funding of Longitudinal Writing Research

LONGITUDINAL WRITING RESEARCH DESIGN

Research Questions. Research questions are at the center of research design, and the longitudinal studies of writing in our review provide a rich landscape of inquiry to consider in the light of lifespan approaches to writing. At the most general level, the research designs employed in the studies we reviewed used three primary methods to frame their inquiries: research questions, hypothesis driven studies, and what we refer to as purpose driven or goal-oriented studies.

Studies framed with research questions use typical interrogative words and phrases such as *how*, *what*, and *to what extent* to guide their studies. Researchers using primarily hypothesis driven approaches usually present their research with phrases like "we hypothesized that. . . ." Purpose driven or goal-oriented studies framed their work around categories of action like investigating, identifying, verifying, and describing.

Of the 54 studies we reviewed, 27 studies were framed primarily with research questions, 13 were framed primarily with hypotheses, and 15 studies used a goal orientation. This is not to say there was no overlap between these categories. Indeed, of the 27 studies primarily organized around research questions, six also included goal statements, and three included hypotheses, though these appeared in a subordinate fashion to the research questions. Likewise, of the 13 hypothesis driven studies, nine also included some kind of purpose statement.

In regards to studies framed around research questions, 12 studies presented a single research question, while 15 used multiple questions (ranging from 2 questions to 7 questions) with an average of almost 4 questions per study for studies with multiple questions. The total number of questions from all of the studies we marked as driven by research questions was 67. The most common question stems were *what* (21), *how* (16), and variations of to which extent and *to what degree* (7). Other interrogative question stems included: *are*, *does*, *will*, *which*, *do*, and *whether*. Of the 10 hypothesis driven studies, 9 pursued multiple hypotheses. Purpose driven or goal-oriented studies used a variety of keywords, the most common of which were *explore*, *examine*, and *investigate* with the objects of these goals most frequently relating to inquiries related to development, specific theoretical claims and models, or particular units of analysis, especially longitudinal relationships, between, for example, reading and writing.

In considering the degree to which longitudinal writing researchers replicate other studies using similar or the same questions, and the degree to which writing researchers conduct studies that can be aggregated with other studies to help build out areas of inquiry and knowledge (Haswell, 2005), the results are mixed. In the main, we found almost no precise replication studies in our corpus. That is, the detailed research design elements differ considerably from study to study whether quantitative or qualitative. Only one qualitative study (Myhill & Jones, 2007) provided enough detail to qualify as a potentially replicable study. However, there are research groups who continue to build out lines of inquiry based on the results of their previous studies (e.g., Bigozzi & Vettori, 2016).

Types of Research Questions. In terms of research questions, we identified three main types. Most common are questions that investigate how writing changes over time in relationship to specific elements, factors, or variables such as increases in content knowledge, the amount and quality of parental support, or the various impacts of particular skills (skills being a very common attribute across the studies). The second most common type of question focused on specific measures and the degree to which those measures are effective predictors of change in writing, usually with a very specific unit of analysis that was related to the measures. The third type of questions focus on descriptive research aims.

Framing of Hypothesis Driven Studies. Similarly, hypothesis driven longitudinal writing research includes three major categories of hypotheses. First are predictor-driven studies that seek to present clear evidence for the predictive value of particular elements and skills associated with writing. Next are hypothesis driven studies that attempt to define more clearly the relationships between and among factors and elements such as correlation studies. A number of the hypothesis driven studies focus narrowly on specific elements of a particular model and the degree to which that model is efficacious in predicting future writing growth. Finally, the purpose-driven studies in our review appear to be approaching their areas of inquiry with an eye towards building out further the larger programs of research and lines of inquiry.

Study Settings (Country, Grade Level, and Public or Private Schools). The longitudinal studies of writing in our corpus were conducted in 13 different countries: United States (23), Italy (5), the UK (3), Portugal (3), China (3), Israel (3), Canada (2), Netherlands (2), Hong Kong (2), Brazil (2), Denmark (2), South Korea (2), Sweden (1), France (1), Australia (1), Russia (1) and Argentina (1). In addition to coding for the geographical location of the studies, we also identified the language under investigation (L1) within each article. Our final data corpus included 14 different languages: Arabic, Cantonese, Chinese, Danish, Dutch, English, French, Hebrew, Italian, Korean, Portuguese, Russian,

Spanish, and Swedish. The three most common languages were English (28), Italian (5), and Portuguese (5). Studies took place across a wide range of grade levels. The most prevalent educational settings for studies of longitudinal writing in our corpus were elementary school (16), university/undergraduate (9), followed by kindergarten (4) and preschool (4), secondary education/high school (3), home (3), middle school (1), university/postgraduate (1), and out of school (1). Eleven studies included settings that crossed typical school designations. These included kindergarten + elementary (3), kindergarten + 1st grade (2), kindergarten + 2nd grade (1), kindergarten + 4th grade (1), kindergarten + 1st grade + 2nd grade (1), kindergarten through 12th grade (1), 1st grade through 6th grade (1), and undergraduate through graduate (1). While the majority of studies did not specify whether the schools were public or private (28/56), of those which did specify, the majority (22) were set in public schools, with only four studies taking place in a private school setting.

Longitudinal and Participant Characteristics. As a part of our coding schema, we looked at the longitudinal characteristics of each study by coding for the number of points of measure and the duration of each study in our corpus. The studies in our corpus of longitudinal writing research averaged 2.9 points of measure per study. Points of measure ranged from 2 (our minimum for inclusion) to 6 points across the 40 articles which specified this information. The remaining studies either had several points of measure (10) but didn't specify how many or were simply unclear (5).

In terms of study duration, the studies in our corpus averaged 3.8 years across which data was collected, ranging from 12 weeks (a quantitative study; Rosário et al., 2017) to 30 years (an ethnographic type of study; Smith & Prior, 2020). Although no study was precisely the mean of 3.8 years in length, one representative study (Yeung et al., 2013a) lasted for 4 years and had 3 points of measure. This funded study was conducted in China, with native Cantonese speakers from 1st to 4th grade, and aimed to examine the relationships between cognitive-linguistic skills that are important to Chinese children's writing development, based on the model of the developmental constraints on writing acquisition (Berninger et al., 1991).

We also coded for the total number of participants, reported age range, and gender distribution. The 54 studies in our corpus involved 6714 total participants at an average of 126.68 participants per study, ranging from 1 to 481 total participants. Coding for age ranges of participants proved problematic as many of the studies reported only grade levels and not age levels. From the studies which did report age averages and ranges, the average reported age was 5.9 years old, ranging from 3.61 (a number of studies looked at the transition from preschool to kindergarten e.g., Skibbe et al., 2013) to 30.95 years old (a number of studies looked at the transition from university to the workplace or graduate school e.g., Chen, 2017).

More clear was the gender distribution of participants in these studies, with only 1.9 percent of articles not clearly reporting the gender distribution of their participants. 82 percent of the studies in our corpus had both male and female participants, with 7.7 percent reporting all male participants and 7.7 percent reporting all female participants. No studies in this corpus reported on gender categories besides male and female. In studies where gender distributions were reported, an average of 58.8 percent of participants were female.

Method of Data Collection and Analysis in Longitudinal Writing Research. One of the most critical elements of any research study involves the systematic collection of data. In this review we coded for the data collection techniques of each study by creating both high-inference and low-inference categories for methods of data collection. While our preference was to use the actual language from the published studies in our analysis (i.e., the low-inference category), we used the high inference categories to generalize more broadly regarding methods of data collection. The high inference categories were: ethnography, observation, interviews, document and artifact collection, descriptive research, correlational research, experimental, quasi-experimental, other, and not specified. (More detailed information on our coding methods can be found in chapter 9.)

The most prevalent methods of longitudinal research in our corpus were quasi-experimental which was employed in almost half of the studies in our corpus (49 percent), followed by experimental research (11 percent), ethnography (9 percent), document and artifact collection (9 percent), other (7 percent), correlational research (6 percent), descriptive research (5 percent) and finally, interviews (4 percent). Within quantitative studies 26 were quasi-experimental (e.g., Aram & Levin, 2004; Kuzeva et al., 2015; Niedo et al., 2014), 6 experimental (e.g., Cordeiro et al., 2020; Drijbooms et al., 2017), and 2 correlational (e.g., Pinto et al., 2009). Three studies which did not fit our initial coding schema were coded as other (10.6 percent). These studies included qualitative studies where the method of data collection was either not stated, unclear, or included more than one type of method (e.g., causal and exploratory quantitative studies or mixed-methods).

Data Collection in Quantitative Studies. In the quantitative studies in our corpus, the most common measures used to research writing were spelling (see Abbott et al., 2010; Beers & Nagy, 2011; Cardoso-Martins et al., 2006; Cordeiro et al., 2020; Kim & Park, 2019; Kim et al., 2015; Limpo & Alves, 2013; Pinto et al., 2015; Treiman et al., 2013; Yeung et al., 2020) and essay and story writing (see Abbott et al., 2010; Bigozzi & Vettori, 2016; Coker, 2006;

Cordeiro et al., 2020; Drijbooms et al., 2017; Limpo & Alves, 2013; Mäki et al., 2001; Oppenheimer et al., 2017; Pinto et al., 2015; Rosário et al., 2017; Tong & McBride, 2016; Woodward-Kron, 2009; Yeung et al., 2013b; Yeung et al., 2020). Spelling was commonly measured through direct dictation tasks (e.g., Yan et al., 2012; Yeung et al., 2013a), the percentage of words spelled correctly in a story (Limpo & Alves, 2013), and by accurately copying characters (Fischer & Koch, 2016). Tasks used to assess writing include narrative writing ("Tell a story about a child who lost his or her pet"; Limpo & Alves, 2013), opinion essays ("Do you think teachers should give students homework every day?"; Limpo & Alves, 2013), persuasive opinion essays (Oppenheimer et al., 2017), descriptive writing ("Describe a happy birthday scene"; Yeung et al., 2013b), expository writing, and scientific writing (Oppenheimer et al., 2017).

Handwriting was another common measure used to investigate writing by the quantitative studies in our corpus (see Cordeiro et al., 2020; Kim & Park, 2019; Limpo & Alves, 2013; Yan et al., 2012; Yeung et al., 2013a) Handwriting was used as a measure in studying fluency (Kim & Park, 2019; Limpo & Alves, 2013; Yan et al., 2012), stroke order tasks (in Chinese; Yeung et al., 2013a) and letter writing automaticity (Kim et al., 2015). Orthographic skills (e.g., hyphenation, capitalization, punctuation, etc.) were also measured in various studies (Bigozzi & Vettori, 2016; Pinto et al., 2012; Pinto et al., 2015; Yeung et al., 2013a; Yeung et al., 2013b). Questionnaires and writing specific scales were also used, such as the motivational orientation writing scale, although less frequently than the measures above (Ahmed et al., 2014; Dunsmuir & Blatchford, 2004; Hamilton et al., 2013; Hooper et al., 2011; Torrance et al., 2000).

A few measures were used in only one or two studies: transcription skills, word length, writing a series of noun-adjective pairs, writing of sentences, writing of short words, early writing by hand and by keyboard (Beers & Nagy, 2011) and early writing concepts (Hooper et al., 2010), emergent literacy abilities, standardized assessments, and syntactic skills (Yeung et al., 2013b; Yeung et al., 2020).

We also investigated the types and number of scales and measures used to collect data by studies in our corpus. Scales or test batteries are one or more tests that aim to assess a particular factor of a person's functioning (Frey, 2018). Our findings show that the majority of studies in our corpus (30/56) relied upon some type of pre-designed scale or measure, and often more than one at a time. The 30 studies in our corpus which used scales and measures used 51 different scales a total of 109 times for an average of 3.6 scales per study which used them. The most frequently used scales (and the number of studies which used the scales in parenthesis) were the WIAT (7), the WJ (5), Raven's Colored Progressive Matrices (6), the WISC-IV (3), the Peabody Picture Vocabulary Test III (2), CELF3 (2), and the TOWRE PDE (2). (See Appendix A for the entire list of scales). These top 7 scales were used 34 different times across the 30 studies in our corpus which used scales and measures. There were 42 other scales used in the studies in our corpus of longitudinal writing research.

Our final corpus of studies included 2 mixed method studies (Skibbe et al., 2013; Svensson, 2018). These studies measured lexicalized figurativeness and genuine figurativeness, with number of units (clauses) and percentage of these measures in the narrative texts (Svensson, 2018), and semistructured writing tasks for both parents and children (Skibbe et al., 2013; Svensson, 2018).

Data Collection in Qualitative Studies. In the qualitative studies in our corpus, the most used method of data collection was ethnography (Chapman, 2002; Compton-Lilly, 2014; Elf, 2016; Roozen, 2008; Smith & Prior, 2020), followed by document and artifact collection (Beaufort, 2004; Chen, 2018; Lammers & Marsh, 2018; Woodward-Kron, 2009), descriptive research (Johnson & Krase, 2012; Sommers & Saltz, 2004; Turnbull et al., 2011), interviews (Driscoll & Powell, 2016; Lunsford et al., 2013), correlational research (Haswell, 2000), and a category we referred to as other (Myhill & Jones, 2007).

Many of these qualitative studies were unclear about the specific number of points of measure, but nonetheless collected data many times across the timeframe of their study (7/14), followed by three points of measure (3/14), five points of measure (1/14), four points of measure (1/14), two points of measure (1/14), and N/A (1/14). These qualitative studies ranged from 6 months to 30 years in duration, averaging 6.53 years of study. The qualitative studies in our corpus rarely reported the ages of participants (12/14), and when they did, they simply gave age ranges (2/14), instead choosing to defer to grade level. Most qualitative studies took place in the secondary grades (8/14), followed by undergraduate (2/14), primary (2/14), middle (1/14), and preschool/kindergarten (1/14). Ranging from 1 participant to 481, the qualitative studies in our corpus averaged 56.28 participants per study. Four of the qualitative studies in our corpus focused on students as the object of study, three focused on texts, and the remaining seven (50 percent) used both texts and students.

Across all qualitative studies, most focused on school-based assigned writing (7/14), or interviews (10/14). For studies which only focused on texts (3/14), two used assigned writing (Chen, 2018; Lammers & March, 2018) and one used extracurricular writing (Turnbull et al., 2011). For studies which only focused on students (Beaufort, 2004; Driscoll & Powell, 2016; Lunsford et al., 2013; Myhill & Jones, 2007), all used interviews and one used observations and interviews (Myhill & Jones, 2007). For studies which focused on both students and texts (7/14), all but one were a combination of assigned texts and interviews, with two of those studies also allowing for extracurricular writing (Roozen, 2008; Sommers & Saltz, 2004).

Data Analysis. We coded data analysis methods for each study in our corpus (the complete coding guide can be viewed online at https://osf.io/tjyu2/?view_only=72272c4f124b4b00bbd41667798edc76). Across all of the studies, predictive, causal, and inferential data analysis methods (i.e., quantitative methods of analysis) remain the most prominent data analysis methods in longitudinal writing research over the past twenty-one years. Among these methods, predictive analysis methods such as correlations (e.g., Hooper et al., 2010) and regressions (e.g., Pinto et al., 2015) were used in 32.1 percent of the articles in our corpus. Qualitative analysis methods were used in 14.3 percent and causal in 8.9 percent of the articles in our corpus. Inferential analysis methods such as ANOVA and t-tests were used in 5.4 percent of studies, the same as Grounded Theory (5.4 percent), and Exploratory (5.4 percent). Studies which used data analysis techniques that did not fit our coding schema were coded as Other (19.6 percent) and mostly involved more than one type of analysis. For quantitative studies specifically, 18 used predictive data analysis, ten used more than one type of analysis, four used causal analysis, three inferential, one descriptive and one exploratory.

Overall, research aims/questions and hypotheses of the quantitative studies in our corpus matched their data analysis methods. For example, studies that aimed to *predict* an outcome, to observe *effects,* or to investigate *relationships* (Sykes, 1993) tended to choose predictive data analysis options, such as regression (see Cordeiro et al., 2020) and CFA and SEM (see Kim & Park, 2019), while studies that used *how* questions, for example "to analyze *how* children are prepared for learning to write and *how* this skill is developed" (see Kuzeva et al., 2015) or *differences* between groups (see Silva et al., 2010), chose data collection methods that lead to the use of inferential data analysis methods such as ANOVA and t-tests (see Beers & Nagy, 2011; Oppenheimer et al., 2017

On the other hand, while qualitative studies asked similar questions to quantitative studies, such as *how* questions and to investigate relationships between writing and other aspects, it is, however, clear that these questions were broader and more intent upon generating new knowledge on a particular topic rather than identifying predictors. For example, the qualitative studies in our corpus which used ethnography used *what* and *how* questions (Chapman, 2002; Compton-Lilly, 2014; Elf, 2016; Roozen, 2008; Smith & Prior, 2020).

Quantitative Data Analysis. Quantitative studies used the following methods of data analysis, with regression being the most used method: ANOVA (Beers & Nagy, 2011; Bigozzi & Vettori, 2016; Levin et al., 2001) and t-tests (Frost, 2001; Oppenheimer et al., 2017) or non-parametric alternatives; correlation (Aram et al., 2013; Dunsmuir & Blatchford, 2004; Frost, 2001; Hooper et al., 2010; Levin et al., 2001; Niedo et al., 2014; Tong & Mcbride, 2016; Torrance et al., 2000), regression, such as bivariate (Bigozzi & Vettori, 2016), multiple regression (Pinto et al., 2015), hierarchical regression (Yan et al., 2012) and logistic and stepwise regression (Pinto et al., 2012) and likelihood-based mixed-effects regression (Rosário et al., 2017); descriptive analysis (Coker, 2006); cluster analysis (Torrance et al., 2000), confirmatory factor analyses (CFA; Kim & Park, 2019), structural equation modeling (SEM; Kim & Park, 2019), content analysis (Yan et al., 2012), exploratory factor analysis (EFA; Pinto et al., 2009), hierarchical linear modeling analysis (Coker, 2006); latent change score modeling (Ahmed et al., 2014); mean proportions (Cardoso-Martins et al., 2006), path analyses (Yeung et al., 2013) and finally relative percentage (Fischer & Koch, 2016).

Qualitative Data Analysis. Qualitative studies of longitudinal writing in our corpus mostly deferred to asking single or multiple questions to frame their inquiry (9/14), with four studies stating a research purpose, and one study stating a research hypothesis; most of the question-driven studies posed a single question (7/9). Questions ranged from "What role do writing performances (particularly outside the classroom) play in early college students' development as writers?" (Sommers & Saltz, 2004), to "How do changes in textual features over time (taken from writing in all classes, not just English/LA) demonstrate emergent genres (and thereby increasingly complex writing)?" (Chapman, 2002). Most of the studies of longitudinal writing which utilized qualitative methods in our corpus took place in the United States (10/14), with two in Canada, one in the UK, and one in Denmark. In all of these studies English was the first language. Only two qualitative studies in our corpus reported the type of community the schools were based in, and both were urban.

The frequency of data analysis methods used in qualitative longitudinal writing research were Grounded Theory (8/14), followed by Qualitative Content (4/14), Discourse Analysis (1/14), Exploratory studies (1/14), and Other (1/14). Five of the studies used some form of coding to perform their analysis (Beaufort, 2002; Myhill & Jones, 2007; Turnbull et al., 2011; Compton-Lilly, 2014; Driscoll & Powell, 2016). Across all studies, most focused on assigned writing (7/14), or interviews (10/14). For studies which only focused on texts (3/14), two used assigned writing and one used extracurricular writing. For studies which only focused on students (4/14), all used interviews and one used observations and interviews. For studies which focused on both students and texts (7/14), all but one were a combination of assigned texts and interviews, with two of those studies also allowing for extracurricular writing (Sommers & Saltz, 2004; Roozen, 2008), and one study strictly based on interviews (Compton-Lilly, 2014). The mixed method studies in our corpus used categorization of narrative texts and its method of analysis of the data (Svensson, 2018) and t-tests, regression, and observation (Skibble et al., 2013).

Publication of Longitudinal Studies of Writing

As a part of our coding schema, we looked at the general characteristics of the publication of each study by coding the authors, journals, and years of publication for each study in order to understand the broader ecosystem of longitudinal studies of writing, which includes the venues in which these studies become public. Our findings show that longitudinal research is on the rise; from 2000–2009 there were 17 articles on longitudinal writing, but from 2010–2020 there were 39 articles on longitudinal writing, meaning that there were 1.7 articles per year for the first decade of this century, but 3.9 articles per year in the most recent decade.

In examining which publication venues had the most longitudinal studies of writing, *Reading and Writing: An Interdisciplinary Journal* published the most with 12 total articles. Five other journals published more than one longitudinal study of writing: The *Journal of Educational Psychology* (5), *Learning and Individual Differences* (3), *European Journal of Psychology of Education* (3), and *Written Communication* (3). The *Journal of Child Language* and *British Journal of Educational Psychology* each had 2; no other journal in our corpus published more than one study.

In terms of authorship, longitudinal writing research proved to be very collaborative, with 49/56 articles written by more than one author with an overall average of 2.8 authors per article. Notably, five of the seven single-authored articles were single-subject case studies. Ten authors had more than one article in our corpus (Giulia Vettori, Claudio Vezzani, Giuliana Pinto, Lucia Bigozzi, Stephen R. Hooper, Teresa Limpo, Young-Suk Grace Kim, Virginia Berninger, Robert D. Abbott, and Dorit Aram), with one of those authors, Lucia Bigozzi, publishing five articles.

Funding of Longitudinal Studies of Writing

Finally, we coded studies for whether they reported funding or not, and if so, the agency which funded the study. We cross-referenced this information to the other coding categories in our study (type of study-qualitative/quantitative or mixed methods; number of participants; points of measure; study duration; study setting) in order to better describe the state of funding in longitudinal writing research. Our results show that 37.5 percent of studies in our corpus were funded, with 35.7 percent explicitly denoting that they received no funding and 26.8 percent of studies not reporting one way or the other. Reported sources of funding appear to be associated most frequently with quantitative studies. Further, most of the funding appeared to be linked to a single project and came from governmental agencies. And, while we identified a number of private funding agencies which granted funding for longitudinal studies, only the Spencer Foundation funded more than one study in our corpus.

Funded studies averaged more participants and longer periods of study, but not more points of measure. Funded studies averaged 163.05 participants per study, while non-funded studies averaged 107.593 participants per study. Among the single-subject studies only one was funded (Compton-Lilly, 2014). Funded studies averaged 3.33 years while unfunded and unclear studies averaged 3.23 years per study. Both funded and unfunded studies took place mostly in public school settings, and there was only one funded study of longitudinal writing in a private school setting.

DISCUSSION

Our study shows that during the past twenty-one years of L1 longitudinal writing research, a wide variety of both qualitative and quantitative studies have been carried out. In addition to the wide range of research methods (in both data collection and analysis) being employed in longitudinal writing research, the number of L1 longitudinal studies of writing appears to be increasing, as represented in our systematic review: from 2000–2009 we identified 17 longitudinal writing research studies; while from 2010–2020 there were 39 studies (1.7 articles per year for the first decade of this century; 3.9 articles per year in the most recent decade). Our review, of course, is not exhaustive, as our inclusion criteria did not include books or book chapters, which we did not consider as peer reviewed, even though these studies, such as Gere (2019) and Krogh and Jakobsen (2019) make valuable contributions to longitudinal writing research and our understanding of writing development. Nonetheless, the increase in L1 studies of longitudinal writing suggests that now is an opportue time to continue developing capacity to carry out longitudinal writing research at scale.

Within the broader range of studies, from large n quantitative to single subject qualitative case studies, we also see a number of studies with similar research methodologies and methods forming into common lines of inquiry; for example, studies that use observations and interviews to gauge parental influence on early literacy development, studies that use literacy measures to predict student performance in and across the early grades, studies that use textual analysis of curricular writing to investigate how collegiate students acclimate to the demands of higher education, etc. Although currently these studies do not lend themselves towards aggregation or replication, these clusters of work do point towards the advancement of longitudinal writing research methods and the refinement of research designs.

From another viewpoint however, the overall number of L1 longitudinal studies of writing remains relatively small, and the field itself is still at an early stage in which replication studies and even aggregation (let alone meta-analyses), remain out of reach. In this regard, we feel strongly that while we need more depth within these clusters of work, (i.e., we need more longitudinal studies of writing that build upon previous work), we also need to encourage an even wider range of research methods. As Bazerman noted, "there is still too much to discover about our multidimensional subject to limit what we are looking for and the way we might be looking" (Bazerman, personal communication, May 1st, 2020).

One important step to take in regard to furthering longitudinal studies of writing is to draw out with greater intentionality the nature of each of these research lines so that future researchers can more easily identify scales and measures, units of analysis, objects of study, and tools for data collection and analysis. Further, it would be beneficial to other researchers to provide more methodological transparency regarding the logistics, barriers, false steps, and the nature of the collaborative activities involved in order to continue to build our collective research capacity and to carry out more sophisticated longitudinal studies of writing that can support the empirical grounding of lifespan approaches to writing.

The wide range of L1 longitudinal writing research reflects the strong interdisciplinary nature of the research communities which study writing. Thus, in addition to a greater awareness of the range of research methods being used, we also see an opportunity in this interdisciplinarity for more mixed methods studies, i.e., the integration of quantitative and qualitative studies of writing. In our view, substantive advances in lifespan perspectives of writing development and longitudinal writing research will depend on these kinds of cross-disciplinary, multidisciplinary, and ultimately transdisciplinary studies of writing being carried out in international contexts around the world.

While longitudinal studies of writing offer a great deal to the work on lifespan writing development, lifespan approaches to writing development also have strong potential to move longitudinal writing research forward across several important dimensions. First of all, given the complexity of writing and the wide breadth of research methods being employed, lifespan perspectives can serve to bring together these disparate lines of inquiry into more coherent and productive models that take into account a variety of writing related influences and outcomes across longer time sequences and especially across major transition points (e.g., preschool to school, elementary to secondary, high school to college, and college to the workplace). While more will still need to be done to provide a full lifespan perspective, this weaving together of insights from across studies can move the entire field forward and away from the myopia of repeatedly focusing on particular areas (such as first year composition in the US) to see writing development across the fuller lifespan and to consider the problems and questions associated with teaching, learning, curriculum, assessment, professional development, etc. in ways that take into account a broader set of socio-cultural experiences and cognitive processes.

Challenges

We encountered three main difficulties while conducting our review. The first challenge was identifying studies in which writing was the central object of inquiry. Determining if writing was the focus of a study proved especially difficult in longitudinal studies in the early grades because the components of literacy are so tightly woven together and there are so many studies of literacy that include elements and sub elements of both reading and writing. Additionally, there exists a wide variety of research studies that use writing as a data source or comparison point among other literacy measures rather than being a study of writing alone (Abbott et al., 2010, p.281).

The second challenge we faced was addressing the potential for conflation in measuring writing development with outcomes of specific writing curricula. No writing curriculum can be created without taking development into account as writing often develops in accordance with curriculum. However, following Bazerman (2018), we found that distinguishing between what counts as writing development and specific curricular outcomes in research is critical because the knowledge, skills, dispositions, and abilities associated with writing extend beyond any particular intervention to include the fullness of a person's literate life (see, for example, Dyson, 2003). This meant looking very carefully at each study's outcomes and the types of curricular interventions that were used (if any) to ensure that the researchers were looking beyond an immediate learning gain to broader issues of writing development over time.

The final challenge we worked through, (which is related to the issue of conflation above) was precisely defining the qualities of longitudinal writing research, and more specifically defining how long a study needed to be to count as longitudinal. We built our screening guide using two points of measurement as our baseline definition of longitudinal. However, we kept in mind the importance of the relationship between development and time, recognizing that development can happen in short periods of time during periods of transition (Bazerman, 2018). However, because the term "periods of transition" is subjective in many cases, we also had long discussions on what can be considered as a longitudinal study in cases of studies lasting for shorter periods of time.

The values which shaped the selection of studies for our corpus, though explicitly and transparently reported in this review, led to a somewhat strict definition of what counted as longitudinal writing research that was contingent on our own specific goals for this inquiry. Much discussion remains to be had by the field regarding the wide ranging and varied conceptions of what constitutes or might constitute longitudinal writing research. There exists a vast spectrum of work which is, or could be considered to be, longitudinal writing research well beyond what is represented in our corpus. Where to draw the line as to what counts has serious implications for reviews like the one reported on here and the generalizations and principles that can be drawn from systematic research reviews. Future research should make clear the specific definition/s of "longitudinal writing" on which the research is predicated.

Throughout our screening and coding processes, a vast majority of exclusions were made on the basis of these distinctions (between curricular outcomes and writing development and writing as the central focus). Further, our review focused explicitly on L1 studies in a K-University context. As a great deal of work on longitudinal writing research takes place outside of school contexts, and as an even larger contingent of this work takes place in L2 contexts, this study reports only a partial view of the work taking place in the broader field of longitudinal research on writing. Future reviews should seek to expand reviews of longitudinal writing research to increasingly broader contexts, and in doing so allow for more fulsome, sophisticated, and nuanced perspectives on longitudinal research of writing and its place in and implications for our understanding of lifespan development.

Improving Longitudinal Writing Research

Our review demonstrates that researchers have an array of research methods and designs to choose from when designing a longitudinal study of writing. However, the wide range of methodological options available to researchers in the field does not necessarily translate into those options of research being equally available to everyone. Disciplinary training and epistemology (especially along the qualitative and quantitative divide) dictate many research design decisions from the beginning of a study, as issues of analytic method and measure often shape the direction which a longitudinal study of writing will take. Thus, one's disciplinary training, though a strength, can also be a limiting factor in addressing nuanced research problems and questions. These considerations of epistemology and disciplinarity and their accompanying methodological choices provide another warrant for encouraging mixed-methods research and cross-disciplinary collaboration in longitudinal writing research. At the field level it will be difficult to build out a robust model of lifespan writing development without a great deal of cross disciplinary collaboration and the richer repertoire of methodological capacities which such collaboration can bring.

For example, our review shows that lines of inquiry can be framed in a variety of ways, (beyond a single research question or even without a research question altogether). An awareness of this wider range of methodological choices at all levels of research is important for making the best possible research design decisions, especially in ways that establish a goodness of fit between problems under investigation, theoretical frameworks, the existing literature, data sources and collection methods, and methods of analysis, and which can best address relevant gaps in the knowledge base.

In order for future researchers to more fully take into account previous work on longitudinal development in writing, future studies will need to advance the clarity and comprehensiveness of their data reporting. Currently, our results show a lack of reporting in some key areas that limit the ability of writing researchers to build on each other's work. For example, every study in our corpus limited gender reporting to male and female. In a world that increasingly values inclusivity and gender fluidity, limiting gender reporting to strictly male and female runs the risk of washing out key differences in participant populations which might further inform longitudinal writing research across the lifespan in important ways.

Reporting issues present an even greater problem when it comes to age ranges, which has serious implications for those interested in constructing lifespan perspectives on writing development. Specifically, many of the studies in our corpus did not report ages or age ranges, often deferring to grade level instead (or not reporting on age or grade at all). Further compounding these reporting issues is the incompatibility of grade levels across contexts of international schooling. Not identifying ages is problematic because longitudinal writing research is time-based; thus, the reporting of participant age ranges is critical for both the tracing of changes across time and the generalizability (and replicability) of results. We strongly encourage all longitudinal writing researchers to seek to identify and report both grade levels and age ranges in their studies.

Our focus in this review was on L1 longitudinal studies of writing in the school years. In relationship to lifespan perspectives, this leaves out important areas. Our larger study, however, not reported on here, includes L2 studies, and studies that extend before and beyond school, as a lifespan view of writing demands widening our horizons beyond the schooling years. However, we acknowledge that the development of writing ability in school age children certainly deserves the attention it has received. In this review, for example, the oldest participant in any of our studies was 30 years old, which does not yet reflect the full potential of lifespan development research. In order to fully build out the lifespan view, researchers will need to account for writing development well beyond the schooling years. In doing so, longitudinal writing research will contribute to a more sophisticated and nuanced understanding of lifespan writing development and cultivate a more accurate knowledge base from which to think about the types of interventions and pedagogies that can advance learning and writing at different ages and stages throughout the lifespan.

Lifespan perspectives on writing development would also benefit greatly from a longitudinal writing research base which produced aggregate results drawn from replicable studies. Due to the great variation in human conditions, interactions, settings, personalities, and other complex contributing variables, it is especially important for longitudinal writing researchers to attend to concretizing methodologies with enough centrifugal force to compare results drawn from a wide range of texts which all aim to convey "a unique message between a unique writer to a particular unique audience" (Bazerman, personal communication, May 1st, 2020). It is through the replication of methods in different settings that comparative results can be found that will be able to illustrate the variations and changes among phenomena that will illuminate differences among participants' development. However, given the relatively young state of lifespan perspectives on writing and longitudinal writing research, at this time, more attention should probably be given to expanding writing research programs and lines rather than narrowing our field of view.

Looking forward, we must continue to generate hypotheses concerning the many interconnected variables and factors which contribute to and shape writing development so that "they can be tested for correlations, their relative importance in contributing to development, as well as the varying degrees in which individual elements contribute to the varying dimensions of writing development" (Rogers, 2009). Finally, we must engage more deeply in model building and hypothesis testing in order to further articulate the impact of specific factors and direction of pedagogical interventions related to the development of writers and writing abilities for people at all points across the lifespan.

REFERENCES

Abbott, R. D., Berninger, V. W. & Fayol, M. (2010). Longitudinal relationships of levels of language in writing and between writing and reading in grades 1 to 7. *Journal of Educational Psychology, 102*(2), 281–298. https://doi.org/10.1037/a0019318.

Ahmed, Y., Wagner, R. K. & Lopez, D. (2014). Developmental relations between reading and writing at the word, sentence, and text levels: A latent change score analysis. *Journal of Educational Psychology, 106*(2), 419–434. https://doi.org/10.1037/a0035692.

Almalki, S. (2016). Integrating quantitative and qualitative data in mixed methods research—Challenges and benefits. *Journal of Education and Learning, 5*(3), 288. https://doi.org/10.5539/jel.v5n3p288.

Aram, D. & Levin, I. (2004). The role of maternal mediation of writing to kindergartners in promoting literacy in school: A longitudinal perspective. *Reading and Writing*, *17*(4), 387–409. https://doi.org/10.1023/B:READ.0000032665.14437.e0.

Aram, D., Korat, O. & Hassunah-Arafat, S. (2013). *The contribution of early home literacy activities to first grade reading and writing achievements in Arabic*. Springer. https://doi.org/10.1007/s11145-013-9430-y.

Bazerman, C. (2018). Lifespan longitudinal studies of writing development: A heuristic for an impossible dream. In C. Bazerman, A. N. Applebee, V. W. Berninger, D. Brandt, S. Graham, J. V. Jeffery, P. K. Matsuda, S. Murphy, D. W. Rowe, M. Schleppegrell & K. C. Wilcox (Eds.), *The lifespan development of writing* (pp. 326–365). National Council of Teachers of English. https://wac.colostate.edu/books/ncte/lifespan-writing/.

Beaufort, A. (2004). Developmental gains of a history major: A case for building a theory of disciplinary writing expertise. *Research in the Teaching of English*, *39*(2), 136–185.

Beers, S. F. & Nagy, W. E. (2011). Writing development in four genres from grades three to seven: Syntactic complexity and genre differentiation. *Reading and Writing*, *24*(2), 183–202. https://doi.org/10.1007/s11145-010-9264-9.

Berninger, V., Mizokawa, D. & Bragg, R. (1991). Theory-based diagnosis and remediation of writing disabilities. *Journal of School Psychology*, *29*, 57–79. https://doi.org/10.1016/0022-4405(91)90016-K.

Bigozzi, L. & Vettori, G. (2016). To tell a story, to write it: Developmental patterns of narrative skills from preschool to first grade. *European Journal of Psychology of Education*, *31*(4), 461–477. https://doi.org/10.1007/s10212-015-0273-6.

Cardoso-Martins, C., Corrêa, M. F., Lemos, L. S. & Napoleão, R. F. (2006). Is there a syllabic stage in spelling development? Evidence from Portuguese-speaking children. *Journal of Educational Psychology*, *98*(3), 628–641. https://doi.org/10.1037/0022-0663.98.3.628.

Caruana, E. J., Roman, M., Hernández-Sánchez, J. & Solli, P. (2015). Longitudinal studies. *Journal of Thoracic Disease*, *7*(11), E537–E540. https://doi.org/10.3978/j.issn.2072-1439.2015.10.63.

Chapman, M. (2002). A longitudinal case study of curriculum genres, K-3. *Canadian Journal of Education / Revue Canadienne de l'éducation*, *27*(1), 21–44. https://doi.org/10.2307/1602186.

Chen, V. (2018). Seeing the world through words: A student writer's journey toward developing her own voice. *Journal for Learning through the Arts: A Research Journal on Arts Integration in Schools and Communities*, *13*(1). https://doi.org/10.21977/D913135150.

Coker, D. (2006). Impact of first-grade factors on the growth and outcomes of urban schoolchildren's primary-grade writing. *Journal of Educational Psychology*, *98*(3), 471–488. https://doi.org/10.1037/0022-0663.98.3.471.

Compton-Lilly, C. (2014). The development of writing habitus: A ten-year case study of a young writer. *Written Communication*, *31*(4), 371–403. https://doi.org/10.1177/0741088314549539.

Cordeiro, C., Limpo, T., Olive, T. & Castro, S. L. (2020). Do executive functions contribute to writing quality in beginning writers? A longitudinal study with second graders. *Reading and Writing, 33*(4), 813–833. https://doi.org/10.1007/s11145-019-09963-6.

Dippre, R. J. & Phillips, T. (Eds.). (2020). *Approaches to lifespan writing research: Generating an actionable coherence.* The WAC Clearinghouse; University Press of Colorado. https://doi.org/10.37514/PER-B.2020.1053.

Doyle, L., Brady, A.-M. & Byrne, G. (2009). An overview of mixed methods research. *Journal of Research in Nursing, 14*(2), 175–185. https://doi.org/10.1177/1744987108093962.

Drijbooms, E., Groen, M. A. & Verhoeven, L. (2017). How executive functions predict development in syntactic complexity of narrative writing in the upper elementary grades. *Reading and Writing, 30*(1), 209–231. https://doi.org/10.1007/s11145-016-9670-8..

Driscoll, D. L. & Powell, R. (2016). States, traits, and dispositions: The impact of emotion on writing development and writing transfer across college courses and beyond. *Composition Forum, 34*. https://eric.ed.gov/?id=EJ1113424.

Dunsmuir, S. & Blatchford, P. (2004). Predictors of writing competence in 4- to 7-year-old children. *British Journal of Educational Psychology, 74*(3), 461–483. https://doi.org/10.1348/0007099041552323.

Dyson, A. H. (2003). *The brothers and sisters learn to write: Popular literacies in childhood and school culture*. Teachers College Press.

Elf, N. (2017). Taught by bitter experience: A timescales analysis of Amalie's development of writer identity. In T. Cremin & T. Locke (Eds.), *Writer Identity and the Teaching and Learning of Writing*. Routledge. https://doi.org/10.4324/9781315669373.

Firestone, W. (1987). Meaning in method: The rhetoric of quantitative and qualitative research. *Educational Researcher, 16*(7), 16–21. https://doi.org/10.3102/0013189X016007016.

Fischer, J. P. & Koch, A. M. (2016). Mirror writing in typically developing children: A first longitudinal study. *Cognitive Development, 38*, 114–124. https://doi.org/10.1016/j.cogdev.2016.02.005.

Fitzmaurice, G. M., Laird, N. M. & Ware, J. H. (2012). *Applied longitudinal analysis.* John Wiley & Sons. https://www.doi.org/10.1002/9781119513469

Frey, B. B. (Ed.). (2018). *The Sage encyclopedia of educational research, measurement, and evaluation. Sage Publications.* https://doi.org/10.4135/9781506326139.

Frost, J. (2001). Phonemic awareness, spontaneous writing, and reading and spelling development from a preventive perspective. *Reading and Writing, 14*(5), 487–513. https://doi.org/10.1023/A:1011143002068.

Greene, J. C., Caracelli, V. J. & Graham, W. F. (1989). Toward a conceptual framework for mixed-method evaluation designs. *Educational Evaluation and Policy Analysis, 11*(3), 255–274. https://doi.org/10.3102/01623737011003255.

Hamilton, E. W., Nolen, S. B. & Abbott, R. D. (2013). Developing measures of motivational orientation to read and write: A longitudinal study. *Learning and Individual Differences, 28*. https://doi.org/10.1016/j.lindif.2013.04.007.

Hartley, J. & Chesworth, K. (2000). Qualitative and quantitative methods in research on essay writing: No one way. *Journal of Further and Higher Education*, *24*(1), 15–24. https://doi.org/10.1080/030987700112282.

Haswell, R. H. (2000). Documenting improvement in college writing: A longitudinal approach. *Written Communication*, *17*(3), 307–352. https://doi.org/10.1177/0741088300017003001.

Hedeker, D. & Gibbons, R. D. (2006). *Longitudinal data analysis*. Wiley-Interscience.

Hooper, S. R., Costa, L. J., McBee, M., Anderson, K. L., Yerby, D. C., Knuth, S. B. & Childress, A. (2011). Concurrent and longitudinal neuropsychological contributors to written language expression in first and second grade students. *Reading and Writing*, *24*(2), 221–252. https://doi.org/10.1007/s11145-010-9263-x..

Hooper, S. R., Roberts, J. E., Nelson, L., Zeisel, S. & Fannin, D. K. (2010). Preschool predictors of narrative writing skills in elementary school children. *School Psychology Quarterly*, *25*(1), 1–12. https://doi.org/10.1037/a0018329

Johnson, J. P. & Krase, E. (2012). Coming to learn: From first-year composition to writing in the disciplines. *Across the Disciplines*, *9*(2), 1–22. https://doi.org/10.37514/ATD-J.2012.9.2.02.

Kim, Y. S. G. & Park, S. H. (2019). Unpacking pathways using the direct and indirect effects model of writing (DIEW) and the contributions of higher order cognitive skills to writing. *Reading and Writing*, *32*(5), 1319–1343. https://doi.org/10.1007/s11145-018-9913-y.

Kim, Y. S., Al Otaiba, S. & Wanzek, J. (2015). Kindergarten predictors of third grade writing. *Learning and Individual Differences*, *37*, 27–37. https://doi.org/10.1016/j.lindif.2014.11.009.

Krogh, E. & Jakobsen, K. S. (Eds.). (2019). *Understanding young people's writing development: identity, disciplinarity, and education*. Routledge.

Kuzeva, O. A., Romanova, A. A., Korneev, A. A. & Akhutina, T. V. (2015). The dynamics of programming, control and the movement sequential organization skills as the basic components of writing. *Russian Education & Society*, *57*(9), 757–782. https://doi.org/10.1080/10609393.2015.1125707.

Lammers, J. C. & Marsh, V. L. (2018). "A writer more than . . . a child": A longitudinal study examining adolescent writer identity. *Written Communication*, *35*(1), 89–114. https://doi.org/10.1177/0741088317735835.

Levin, I., Ravid, D. & Rapaport, S. (2001). Morphology and spelling among Hebrew-speaking children: From kindergarten to first grade. *Journal of Child Language*, *28*(3), 741–772. https://doi.org/10.1017/S0305000901004834.

Lewis-Beck, M., Bryman, A. E. & Liao, T. F. (2004). *The Sage Encyclopedia of Social Science Research Methods*. Sage. https://doi.org/10.4135/9781412950589.

Limpo, T. & Alves, R. A. (2013). Modeling writing development: Contribution of transcription and self-regulation to Portuguese students' text generation quality. *Journal of Educational Psychology*, *105*(2), 401–413. https://doi.org/10.1037/a0031391.

Lunsford, A. A., Fishman, J. & Liew, W. M. (2013). College writing, identification, and the production of intellectual property: Voices from the Stanford study of writing. *College English*, *75*(5), 470–492.

Mäki, H. S., Voeten, M. J. M., Vauras, M. M. S. & Poskiparta, E. H. (2001). Predicting writing skill development with word recognition and preschool readiness skills. *Reading and Writing, 14*(7), 643–672. https://doi.org/10.1023/A:1012071514719.

Myhill, D. & Jones, S. (2007). More than just error correction: Students' perspectives on their revision processes during writing. *Written Communication, 24*(4), 323–343. https://doi.org/10.1177/0741088307305976.

Niedo, J., Abbott, R. D. & Berninger, V. W. (2014). Predicting levels of reading and writing achievement in typically developing, English-speaking 2nd and 5th graders. *Learning and Individual Differences, 32*, 54–68. https://doi.org/10.1016/j.lindif.2014.03.013.

Oppenheimer, D., Zaromb, F., Pomerantz, J. R., Williams, J. C. & Park, Y. S. (2017). Improvement of writing skills during college: A multi-year cross-sectional and longitudinal study of undergraduate writing performance. *Assessing Writing, 32*, 12–27. https://doi.org/10.1016/j.asw.2016.11.001.

Pinto, G., Bigozzi, L., Gamannossi, B. A. & Vezzani, C. (2009). Emergent literacy and learning to write: A predictive model for the Italian language. *European Journal of Psychology of Education, 24*(1), 61. https://doi.org/10.1007/BF03173475.

Pinto, G., Bigozzi, L., Gamannossi, B. A. & Vezzani, C. (2012). Emergent literacy and early writing skills. *The Journal of Genetic Psychology, 173*(3), 330–354. https://doi.org/10.1080/00221325.2011.609848.

Pinto, G., Tarchi, C. & Bigozzi, L. (2015). The relationship between oral and written narratives: A three-year longitudinal study of narrative cohesion, coherence, and structure. *The British Journal of Educational Psychology, 85*(4), 551–569. https://doi.org/10.1111/bjep.12091.

Rogers, P. (2009). The contributions of North American longitudinal studies of writing in higher education to our understanding of writing development. In C. Bazerman, R. Krut, K. Lunsford, S. McLeod, S. Null, P. Rogers & A. Stansell (Eds.), *Traditions of writing research* (pp. 337–389). Routledge.

Roozen, K. (2008). Journalism, poetry, stand-up comedy, and academic literacy: Mapping the interplay of curricular and extracurricular literate activities. *Journal of Basic Writing, 27*(1), 5–34. https://doi.org/10.37514/JBW-J.2008.27.1.02

Rosário, P., Högemann, J., Núñez, J. C., Vallejo, G., Cunha, J., Oliveira, V., Fuentes, S. & Rodrigues, C. (2017). Writing week-journals to improve the writing quality of fourth-graders' compositions. *Reading and Writing, 30*(5), 1009–1032. https://doi.org/10.1007/s11145-016-9710-4.

Shulruf, B., Hattie, J. & Dixon, R. (2007). Development of a new measurement tool for individualism and collectivism. *Journal of Psychoeducational Assessment, 25*(4), 385–401. https://doi.org/10.1177/0734282906298992.

Skibbe, L. E., Bindman, S. W., Hindman, A. H., Aram, D. & Morrison, F. J. (2013). Longitudinal relations between parental writing support and preschoolers' language and literacy skills. *Reading Research Quarterly, 48*(4), 387–401. https://doi.org/10.1002/rrq.55.

Smith, A. & Prior, P. (2020). A Flat CHAT perspective on transliteracies development. *Learning, Culture and Social Interaction, 24*. https://doi.org/10.1016/j.lcsi.2019.01.001.

Sommers, N. & Saltz, L. (2004). The novice as expert: Writing the freshman year. *College Composition and Communication*, *56*(1), 124–149. https://doi.org/10.2307/4140684.

Sullivan, G. M. & Sargeant, J. (2011). Qualities of qualitative research: Part I. *Journal of Graduate Medical Education*, *3*(4), 449–452. https://doi.org/10.4300/JGME-D-11-00221.1.

Svensson, B. (2018). The development of figurative competence in narrative writing: A longitudinal case study. *International Journal of Language Studies*, *12*, 75–102.

Tong, X. & McBride, C. (2016). Reading comprehension mediates the relationship between syntactic awareness and writing composition in children: A longitudinal study. *Journal of Psycholinguistic Research*, *45*(6), 1265–1285. https://doi.org/10.1007/s10936-015-9401-3.

Torrance, M., Thomas, G. V. & Robinson, E. J. (2000). Individual differences in undergraduate essay-writing strategies: A longitudinal study. *Higher Education*, *39*(2), 181–200.

Treiman, R., Pollo, T. C., Cardoso-Martins, C. & Kessler, B. (2013). Do young children spell words syllabically? Evidence from learners of Brazilian Portuguese. *Journal of Experimental Child Psychology*, *116*(4), 873–890. https://doi.org/10.1016/j.jecp.2013.08.002.

Turnbull, K., Deacon, S. H. & Kay-Raining Bird, E. (2011). Mastering inflectional suffixes: A longitudinal study of beginning writers' spellings. *Journal of Child Language*, *38*(3), 533–553. https://doi.org/10.1017/S030500091000022X.

Woodward-Kron, R. (2009). "This means that . . . ": A linguistic perspective of writing and learning in a discipline. *Journal of English for Academic Purposes*, *8*(3), 165–179. https://doi.org/10.1016/j.jeap.2009.07.002.

Yan, C. M. W., McBride-Chang, C., Wagner, R. K., Zhang, J., Wong, A. M. Y. & Shu, H. (2012). Writing quality in Chinese children: Speed and fluency matter. *Reading and Writing*, *25*(7), 1499–1521. https://doi.org/10.1007/s11145-011-9330-y.

Yeung, P., Ho, C. S., Chan, D. W. & Chung, K. K. (2013a). Modeling the relationships between cognitive-linguistic skills and writing in Chinese among elementary grades students. *Reading and Writing*, *26*(7), 1195–1221. https://doi.org/10.1007/s11145-012-9411-6

Yeung, P., Ho, C. S., Chan, D. W. & Chung, K. K. (2020). Longitudinal relationships between syntactic skills and Chinese written composition in Grades 3 to 6. *Journal of Research in Reading*, *43*(2), 201–228. https://doi.org/10.1111/1467-9817.12298.

Yeung, P. S., Ho, C. S. H., Wong, Y. K., Chan, D. W. O., Chung, K. K. H. & Lo, L. Y. (2013b). Longitudinal predictors of Chinese word reading and spelling among elementary grade students. *Applied Psycholinguistics*, *34*(6), 1245–1277. https://doi.org/10.1017/S0142716412000239.

Zeanah, C. H., Boris, N. W. & Larrieu, J. A. (1997). Infant development and developmental risk: A review of the past 10 years. *Journal of the American Academy of Child & Adolescent Psychiatry*, *36*(2), 165–178. https://doi.org/10.1097/00004583-199702000-00007.

APPENDIX A. SCALES IN LONGITUDINAL STUDIES

All Scales Used by the Studies in Chapters 9 and 10	
PAL-II	ORF 1
CTOPP	ORF2
PPVT-4	Peabody Picture Vocabulary Test III
CREVT-2	HKT-SpLD
VIGIL	WUR
WJ-III	Raven's Colored Progressive Matrices
WRAML-2	Big-Small Stroop-like task
WISC-IV	WISC-III
WIAT-II	BANC
WorkingMem z-score	ERRNI
ReceptiveLang z-score	Systematic Screen of Handwriting Difficulties
Phonemes z-score	PI-dictee
ERA	PPVT-III-NL
Reading Interest Orientation	Tea-Ch
Reading Mastery Orientation	Sky Search
Writing Avoidance	LDST
Ego Orientation	D-KEFS-Letter
TOWRE PDE	LDST
WJ Passage Comp	D-KEFS-Letter Fluency
D-KEFS-TMT	GRE Issue Task
PPST	TOEFL
Kaufman IQ Test	Test of Word Reading Efficacy
SWAN	CTOPP
PAL	UW
WPPSI	BAS
CELF3	KTI

PART 2.
A SELECTION OF "ANDS": IMAGINING METHODOLOGICAL FUTURES IN LIFESPAN WRITING RESEARCH

The first portion of this volume demonstrates, if not conventional, then at least conventional-ish methodological approaches to studying writing through the lifespan. These are approaches with considerable histories that have been proven useful not only in particular sites and with particular participants, but across a wide range of settings, circumstances, and populations. In Part II, we enter the "yes, and" of improvisation: our contributors offer new considerations, new visions, and new critiques that can usefully inform the ongoing work of LWR.

We begin with "An Autoethnographic Springboard to More Extensive Lifespan Writing Research" by Kathleen Shine Cain, Pamela Childers, and Leigh Ryan, which offers insights into the uses of autoethnography for LWR. Their chapter intentionally sits between Parts I and II as their autoethnographic account traces the ongoing improvisations of research-in-process. Their chapter also provides a compelling case for the possibilities that autoethnographic work offers to lifespan writing research.

The next two chapters identify important considerations for methodological design in LWR. Joe Cirio and Jeff Naftzinger's "A Matter of Time and Memory: A Methodological Framework of Memory for Lifespan Writing Research" calls our attention to the role of memory, how it might be conceptualized, and how we might theorize with and through memory when studying writing through the lifespan. In Chapter 13, Soledad Montes and Karin Tusting offer powerful suggestions for conceptualizing transitions in "Writing in Transitions Across the Lifespan." They ask us to re-examine our definitions of "transition," drawing on a considerable body of work in New Literacies to challenge assumptions about writing, literacy, and the lifespan that may then productively complicate future lifespan writing research.

The next four chapters suggest novel applications to LWR for more recent and emerging methodologies. Erin Workman's "Centering Positionalities in Lifespan Writing Research through Institutional and Auto/Ethnographic Methodologies" uses her personal experience as a lens into institutional and auto-ethnography, calling attention to the lived, material, practiced world of institutions and their roles in shaping the complexity of our literate lives. In Chapter 15, Karen

Lunsford, Carl Whithaus, and Jonathan Alexander draw connections between their project of "wayfinding" and writing through the lifespan in "Wayfinding: The Development of an Approach to Lifespan Writing." Then Matthew Zajic and Apryl Poch consider LWR from a quantitative perspective, offering a range of ways to take up quantitative approaches to LWR questions in "How Might We Measure That? Considerations from Quantitative Research Approaches for Lifespan Writing Research." Flexing the range of valuable approaches to LWR, Chapter 17 turns us to poetry and the role that it can play to make sense of the complicated and nonlinear literate lives that we and our research participants live. Sandra Tarabochia's "Becoming Researcher-Poets: Poetic Inquiry as Method/ology for Writing (through the Lifespan) Research" gives productive examples of what poetry can do for researchers, an effective rationale, and a straightforward approach to getting started.

We close our volume by turning to several larger issues underlying our individual and collective methodological choices. The final four chapters provide a range of important, challenging critiques to the existing agenda of Lifespan Writing Research, including important considerations as we design future studies. These chapters ask us to think carefully about what comes next, about how we proceed (individually and, insofar as we are able, as a group), and about how LWR might serve as a vehicle to meaningfully engage a range of issues in and beyond the work of academic writing and research.

In Chapter 18, "Approaching Lifespan Writing Research from Indigenous, Decolonial Perspectives," Bhushan Aryal argues that lifespan writing researchers should give explicit attention to the home languages and literacies of our participants and the ways that all of our participants' languages and literacies are caught up within structures of power. He challenges lifespan writing researchers to consider whether and how our work represents Indigenous voices, victims of colonialism, and those whose literacy practices fall outside of white Englishes.

Next, Jeremy Levine comes at school-fostered literacies from a very different angle in "Motivating Lifespan Writing Research Toward Education Policy," asking what lifespan writing researchers really aim to achieve. Levine suggests that if our collective research accomplishments are going to change the systems in which our writer-participants find themselves, then we likely need to give more serious consideration to making that work both intelligible and powerful to policy makers. He outlines key factors driving much of the educational policymaking around writing, providing a range of possibilities for lifespan writing researchers interested in designing studies for policy impact.

We conclude with Suellynn Duffey's case study of Kim's rich, powerful set of literacies that make stark the limits of methodologies. In Chapter 20, "A

Graduate School "Drop-Out"—After School," Duffey demonstrates how Kim's literacies were decoupled from schooling and thus were likely to be overlooked by any kind of academy-based research project. Even more significant, Kim's profound literacies were revealed gradually to Duffey across many years of many different kinds of contact; their depth and complexity is incompatible with many data collection plans. Kim's story also bears on how we construct literacy success as both researchers and teachers and how we employ methodologies to understand it.

CHAPTER 11.
AN AUTOETHNOGRAPHIC SPRINGBOARD TO MORE EXTENSIVE LIFESPAN WRITING RESEARCH

Kathleen Shine Cain
Merrimack College

Pamela B. Childers
The McCallie School

Leigh Ryan
University of Maryland

Research is messy! It begins with a question or a curiosity about something; attempts to find answers can lead down various paths that typically clarify what the project is *really* about and suggest ways to get information that might provide answers. This project began with discomfort about our retirement. With our identities so tightly linked to our writing center work, what would we do and who would we be when we left our positions as directors? Did others in our place have the same questions and apprehension? Would sharing our stories help us to find answers that might be useful to us and others? This narrative focuses on our experience as researchers and how the messiness and evolution of our research experiences led us to continued improvisations in our methodology as our topic kept expanding and developing. We began with methodologies familiar to us and to those in the field, but as our work progressed, we developed a lifespan perspective and were drawn to autoethnography, a methodology relatively new to our field of writing center studies.

We offer here an autoethnographic case study of how one research project actually grew and evolved over time. We describe our own project—a research journey of three academic colleagues and friends, evolving from casual conversations through formulating tentative research questions to factoring in expanded questions as we explored, framed, and finally conducted our project collaboratively. We begin this chapter with the questions and conversations that led us to use autoethnography, moving from there to our decision to survey others, and

DOI: https://doi.org/10.37514/PER-B.2024.2289.2.11

then on to the implications for lifespan writing research. We conclude with the acknowledgment that our project continues to evolve.

BEGINNING WITH CONVERSATIONS AND QUESTIONS

Our research began, as many projects do, with conversations and questions among colleagues that took place over years with increasing intensity. As long-time and active writing center directors, each for more than thirty years, we were well acquainted with one another through attending and presenting at regional, national, and international conferences. We usually got together to socialize and "talk shop," most often at the many international conferences in which we participated. Each of us took on unique individual or collaborative work that sometimes intersected and often supported the work of the other two. Throughout those years, Pam Childers and Leigh Ryan occasionally presented jointly, and Kathy Shine Cain and Leigh were active in the National Conference on Peer Tutoring in Writing (NCPTW). All three participated in other professional organizations for writing and writing center researchers and teachers, serving as officers and mentors, hosting conferences, and, of course, presenting and publishing. And then, ten plus years into the twenty-first century, we each found ourselves planning retirement and thinking about our transitions into that new "life" after leaving a profession we loved.

Chronologically, Pam retired in 2010 as Caldwell Chair of Composition and Caldwell Writing Center Director from the McCallie School, a college preparatory independent boys' school in Tennessee, after previously directing the writing center at a public secondary school in New Jersey. In 2016, Leigh retired as Director of the Writing Center at the University of Maryland, a large public research and flagship university. Finally, Kathy retired in 2018 from Merrimack College, a private college in Massachusetts, after directing the writing center and holding other Writing Program Administrator (WPA) positions. We considered the diversity of our positions to be an advantage, since we represented a range of institutions and possible writing center director positions. Unlike many other authors in this collection, we conducted our research study independent of any academic institution, although we brought to our work the collaborative input from our previous positions.

As we individually stepped away from our full-time jobs, our paths continued to cross at conferences. Pam presented on a panel with other retired writing center directors at the International Writing Centers Association (IWCA) conference in 2014, where she roomed with Leigh, and they presented with Steve Sherwood at the 2016 IWCA conference on a retrospective of writing center research promise and progress. Then Pam spoke on life after retirement at the 2017 Conference on College Composition Communication (CCCC), which Kathy attended.

When we met at conferences to share a meal or two, increasingly retirement became a significant topic of conversation. Though published long after we began sharing articles on retirement, Arthur C. Brooks's (2020) article "How to Build a Life: Why So Many People are Unhappy in Retirement" sums up much of what we have since discovered about retirement:

> Unless you keel over in the prime of life, your victories will fade, your skills will decline, and life's problems will intrude. If you try to hang on to glory, or lash out when it fades, it will squander your victories and mark an unhappy end to your journey. If you're still in the middle of your hero's journey, it would behoove you to make tangible plans now to show true strength and character in the final phase. Plan to spend the last part of your life serving others, loving your family and friends, and being a good example to those still in the first three stages of their own hero's journey. Happiness in retirement depends on your choice of narrative.

What would our narratives be and how would we find them? Having retired from different kinds of institutions and writing center director positions, we wondered if we were each facing similar issues as we considered how to retain and balance professional and personal activities in this new phase of our lives.

TURNING TOWARDS AUTOETHNOGRAPHY

When Leigh suggested that we reread the late Wendy Bishop's essay, "You Can Take the Girl Out of the Writing Center, But You Can't Take the Writing Center Out of the Girl" (1997), we began to consider more seriously how our experiences as writing center directors informed and influenced our post-writing center lives. We had each spent many years in the field, and so it made sense to contemplate relationships between our professional lives and our subsequent or anticipated civic, professional, and personal retirement activities—both ongoing and new—that seemed natural continuations of our writing center work. We were considering possible ideas to address our own concerns, while also improvising ways to help others in similar positions. And, at this point we were not familiar with lifespan writing research.

The 2018 IWCA conference in Atlanta provided an opportunity to explore this idea further, so we proposed a session grounded in autoethnography. As mentioned in some of the earlier chapters, this research method allowed us to tell our own stories, mining our pasts for details, linking them to the present, and tentatively forecasting their presence in the future. According to Margot

Duncan (2004), autoethnography presents "reports that are scholarly and justifiable interpretations based on multiple sources of evidence. This means autoethnographic accounts do not consist solely of the researcher's opinions but are also supported by other data that can confirm or triangulate those opinions" (p. 3). We were able to draw on copious documented evidence from our various professional positions; regional, national, and international leadership roles; awards; workshops; presentations; and publications from a wide range of organizations to support our personal reflections. Carolyn Ellis and colleagues (2011) describe our choice of methodology in their description of autoethnography:

> When researchers write autoethnographies, they seek to produce aesthetic and evocative thick descriptions of personal and interpersonal experience. They accomplish this by first discerning patterns of cultural experience evidenced by field notes, interviews, and/or artifacts, and then describing these patterns using facets of storytelling (e.g., character and plot development), showing and telling, and alterations of authorial voice. Thus, the autoethnographer not only tries to make personal experience meaningful and cultural experience engaging, but also, by producing accessible texts, she or he may be able to reach wider and more diverse mass audiences that traditional research usually disregards, a move that can make personal and social change possible for more people. (Ellis, Adams & Bochner, 2011, p. 5)

Likewise, Tony Adams and others describe autoethnography as

> radically inductive. The categories and the themes of the study emerge from the writing explorations. Written reflection emerges in a dialectic that alternates between the collection of data (written fieldnotes, documents, journals, other written ephemera) and the theorizing of that data on its own terms. (Jones et al., 2015)

Calling this theorizing of data "thematicizing," they suggest that it involves "a continual rereading of this mass of writing and then reflecting in writing that looks for themes, which may be signaled by repeated words, 'images, phrases, and/or experiences'" (Jones et al., 2015).

It should be noted, as Jodi Skipper (2022) points out, that "some other academics tend to segregate [autoethnography] as an activist and, not [as an] academic, which is not how I was trained to think. I also just believe that academic work is innately political and that such a separation isn't optional" (quoted in

Henery, 2022). Given that our own reflections continue to emphasize the values inherent in writing center work, and that many respondents shared our association of this work with social justice, we would share Skipper's assessment of this methodology.

Elliot Eisner (1991) describes the ways in which qualitative studies like autoethnographies find usefulness: if they help readers understand a situation that is otherwise confusing, if such studies in some way help readers to anticipate future possibilities, and if they act as guides to highlight specific aspects of a situation that may go unnoticed (paraphrased in Duncan, 2004, p. 9). And that is precisely what happened with our autoethnographic study. As Kathy wrote in hers,

> So what to do [in retirement]? I'm beginning to formulate an answer to that question, focusing on two essential elements of my writing center experience: 1) I want to maintain my professional identity, and 2) I want to continue to engage in the kind of social justice-oriented work that I believe is inherent in writing center work.

Pam considered,

> Just as in our writing center positions, we have dealt with family joys, losses, major health issues, and our own aging processes. I have flown cross country monthly for 3 ½ years caring for my parents, traveled throughout the world, taken on many new adventures, and re-examined how I am approaching this project [called retirement].

Finally, Leigh noted the significance of bringing interests together, both on and off the job:

> For me it was social justice. I began volunteering at an historic house museum in 1994 because I loved the mansion, but quickly became primarily interested in an enslaved family, the Plummers, and their stories. My activities at the mansion aligned with my interests and activities at work, where my tutors and I actively sought to promote inclusivity, diversity, and social justice in our tutoring and other projects.

All three of us have continued our involvement in social justice issues, both old and new, in our retirement activities, but was that true of other retired writing center directors? And as messy as they might be, what avenues could we explore to discover that information?

FROM AUTOETHNOGRAPHY TO RESEARCHING OTHERS

These self-reflective autoethnographies were just the beginning of what would evolve into a far different research project than we had originally envisioned. A lively discussion among participants in our Atlanta presentation made it clear that some of our former writing center colleagues had left their directorships not to retire, but to move into other positions inside and outside academia. Some had advanced to key administrative positions, while others focused on different but related academic interests, took full-time teaching positions, or started their own businesses. Fortunately, we had kept in touch with many colleagues over the decades through conferences and collaborative projects connected to IWCA, CCCC, NCPTW, and WAC. How had their writing center directorships influenced their choices and work after leaving that position? As we examined our individual qualitative studies and listened to others who shared their own stories, we asked ourselves, "Why not broaden our study to include 'former' rather than 'retired' writing center directors?" This simple change in language shifted our perspective and greatly expanded the implications of the project.

At this point, we began to reconsider and refine our research questions. We now had information gleaned from our 2018 IWCA autoethnographies, along with feedback from that audience and other former, current, and future writing center directors with whom we had shared our ideas. In addition, we had determined that our research needed to include a larger, more diverse, and international group of subjects. We also considered the relevance of prior writing center research. The work of Kenneth Bruffee (1984), particularly his definitions of collaborative learning and of knowledge as a social construct, along with Pam and Leigh's reflections on Steve Sherwood's presentation on writing center careers (2011), helped inform our thinking. Also relevant were Brad Hughes, Paula Gillespie, and Harvey Kail's (2010) analysis of the lasting impact of the writing center experience on undergraduate tutors' professional lives and Andrew Jeter's (2016) conclusion from his research on high school peer tutors: "peer tutoring taught [student tutors] how to find the joy in collaboration with others" (p. 110). Our research questions reflected these studies: What, if any, similar conclusions could be reached about the impact of writing center work on former directors? And to what extent might our experiences help current directors consider what facets of their writing center work might carry over into retirement or future positions and how? Also, could this research impact the way others approached their lifespan writing projects involving retirees?

As we deliberated, we looked more closely at the Peer Writing Tutor Alumni Research Project's (PWTARP) interest in learning "which abilities, values, and skills tutors developed from [students'] education and experience as peer writing tutors and how, if at all, they had used those abilities, values, and skills in their lives beyond graduation" (Hughes et al., 2010). That study's framework led us to ask about the talents, skills, and abilities former writing center directors put into practice or learned in their positions, and how those might have served them in the professional, civic, and personal aspects of their lives after leaving to assume other positions or retire.

The PWTARP results also reinforced our notion of writing centers as communities of practice (Lave, 1993; Lave & Wenger, 1990; Wenger, 1998), featuring collaboration and interaction on an ongoing basis, with a focus on exploring and sharing best practices and creating new knowledge. We wondered what being part of a community of practice meant to former directors, and if and how they saw it influencing or being a part of their subsequent activities. We also began regular online discussions to determine our next steps. To gather information from others who had left their writing positions, we decided to compose a survey of former directors modeled on Hughes and his colleagues' (2010) survey of peer writing tutors.

We initially coded our own autoethnographies, and then turned to crafting questions for our survey. This shift moved us from our original qualitative study (autoethnography) to a quantitative one (survey) that would also include data we could analyze as correlative and code as descriptive. Guidelines for developing surveys and questionnaires (Anthony et al., 2014) served as a kind of brief refresher course, reminding us to focus on our objectives, design ways to best obtain information (e.g., demographic questions, closed or open questions, use of scales such as Likert), and determine the structure and order of the survey itself. And, of course, we continued reading what we termed "background material."

Development of the survey, which went through many iterations before being finalized, involved weekly online meetings, email discussions of drafts, and feedback from participants at several conferences, and finally, some discussions at our weekly online meetings. Though sometimes messy, drafts we presented at conferences received spontaneous suggestions and comments from attendees that we quickly recorded. Finally, we discussed, critiqued, revised, and reordered our questions, then tested the final version (Appendix A) with our own responses. We were participants in our own survey! That final survey included basic demographic information (i.e., age, education, years of experience as writing center directors, institutional affiliations), involvement in professional organizations, publications, and presentations. The last six open-ended questions allowed participants to expand on specifics related to their work as writing center directors and future career/personal choices they had made during and after leaving the writing center. The survey ended with a question requesting contact information for respondents willing to complete more detailed follow-up interview questions. Meanwhile, we secured a mutually accessible Survey Monkey account.

We began our survey distribution process in the spring of 2020, sending invitations (Appendix B) through more than a dozen regional, national, and international listservs that might include former secondary and postsecondary writing center directors. Since more people were working online during the pandemic, we may have been able to contact a greater number of respondents through listservs than we might have otherwise. Because some who had left writing center positions were no longer on any of these listservs, we contacted those we knew directly and solicited names and contact information from other colleagues. What began as three individual autoethnographic research studies had grown into a full-fledged, internationally diverse and inclusive research survey that could impact the personal and professional work of former, current, and future writing center directors.

CONNECTING EARLY FINDINGS TO LIFESPAN WRITING RESEARCH

As of this writing, we have received 260 responses, with over half volunteering to respond to follow-up interview questions. The former writing center director respondents included high school, community college, and four-year college and university directors from such countries as Iceland, Canada, Turkey, Norway, Sweden, the Netherlands, Philippines, Taiwan, Oman, Chile, Namibia, Denmark, Germany, and the United States. Only 18 percent were under 45 years of age, with 25 percent between ages 45 and 55, 21 percent from 55–64, and 36 percent over 65. It was interesting to discover that many had left their writing center positions early in their careers but still felt a strong connection to those experiences that influenced them in other positions in academia or elsewhere. In fact, 60 percent had been directors for less than ten years. Although 18 percent of respondents had retired, most have continued volunteer work that reflects what they learned as directors, and at least 46 percent moved into full-time faculty or administrative positions where they have applied what they learned as writing center directors. We would never have received these kinds of responses or amassed such detailed information if we had not changed our original research question from its focus on "retired" to "former" writing center directors.

As responses slowly came into the new Survey Monkey email we created, we began to focus on the data we were receiving. This was messy work, as we alternated checking periodically to identify trends and reaching out to additional potential participants. Between and during our weekly online meetings, we analyzed and shared our coding of the survey data to determine what follow-up information to gather. Then, we created six questions (Appendix C) to distribute in early 2021 to those (130) who had volunteered to participate further. By summer 2021, we had received 64 follow-up interview responses, offering more qualitative research with an abundance of useful specific personal data to investigate. Throughout this time, we continued sharing drafts of data, gathering new research, and collaborating on writing conference proposals, presentations (Appendix D), and applications for grants.

As our work progressed, we noticed that more and more attention was being paid to intellectual and scholarly connections between the academic and post-academic life, all of which suggested we were on a good path. One valuable resource was our involvement in the Writing Through the Lifespan Collaboration starting early in 2018. This group began in 2016 in response to Charles Bazerman's call for research on writing across the lifespan, from cradle to grave. We were fortunate to attend virtual presentations and discussions, and presented our own *Work in Progress*, "Identity, Activity, and Community Practice in the Writing Center and Beyond: What Departing Directors Carry with Them," in October 2020. Participants offered valuable suggestions for further research, shared their own experiences, and asked beneficial questions. It is at this point that we began to more fully understand and articulate the inextricable connection between our identities as writing center directors and as lifelong writers. Pam and Leigh also became subjects in an ongoing study involving retired members of rhetoric, composition, and writing studies that looks at retirement as an active part of the disciplinary lifecycle (Bowen & Pinkert, 2020). In addition, we noted an increase of formal organizations for intellectual exchange, cultural enrichment, and social interaction forming on campuses and within organizations. The University of Maryland Emeritus/Emerita Association, for example, allows retired faculty to continue engaging with the university, while the CCCC "Standing Group for Senior, Late-Career, and Retired Professionals in Rhetoric, Composition, and Writing Studies" likewise provides an arena for continued professional activity and interaction. All three of us benefited from these further sources of information we had not considered or that were not available when we started our own research.

A PROJECT THAT CONTINUES TO EVOLVE

Our project remains one "in progress." Not only is there much more to do, but that work takes us down several paths simultaneously. As Maureen Daly Goggin and Paul N. Goggin describe in their introduction to *Serendipity in Rhetoric, Writing, and Literacy Research* (2018), "What one can rely on is an open mind, one that is ready for the messiness and one that learns to stay comfortable within the mire of unknowing as well as a process of preparing that mind" (p. 6).

Sometimes it is chaotic; always it is a bit muddied because there's never just one thing going on at a time while we examine and code the surfeit of information we have gathered. We also continue to read and listen, learning and adding to what we know, and to investigate links to similar research, past and present. In this collection alone are multiple resources from existing research, and the chapters that follow offer innovations we had not previously considered.

Repeatedly, we have discovered that sometimes the "messiness" that Goggin and Goggin (2018) refer to appears simply because life intrudes. Economic or political realities, natural disasters, a pandemic, or an unexpected international war may interrupt the progress of a project like ours. Personal and family health issues, as well as unexpected situations encountered in other areas where we had commitments, affected our work and required us to be flexible. With three of us, it was not unusual for one or two of us to cover for a third, to make small or large changes for the common good, or to fill in gaps for one another; and we simply accepted it as a part of the research process. That is one of the advantages of lifespan writing research that is collaborative, as noted in so many of the chapters in this collection.

Our lifespan writing research is not complete. We continue to find ways to share portions of what we have gleaned so far through conference presentations and other activities. These opportunities allow us to focus ever more closely on not only what we are discovering, but also how we are discovering it and how it might be used. That means writing proposals to present at conferences, and then creating appealing and informative presentations. Also, we have taken parts of our research to use in more specific studies regarding lifespan writing. For instance, why did such a large percentage of our respondents leave writing center positions after less than ten years? How might we conduct case studies on the impact of writing center work on directors' moves to other positions in academia? How does or does not the role of mentoring change over the lifespan of former writing center directors? Individual responses to our survey and follow-up questions take on different meaning as we reread them and reflect on new improvisational directions for our research.

We have already connected diversity, equity, and inclusion (DEI) responses to our interview questions in a presentation at CCCC in March of 2022 and participated in the CCCC Standing Group for Senior, Late-Career, and Retired Professionals in Rhetoric & Composition/Writing Studies. We have several other research avenues currently in progress on this endless journey of lifespan writing research. The dissemination of information has also involved writing this chapter and proposing a book explaining and exploring our findings, possibly as part of a series of publications on lifespan writing research, and writing a chapter for a forthcoming book on the role of collaboration in our ongoing research. Most recently, we organized an international session at IWCA 2021 to discuss forming a Special Interest Group (SIG) of "Past, Present, and Future Writing Center Directors." The fifteen attendees at that online session were early career, mid-career, late-career, and retired writing center directors. They decided that the SIG would be important to "support, exchange, advise, and collaborate (SEAC)" with one another. We proposed another SIG for the fall of 2022, and IWCA has made our SIG permanent. Through that group, we have also met new writing center directors who have moved our work in a new direction of multigenerational writing center research and mentorship. Finally, we continue to consider ways to establish new initiatives—activities that will serve others in the future, such as a blog, a listserv, a regular journal column, or a formal mentoring project. Who knows what a Call for Proposals, suggestion from a former writing center director, rereading of an article, or critical thinking among the three of us might lead to in the future? We may come up with some new "messiness" based on the innovative research in the chapters that follow this one!

IMPLICATIONS FOR OTHERS DOING LIFESPAN WRITING RESEARCH

For novice researchers and those new to lifespan writing research, we hope readers will see the trajectory of our work as an example of the organic, experimental, experiential, and sometimes chaotic quality of each research experience and the often improvisational journey from one research project to a related, more specific, or different one. Our lifespan writing research involves questioning ourselves and others, taking risks that may change our methods and lead us into new directions, listening to the voices and ideas of others, and adapting old or creating new methods of research. Managing this ever-evolving research project and juggling all its pieces is often messy and not always easy, but the process of conducting and sharing it continues to keep each of us engaged in a very fulfilling and rewarding example of lifelong learning and sharing what we learn in the form of lifespan writing research.

REFERENCES

Adams, T., Jones, S. H. & Ellis, C. (2015). *Autoethnography*. Oxford University Press. https://doi.org/10.1002/9781118901731.iecrm0011.

Anthony, Jr., A. R., La Rochelle, J. S., Dezee, K. J. & Gehlbach, H. (2014). Developing questionnaires for educational research: AMEE Guide No. 87, *Medical Teacher*, 36(6), 463–474. https://doi.org/10.3109/0142159X.2014.889814.

Bazerman, C. (2020, July 10). *Trajectories, moments, dimensions: Some neighborhoods I have passed through*. [Conference presentation]. Lifespan Writing Online Conference.

Bishop, W. (1997). You can take the girl out of the writing center, but you can't take the writing center out of the girl: Reflections on the sites we call centers. [1996 SWCA Keynote Address]. In W. Bishop (Ed.), *Teaching lives: Essays & stories*. (pp. 157–166). Utah State University Press.

Bowen, L. M. & Pinkert, L. A. (2020). Identities developed, identities denied: Examining the disciplinary activities and disciplinary positioning of retirees in rhetoric, composition, and writing studies. *College Composition and Communication, 72*(2), 251–281. https://doi.org/10.58680/ccc202031037.

Brooks, A. C. (2020, May 7). How to build a life: Why so many people are unhappy in retirement. *The Atlantic*. https://tinyurl.com/57xtkwkv/.

Bruffee, K. (1984). Collaborative learning and the 'conversation of mankind.' *College English, 46*(7), 635–652.

Duncan, M. (2004, December). Autoethnography: Critical appreciation of an emerging art. *International Journal of Qualitative Methods*, 3.

Ellis, C., Adams, T. E. & Bochner, A. P. (2011). Autoethnography: An overview. *Forum: Qualitative Social Research, 12*(1). https://www.qualitative-research.net / index.php/fqs/article/view/1589/3095.

Fuchs, M. (2021). Don't want to retire? Here's how to maintain a fulfilling career into your 80s and beyond. *The Washington Post*. https://tinyurl.com/3xvbhbse.

Goggin, M. D. & Goggin, P. N. (Eds.). (2018). Stumbling into wisdom in rhetoric, writing, and literacy research: An introduction. *Serendipity in rhetoric, writing, and literacy research*. Utah State University Press, 3–9.

Henery, C. (2022, April 19). Public history, autoethnography, and community: An interview with Jodi Skipper. *Black Perspectives*. https://tinyurl.com/4ft2c6eu.

Hughes, B., Gillespie, P. & Kail, H. (2010). What they take with them: Findings from the peer writing tutor alumni research project. *The Writing Center Journal 30*(2). https://writing.wisc.edu/pwtarp/.

Jeter, A. I. (2016, December). *The high school peer tutor alumni research project*. [Dissertation]. Indiana University of Pennsylvania.

Lave, J. (1993). The practice of learning. In S. Chaiklin & J. Lave (Eds.), *Understanding practice: Perspectives on activity and context* (pp. 3–32). Cambridge University Press.

Lave, J. & Wenger, E. (1990). *Situated learning: Legitimate peripheral participation*. Cambridge University Press.

Penrose, A. (2012). Professional identity in a contingent-labor profession: Expertise, autonomy, community in composition teaching. *WPA: Writing Program Administration, 35*(2), 108–126.

Sherwood, S. (2011, February). A career in the writing center: Entering academe through the back door. [Conference presentation]. South Central Writing Centers Association, Houston, TX.

Wenger, E. (1998). *Communities of practice: Learning, meaning, and identity*. Cambridge University Press.

APPENDIX A. THE WRITING CENTER DIRECTOR ALUMNI RESEARCH PROJECT SURVEY

Participants: Former writing center directors who have either retired or moved on/back to other careers, in or out of academe.

Purpose: To examine how the experience of directing a center has informed/influenced participants' civic/professional/volunteer life after leaving the center.

Methodology: Survey followed by interviews and/or focus groups.

SURVEY

Purpose of Research

You are being asked to participate in a research study that will gather information on the extent to which your identity as a writing center director has influenced you in re-shaping your professional identity and the ways in which you have adapted your scholarly and professional expertise to address issues and audiences beyond the discipline. Specifically, you will be asked to answer questions about your experiences beyond those as writing center director in other careers or retirement.

Benefits to the Individual

There are no direct benefits to you other than the opportunity to reflect on your own experiences; however, there may be benefits to others in the profession or in society, such as mentoring and material for further research.

Confidentiality

Survey results will be delivered and reported anonymously. Even if participants reveal themselves by naming specifics in their responses that might identify them, the research team will not reveal the specific participant. We may ask participants to volunteer participation in follow-up interviews, but those interviews will also be anonymous unless the participant chooses to become known.

Survey Questions

1. What is your current age?
   __under 30   __30–39   __40–49   __50–59   __60–69   __70/over

2. What is your gender/sexual identity *[if determined to be relevant to this study]*?

3. What is your race/ethnicity *[if determined to be relevant to this study]*?

4. How long did you work in a writing center? How long as director?

5. What other positions, if any, did you hold in the writing center?

6. How long ago did you leave your last writing center work as director?

7. What academic training prepared you for a writing center position (check all that apply):
   __Postdoctoral study __PhD/EdD __MA/MFA/MS
   __Certificate of Advanced Graduate Study in __Rhet/Comp
   __English __other (name)

8. What avenues of ongoing professional development did you pursue (check all that apply):
   __coursework __additional degree(s) __IWCA Summer Institute
   __conferences __reading/research __collaborative work with other writing center directors ___ self-directed research __other (name)

9. In what ways did you contribute to writing center scholarship (check all that apply):
   a) publication of __ scholarly books __ articles __chapters __tutor guides __ regular columns;
   b) conference presentations __international __national __regional __keynote addresses
   c) __invited presentations/workshops
   d)__held leadership positions in regional/national/ international writing center organizations

10. How were you appointed to the directorship?
    __result of national search __promoted from within
    __directed by administration __other (name)

11. What was the nature of your position?
    __TT Faculty __Non-TT Faculty__Administration __Staff
    __Part-time Faculty/Part-time Director __other (name)

12. If your position was faculty, how was it counted?
    __release time (how much?) __part of teaching load __other (name)

13. Where was your writing center housed?
    __stand alone __department/program (name)
    __college/school within institution __learning center (or similar entity)

14. What was the reporting line for your position?
    __Department Chair(name) __WAC Director __Learning Center Director/ Dean (or similar entity) __Academic Dean (name) __Provost/Academic Vice President __other (name)

15. Why did you leave writing center work?
   __choice __position eliminated __terminated __position/operation of writing center altered __other (name)

16. What did you do upon leaving writing center work?
   __retired __returned to faculty __moved to administrative position __moved to another academic institution __left academe

17. If retired, what have you done since retiring (check all that apply):
   __volunteer work __consulting __writing/publishing in the field
   __writing/publishing outside the field __presenting at conferences
   __attending conferences __adjunct teaching __activist work __other (name)

Respondents will be able to answer questions 10–15 for each center they've directed.

Narrative responses:

In what ways has your experience as a writing center director informed your subsequent work/activity?

Are there any ways in which your experience as a writing center director may have impeded your subsequent work/activity? If so, how?

How might you have better prepared yourself for life after the writing center?

What is the most valuable thing that you've taken from your experience as a writing center director?

What do you wish you had known before becoming a writing center director?

Would you like to add anything to your responses?

If you are willing to participate in a follow-up interview, please leave your email address here so that we may contact you.

APPENDIX B. EMAIL INVITATIONS

Email Invitation to Listservs

Are you no longer a writing center director? Have you moved out, moved up, moved on, or retired? If so, we would appreciate your going to https://www.surveymonkey.com/r/RCKPVGG and completing our anonymous survey. We will be sharing the results of our survey at future regional, national, and international conferences as well as in a future publication. We appreciate your taking the time to reflect on your own experiences as a writing center director to help current and future writing center directors. If you are willing to offer suggestions or answer follow up interview questions, please respond at the end of the survey. We hope you enjoy this experience as much as we did completing the survey ourselves!

Email Invitation to Individuals Known to Have Been Writing Center Directors

Because you have worked as a writing center director, we would appreciate your going to https://www.surveymonkey.com/r/RCKPVGG and completing our anonymous survey. We will be sharing the results of our survey at future regional, national, and international conferences as well as in a future publication. We appreciate your taking the time to reflect on your own experiences as a writing center director to help current and future writing center directors. If you are willing to offer suggestions or answer follow up interview questions, please respond at the end of the survey. We hope you enjoy this experience as much as we did completing the survey ourselves!

Email Invitation to Individuals Who May Have Been Writing Center Directors

If at any time in your career you have worked as a writing center director, we would appreciate your going to https://www.surveymonkey.com/r/8VFZJM9 and completing our anonymous survey. As we receive responses, we will be sharing the results of our survey at future regional, national, and international conferences as well as in a future publication. We appreciate your taking the time to reflect on your own experiences as a writing center director to help current and future writing center directors. If you are willing to offer suggestions or answer follow up interview questions, please respond at the end of the survey. We hope you enjoy this experience as much as we did completing the survey ourselves!

Follow-up Email

Thank you so much for agreeing to respond to some follow-up questions for our project, "Identity, Activity, and Community Practice in the Writing Center and Beyond: What Departing Directors Carry with Them" (or essentially, The Former Writing Center Director Project).

This research project began as we each dealt with retirement and discussed among ourselves what it meant. After years directing a writing center, what were we taking with us as we left? For this study, we expanded our questions and concerns to include all people who had directed a writing center at any point in their careers. When we asked you that question, your answers were similar to ours—broad things like "management skills" and "an appreciation for collaborative learning." Now we would like you to dig a little deeper and tell us even more.

We have returned to Wendy Bishop's comment, made when she left directing a writing center to assume another administrative position: "you can take the [person] out of the writing center, but you can't take the writing center out of the [person]." We wondered, what does it mean that the writing center is in us? We decided it meant that we infused the writing center with aspects of our identity and vice versa. To get at how that happens, we'd appreciate your exploring more fully the ways in which your identity has been shaped by your writing center experience, and how you shaped the identity of your writing center(s). To do that, please respond to the following questions, elaborating as you see fit.

APPENDIX C. FOLLOW-UP INTERVIEW QUESTIONS

1. In what ways, if any, did your writing center(s) reflect you? How would you characterize the ethos of your writing center(s)? And how have you carried that ethos into your work after leaving the director's position?
2. What challenges did you have to overcome as director of a writing center (e.g., physical space, funds, needed items to function, clear mission, administration, taking over from a previous director)? Any specific examples would be helpful.
3. What other interests were you engaged in outside the writing center while you worked as director? Have you continued to pursue those interests, or what new interests/activities/hobbies have you pursued since leaving the center? Have any been connected to your experience as a writing center director? If so, how?
4. What are you most proud of accomplishing in your center(s)? What did that accomplishment reveal about you, personally and professionally? How have those qualities served you in your work after leaving your writing center position?
5. What skills, values, and abilities served you best during your writing center career? In what ways has the knowledge you gained as writing center director served you in any of your work since stepping away from the writing center? Give any specific examples from your own experience.
6. A writing center is often described as a community of practice, one that is defined by collaboration. What does this description mean to you? In what ways might this description fit with your experience(s) as a writing center director and your experiences since leaving the director's position?

APPENDIX D. FURTHER PRESENTATIONS AND WORKSHOPS

"The (HE)ART of It All: What Departing Writing Center Directors Carry with Them" (IWCA, 2019)

"Identity in the Writing Center and Beyond" (Mid-Atlantic Writing Centers Association, 2019)

"The Writing Center Director Alumni Research Project: Re-shaping Professional Identities" (European Association of Teachers of Academic Writing, 2019)

"Beyond the Writing Center: What's in Your Backpack?" (Writing Through the Lifespan Collaboration, 2021)

"Re-shaping Professional Identities: The Writing Center Directors Alumni Project" (CCCC, 2021)

"Past, Present and Future Writing Center Directors' SIG (IWCA, 2021)

"'Welcome to the Writing Center': Encouraging Inclusivity in the Writing Center" (CCCC, 2022)

"Taking the Commonplace Out of the Common Place: How Do Former Directors Adapt Writing Center Culture in New Venues?" (CCCC, 2022)

"Empowering Writing Centers: What We Can Learn from Former Directors" (European Writing Centers Association, 2022)

CHAPTER 12.

A MATTER OF TIME AND MEMORY: A METHODOLOGICAL FRAMEWORK OF MEMORY FOR LIFESPAN WRITING RESEARCH

Joe Cirio
Stockton University

Jeff Naftzinger
Sacred Heart University

This chapter considers memory as a methodological concept, one that can clarify our relationship to the knowledge we seek to make about lifespan writing for interested researchers. If lifespan writing research is interested in "studying literacy development *over wider segments of time*" (Dippre and Phillips, 2020, p. 3, emphasis added), then *memory work*—the processes and products of remembrance—appears to be a necessary entry point to understand this expanse of (life)time. We specifically draw upon social theories of memory which approach the past as a shared text, one that is constantly being reshaped and revised given present needs. Given that lifespan writing research is interested in how writers negotiate their past and prior writing experiences, a focused consideration of memory as methodology provides perspective about the questions and epistemologies that go into such remembrance. However, although there have been efforts to rehabilitate the concept of memory in writing and rhetorical studies (e.g., Reynolds, 1993 and Horner, 2000), there has not yet been an articulation of how memory could operate as a methodological basis to guide writing and literacy research—both for lifespan writing research specifically and for composition theory more broadly.

In what follows, we first define the relationship that lifespan writing research has with inquiries of time. Establishing this relationship to time is important because it provides the justification to consider memory, which we define as the rhetorical process and product through which the past is constructed. We then propose five principles that forward our methodological framework. These principles are adapted from the assumptions for public

DOI: https://doi.org/10.37514/PER-B.2024.2289.2.12

memory offered by Blair, Dickinson, and Ott (2010) in their introduction to *Places of Public Memory*. The principles that we articulate reimagine how Blair, Dickinson, and Ott's assumptions can serve to reframe the work in lifespan writing research and offer a basis for continued work in this area of research. The five principles are:

1. Memory is concerned with representations of the past for a present purpose.
2. Memory is a material, constructed, rhetorical process that is necessarily in flux, mutable, and porous.
3. Memory is cultural, collective, and inter-generational.
4. Memory is distributed cognition involving infrastructures and systems that support and impact memory processes.
5. Memory can address questions about "stickiness."

In each discussion, the principle is defined and situated within existing lifespan writing research. Particular attention is given to what a framework of memory can draw attention to: the processes and products of memory that researchers can seek from writers, the methods and techniques to gather information on the processes and products of memory, and the inquiries and knowledge that are possible from orienting towards memory.

WRITING THROUGH THE LIFESPANS: A MATTER OF TIME AND MEMORY

This inquiry into memory as methodology must begin with defining the relationship lifespan writing has with time. The focus on writing across the life*spans* directs inquiry towards people's literacy experiences through the expanse of life— or the literacy experiences "from cradle to grave" (Dippre & Phillips, 2020, p. 6). Lifespan writing research, then, is tethered to inquiries of time, particularly in the ways writers represent and imagine the moments and movements of literacy experience across a lifetime. The centrality of time is in part acknowledged in the first of eight principles offered by the Lifespan Writing Development Group (Bazerman et al., 2017). Namely, the authors emphasize that lifespan writing research attends to how writers across the lifespan draw upon, repurpose, and make use of their past and prior writing knowledge and experiences. The authors explain,

> As roles and responsibilities expand across the lifespan, people reconsolidate past learning while encountering new demands and challenges. How people are able (and invited) to bring

their writing pasts in new contexts provides a basis for further writing development. . . . (Bazerman et al., 2017, p. 354)

Lifespan writing research poses compelling questions about how writers invoke and repurpose their *past* writing experiences; about what mechanism and materials activate and mobilize those *past* experiences; about how writers invoke the *past* to engage in a *present* writing task; about how we can prepare for *future* writing activities; and about how we preserve and make way for the recirculation of literacy objects for the *future*. The temporality of literacy experiences, in this sense, is the *object* of study in lifespan writing development: for writing-researcher and writing-subject alike, our gaze turns toward the movements and moments in time that collectively compose the writer and our writerly experiences. But if time is the object of study, then memory is the methodology.

Social frameworks of memory, influenced by social theorists like Maurice Halbwachs (1980), will often define memory in its relationship to time. Namely, that memory is the rhetorical product that is constructed to make sense of one's past. In their introduction to *Places of Public Memory*, Blair, Dickinson, and Ott (2010) describe an analogy posited by Halbwachs to understand memory in relationship to time, drawing a connection to the relationship between place and space:

Place : space :: memory : time

In other words, place is to space what memory is to time.[1] The authors explain,

If places are differentiated, named 'locales,' deployed in and deploying space, we might suggest that memories are differentiated, named 'events' marked for recognition from amid an undifferentiated temporal succession of occurrence. Both place and memory, from this point of view, are always rhetorical. They assume an identity precisely in being recognizable—as named, bordered, and invented in particular ways. They are rendered recognizable by symbolic, and often material, intervention. (Blair, Dickinson & Ott, 2010, p. 24)

Time and the sequences of time are the resources for rhetorical knowledge—memory is the meaning-making process to make sense of time. Writing

---

1   This analogy likewise poses the possibility of *place* as a methodological concept for life*wide* writing research. In other words, if lifewide refers to an interest in the "many social spheres that writers participate in" (Dippre & Phillips, 2020, p. 5–6), then place-based inquiries and metaphors of "wayfinding" (Alexander, Lunsford & Whithaus, 2019) can describe how writers make sense of the expanse of "lifespaces."

knowledge might be understood as a stable-for-now or just-in-time assemblage of undifferentiated temporal resources: prior writing experiences, writing processes, writing beliefs, dispositions, knowledge, points of departure, and so on (Yancey, 2017). Writers activate, mobilize, and assemble these priors to engage in an immediate writing task. This is a process of memory, and memory assemblages are rhetorical actions.

Framing memory as a rhetorical process would also allow us to break away from understanding memory and the past as located within various cognitive functions; rather, the value of a public, collective approach to memory is its attention to representation which moves memory beyond simply a storage system within an individual's brain. Memory work, then, involves the construction of discursive, rhetorical products that reveal and facilitate shared ideology and shared social practices. Framing memory in this way, an attention to memory prompts methodological questions about what factors influence the *articulation* and the *becoming* of memory—or maybe more broadly, the articulation and becoming of the past.

Taken together, framing memory as both a rhetorical process and product of time provides an avenue to consider memory as a methodological framework, especially in the study of lifespan writing development where there is a particular interest in reflecting upon the convergences of past, present, and future. If this emergent area of research on lifespan writing has an interest in how writers—from cradle to grave—invoke and re-invoke their writing pasts to navigate writing presents and futures, then the processes and products of memory work become our entry point to begin that methodological inquiry.

FIVE PRINCIPLES OF METHODOLOGICAL FRAMEWORK OF MEMORY

Our goal in proposing memory as a methodological framework is not to dramatically alter the way research into lifespan writing is conducted; rather, our interest is to flesh out a methodological orientation that appears already threaded in the work being produced in this area. The five principles we offer below function more as observations from research interested in writers' priors, including prior "processes, dispositions, beliefs, knowledge, and points of departure" (Yancey, 2017, p. 314). With them, we hope to articulate what a memory methodology can offer lifespan writing and composition studies given our particular interest and goals. Though the distinction between methodology and method has been notoriously slippery in writing research (Nickoson & Sheridan, 2012), we approach our methodological framework as a "theory and analysis of how research does or should proceed" (Harding, 1987, p. 2 qtd. in Schell, 2010,

p. 2). Our reference to this memory methodology as a "framework" has been deliberate since a frame functions to shape and unify an understanding of our circumstances. As Adler-Kassner and O'Neill (2010) describe, "the ideas of frames and framing can be applied to the constructions of what individuals and groups perceive to be realistic and feasible, or unrealistic and out of the realm of possibility" (p. 16). In articulating our methodological framework, we have sought to define what is possible and feasible in three areas of conducting research: *ontologically*, i.e., what is considered meaningful data?; *procedurally*, i.e., what methods or techniques can gather such meaningful data?; and *analytically*, i.e., what questions can such data answer for us? For each principle, we seek to address some of these three questions by pointing to extant research already circulating in lifespan writing scholarship as well as speculate at the kinds of data, methods, and questions that are possible if we frame our research under the banner of memory.

1. Memory is Concerned with Representations of the Past for a Present Purpose.

Though memory is focused on the past, it is a rhetorical process that we engage at a present moment in order to solve immediate problems. Blair, Dickinson, and Ott (2010) begin their assumptions on public memory with this very idea: memory work is rhetorical work, meaning that selecting and re-constructing aspects of the past can communicate for ourselves or others who we are at the current moment—the conditions, beliefs, ideologies, and goals. In lifespan writing scholarship, researchers will often rely on writers to reflect on their past and prior writing experiences to help us understand their development over time as a way to understand what has shaped their current literacy actions. In oral historical research, oral historians recognize that a narrator's testimony reveals something about their *relationship to the past* rather than a whole and accurate conduit to the past. In his foundational theoretical work on oral history, Alessandro Portelli (1981) notes that narrators of the past "tell us not just what people did, but what they wanted to do, what they believed they were doing, and what they now think they did" (p. 99–100). In doing so, narrators are communicating something about what is presently valuable about the past and their relationship to it. For writing and literacy researchers, such thinking appears to be aligned with our particular interests: what are the literacy experiences and actions in a writer's development that have shaped who the writer is now and what they will do?

Procedurally, in writing research, researchers will invite writers to access their prior knowledge and experiences by engaging in some form of reflection, conceived by Yancey (1998) as a dialectical process that entails "casting backward to see where we have been" and based on "what we know, what we have learned, and what we might understand" (p. 6). Yancey's conceptualization of reflection focuses on how the invocation of the past is goal-oriented and geared toward understanding something about who the writer is and where they are going—it bridges temporal concepts of past, present, and future. Roozen (2016) applies this concept through a method of reflective interviewing, through which a researcher uses a writer's own writing artifacts to stimulate the writer's recall and trace their literacy histories and motivations. Roozen makes clear how the past bridges into the present and future. Certainly, such reflective practices can offer researchers a "means of understanding a person's experiences with texts and textual practices from other times and places;" yet, he also notes how such invocations of the past also reveal what literacy practices are shaping the writer "in the immediate here and now of the ethnographic present" (p. 255). Inviting writers to reflect upon their past—whether with reflective interviewing, literacy narratives, textual personal narratives, or life-stories (Knappick, 2020) necessarily involves writers making sense of their literate lives. As Knappick notes, by "creating a coherent story, segmenting and ordering *their past*, research subjects are making sense of *their present*" (p. 68; emphasis added).

These techniques of collecting data on writers' development through reflection recognize the contingent and selective nature of this memory work. The methodological framework of memory values ambiguity as a necessary component to its work because such ambiguity invites analysis and interpretation about one's *link* to the past—and the material, social, and ideological contingencies that make that link possible. In engaging writers in these reconstructions of the past, we are not accessing a singular and "accurate" moment from a writer's life as we discuss their development. Instead, we're encountering a *reconstruction* of that memory that can reveal something about their relationship to that moment in the past and the current conditions that make that reconstruction possible.

2. Memory is a Material, Constructed, Rhetorical Process that is Necessarily in Flux, Mutable, and Porous.

Memory is also an externalized, material practice that is supported by various memory objects, systems, and technologies. Memory theorist Jan Assmann (2008) explains that cultural memory operates as a kind of institution that is built and sustained through objects and materials that are "exteriorized, objectified, and stored away in symbolic forms" (p. 110). As he explains, "Things do not 'have' a memory of their own, but they may remind us, may trigger our memory, because they carry memories which we have invested into them, things such as dishes, feasts, rites, images, stories and other texts. . . ." (Assmann, p.

111). Assmann provides a way for us to explore the kinds of literacy artifacts, materials, and objects that are necessarily wrapped up in a writer's lifespan. If we want to have a full discussion about a writer's past and how they conjure and invoke that past, then we necessarily need to inquire into the kinds of literacy objects and materials that circulate in their literate practices.

Yet, objects are not always stable conduits of memory. Objects, like the memory work they can facilitate, are in flux, mutable, and porous. How we use certain objects, what meanings we attach to them, and how we relate to them might change depending on when and how we interact with them. For example, among the scenes of everyday writing discussed in Yancey et al. (2020) is a notebook from Bessie Dominick Suber, "poorly preserved with dates ranging from December 19, 1964 to November 4, 1979" (p. 17). The authors describe how the notebook is a dynamic intertext "which changed over the years as Bessie's life did" (p. 18). For Bessie, the notebook is a space of becoming where she can engage in reconstructing her identity and her relationship to her communities by returning to and revising this material document. Such a complex object does not represent a single moment or a clear set of sequences of development but, instead, represents layers of literacy experiences that the authors call an "a-chronological" "intertextual palimpsest" (p. 20). Though this notebook appears to be of particular complexity, it invites researchers to view any literacy object as intertextual palimpsests. In other words, literacy objects like these will change as they move through time and space. As they are witness to these passages of time, they change as they are written in, revised, grafted, or stored with other objects, yellowed and damaged with age, or become lost completely. And likewise, the memories associated with these objects are capable of manipulation, of getting lost, of degrading, of being repaired, of being hidden or displayed, and of being shaped by the situations in which they are recalled.

In research on writers' lifespan development, several methods and techniques of gathering data have engaged writers in discussing and reflecting upon materials and objects to help in their recall. In Bowen's (2020) literacy tours, for example, participants lead Bowen through the spaces where they engage in literate activity and highlight objects that point towards the "role of materiality in literacy development" (p. 116). These literacy tours involve a wide variety of literacy objects and materials: "predictably literacy-related objects, such as books, computers, writing instruments, and notebooks, as well as less obviously literacy-related artifacts: photographs, chairs, maps, model vehicles, clocks, and other objects" (Bowen, 2020, p. 117). As they point out the materials that play a role in their literate activity, they are necessarily invoking and constructing their past and prior experiences and negotiating the public memories surrounding those objects.

Writers' literate lives are inextricably entwined with resources, materials, objects, and technologies that anchor and give shape to our literacy development. Researchers' engagement with these objects—these companions to literate lives—is rhetorical memory work. Such objects can operate as prisms that can shape how a writer articulates and reflects upon their past literacy experiences.

3. Memory is Cultural, Collective, and Intergenerational.

In framing memory as "exteriorized, objectified, and stored away" (Assmann, 2008, p. 111), we can begin to consider memory as collective—as something that groups can share and, both figuratively and literally, pass on to others. Objects, as Assmann claims, have a certain degree of stability and "may be transferred from one situation to another and transmitted from one generation to another" (p. 111). Objects carry with them common ritual that groups can share in re-enacting or common practices that are re-produced across different individuals and people. These objects thus become a point of convergence to orient groups together and form a common, collective sensibility.

This orientation is illustrated by White-Farnham's (2014) concept of *rhetorical heirlooms* where writing practices and genres are passed down, inherited, and repeated from generation to generation. White-Farnham offers the "household literacy practices" of Edna who mediates her life through "writing recipes, planning meals, writing grocery lists, and maintaining a budget;" yet these writing practices also "reflect and perpetuate values central to Edna's family life, such as their Italian heritage and eating meals together" (p. 210). The re-use and re-creation of these household literacy practices operate as ritual, repeated practices that can link the present to the past and link the individual with the collective. Ritual practices like these rhetorical heirlooms are memory work; these textual objects and rituals serve to define our relationship to our shared past and navigate our shared present.

Ritual can also serve as a particular technique of research—as a mode of knowledge-making through re-inhabiting or re-playing the movements and behaviors of another as a way to gain a view from their particular perspective. Shipka (2021), for example, uses repeated practice to form a bridge between herself and a couple named Dorothy and Fred, ordinary people whose boxes of memoria were bought by Shipka at a yard sale. Shipka describes being moved to "try to understand something of these strangers' lives, relationship, and experience while adding to and reflecting on my own" (p. 114). Her method of seeking this connection was through re-staging and re-tracing a trip, documented in Dorothy's travel diaries, that Dorothy and Fred made from Baltimore to St. Louis in the summer of 1963. As Shipka (2021) explains:

> While my partner and I based our movements on those of strangers, we inevitably transformed that trip, making it our own—populating it with our own rhythms, histories, and intentions. In this way, their experiences, practices, and memories became folded into, and thus transformed, our own. (p. 114)

Like memory work more broadly, ritual is not a perfect gateway to the past—it is not that Shipka retraces the trip to form a whole and accurate account of this experience from 1963; rather, Shipka sought to form a relationship to the past and, in particular, these people she never met. Retracing this trip allowed Shipka a new perspective on who this couple was—not necessarily as a project for preservation, but to collaborate with the dead "to learn how the past might 'break through into the present in surprising ways'" (Cresswell 2010, p. 19, qtd. in Shipka, 2021, p. 115).

Shipka demonstrates a compelling method of collaborating across generations of dead and not-yet-born—working across documents and memoria to recreate and retrace a past experience which could, in turn, be recreated in the future. The implication of such a process is that some sensibility, affect, and/or knowledge is being handed off, generation after generation.

Shipka does not speak directly to what exactly such re-staging and re-tracing *does*, yet there are certainly deeper implications to these ritual practices in terms of circulating particular ideologies. Consider, for instance, an historical inquiry from Fullmer (2012) into typewriter technologies in the early 20th century. As he observes, the typewriter was used in the classroom to reinforce and recreate a formalist writing pedagogy and the typewriter itself "provides a means of 'standardized' and 'form-alized' writing" (p. 60). As a technology, the typewriter is imbued with a particular ideology through the rituals and practices that we attach to them *in the classroom*. But Fullmer observes how these same ideologies moved into the *household* as typewriters became a common household appliance and these efforts "seemed suppressed by the mechanical constraints of the typewriter and the form-alist pedagogy" that framed its use (p. 69). Fullmer's example demonstrates the deeper implications of a ritual literacy practice centered around a literacy object: they circulate particular ideologies, even harmful ones, as these objects move through various spaces in life. And while the typewriter is distributed across individual homes, the ritual practices are nonetheless shared and collected which influence the way writers act and frame writing as a collective.

White-Farnham, Shipka, and Fullmer exemplify the ways that ritual, repeated practice can have the dual function of tethering past to present (and future) and individual to collective. Thus, memory work operates not simply at the nexus of temporal questions of representing past, present, and future—it also simultaneously operates to conjure and build a *shared* past, present, and future. This principle of memory, then, can help us extend our research beyond thinking about writing development as involving a single lifespan and can instead help us think about development across *lifespans* and the ways in which these shared processes or collective connections can shape that development.

4. Memory is Distributed Cognition Involving Infrastructures and Systems That Support and Impact Memory Processes.

As we work with social and material approaches to memory, our attention must necessarily include the relationship between the process of remembrance and the systems of objects, materials, and environments that are necessarily part of that process. Scholars researching memory, like Derek Van Ittersum (2009), have offered distributed cognition as a model to understand memory and the ways that externalized systems of materials augment the capacity of an individual's memory. Framing lifespan writing research in the context of memory frameworks can help us develop inquiries into the ways writers exist and construct environments, systems, or infrastructures that invoke particular kinds of prior writing knowledge and thus affect literacy. When we understand memory as distributed cognition, then we might frame memory not simply as something we invoke, but rather something we can *inhabit.* Memory may operate similarly to what Johnson-Eilola (2004) refers to as the datacloud, the environments or spaces that information workers inhabit in order to "work with information, rearranging, filtering, breaking down, and combining" (p. 4). These spaces go beyond simply information stored on a computer (read: computer memory); they also extend to environments that include a variety of technologies and tools to mediate the composing process. The datacloud offers a compelling parallel to memory work where writers construct environments that render certain kinds of remembrance—and likewise certain kinds of literacy—possible.

Some of the possibilities in observing the relationship between memory, environment, and literacy—and the benefits of these observations for lifespan writing research—can be seen in Jacob Craig's (2019) research into the "writing sanctuaries" that writers construct to support their writing processes. One participant of Craig's study, Maggie, sought to recreate a workflow environment that echoed that of her childhood despite being in a new location and faced with new, college-level writing tasks. Craig writes that Maggie

> [n]ot only found focus as she had in childhood and mitigated the stress of the writing task as she had on the couch

in her first apartment, she 'felt creative,' realizing the affective potential of her mobile sanctuary to help her invent discourse. (n.p.)

Maggie's experiences demonstrate a compelling link between a writer's prior writing knowledge and the writing environments that they construct. Maggie's re-creation of a childhood writing sanctuary allowed her an avenue to a writing past in order to accomplish an immediate goal. Such writing sanctuaries offer a material space for research inquiry in lifespan development: not simply what objects and materials exist in that space, but how it's arranged and facilitates a writer's work flow.

Craig's work aligns well with inquiries posed by social memory theorists like Olick (2007) who, likewise, understands memory as distributed across a collection of representations and symbols; yet he notes that memory researchers attend particularly to publicly available resources of remembrance. Specifically, memory inquiries must necessarily involve attention to "what symbols and words were available to [people] in which times and places and hence with how those cultural frameworks are prior to, and thus shape, their intentions" (Olick, 2007, p. 7). Olick pushes us to consider questions of accessibility and availability of materials and technologies of remembrance—as well as the barriers and gateways that make certain resources accessible. In other words, we should consider how the objects and technologies that augment and enhance human memory can also define the bandwidth of what's possible by defining how that memory is accessed: what can be remembered and what is supposed to be forgotten? These regimes of remembering and forgetting are what Nathan Johnson (2020) has referred to as memory infrastructures. These memory infrastructures are not simply environments that individuals can construct; rather, it refers to the institutional forces involved in designing what is remembered for a public. Johnson offers examples of libraries and archives that use systems of selection and documentation, labor forces, and often institutional and hegemonic imperatives that, according to Johnson, "do not merely document pieces of the past; they anchor, shape, and compose remembering and forgetting" (p. 15).

5. Memory Can Address Questions About "Stickiness."

A methodology of memory also allows attention to questions about what sticks, which is particularly salient for writing researchers because it addresses what kinds of writing knowledge, experiences, and practices find resonance with our students: what is going to be remembered? What is kept, what is recirculated, and what is transferred from one context to the next? What's going to be invoked by students in the future and why? Invoking "student" is deliberate since the teaching of writing often forms the center of our disciplinary work. For many of us, educational institutions are our dominion: it's where we work, it's where we regularly share and circulate our knowledge, and is often the site of our research and where we *make* our knowledge about writing. But in terms of a lifespan, K-12 and college education are only a relatively brief and transitional moment in the life of a writer; however, school literacies remain deeply embedded in writers' approaches to writing in the lifespan. Barton and Hamilton (2012) remark that they had assumed that their study of the literacy activities of everyday people in Lancaster, UK would uncover a "distinct home literacy which could be contrasted with work literacy or school literacy," but instead, they discovered how work, school, and home literacies "mingle together" in the home (p. 188). Since school can so often be a sticking point for writers, the question of *what sticks* occupies a great deal of attention for researcher-educators: if we only have a handful of brief moments to engage students in writing knowledge, then we really need to think about what sticks and what is going to be remembered. Stickiness, in this sense, frames memory as both a question directed to the present (What prior experiences or knowledge will a writer uptake in a given moment?) and future (What will resonate?).

Researchers in the transfer of writing knowledge have sought to address this question of stickiness. The teaching for transfer curriculum, for instance, from Yancey, Taczak, and Robertson (2014), seeks to address how we, as teachers, "can help students develop writing knowledge and practices that they can draw upon, use, and repurpose, for new writing tasks in new settings" (p. 2). But even before we point to the future, we already know the major writing knowledge that sticks with our students. Wardle (2012) has noted the ways students' learning dispositions are a reflection of the institution of which they are a product. And specifically, the over-reliance of standardized testing and the corresponding culture of such testing creates an environment that socializes students in a way that limits "the kinds of thinking that students and citizens have the tools to do" (Wardle, 2012, n.p.). In demonstration of the impact of such socialization of writing knowledge, research from Cirio (2019) underscores Wardle's conclusions: students in Cirio's study on classroom rubric negotiation had drawn upon their previous experiences with rubrics that they were already familiar with and would offer rubric criteria that teachers had hoped to disrupt in negotiating the rubric. Put simply, certain writing knowledge is, indeed, sticking with students as they move through the education system and move beyond it—yet it appears that not all that writing knowledge is particularly useful for students and may misinform them about how writing works as they move in new, unfamiliar writing situations.

These are concerns of memory. Rounsaville (2012), in fact, argues that the focus on "uptake" in research on writing transfer is dealing with the complexities of memory work. Uptake, for Rounsaville, provides a language and frame to describe how knowledge transfer is a process of *selection* and *translation* of "heterogeneous and even contradictory memories" (n.p.). Rounsaville recognizes that prior writing knowledge and experiences are invoked to solve new, unfamiliar writing problems; namely, "past experiences serve as platforms and interpretive frames for solving problems of new and unfamiliar genres and are recalled precisely because of the task at hand" (n.p.). An attention to uptake would invite researchers to "trace and track those memories within textual and generic systems that are grounded in the student's own writing logic" (n.p). In this sense, uptake draws attention to the interfaces that make certain connections to the past possible—or not. Rounsaville discusses John, a first-year student who had trouble linking his past writing experiences in a college preparatory school with an assignment in his first-year writing course. Although John was able to point to a variety of past writing experiences and complex writing practices (e.g., the role of scholarly texts in academic writing), he was unable to bridge those experiences in a meaningful way to a particular writing task in first-year writing. As an issue of stickiness, John demonstrates how even complex and useful prior writing experiences may not always stick or be taken up to solve a particular problem.

Educational institutions and specifically our classrooms, then, operate in much the way that Johnson (2020) describes memory infrastructures. In that sense, certain writing experiences appear particularly salient for students and, by design, define the scope of what's possible in the future. Yet, students also have rich, literate lives both in and out of a writing classroom, so a memory methodology can address the kinds of writing that are most useful for our students and how educators design regimes of remembering and forgetting that can prescribe certain kinds of knowledge. Put another way, memory methodology poses inquiries into how we create stickiness, how we invoke particular kinds of uptake, and how we can trace futurity, but not simply as educators, as researchers. Memory methodology invites researchers to consider the writing knowledge and prior experiences that writers carried with them and why.

CONCLUSION

Our intention with offering a methodological framework of memory was to identify and describe a thread that we believe was already embedded in lifespan writing research. As we have forwarded, memory can describe (a) a process of invoking, reconstructing, and remembering the past; and (b) the material, rhetorical products that construct the past. Memory's relationship to the past appears well suited to provide a unifying methodological framework to lifespan development research since this emergent field of study seeks to understand how the prior experiences of a writer's life(time) is constitutive of their current writing practices. The lifespan perspective is unique in its consideration of a writer's movement through time and how they make sense of such development over time. In that sense, memory is something that's always being engaged in the research process. And framing the research process under the banner of memory can offer a scope of (a) the kinds of data to collect that can speak to writers' priors, (b) what methods to use in order to collect that data, and (c) what questions such past-oriented data can address for us.

Drawing upon rhetorical and social approaches to memory offered an understanding of the materiality of memory: that memory is mediated by *things* that have a relationship with or have some tether to a shared past. For lifespan writing research, exteriorizing memory as material *things* is necessary for the research process since representations of the past are the basis of our data. And like any *thing* of memory, what we encounter as researchers can be collected, selected, constructed, arranged, shared, circulated, destroyed. But most importantly, these things move through time and shift as they encounter the social and material world. These things of memory are companions to one's life, witnesses to one's past, and an insight into one's development. Likewise, these things can be touchstones to writers' pasts as well as touchstones to their collective communities. With a rhetorical-material approach to memory, lifespan development research's interest in wider segments of time can go beyond simply the individual writer and extend outwards to the multi-generational collective.

We've also observed how existing research in lifespan writing already engages techniques of data collection that align with a memory framework. Methods like document-based, reflective interviews (Roozen, 2016) and literacy tours (Bowen, 2020) use objects, tied to one's prior writing experiences, to, in part, stimulate a writer's recall. But even those methods go beyond simply recalling one's past and instead, work towards bridging how the writer's prior writing development informs their current literacy knowledge and practices. And methods like Knappick's (2020) literacy narratives explicitly understand such narratives as revealing more about one's present and immediate circumstances, even if it's pointed to the writer's past. We've also noted the possibilities of less conventional techniques such as ritual as a method of knowledge-making: Shipka (2021) reimagines a researcher's relationship to the memory objects they may encounter, even from everyday or personal archives like estate sales or your attic. A researcher can gain insight into a collective literacy experience by recreating and re-inhabiting the movements of complete strangers, accessed through the literacy materials they've left behind. Our principles also open questions about the site of our research, whether the ways writers construct and inhabit writerly pasts (see Craig, 2019) or different kinds of archives of literacy objects. Johnson (2020), in particular, invites conversations about how regimes of remembrance, like archives, can reveal *what* a community remembers about their past and *how* that community should remember that past.

Turning toward the future of lifespan writing research, we believe a memory framework can reorient the kinds of questions that we can seek to answer through the collection of data oriented towards one's past. Just as a theorist of public memory will seek to understand the social function of monuments in public space, lifespan writing researchers might turn our attention to what we believe our "monuments to literacy" may be and what that may mean. And here we mean "monuments" literally: what are those material things that unify communities of writers? How are those things tied to a shared past? How do these things bring a writer's past to bear on their literacy practices and writing knowledge? How are those things constructed and responsive to various social, cultural, and collective entanglements? The frame of memory that we've proposed prioritizes questions that recognize literacy development as constelled in communities, as grounded in materiality, and as rhetorically constitutive.

Like any methodological approach, our framework provides only a beginning, a prospectus about what is possible in our understandings of lifespan writing. We have offered a point of departure from which we believe all lifespan writing research can branch: an orientation towards wider segments of time and the multiple ways writers conjure and make sense of those literacy moments and movements through a constellation of lifetimes.

REFERENCES

Adler-Kassner, L. & O'Neill, P. (2010). *Reframing writing assessment to improve teaching and learning*. Utah State University Press. https://doi.org/10.2307/j.ctt4cgrtq.

Alexander, J., Lunsford K. & Whithaus, C. (2019). Toward wayfinding: A metaphor for understanding writing experiences. *Written Communication, 37(1),* 104–131. https://doi.org/10.1177/0741088319882325.

Assmann, J. (2008). Communicative and cultural memory. In A. Erll & A. Nünning (Eds.), *Cultural memory studies: An international and interdisciplinary handbook* (pp. 109–118). De Gruyter. https://doi.org/10.1515/9783110207262.2.109.

Barton, D. & Hamilton, M., (2012). *Local literacies: Reading and writing in one community*. Routledge. https://doi.org/10.4324/9780203125106.

Bazerman, C., Applebee, A. N., Berninger, V. W., Brandt, D., Graham, S., Matsuda, P. K., Murphy, S., Rowe, D. W. & Schleppegrell, M. (2017). Taking the long view on writing development. *Research in the Teaching of English, 51,* 351–360. https://doi.org/10.58680/rte201728980.

Bowen, L. M. (2020). Literacy tours and material matters: Principles for studying the literate lives of older adults. In R. J. Dippre & T. Phillips (Eds.), *Approaches to lifespan writing research: Generating an actionable coherence* (pp. 111–125). The WAC Clearinghouse; University Press of Colorado. https://doi.org/10.37514/PER-B.2020.1053.2.07.

Blair, C., Dickinson, G. & Ott. B. L. (2010). Introduction. In G. Dickinson, C. Blair & B. L. Ott (Eds.), *Places of public memory: The rhetoric of museums and memorials* (pp. 1–55). University of Alabama Press.

Cirio, J. (2019). Meeting the promise of negotiation: Situation negotiated rubrics with students' prior experiences. *WPA: Writing Program Administration, 42*(2), 100–118.

Craig, J. (2019). Affective materialities: Places, technologies, and development of writing processes. *Composition Forum, 41.*

Dippre, R. J. & Phillips, T. (2020). Generating murmurations for an actionable coherence. In R. J. Dippre & T. Phillips (Eds.), *Approaches to lifespan writing research: Generating an actionable coherence* (pp. 3–11). The WAC Clearinghouse; University Press of Colorado. https://doi.org/10.37514/PER-B.2020.1053.1.3.

Fullmer, S. (2012). "The next takes the machine": Typewriter technology and the transformation of teaching. In S. Borrowman (Ed.), *On the blunt edge: Technology in composition's history and pedagogy* (pp. 52–71). Parlor Press.

Halbwachs, M. (1980). *The collective memory* (2nd ed.). Harper & Row. (Original work published 1950)

Horner, W. B. (2000). Reinventing memory and delivery. In M. D. Goggin (Ed.), *Inventing a discipline: Rhetoric scholarship in honor of Richard E. Young* (pp. 173–184). National Council of Teachers of English.

Johnson-Eilola, J. (2004). *Datacloud: Toward a new theory of online work.* Hampton Press.

Johnson, N. (2020). *Architects of memory: Information and rhetoric in a networked archival age.* University of Alabama Press.

Knappick, M. (2020). Making sense of a person's literate life: Literacy narratives in a 100-year-study on literacy development. In R. J. Dippre & T. Phillips (Eds.), *Approaches to lifespan writing research: Generating an actionable coherence* (pp. 67–80). The WAC Clearinghouse; University Press of Colorado. https://doi.org/10.37514/PER-B.2020.1053.2.04.

Nickoson, L. & Sheridan, M.P. (2012). *Writing studies research in Practice: Methods and methodologies.* (1st ed.). Southern Illinois University Press.

Olick, J. K. (2007). *The politics of regret: On collective memory and historical responsibility.* Routledge.

Portelli, A. (1981). The peculiarities of oral history. *History Workshop Journal, 12*(1), 96–10. https://doi.org/10.1093/hwj/12.1.96.

Reynolds, J. F. (1993). Memory issues in composition studies. In J. F. Reynolds (Ed.), *Rhetorical memory and delivery: Classical concepts for contemporary composition and communication* (pp. 1–16). Lawrence Erlbaum Associates.

Roozen, K. (2016). Reflective interviewing: Methodological moves for tracing tacit knowledge and challenging chronotopic representations. In K. B. Yancey (Ed.), *A*

Rounsaville, A. (2012). Selecting genres for transfer: The role of uptake in students' antecedent genre knowledge. *Composition Forum, 26.*

Schell, E. E. (2010). Introduction: Researching feminist rhetorical methods and methodologies. In E. E. Schell & K. J. Rawson (Eds.), *Rhetorica in motion: Feminist rhetorical methods and methodologies.* (pp. 1–22). The University of Pittsburgh Press. https://doi.org/10.2307/j.ctt5vkff8.5.

Shipka, J. (2021). Rethinking past, present, presence: On the process of mobilizing other people's lives. In B. Horner, M. F. Hartline, A. Kumari & L. S. Matravers (Eds.), *Mobility work in composition* (pp. 112–126). Utah State University Press. https://doi.org/10.7330/9781646420209.c007.

Van Ittersum, D. (2009). Distributing memory: Rhetorical work in digital environments. *Technical Communication Quarterly, 18*(3), 259–280. https://doi.org/10.1080/10572250902942026.

Wardle, E. (2012). Creative repurposing for expansive learning: Considering "problem-exploring" and "answer-getting" dispositions in individuals and fields. *Composition Forum, 26.*

White-Farnham, J. (2014). "Revising the menu to fit the budget": Grocery lists and other rhetorical heirlooms. *College English, 76*(3), 208–226. https://doi.org/10.58680/ce201424523.

Yancey, K. B. (1998). *Reflection in the writing classroom.* Utah State University Press. https://doi.org/10.2307/j.ctt46nsh0.9.

Yancey, K. B. (2017). Mapping the prior: A beginning typology and its impact on writing. In P. Portanova, J. M. Rifenburg & D. Roen (Eds.), *Contemporary perspectives on cognition and writing* (pp. 313–330). The WAC Clearinghouse; University Press of Colorado. https://doi.org/10.37514/per-b.2017.0032.2.16.

Yancey, K. B., Cirio, J., Naftzinger, J. & Workman, E. (2020). Notebooks, annotations, and tweets: Defining everyday writing through a common Lens. *South Atlantic Review, 85*(2), 7–34.

Yancey, K. B., Robertson, L. & Taczak, K. (2014). *Writing across contexts: Transfer, composition, and sites of writing.* Utah State University Press. https://doi.org/10.2307/j.ctt6wrr95.

CHAPTER 13.

WRITING IN TRANSITIONS ACROSS THE LIFESPAN

Soledad Montes
Lancaster University

Karin Tusting
Lancaster University

Lifespan Writing Research (hereafter, LWR) has focused on observing writing practices over time as they move and change throughout the lifespan. Dippre and Phillips (2020) refer to the lifespan as the "entirety of a lifetime" as it unfolds "across the many social spheres that writers participate in" (p. 5–6). They call for both life-long and life-wide inquiry that leads us to observe the developing writer's multiple activities in their naturally dynamic and not necessarily linear forms.

Observing writing development along the entire lifespan is a challenging task. That is why LWR has regarded itself as a methodologically eclectic approach. This heterogeneity allows us to build the whole picture of writing development collaboratively. There are, in fact, different angles through which we can observe the lifespan of a writer and how their writing practices change all along the way. We can look at how writers master different genres or focus on how knowledge about writing is transferred from one context to another. This chapter contributes to this choral effort by reflecting on one particular angle of the human life course: transition.

Life-course transitions, such as changing jobs or moving from school to the workplace, could be a valuable entry point from which to observe developing writers' challenges, struggles, achievements, and learnings across time. While some studies on transitions rely on rigid understandings of change—as some authors have already pointed out (see Quinn, 2010; Colley, 2007; 2010)—we would like to explore other approaches that give us some analytical and methodological tools to explore transitions in alignment with lifespan writing research's main insights. This chapter will examine some of the latest contributions to the comprehension of transitions, mainly based on feminist theory and on critical concepts from Deleuze and Guattari (1987), highlighting the notion of *transition as becoming* and the inherent diversity of life course transitions. We will consider several aspects of this diversity, including diversity in contexts, identities, and time, drawing on insights from New Literacy Studies. Finally, we will discuss some implications of these perspectives on transitions for LWR methodologies.

WHAT IS TRANSITION?

Transitions have been traditionally referred to as changes in the life course that involve shifts of context, identities, and social roles (Colley, 2010; Ecclestone et al., 2010). Some transitions are regulated by educational institutions, such as passing from kindergarten to school, from primary to secondary education, or from secondary school to university. These movements encompass new identities and writing practices that shape and are shaped by those contexts. Other transitions, such as the one from single to married status, involve our social relationships and inscribe them in a civil law framework, shaping, for instance, the way we are referred to in legal documents. A job change implies getting involved in a new community in new roles and perhaps writing emails from a different interpersonal position. All these life course changes imply identity negotiations, as transitioning subjects change their social roles and the way they engage in daily activities with others. They also concern writing practices, as writers engage in different literacy events while transitioning across contexts and identities.

Within the literature on educational research and practice, transitions have been widely understood as periods of crisis. Researchers have depicted them as delimited periods of intense change that lead to a final stage of stability and adaptation to a new culture or social status. This comprehension of transitions has one of its roots in the concept of *rites of passage*, first introduced by Van Gennep (1960). He understood that human development is structured by a series of passages that function as markers of life change. According to Van Gennep, transitions follow a pattern of pre-liminal rites (rites of separation from a previous stage); liminal rites (during the transitional phase); and post-liminal rites, those unfolding when the individual is incorporated into a new world and status. Some works on "liminality" have paid attention to the "spaces in between," foregrounding the uncertainty and indeterminacy of the process (Gourlay, 2009; Turner, 1995). Other studies describe transitions as a sequence of stages, such as Nicholson and West's (1995) description of the transition to higher education organized in the phases of preparation, encounter, adjustment, and stabilization. Thus, transitions have been seen as time-limited periods preceded and followed by periods of stability. The extension of this period has also been outlined with specific landmarks. For example, Coertjens et al. (2017) define the end of the transition to higher education when the moment of the first assessment comes. These fixed depictions tend to neglect the fact that change and movement are constantly unfolding and disregard individuals' positionings in the social structure as if people all have the same opportunities, social repertoires, and economic capital when they go through transitions.

Since the pivotal work of Van Gennep, it has been recognized that transitions involve a social component in the form of social expectations and regulations. They are often socially regulated by institutions such as schools or the civil law. These institutions hold discourses and ideologies that also shape our understandings and expectations. Just as we could sustain an "autonomous model" of literacy (Street, 2005) by disregarding social conditions and cultural understandings of what it is to read and write, we could also do the same with transitions by depicting them according to what is expected from a normative perspective. The representation of a linear progression from kindergarten to primary school, from secondary education to higher education, and so forth tends to subsume many people's diverse realities into one universal process, often regarded as *the* successful progression.

As many authors point out, such a view neglects many experiences, struggles, and trajectories (Quinn, 2010; Colley, 2007; Nordquist, 2017). The fact that transitions are socially determined makes them highly diverse depending on social class, gender, ethnicity, among others. At the same time, even though there are social expectations regarding when and how specific transitions "should" occur, such as the age when students "should" enter university, contemporary individuals' trajectories are more diverse. People are more likely to change jobs as the labor market is more dynamic (Ecclestone, 2009), and students traditionally excluded from higher education are now entering university (Cupitt & Trinidad, 2017; Lillis, 2001; Villalobos et al., 2017).

This scenario pushes us to build new understandings of transitions in the lifespan. Recent research describes transitions as more fluid processes using terms like *transition as becoming* (Gale & Parker, 2014) or *life as a transition* (Colley, 2007). From this perspective, transitions are not described as shifts from one homogeneous and stable context or identity to another; rather, transitioning is a permanent condition of people's lives. We will discuss some of the contributions of this approach to transition, and their potential usefulness for studying writing across the lifespan.

TRANSITION AS BECOMING: A RHIZOMATIC UNDERSTANDING

Many recent works in transitions rely on the notions of *rhizome* and *becoming* developed by Deleuze & Guattari (see Amundsen, 2021; Gravett, 2019; Taylor & Harris-Evans, 2018). The concept of the *rhizome* (Deleuze & Guattari

1987) refers to a non-linear and non-hierarchical system with multiple entryways and exits. This helps us think of transitions as nonpredictable *becomings* that can spread in various directions. Changes of context and identities across time should not be depicted as predictable or occurring in developmental stages but as dynamic processes that vary from person to person. This contrasts with approaches to writing development which compare two points (e.g., primary and secondary school) and assume the latter will be superior (Smith 2020). This common expectation fails to acknowledge the multiple writing contexts in which students participate (Ivanič et al., 2009; Barton & Hamilton, 1998) and the many influences on their writing abilities beyond school.

We suggest that transitions in the lifespan should be understood as processes within a more complex orchestra of simultaneous changes and becomings, which can evolve in multiple ways. Mainstream paths in transitions, such as from secondary to higher education, are not the only "correct" or "logical" sequence. Seeing transitions as rhizomatic pushes us to regard them without a predefined idea of their direction and order. Expectations of what a "typical" transition looks like are significantly determined by our social position and views.

Trajectories such as school to workplace, job to further education, or in and out of university are common for people traditionally not represented in mainstream educational paths. Such is the case of Kurdish women refugees entering and leaving formal education in cycles described by Mojab (2006) and analyzed by Colley (2007; 2010), or the working-class and first-generation students interviewed by Quinn et al. (2005), who dropped out of university before completion but desired to return. Students from our current research on transitions after school in Chile also have shown far from linear trajectories. One of our participants, a student in her last year of secondary education, is not planning to enter university after finishing school but to join her father's gardening business, which she started to learn at ten-years-old. For her, this choice is compatible with studying in university after a period or while working:

> I have to see how I will sort it out because, to be honest, even if I study advertising I would like to keep my job maintaining gardens because it is what I know most about and if it comes a moment when I am tired of carrying the machines, cutting the grass, the heat and everything, so if it comes the moment when I say, 'I cannot do it anymore', I can work in that what I studied.

Transitions have been regarded as shifts of *contexts* and *identities* across time. They are socially regulated and shaped by social expectations, discourses and socially determined possibilities, access, and opportunities. They are concerned with changes situated in core areas of our human activity; our social practices and the identities that we create within them. A clear understanding of contexts and identities could provide many clues of how to study transitions and writing across the lifespan.

Transitions and Contexts

Transitions, as life-course phenomena, should be regarded from both a *life-long* and *life-wide* perspective in the same way that lifespan writing practices should be (Dippre & Phillips, 2020). The life-wide perspective helps us to see how the multiple contexts in which people engage change simultaneously around significant life transitions. In transition to higher education, for example, this means taking into account not just the movement from school to university but also all the daily activities in different contexts occurring on a smaller scale. This means understanding transitions across the lifespan as multidimensional rather than as a change from one unified context to another.

This multidimensionality has been considered in transition research using metaphors like 'vertical' and 'horizontal' transitions (Kagan & Neuman, 1998). Vertical transitions indicate movements between more extensive periods of an individual's life (Zigler & Kagan, 1982), such as the one from primary to secondary education. As they commonly represent progress across educational levels (Johansson, 2006), vertical transitions tend to be regulated by social institutions, such as ministries of education, national curricula, and lifelong learning policies. In contrast, horizontal transitions refer to those movements happening in shorter time frames, even daily, when individuals move across life spheres (Kagan & Neuman, 1998). Another scale is introduced by Spelman Miller & Stevenson (2018) with the idea of micro transitions in writing, referring to the negotiation of different genres, learnings, and modalities or semiotic systems. These various dimensions (vertical, horizontal, micro) require an ecological approach to fully capture them. In this vein, Johansson (2006) highlights the importance of looking at the interactions between different scales of transitions as they occur in the entire experience of individuals. These perspectives suggest a layered idea of writing practices and contexts in transition.

Changes in context are frequently associated with changes in writing practices, a connection highlighted by the New Literacies Studies understanding of literacies as a social practice. One of the central precepts of this approach is that "there are different literacies associated with different domains of life" (Barton & Hamilton, 2000, p. 8). The workplace, school, university, home, and healthcare, among others, are all different life domains in which we can see a range of literacy practices that materialize in concrete writing events mediated by texts.

Life transitions across time are rarely a movement from just one isolated context to another. On the contrary, when transitions occur, many contextual changes frequently unfold simultaneously. For example, when students move from school to university, they are not just shifting from school culture to university culture; they participate in a more diverse range of social domains such as home and family, political groups, and the workplace. In this vein, depicting "the transition from school to university"—or any other—as a movement between just two homogeneous contexts does not recognize the complexity of human activity and the literacy practices shaping and being shaped by those activities.

Transitions and Identities

The concept of *becoming* (Deleuze & Guattari 1987) is also illuminating to understand the relationship between transitions and identity. It refers to the continual production of differentiation in which the self is permanently unfolding in an ongoing process of change. The process of becoming does not begin with a delimited entity; this is not *someone* becoming *someone else*. On the contrary, our entire subjectivity goes through a constant movement of becoming. This means that when we look at people's life transitions—and writing practices within them—we might want to avoid representations of change as a movement from instability to stability, from struggling to adaptation, or from an unsettled identity to a complete one. Rather, individuals constantly negotiate their identities as they participate in diverse life domains. This understanding pushes us to look at these change processes with an open mindset, without hoping for a "final stage" where the transition is over but looking at transitional movement through more extended observations to see the nuances of changing processes as they unfold through time.

Identity positions us in relationships with others and is built through social participation in concrete activities mediated by cultural tools and artifacts (Russell, 1997). Ivanič (1998) writes of *identification* as the "process whereby individuals align themselves with groups, communities, values, beliefs and practices" (p. 11). Wenger's (1998) notion of identity as an experience negotiated through participation in communities of practice shows how subtle the edge between identity and context is. Understood in this way, it becomes clear that there are multiple identities as we participate in various life domains.

For example, when students enter university, they are not "becoming somebody" but adding new nuances and possibilities to their multiple identifications with others' values, beliefs, and discourses, some of which might even conflict with each other, as Lillis (2001) showed in her research with non-traditional students. Similarly, Zavala (2011) explores tensions between Quechua students' identities and academic cultures. These identity negotiations are a crucial element of any transition and commonly occur in the interaction of artifacts, institutions, and social actors in different positions of power.

Hamilton (2010), analyzing transitions in adult learning, understands identities—following sociocultural theories—as relational in nature, emphasizing how they are built and rebuilt through interaction. She explores transitions into and through the Skills for Life program for adult literacy and numeracy developed in 2001 in the UK and observes how artifacts and social actors mediate the construction of narratives and identities of both students and tutors in the program. She shows how identity is not only in a permanent state of becoming but is also socially and culturally negotiated. Regarding educational transitions, these identity negotiations are frequently determined by institutional narratives about what it is to be, for instance, a university student, or a student in an adult literacy program.

The role of institutional narratives and the *possibilities for self-hood* (Ivanič, 1998) they offer to individuals are key to understanding the multilayered complexities of identity negotiations in transitions. As Ecclestone (2009; Ecclestone et al., 2010) has pointed out, transitions are changes of contexts and identities where individuals have a space for agency but are also regulated by social expectations and institutional constraints. This means that identity negotiations in transitions could be observed in individual participation and interactions and in the relationship with institutional regulations, which are frequently built through cultural artifacts such as texts. In this vein, Hamilton (2010) shows how guidelines, exams, screening tests, program descriptions, etc., in the Skills for Life adult learning program helped to construct institutional narratives and sometimes promoted stigmatized identities. Following Hamilton, it is critical to think about such intersections among texts and socially constructed identities in transitions. We suggest that both a multi-context and a multi-identity approach are needed, allowing us to understand the natural dynamic of these life-course changes and their connections with meaning-making processes through writing.

Transitions and Time

Time is a fundamental concept for transitions as every transition constitutes changes of contexts or/and identities *over time*. Just as contexts and identities are multiple, time can be conceptualized as multiple and diverse rather than simply linear.

Colley (2010) argues that the most widespread understanding of time in transition research and theory is triadic; time is organized into past, present, and future. For instance, Biesta and Tedder (2007) depict human agency as iterational orientations (influences from the past), projective orientations (to the future possibilities), and practical-evaluative orientations (regarding the present). From this point of view, agency regards "the formulation of projects for the future and the realization of those projects in the present" (Colley, 2010, p. 134). This understanding, criticized by Colley, shows a positivistic approach to time as a one-direction progression projected according to the individual's will.

However, time is not necessarily linear but can be perceived in diverse ways in people's actual experiences. As Tusting (2000) points out following Zerubavel (1981), time can indicate boundaries between one social domain and another. Students inhabit different social roles in higher education, for instance in "class time" versus "break time." In these different times, "ways of doing things" in social practices (Wenger, 1998) dramatically change, such as rules for making questions or interrupting a conversation.

By looking at how time unfolds at this more micro level, we can see how its linearity vanishes. Time passing leads us from one context to the other. A popup message could make us think about a future holiday destination; a few minutes later, we return to the chapter that we were writing before. At the same time, we can recognize different time scales (Burgess & Ivanič, 2010). Following Adam, Tusting (2000) emphasizes the "multiplicity of times" (p. 41); the time frame of an individual's life history is very different from the broader historical sweep. We could add to these the time experienced in daily activities while people engage in concrete events mediated by writing.

Nordquist & Lueck (2020) challenge the tendency to separate literacy development into homogeneous levels like "high school writing" and "college writing," which neglects actual diverse students' experiences with reading and writing in their daily lives. These linear representations of time set social expectations attached to age and cognitive development: "These stages are reinforced with appeals to ostensibly predictable relations among age, grade level, and cognitive, curricular, and social processes of development" (Nordquist & Lueck, 2020, p. 254). Following these ideas, we attempt to reinforce the multiple nature of time and how the experience of time as it progresses in an individual's concrete life events is not necessarily reflected in broader narratives of time as a linear progression.

STUDYING TRANSITIONS AND WRITING IN TRANSITIONS ACROSS THE LIFESPAN: METHODOLOGY AND METHODS FROM A RHIZOMATIC PERSPECTIVE

Researching writing across the lifespan is a significant challenge that requires collaborative efforts and multiple gateways to approach the complexity of people's writing practices in the frame of their life-long and life-wide trajectories.

We have suggested that transitions in the lifespan are just one more angle to explore, but a meaningful one as transitions represent shifts in core areas of human development. A focus on transitions could encompass questions such as: how are changes of context involving new social roles and identities in someone's life course linked with writing practices in meaningful ways?; how do social expectations and individuals' agency shape changes across contexts and identities?; how do social institutions regulate life-course transitions, and what is the role of artifacts such as text within them? We might want to look at specific transitions, for instance, the movements in and out of university or the entry to an adult learning program. Looking at those changes as transitions involves accounting for an individual's life history of participation in multiple contexts where identities and social roles are negotiated.

Transitions could be looked at vertically, along time and across institutions, or horizontally across contexts in a smaller time range. In particular, horizontal transitions could also be understood from writing across contexts (Prior & Smith, 2020; Kell, 2011) or transliteracies approaches (Stornaiuolo et al., 2017), contributions that have played a pivotal role in LWR. Finally, the angle of transitions focuses on changes encompassing identity negotiations and forms of participation in different time scales.

Transitions and the ways we understand context, identity, and time are not neutral. On the contrary, they have been depicted in diverse manners that imply particular epistemologies, methodological approaches and methods of inquiry. Looking at transitions is a rich node for exploring writing practices across the lifespan, but this could be looked at through different lenses. Consequently, it is critical to be aware of our own lenses and their implications.

Looking at transitions from a rhizomatic perspective has several methodological implications. It involves understanding writing practices as contextualized activities in peoples' lives, unfolding in diverse and dynamic trajectories of change across multiple levels of contexts, times, and identities. We suggest at least three main methodological orientations to study transitions and writing across the lifespan. We will also give examples of particular methods that lifespan researchers could incorporate when they take this stance.

1. Openness

When we look at one specific transition, we are always at risk of assuming a previously defined trajectory. For instance, we might be tempted to explore school to university or university to workplace without recognizing that these trajectories are not necessarily the same for everybody. When we decide to study a particular transition, it is always worth asking ourselves: what diversity of possible trajectories could we consider? Are there movements that we are not taking into account? How could we be open to unexpected movements? Which social factors such as social class, gender, ethnicity, among others, could be shaping how transitions unfold?

Being aware of the variety of possible trajectories, and being open to exploring those we did not predict, could be helpful at different levels of research. For instance, in the sampling phase, we can choose participants who could experience transitions differently rather than work just with those who will follow mainstream careers. Moreover, we could incorporate openness during interviews by not assuming a specific direction in participants' transitions. Participants of our current research who were interviewed in their last year of secondary education were from economically deprived neighbourhoods in Chile. Even though they were part of an inclusion program to access higher education, going to university was not taken for granted for many of them. We tried to keep open to and hear their desires and expectations, often attached to the social valuing attributed to tertiary education but sometimes linked to other careers or possibilities.

An open mindset could also be adopted during the coding process. Broadly speaking, coding involves organizing data by labeling them within themes or categories. Coding is in itself an exercise of data simplification, reduction, and abstraction. It takes us "away from the data—from their detail, complexity and singularity" (MacLure, 2013, p. 169). Following Deleuze's critiques of representational thinking, MacLure points out that coding tends to use a tree-like hierarchical structure that organizes data in categories and subcategories in static relationships. This logic could lead us to "recode what is already coded by language culture, ideology and the symbolic order" (p. 170) and, more importantly, it could prevent us from taking into consideration those elements that might not fit with our previous understanding of a phenomenon or with our coding scheme. This openness to unpredicted interpretations is especially critical when social contexts become particularly unpredictable or unwieldy, as was explored by Ávila et al. (2021) in their research in times of social unrest and pandemic.

Regarding transitions, as we seek to capture change over time and across contexts in a way that involves multiple identity negotiations, it seems particularly important to avoid coding schemes that might restrict our capability to see how change is inscribed in the data along a period of time. This is also relevant to capture identities in their plurality and intrinsically dynamic becoming. In other words, if we want to observe the negotiation of identities that are not only multiple but changing over time, fixed tree-like themes and categorizations might not always be helpful. From our perspective, this view on coding does not imply abandoning themes and categories but using them more flexibly by allowing us to hold those fragments that do not fit or enabling the emergence of more rhizomatic connections between different elements of our data.

Some researchers in transitions have applied a rhizomatic approach to data analysis (see Taylor & Harris-Evans, 2018; Amundsen, 2021) by focusing on "data hot-spots" that seem to carry complex relationships of language, emotions, and thoughts. In this vein, MacLure suggests incorporating the practice of *unforgetting* by holding fragments and details in slow and intimate work with data. We encounter various elements that resist coding in our current study. For instance, one of our participants repeatedly used a question prosody when asserting or answering a question. This was a persistent tendency in our interviews with her, showing us the interpersonal nature of our interactions and the imbalance of power in them. Her silences, doubting prosody, and conciseness could also be expressing something else, something that escapes our current ways of thinking, but we are committed to not forgetting those signs, even though we still wonder about their meaning.

2. Motion

As some lifespan researchers (Bazerman, 2013; Dippre & Phillips, 2020) and researchers of writing across contexts (Prior & Smith, 2020; Kell, 2011) have pointed out, writing has commonly been studied from a one-context perspective. Since the turning of the new century, the notion of context has gained increasing attention from writing research (Lillis, 2008). Linguistic ethnography has frequently explored one setting by prolonged immersion in the context, using field notes and detailed observations, among other methods. These techniques have enormously contributed to writing studies, focusing on the writing event or the activities mediated by texts rather than on the written piece as the main object of inquiry. However, exploring writing practices across contexts remains a central challenge (Prior & Smith, 2020).

We commonly depict a movement from one context to another when studying transitions (e.g., from a job to another, from university to a job, etc.). However, research on transition usually focuses on the "new setting," where the person is transitioning to (see Hebdon, 2015; Megwalu, et al., 2017; Elliott et al., 2019). A step forward to capture the complexity of transitions could be to explore the two reference points in our transition, such as school and university, for example, through a longitudinal study across educational levels. We can take another step forward by looking at the diversity of contexts students engage with while moving from school to university, from one job to another, or from university to work. This multisite approach allows us to explore how people experience transitions in the context of their life as a whole rather than as an isolated phenomenon. In this vein, if we observe transitions at the end of schooling, we can look at people's movements across context and identities as their life trajectories unfold and explore the diverse roles of writing across these.

To observe movement across time imposes significant methodological stakes. It implies the need to perhaps follow our participants across settings or find meaningful ways to talk with them about their several spheres of social activity. Various studies have challenged the one-setting approach by moving with participants across time and contexts. Nordquist (2017) incorporates time-space mappings and *shadowing* (Jirón, 2011) in his research about writing and mobilities. He "became the shadow" of his participants by walking with them in their daily activities from school to home, from home to extracurricular activities, work, etc. While shadowing participants' routines, he took field notes, had more informal conversations, and recorded interviews throughout the day. This seems to be a valuable tool to observe transitions as they unfold across time and context and to explore the writing practices that shape both those movements and settings.

Barton et al.'s (2007) repeated interviews across time with adult learners is also worth mentioning. The researchers conducted several interviews focusing not just on participants' experiences with reading and writing but on the broad context of people's lives in different careers: work, health, education, etc. They use temporal representations of events within these trajectories and explore how writing practices are entangled with individuals' experiences in several life domains. The authors also capture the materiality and spaces of social practices by using photographs of places or meaningful objects. In our current research, we discuss with our participants some of the texts they wrote for school and other contexts. We regard these texts as artifacts mediating concrete activities and ask for them in their original format to see how these cultural tools were used. For instance, some of these texts were notes on a wrinkled piece of paper; other times, they were cellphone notes with letters and emojis. Working with artifacts as they exist in the context of the activity that they mediate allowed us to see through them our participants' several social practices and writing practices.

3. Repetition

Researching transitions as a permanently unfolding process of change over time and across contexts requires detailed observation of people's practices. As other researchers within LWR have stated, longitudinal observations comparing two predefined points—for instance, first and second year of university—do miss the spaces in between. In transition research, those spaces in between are regarded as transitional stages or liminal sites in transition studies. These spaces are precisely one of the defining aspects of transitions, as moments where changes of contexts and negotiation of multiple identities show the mobility and unsettledness of individuals' experiences. One observation of a particular context or one interview before and after is not enough to capture this subtleness of transitions; on the contrary, we need sustained engagement through repeated interactions or/and observations across time.

A central methodological principle of ethnography is sustained engagement (Hammersley, 2006; Lillis, 2008) in a particular setting. This could be challenging when observing writing practices in transitions as they unfold across several contexts. However, as Lillis (2001; 2008) and Ávila (2021) suggested, long term engagement could be incorporated in research as long conversations with participants. Lillis suggests conducting cyclical talking around text interviews with several encounters with participants. This methodological tool seeks to consider students' perspectives on their processes of meaning-making through writing. This *emic perspective* helps us hold the principle of openness described above and is a valuable way to avoid the *reification* (Lillis, 2008) of what participants say or describe as immutable and easy to translate into general principles.

In our current research, we engage in repeated encounters with our participants. We seek to understand the role of writing practices as students move out from school to new settings after secondary education. Through our interviews, we found many horizontal and micro-level transitions while students were in their last year of school. They faced an unprecedented pandemic that forced schools to shift to online learning. Writing practices mediated by technologies became preponderant in the school classroom with laptops, cellphones, emails, online platforms as new tools for communication and learning. In our first interview, one of our participants told us how difficult it was for her to write on her laptop. Her dad was a porter and a resident of the building he was working in gave him a disused laptop. This was now the computer of our participant, and she was getting familiar with this new tool: "Technology was difficult for me . . . even though we are the youth that knows, for me was too difficult," she says. However, at our second interview a few months later, she had become accustomed to using her laptop for school homework and even for personal fictional writing which she used to write in a notebook. After the first interview, our impression was that technologies could be challenging for students who did not have earlier access to them; the reification of this judgment would have led us to a misunderstanding. We would have missed how new mediational tools could have evolving meanings for our participants and play changing roles in their practices.

CONCLUSION

In this chapter, we have explored the concept of transitions and shown the importance of considering transitions as a diverse and rhizomatic phenomenon. We have argued that the concept of *transition as becoming* is likely to be a more fruitful way to approach transitions for lifespan writing researchers than seeing transitions as simple linear shifts over time. Drawing on researchers from New Literacy Studies and from LWR, we have emphasized the importance of understanding context, identity and time as dynamic phenomena of multiple layers, and discussed methodological implications of this for writing research across the lifespan. In particular, we call on lifespan researchers to adopt the principles of openness, movement across contexts, and repeated data collection across time, to develop fuller understandings of how writing practices develop, transform, and remain, as people transition between different contexts throughout their lifetimes.

REFERENCES

Amundsen, D. (2021). Life is not always linear: expanding the notion of transitions in higher education to challenge structural, static and linear processes facing Indigenous and older adult students. *Studies in Higher Education 47*(8), 1–13. https://doi.org/10.1080/03075079.2021.1948526.

Ávila, N. (2021). Literacy histories and talk around texts. Emphasizing the emic to explore student's perspectives on academic writing. In I. Guillén-Galve & A. Bocanegra-Valle, *Ethnographies of academic writing research. Theory, methods, and interpretation.* John Benjamins. https://doi.org/10.1075/rmal.1.

Bazerman, C. (2013). Understanding the lifelong journey of writing development. *Infancia & Aprendizaje, 36*(4), 421–44. https://doi.org/10.1174/021037013808200320.

Barton, D., Ivanič, R., Appleby, Y., Hodge, R. & Tusting, K. (2007). *Literacy, lives and learning.* Routledge. https://doi.org/10.4324/9780203608302.

Barton, D. & Hamilton, M. (2000). Literacy practices. In D. Barton, M. Hamilton and R. Ivanič (Eds.), *Situated literacies: Reading and writing in context* (pp. 7–15). Routledge. https://doi.org/10.4324/9780203984963.

Barton, D. & Hamilton, M. (1998). *Local Literacies. Reading and writing in one community.* Routledge.

Biesta, G. & Tedder, M. (2007). Agency and learning in the lifecourse: Towards an ecological perspective. *Studies in the Education of Adults, 39*(2), 132–149. https://doi.org/10.1080/02660830.2007.11661545.

Burgess, A. & Ivanič, R. (2010). Writing and being written: Issues of identity across timescales. *Written Communication, 27*(2), 228–255. https://doi.org/10.1177/0741088310363447.

Coertjens, L., Brahm, T., Trautwein, C. & Lindblom-Ylänne, S. (2017). Students' transition into higher education from an international perspective. *Higher Education, 73*(3), 357–369. https://doi.org/10.1007/s10734-016-0092-y.

Colley, H. (2007). Understanding time in learning transitions through the lifecourse. *International Studies in Sociology of Education, 17*(4), 427–443. https://doi.org/10.1080/09620210701667103.

Colley, H. (2010). Time in learning transitions through the lifecourse: A feminist perspective. In K. Ecclestone, G. Biesta & M. Hughes (Eds.), *Transitions and learning through the lifecourse* (pp. 130–147). Routledge. https://doi.org/10.4324/9780203867617.

Cupitt, C. & Trinidad, S. (2017). What is widening participation and why does it matter? In M. Shah & G. Whiteford (Eds.), *Bridges, pathways, and transitions: International innovations in widening participation* (pp. 17–32). Chandos Publishing/Elsevier. https://doi.org/10.1016/B978-0-08-101921-4.00002-6.

Deleuze, G. & Guattari, F. (1987). *A thousand plateaus: Capitalism and schizophrenia*. Continuum.

Dippre, R. J. & Phillips, T. (2020). Introduction. Generating murmurations for an actionable coherence. In R. J. Dippre & T. Phillips (Eds.), *Approaches to lifespan writing research: Generating an actionable coherence* (pp. 3–11). The WAC Clearinghouse; University Press of Colorado. https://doi.org/10.37514/PER-B.2020.1053.1.3.

Ecclestone, K., Biesta, G. & Hughes, M. M. (2010). Transitions in the lifecourse: the role of identity, agency and structure. In K. Ecclestone, G. Biesta & M. Hughes (Eds.), *Transitions and learning through the lifecourse* (pp. 1–15). Routledge. https://doi.org/10.4324/9780203867617.

Ecclestone, K. (2009). Lost and found in transition: educational implications of concerns about 'identity', 'agency' and 'structure' In J. Field, J. Gallacher & R. Ingram (Eds.), *Researching transitions in lifelong learning* (pp. 9–27). Routledge. https://doi.org/10.4324/9780203875179.

Elliott, S. et al. (2019). 'On the outside I'm smiling but inside I'm crying': Communication successes and challenges for undergraduate academic writing. *Journal of Further and Higher Education*, *43*(9), 1163–1180. https://doi.org/10.1080/0309877X.2018.1455077.

Gale, T. & Parker, S. (2014). Navigating change: A typology of student transition in higher education. *Studies in Higher Education*, 39(5), 734–753. https://doi.org/10.1080/03075079.2012.721351.

Gourlay, L. (2009). Threshold practices: Becoming a student through academic literacies. *London Review of Education,* *7*(2), 181–192. https://doi.org/10.1080/14748460903003626.

Gravett, K. (2019). Troubling transitions and celebrating becomings: From pathway to rhizome. *Studies in Higher Education*, 1–12. https://doi.org/10.1080/03075079.2019.1691162.

Hamilton, M. (2010). Managing transitions in Skills for Life. In K. Ecclestone, G. Biesta & M. Hughes (Eds.), *Transitions and learning through the lifecourse* (pp. 69–86). Routledge. https://doi.org/10.4324/9780203867617.

Hammersley, M. (2006). Ethnography: Problems and prospects. *Ethnography and Education*, *1*(1), 3–14. https://doi.org/10.1080/17457820500512697.

Hebdon, S. (2015). Embedding support for students transitioning into higher education: Evaluation of a new model. *International Journal of Training Research*, *13*(2), 119–131. https://doi.org/10.1080/14480220.2015.1082926.

Ivanič, R. et al. (2009). *Improving learning in college. Rethinking literacies across the curriculum.* Routledge.

Ivanič, R. (1998). *Writing and identity: The discoursal construction of identity in academic writing.* John Benjamins. https://doi.org/10.1075/swll.5.

Johansson, I. (2006). Horizontal transitions: what can it mean for children in the early school years? In A. W. Dunlop & H. Fabian (Eds.), *Informing transitions in the early years* (pp. 33–44). McGraw-Hill Education.

Jirón, P. (2011). On becoming the shadow. In M. Büscher, J. Urry & K. Witchger (Eds.), *Mobile methods* (pp. 36–53). Routledge. https://doi.org/10.4324/9780203879900.

Kagan, S. L. & Neuman, M. J. (1998). Lessons from three decades of transition research. *Elementary School Journal, 98*(4), 365–379. https://doi.org/10.1086/461902.

Kell, C. (2011). Inequalities and crossings: Literacy and the spaces-in-between. *International Journal of Educational Development, 31*(6), 606–613. https://doi.org/10.1016/j.ijedudev.2011.02.006.

Lillis, T. M. (2008). Ethnography as method, methodology, and "deep theorizing": Closing the gap between text and context in academic writing research. *Written Communication, 25*(3), 353–388. https://doi.org/10.1177/0741088308319229.

Lillis, Theresa M. (2001). *Student writing: Access, regulation, desire.* Routledge.

Mojab, S. (2006). War and diaspora as lifelong learning contexts for immigrant women. In C. Leathwood & B. Francis (Eds.), *Gender and lifelong learning: Critical feminist engagements.* Routledge. https://doi.org/10.4324/9780203969533.

Megwalu, A., Miller, C. & Haller, C. R. (2017). The library and the common reader program: a collaborative effort to college transition. *Reference Services Review, 45*(3), 440–453. https://doi.org/10.1108/RSR-11-2016-0081.

Nordquist, B. (2017). *Literacy and mobility. Complexity, uncertainty, and agency at the nexus of high school and college.* Routledge.

Nordquist, B. & Lueck, A. (2020). Educational progress-time and the proliferation of dual enrollment. *Journal of Adolescent and Adult Literacy, 64*(3), 251–257. https://doi.org/10.1002/jaal.1097.

Nicholson, N. & West, M. (1995). Transitions, work histories, and careers. In M. B. Arthur, D. T. Hall & B. S. Lawrence (Eds.), *Handbook of career theory* (pp. 181–201). Cambridge University Press. https://doi.org/10.1017/CBO9780511625459.

Prior, P. & Smith, A. (2020). Editorial: Writing across: Tracing transliteracies as becoming across time, space, and settings. *Learning, Culture and Social Interaction, 24*, 2018–2021. https://doi.org/10.1016/j.lcsi.2018.07.002.

Quinn, J. (2010). Rethinking 'failed transitions' to higher education. In K. Ecclestone, G. Biesta & M. Hughes (Eds.), *Transitions and learning through the lifecourse* (pp. 118–129). Routledge. https://doi.org/10.4324/9780203867617.

Quinn, J., Thomas, L., Slack, K., Casey, L., Thexton, W. & Noble, J. (2005). *From life crisis to lifelong learning: Rethinking working class 'drop out' from higher education.* Joseph Rowntree Foundation.

Russell, D. R. (1997). Writing and genre in higher education and workplaces: A review of studies that use cultural-historical activity theory. *Mind, Culture, and Activity, 4*(4), 224–237. https://doi.org/10.1207/s15327884mca0404_2.

Smith, A. (2020). Across, through, and with: Ontological orientations for lifespan writing research. In R. J. Dippre & T. Phillips (Eds.), *Approaches to lifespan writing research: Generating an actionable coherence* (pp. 15–25). The WAC Clearinghouse; University Press of Colorado. https://doi.org/10.37514/PER-B.2020.1053.

Spelman Miller, K. & Stevenson, M. (2018). Transitions in writing: An introduction. In K. Spelman Miller & M. Stevenson (Eds.), *Transitions in writing* (pp. 1–10). Brill.

Stornaiuolo, A., Smith, A. & Phillips, N. C. (2017). Developing a transliteracies framework for a connected world. *Journal of Literacy Research, 49*(1), 68–91. https://doi.org/10.1177/1086296X16683419.

Street, B. V. (2005). At last: Recent applications of new literacy studies in educational contexts. *Research in the Teaching of English, 39*(4), 417– 423.

Taylor, C. A. & Harris-Evans, J. (2018). Reconceptualising transition to higher education with Deleuze and Guattari. *Studies in Higher Education, 43*(7), 1254–1267. https://doi.org/10.1080/03075079.2016.1242567.

Tusting, K. (2000). New literacy studies and time. In D. Barton, M. Hamilton & R. Ivanič. *Situated literacies. Reading and writing in context*. Routledge. https://doi.org/10.4324/9780203984963.

Turner, V. (1995*). The ritual process. Structure and anti-structure*. Aldine. https://doi.org/10.4324/9781315134666.

Van Gennep, A. 1960. *The rites of passage*. Routledge & Kegan Paul.

Villalobos, C., Treviño, E., Wyman, I. & Scheele, J. (2017). Social justice debate and college access in Latin America: merit or need? The role of educational institutions and states in broadening access to higher education in the region. *Education Policy Analysis Archives, 25*, 73. https://doi.org/10.14507/epaa.25.2879.

Wenger, E. (1998). *Communities of practice. Learning, meaning, and identity*. Cambridge University Press.

Zavala, V. (2011). La escritura académica y la agencia de los sujetos. *Cuadernos Comillas, 1*, 52–66.

Zerubavel, E. (1981). *Hidden rhythms: Schedules and calendars in social life*. University of California Press.

Zigler, E. & Kagan, S. L. (1982). Child development knowledge and educational practice: Using what we know. In A. Lieberman & M. McLaughlin (Eds.), *Policy making in education. Eighty-first yearbook of the National Society for the Study of Education* (pp. 80–104). University of Chicago Press.

CHAPTER 14.

CENTERING POSITIONALITY IN LIFESPAN WRITING RESEARCH THROUGH INSTITUTIONAL AND AUTO/ETHNOGRAPHIC METHODOLOGIES

Erin Workman
DePaul University

In this chapter I re-analyze a descriptive study on students' writing conceptions using institutional ethnography (IE) and autoethnography (AE). However, this is a very different chapter than I would have written six years ago, just after completing the study. Reframing that study through IE, as I initially proposed for this volume, became challenging for reasons beyond the horrors of the pandemic, pre-tenure administrative workload, caregiving, and burnout. The spark of excitement I felt about making connections between IE and lifespan writing research (LWR) gave way to frustrated writing episodes of cycling through sentence-level work, second-guessing my ideas and conceptual grasp of others' ideas, sometimes looping on the same sentence for *hours*, typing, backspacing, retyping, deleting, over and over again: I get stuck in a rut, constructing sentences that don't foreground my contributions or feature "my voice,"—however that term signifies to you—a rut that is all too familiar. . . .

~~~

"You're skilled with synthesizing scholarship," a dissertation committee member says as we review practice preliminary exam responses. "But it's difficult to tell what *your* contribution is." As this statement washes over me, I remember advice from a thesis committee member several years prior—to succeed in a literature Ph.D. program, I will need to change my *way of being in the world*, come out of my shell, speak up, stake out a claim, defend it; otherwise, they'll eat me alive.

I don't reply, "I've spent *years* making myself small and quiet out of necessity, tiptoeing and whispering, peering cautiously around corners, hypervigilant for early signs of danger in a gesture or heavy footfall, concerned about drawing attention, about getting 'it' wrong, about *being* wrong."

Either way, assertive or not, my being feels wrong. I don't yet know the psychiatric discourse that frames this symptomatology as "autonomic overactivation manifested by chronic anxiety, irritability, and startle responses" (Chu, 2011, p. 36). All I know is I'm anxious all the time, prone to freeze rather than fight or take flight, and filled with so much self-doubt that asserting *anything* with any level of confidence can be an emotionally exhausting task.

Having "jumped ship," as my MA advisor put it, to rhetoric and composition, I'd managed to get through doctoral coursework without transforming myself into Erin 2.0 Extrovert Extraordinaire, but as I sit reviewing practice exam responses and taking in this familiar assessment of my strengths and weaknesses, I find myself confronted again with the imperative to not only stake out a claim but to make a *contribution*.

~~~

Seven years later, I'm stuck again, performing rhetorical gymnastics to efface myself from my writing, more through habit than intention, autonomically cutting up and stitching together bits of others' words in a way that, as the coeditors of this collection helpfully observed, "takes a real toll on a reader's energy" as they try "to hold on to a larger point or argument when you're doing that much work in each sentence." Despite forcing my way into a previous draft by way of autoethnography, dense thickets of quotations remained, calling out for "that old paraphrasing trick of reading what you have now and then rewriting it from memory to see if that results in a simpler style," much like Marjorie DeVault's (2019) observation that "using simple, concrete language" in institutional ethnographies is "useful for recognizing and avoiding institutional concepts and categories that too often erase or obscure people's active construction of the social" (p. 98).

Yet, I still struggle to write outside of institutional categories and concepts, partially because disciplinarity opened a path for me, a way to keep climbing, an assurance that I'll never have to go back home. Erasing myself from my writing—as I've discovered through a collaborative autoethnography on navigating academe with psychosocial disabilities (Larrowe & Workman, 2022)—is a self-protective habit to cope with the entanglement of my writing and lived experience of complex post-traumatic stress disorder (CPTSD). Characterized by severe and ongoing trauma, CPTSD has "a profound effect on cognitive, affective, and psychosocial developments, leading to an inadequate sense of self, impaired schemas, [and] deficits in affect regulation and impulse control" (Korn, 2009, p. 264). Those of us with CPTSD are "frequently overwhelmed with intense feelings," and, "unable to tolerate such intense affects, may resort to a variety of dysfunctional behaviors, such as self-destructive acts [and] repetitive self-injury as a form of tension release" (Chu, 2011, p. 36).

As Jesse Rice-Evans and Andréa Stella (2021) write about their experiences as doctoral students with CPTSD, we "have emerged from our worlds with scars: many metaphorical and literal" (p. 20). Whether in flesh or on screen, inscriptions mediate affect and trauma.

～～～

Beginning with positionality is crucial to the ethnographic methodologies I explore in this chapter. As Trude Klevan (Klevan & Grant, 2022) observes about her dissertation, "parallel to the development of knowledge, there is also another story that has been unfolding . . . the story of *my becoming a researcher*" (p. 3). Like Klevan, I recognize that my *becoming a researcher* is inseparable from the data I collect and analyze, the findings I construct, and the discourses I engage along the way. Taking up auto- and institutional ethnography, I consider how my education in "damn-near-all-white graduate programs" in "damn-near-all-white institutions" (Kynard, 2021, p. 188), my engagement with disciplinary discourses, and my positionality as a neurodivergent white woman with a psychosocial disability contoured my research design, reinscribing "writing normativities" without my realizing it (Dippre & Phillips, 2020, p. 7). As Dorothy Smith and Alison Griffith (2022) observe about their early IE work, "[o]nce we could recognize how we participated in [the mothering discourse], we could see that we had taken it for granted and built it into how we organized our interviews" with participants (p. 38). Similarly, I approached my study on students' writing conceptions thinking that the survey and interview protocols adapted from transfer research (Yancey et al., 2014; Reiff & Bawarshi, 2011) would, as Eric Darnell Pritchard (2016) writes of his own well-defined methods, "cente[r] the meanings that research participants give to literacy"—or, in my case, to writing (p. 35). However, I didn't recognize the ways in which my positionality and research design imposed disciplinary concepts onto participants' responses, thereby obscuring their "active construction of the social" (DeVault, 2019, p. 98). As I discuss below, this process illustrates how writing normativities persist.

To make this argument and model the affordances of AE and IE for lifespan writing research, I define core methodological concepts, foregrounding their use for social justice-oriented research. After situating these methodologies in relation to Ryan Dippre's (2019) approach to literate action research, I turn to my earlier study (Workman, 2020), briefly describing the research design and re-analyzing data from one participant, Imani, for hooks and traces of disciplinary discourses, illustrating how my study reinscribed writing normativities I sought to avoid and revealing how these persist regardless of intentionality. I conclude by reiterating the methodological affordances for lifespan writing research and identifying lines of inquiry for which AE and IE are well-suited.

DEFINING AUTOETHNOGRAPHY AND INSTITUTIONAL ETHNOGRAPHY

Ethnography has been prevalent in composition studies since 1981, but the crisis of representation in the social sciences problematized its accuracy in depicting participants' lived experience, necessitating participant-centered approaches such as autoethnography (AE) and institutional ethnography (IE). AE, first enacted by Zora Neale Hurston (Maraj, 2021), and IE, developed by Smith (2005), are social justice-oriented methodologies that center participants' perspectives, adapt qualitative methods to pursue open-ended projects of discovery, and seek to intervene in dominant cultural narratives (AE) or reveal the invisible social relations coordinating participants' work (IE). These similarities, however, give way to different analytical foci, with AE taking up "autobiographical, phenomenological concerns" and IE attending to "critical, social concerns" (Jubas & Seidel, 2016, p. 62).

AE is written from and about the researcher's personal experiences, not "to make an argument a priori," but rather to "pose a question, collect relevant data, and listen . . . to see what findings emerge" (Jackson & McKinney, 2021, p. 11). AEers collect data systematically through traditional qualitative methods like "interviews, artifacts, fieldnotes, photographs, or videos," and less typical methods, such as "memories, diaries, self-interviews, and systematic introspection" (p. 7). Autoethnography also refers to a written product that can take different forms, such as analytic AE, which is "characterized by the genre conventions . . . social science writing," and evocative AE, which "takes the form of 'stories that fuse ethnography with literary art'" (p. 8). Because "evocative autoethnography is a blended, bended genre that . . . transgresses traditional conventions and categories of expressing or 'representing events that really occurred,'" researchers composing evocative autoethnographies might encounter resistance from publication venues (p. 8). Louis Maraj (2021) recounts submitting an autoethnographic manuscript "that not only tells various stories about im/migrant Blackness but also carefully plots a Black/feminist tradition of autoethnographic work in rhetoric, writing, and literacy studies" to "a largely traditional writing studies venue," only to receive a desk rejection "detail[ing] the very aspects of disciplinary anti-Blackness that the essay pushes against" (p. 175). Summarizing the white woman editor's "demeaning letter," Maraj reveals how these "marginalizing moves" reproduce the status quo:

> From the editor's assumption about the ethics of my data collection, to their proposed alternative between creative nonfiction and analytical research essay in revision, to the

insinuation that a Black im/migrant remains unaware of the precut formulas for research writing that still form the basis of dominant pedagogies, we can see the distinct hegemonic circumstances autoethnography—and particularly Black and Black feminist autoethnography—faces in finding validation in our fields. (p. 176)

Like Maraj, Venus Evans-Winters (2019) centers "the standpoint of Black women and other women of color," describing how disciplinary approbation of qualitative methodologies is contingent upon positionality, such that "Black women's ways of knowing, cultural and spiritual beliefs continue to be marginalized, suppressed, or bastardized and propagated as trite or esoteric" while methodological conversations remain "dominated and policed by those of the White educated elite" whose scholarship is "more reflective of White middle class culture, or a limited worldview, than representative of the richness and dynamism of those of us who live and exist on the margins of society" (p. 2). As Maraj and Evans-Winters illustrate, the marginalizing moves and anti-Blackness pervasive in our disciplines and institutions persist through "ordinary working practices," necessitating methodologies like AE and IE that are attuned to embodiment, material texts, routine practices, disciplinary discourses, and institutional regimes.

Like AE, institutional ethnography "remain[s] always with actual people and what they do," but IE aims to uncover "*for people's use* how people are active in the objectified (or ruling) relations that exist independently of us and overpower our lives" (Smith & Griffith, 2022, p. 23). IE has gained disciplinary currency following Michelle LaFrance and Melissa Nicolas's (2012) call for "more institutional ethnographies in our field" (p. 145) and LaFrance's (2019) subsequent monograph outlining and modeling IE for writing studies research. For researchers interested in writing program administration, institutional policies and procedures, diversity work, and local instantiations of professional statements of best practices, IE offers concepts to flexibly pursue inquiry, starting with an embodied *standpoint* from which the direction of research—what Smith refers to as a *problematic*—is discovered. Starting with her standpoint as a white single mother working in institutions and professional discourses that "had almost nothing to say about" her lived experience, Smith (1999) used this disjuncture to develop IE as an alternative sociology informed by Marxist materialism, feminist consciousness-raising practices, and ethnomethodology (p. 11). Unlike sociological research that samples populations and generalizes from "prescriptive categories of . . . social order" (Kynard, 2013, p. 235), IE seeks to "lear[n] from actual people in their everyday lives and how what they do coordinates with the actions of others" (Smith & Griffith, 2022, p. 5).

Using traditional qualitative methods, the IEer listens and looks for disjunctions when individuals interface with institutions, taking note of "connections, links, hookups, and various forms of coordination that tie people's work and work processes into those of others" (Smith, 2005, p. 144). *Work* is conceptualized as "whatever people are doing that is intentional, takes time and effort, and is getting done at a particular time and in a particular place," such that students are understood as working much like faculty, and, as I illustrate below, attending to what students do as *work* reveals much that would otherwise remain hidden (Griffith & Smith, 2014, p. 10). Documenting people's work processes involves mapping *institutional circuits*—"sequences of text-coordinated action making people's actualities representable and hence actionable within the institutional frames that authorize institutional action" (Smith & Turner, 2014, p. 10). For example, Imani, like many new admits at our R1 institution in 2015, thought she earned credit for both required FYW courses through AP and dual enrollment, and had she started college in 2014, she would have been right. However, to mitigate the impact of declining FYW enrollments on the number of graduate teaching assistantships the English department could offer, the second required course was moved to the sophomore level, ensuring that all students would enroll because comparable 2000-level composition courses were rare. Even though Imani's "actualities" did not change, how they were framed and the institutional action they authorized certainly did.

Ultimately, IE "traces the ways in which texts stitch together smaller social groupings into larger institutional contexts, which in turn leads to even larger power structures," or *ruling relations* (Taber, 2010, p. 11). Though integral to IE, the *ruling relations* construct can be opaque, but Nancy Taber's metaphor is illuminative: "IE tends to show us the trees that were hidden in the forest; once we can see the trees (ruling relations), they can never again recede. And once we can see the ruling relations, we can begin to interrogate and challenge them" (p. 20). While an IE project begins with standpoint, entry-level data analysis will move beyond the individual to "second level data [like] texts and policies and/or interviews with policy makers, to explore how participants' lives are socially organized," opening opportunities for intervention and change (p. 11).

Writing studies IEs have focused on connections between professional discourses and local institutional complexes, such as writing centers (e.g., Miley, 2018; Crozier & Workman, 2022), writing programs (LaFrance, 2019), and university writing sites (Workman et al., 2023) rather than on "the experience of the person performing . . . literate action" (Dippre, 2019, p. 5), as autoethnographic research might do. Given their complementary affordances, AE and IE can be productively used together, as Taber exemplifies by using AE "to foreground [her] own experiences" as a woman in the military and IE to "investigate policies and social practices" hooking her into ruling relations of the military and institutional regimes (p. 9). Since Taber argued for incorporating AE and IE, researchers across disciplines have taken up her call (Jubas and Seidel, 2016; Fixsen et al., 2022), but none have used these methodologies for studying lifespan writing development, as I do here.

Next, I place AE and IE in conversation with Dippre's approach to lifespan literate action research, but first, I define each methodology in Table 14.1.

Table 14.1. Definitions of Autoethnography and Institutional Ethnography

Methodology	Definition for Writing Studies
Autoethnography	a method of inquiry and a written product in which the researcher:
	writes from personal experiences within writing/writing studies
	uses an inductive, qualitative approach for project design, data collection, and analysis;
	writes in conversation with other texts; and
	writes back or intervenes in a cultural narrative or conversation (Jackson & McKinney, p.11).
Institutional Ethnography	a theory of institutional organization,
	a set of analytic moves that allow for a distinctive approach to analyzing and understanding a site and the people who carry out their work within that site, and
	a practical tool that aids writing researchers interested in how writing constitutes our work" (LaFrance, 2019, p. 18).

AUTO- AND INSTITUTIONAL ETHNOGRAPHIC METHODOLOGIES FOR LIFESPAN WRITING RESEARCH

For lifespan writing researchers who understand that "writers develop in relation to the changing social needs, opportunities, resources, and technologies of their time and place" (Bazerman et al., 2018, p. 28, p. 31), autoethnography likely registers as a productive methodology. Indeed, James Zebroski (2020) takes up AE for lifespan writing research (LWR) to make sense of his transition to retirement. Well-suited to LWR, AE affords the researcher:

> unlimited access without temporal and spatial constraints,
> possibly even access to a lifetime of time 'in the field,'
> . . . the ability to ask the hard questions, . . . and press

themselves to think, feel, and remember things they might not press others to remember. [AE creates] a dual role . . . as both subject and researcher, [which] means they both produce and analyze the data, thus closing the gap in interpretation between a subject's and researcher's perspective (Jackson & Grutsch McKinney, p. 8).

Alternatively, IE's institutional emphasis may seem counterintuitive; however, like Dippre's (2019) "logic-in-use" for literate action research, IE is adapted from ethnomethodology, or "the study of how people work together to create social order through interaction" (p. 13). Consequently, IE and Dippre's logic-in-use focus on "the ways in which individuals construct and are constructed by situations via *material interactions* with talk, tools, and *texts activated* in those situations" (p. 25; emphasis added).

Though both focus on material texts, practices, and individuals' activation of texts in the ongoing co-production of social reality, each approach directs inquiry differently, with the IE zooming out to discover ruling relations "beyond our practical and direct knowledge" that invisibly constrain knowledge and action (Smith, 1999, p. 44) and the logic-in-use zooming in on individuals' practices as they develop and transform over time. Just as IE begins with standpoint and traces individuals' activation of material texts in the trans-locally coordinated work processes that hook them into ruling relations beyond their view, Dippre's logic-in-use likewise focuses on "individuated actors, participants in producing social order with unique footings in the social space that they are co-constructing" through material practices (p. 34). Offering a case study of seventh-grade student Alice, Dippre highlights "moments that serve as a 'microscope of Nature' (Merton, 1987, p. 11) for seeing literate action *in action*," illustrating how the material practice of writing unfolds in real time as Alice, her peers, and their teacher engage in the ongoing co-production of social order in the classroom. An IE project would ask how classroom work happens as it does, perhaps by interviewing Alice's teacher and locating documents and policies constraining her work to discover the hidden ruling relations of the educational industrial complex.

For IE and the logic-in-use, disjunction and disruption are generative for directing inquiry into individuated actors' situated practices as they interface with institutional discourses or as their practices transform and endure throughout the lifespan. Smith's (2005) experience of disjunction between her lived experience as a single mother and her work as an academic led her to develop IE as an alternative sociology for "mak[ing] visible what is ordinarily taken for granted, that the very organization of the everyday is permeated with connections that extend beyond it" (p. 40). Just as tension and disruption signify an emerging problematic and warrant careful consideration in IE, Dippre observes that "[t]here are opportunities for complication that can disrupt a given instantiation of a practice and, in doing so, perhaps provide an opportunity for further literate action development by transforming such a practice" (p. 161). Development and transformation are catalyzed by failures of routine practice, making disjunction and disruption integral to (the study of) institutions *and* individuals; otherwise, "ordinary working practices" continue to operate "below the level of consciousness," thereby "ensuring that . . . whatever knowledge is produced is not oriented to the needs and interests of the mass of people, but to the needs and interests of ruling" (Smith, 1999, p. 40, p. 16). This perspective exposes how the marginalizing moves documented by Maraj and Evans-Winters are continuously reenacted through mundane, material practices and habitual work processes.

Considering IE alongside Dippre's logic-in-use reveals how their ethnomethodological heritage orients them similarly to individuals' material practices of co-constructing social order through "recurrent . . . intersubjective accomplishment" (Dippre, p. 17). Both approaches set out from *a lived reality perspective* to pursue inquiry into individuated actors' literate action development, or to "mak[e] visible how we are connected into extended social relations of ruling and economy" (Smith, 2005, p. 29). Autoethnography can complement both approaches by offering unlimited access to participants' material texts, closing the subject-researcher gap, and surfacing tensions between lived experience and institutional discourses and ideologies (Jackson & Grutsch McKinney, p. 3). The methodological differences enacted through AE, IE, and the logic-in-use open ways of studying individual development in relation to institutional reproduction and transformation, most crucially for "those who do not quite inhabit norms" or fit neatly within institutional categories (Ahmed, 2017, p. 115).

DIVERSIFYING ETHNOGRAPHIC APPROACHES TO INDIVIDUAL AND INSTITUTIONAL PRACTICES

Much like Black feminist traditions of autoethnography, institutional ethnography is a descriptive and activist project premised on the assumption that "problematic institutional practices lying within practicable reach can be identified, creating possibilities of change from within" (Smith, 2005, p. 32). IE starts with a rupture between lived experience and institutional discourses, a phenomenon that Sara Ahmed (2021), drawing from Rosemarie Garland-Thomson, calls "misfitting": "You have a fit when an environment is built to accommodate you. When you are accommodated, you don't even have to notice that environment. You are a misfit when there is an incongruous relation of your body to thing or body to world" (p. 140). Rice-Evans and Stella (2021) describe the visceral experience of misfitting within academe using language that resonates with my experiences of CPTSD: "I feel wrong all. of. the. time. I have acted wrong, I've spoken out of turn, I've taken a risk I shouldn't have, I've offended, I haven't followed the simple rules. *And this wrongness is that I, me as a person, is actually wrong*" (p. 27; emphasis added). When my professor said I would need to change my way of being, they were explicitly saying that *I am wrong*, that I will assuredly *misfit* within the combative social order of a literature Ph.D. program. The problem is me, not the institution.

Yet, as Dejah Carter (2020) contends, "[h]igher education institutions were created to center heteronormativity, white supremacy, patriarchy, and classism" (p. 26–27), not to mention able-bodiedness and able-mindedness (Dolmage, 2017; Price, 2011), white linguistic supremacy and Anti-Black Linguistic Racism (Baker-Bell, 2020), and literacy normativity (Pritchard, 2016). This scholarship reveals how "some more than others will be at home in institutions that assume certain bodies [and minds] as their norm" (Ahmed, 2012, p. 3). However, as Ahmed's research demonstrates, experiences of misfitting can teach us much about institutional mechanics because "[i]t is from difficult experiences, of being bruised by structures that are not even revealed to others, that we gain the energy to rebel. It is from what we come up against that we gain new angles on what we are against" (2017, p. 255).

Students for whom the university wasn't made, students with rich arrays of literacies, languages, and discursive resources that are not valued within disciplinary and institutional discourses often hit a wall in FYW courses, and when students hit a wall in FYW, *FYW is a wall,* one that excludes some while allowing others to easily pass through or skip the requirement altogether. This barrier is well-documented by Black composition-literacy scholars like Elaine Richardson (2004), who writes of her college experience, "[i]t wasn't long before I figured out that I could succeed by relinquishing my language variety and my history, experience, culture, and perspective for theirs. All I had to do was let them Whitenize my papers" (p. 2). "Consequently," she continues, "most African American Vernacular English-speaking students become further indoctrinated in the precepts of White dominant discourse in the process. What the student brings to the classroom is not valued or recognized; no transcultural dialogism takes place" (2). Richardson describes what Pritchard (2016) has termed "literacy normativity," or "the use of literacy to create and impose normative standards and beliefs onto people who are labeled alien or other through textscapes that are experienced as painful because they do damage or inflict harm" (p. 28).

Deficit-based perspectives of student writers persist, inscribed in institutional documents, learning outcomes, writing requirements, and professional statements of best practices (e.g., WPA Outcomes Statement for First-Year Composition) such that our routine activation of these texts in our local contexts can enact marginalizing moves and perpetuate writing normativities. For instance, Yancey et al. (2014) report that every student in their study "when asked to define writing, used a single word: *expression*," and they frame this finding as an "*absence* of prior knowledge," specifically "in two important areas: (1) key writing concepts and (2) nonfiction texts that serve as models" (p. 111, p. 108). When students "see writing principally as a *vehicle for authorial expression*," they struggle to develop foundational rhetorical knowledge necessary for writing effectively across contexts (111). Yet, Sheila Carter-Tod (2021) problematizes this "singular" and "generally Aristotelian" conception of rhetoric, describing her struggle "to figure out ways to merge my professional administrative practices with what I know is a more inclusive approach to writing instruction and writing program curricular development." Drawing from African American rhetorics, Carter-Tod proposes "expand[ing] the traditional rhetorical triangle to a star that includes *language, style, discourse, perspective, community* and *suasion*." Retrospectively, I recognize how this expansive rhetorical approach could have better served my student-research-participants. With this framework, I turn to my study on students' writing conceptions, offering some context before re-reading data for hooks and traces of the institutional and disciplinary discourses coordinating writers and their work of writing *through* lifeworlds.

UNCOVERING AND STUDYING CONCEPTIONS OF WRITING

Conducted over nine months at a large, southeastern R1 university, my descriptive study (Workman, 2020) aimed to document and trace changes in first-year college students' representations of their conceptual writing knowledge. Participants were recruited from a new 2000-level transfer-focused composition course that engaged students in developing theories of writing informed by rhetorical concepts and composed iteratively through sustained reflective activities (Yancey et al., 2014). Students defined writing, identified key terms important for that definition, and visually depicted connections among terms through a process that I call *visual mapping*, and, once grades were posted, eight participants completed an exit survey and interview, during which they reflected on three visual maps and writing assignments from the course. Participants completed two additional document-based interviews the following semester, creating a new visual map each time and, for the final interview, sharing self-selected samples of academic and non-academic writing to anchor reflection on how their conceptions of writing and writing practices had changed or stabilized over time.

When I began the study in 2015, I was engrossed with writing transfer scholarship and understood transfer-focused writing instruction to be grounded in empirical research and responsive to disciplinary best practices. Although I intentionally modeled my course and research design on Yancey et al.'s (2014), I failed to recognize how immersed I was in Teaching for Transfer (TFT) discourse—much like Smith and Griffith (2022) discovered about the mothering discourse—and how I was imposing TFT concepts on data before I even collected them. To use the parlance of IE, my research was *institutionally captured*, "regulated by the institutional procedures of text-reader conversations, through which institutional discourse overrides and reconstructs experiential talk and writing" (Smith, 2005, p. 119). My use of TFT key terms, which represent dominant discourses of postsecondary writing pedagogy (Brown, 2020), precluded any possibility of attending to linguistic diversity, cultural rhetorics, Black language, and Black rhetorical traditions (Kynard, 2013; Carter-Tod, 2021).

Having been hooked into writing studies via scholarship on Writing about Writing (WAW), transfer, and reflection, I lost sight of how *I* had been disciplined, how these were just some of the *many* discourses circulating within writing studies. Unlike Tessa Brown (2020), who experienced the kind of productive disjuncture that would direct an IE project when moving from her MA program, with its focus on Students Rights to Their Own Language (SRTOL) and Hip Hop Literacies, to her Ph.D. program, with its focus on threshold concepts for writing studies outlined in *Naming What We Know* (*NWWK*) (Adler-Kassner & Wardle, 2015), I felt no such tension when transitioning to my doctoral program, even though my MA coursework included sustained engagement with SRTOL and linguistic diversity. When *NWWK* was published, I failed to consider how racially, culturally, and linguistically exclusive that *we* and *what we know* actually was—in part because my faculty mentors made multiple contributions to the crowdsourced collection, and in part because my disciplinary engagement during graduate study was primarily with white scholars and faculty, studying mostly white students and unmarked white racialized discourses that continually reconstitute the discipline and higher education institutions across the US. However, despite the disciplinary discourses *capturing* my study, the visual mapping method that I designed to elicit participants' conceptions of writing enabled them to language in ways that were meaningful to them in that moment, especially as they moved into their second semester of college.

RE-READING DATA TO SURFACE TENSIONS IN CONCEPTIONS OF WRITING

> "I would love to love writing again since my high school writing experience wasn't something I enjoyed."
>
> – Imani, course goals reflection

Having outlined the affordances of IE for studying individual development in relation to institutional reproduction and transformation, I turn now to modeling these affordances for lifespan writing research. To do so, I follow Rebecca Lund's (2020) model of "re-engag[ing] critically" with my earlier study, "drawing on the conceptual resources of IE . . . to examine, with hindsight," missed opportunities for disrupting writing normativities (p. 103). Rereading data from Imani, an 18-year-old, self-identified middle-class Black woman majoring in pre-med biology, I demonstrate how an IE approach to analysis "helps the ethnographer to uncover the disjunctions, divergences, and distinctions experienced by individuals" as they engage in daily work processes and co-construct social reality (LaFrance, p. 35). This analysis surfaces lines of inquiry into Imani's writing development and tensions Imani felt as institutional and ideological discourses shaped and constrained her ways of writing and making meaning. I highlight moments when Imani indicated "elevated levels of uncertainty" about writing and examine the socially and culturally situated practices Imani engaged to address the tension she felt between personal and institutional writing tasks (Dippre, p. 65).

Returning to Yancey et al.'s (2014) observation that all student participants in their study defined writing as expression—a finding replicated by my study—we can think about this commonality across students and institutional contexts as indicative of the ruling relations of secondary and postsecondary educational discourses. Imani speaks to this directly in her final course reflection when she states, "I think [expression] describes *everyone's* idea of writing *prior to taking a college level* English course. It is somewhat of the basis of *the idea of writing that most students grew up on*" (3; emphasis mine). Imani is right, yet, as indicated above, some teacher-researchers, including me, perceive this conception as a barrier to developing and enacting writing knowledge and practices "appropriate" for postsecondary learning contexts. Describing the link between students' conceptions of writing and writing practices, Mar Mateos and Isabel Solé (2012) explain that "personal conceptions are constructed within the framework of scientific and popular conceptions about writing as well as within the writing practices promoted by these conceptions" (p. 53). Reframing this observation through IE reveals how scientific and popular discourses about writing can invisibly constrain students' instantiation of writing conceptions as they engage in writing practices promoted by these conceptions. It's this effect on writing practice that seems implicit in the move against *expression*: you can express yourself, but there's a time and place for doing so, and the time and place for doing so is not in the college-writing classroom. Correcting students' *mis*conceptions, or expanding limited and limiting conceptions, of writing is one goal of curricular models like TFT and WAW; however, these and related approaches to writing pedagogy have been critiqued for perpetuating whiteness and white language supremacy.

As the epigraph for this section illustrates, Imani and others in my study who reported positive early childhood experiences with writing would experience a change as they moved through secondary schooling. In Imani's reflection on her prior writing experiences, she contrasts writing she enjoys with academic writing that comes with critical, even harmful, responses from others:

> I mostly enjoy writing lyrics, writing in a journal, and sometimes short stories. This type of writing is more enjoyable because I have the opportunity to write as I please with no specific restrictions and I can write at anytime I feel with no guideline or restrictions on time. . . . Usually, I write in a journal at home (well in my dorm now) *because it is my own space and others can't criticize me in my own comfort zone*. I do not enjoy writing essays because there is usually a specific topic or certain criteria to complete while writing and I usually overthink or over analyze what actually needs to be said in the essay. Although I do write essays at home, *most essays I have written have been at school, and usually have had to face the opinion of others who may have criticized more than critiqued*. (emphasis added)

Imani discloses her strong affective response to academic writing based on prior experiences when others "may have criticized more than critiqued," and although she doesn't explicitly name those others here, in subsequent interviews all references to negative writing experiences are linked exclusively to teachers. As indicated on her first visual map (see Figure 14.1) where she begins with *freedom* and *expression* in the top and bottom left corners, Imani does not believe that successful writing is contingent upon having others agree with her, explaining that "getting a point across through communication is successful" and "expressing is a success as long as you say what you feel, even if others disagree." For Imani, being passionate and expressive is not at odds with communicating effectively because "any type of expression is a way of communicating."

This emerging tension between having freedom to creatively express herself using the genres, materials, and practices of her choosing and feeling constrained to produce whatever "different teachers like" is evident throughout

Imani's dataset, beginning with her own goal of learning to love writing again, and continuing through reflections and interviews in which Imani discloses the damaging impact of these lessons on her relationship to and conception of writing. As noted previously, within the pedagogical model guiding my teaching and the disciplinary scholarship shaping my research, to express is *not* to write rhetorically, but rather to reify a problematic construct from literature and creative writing—the exclusion of which "limit[s] contributions and theorizations from writers of color" and further perpetuates writing normativities (Brown, p. 607). This discourse suggests that students shouldn't (only) express themselves; they should learn how to communicate effectively for institutionally mandated purposes. However, as Imani's second visual map (see Figure 14.2) illustrates, she understands expressive writing to have rhetorical power, to make an impact and spark conversation among her audience(s):

[A]s a writer, I feel that is important for my writing to make people ask questions and to talk to others about what their take on the topic would have been. I want people to be intrigued and inquisitive about what I write. I think that making buzz and making people question and have conversations about my writing is what makes it successful" (5).

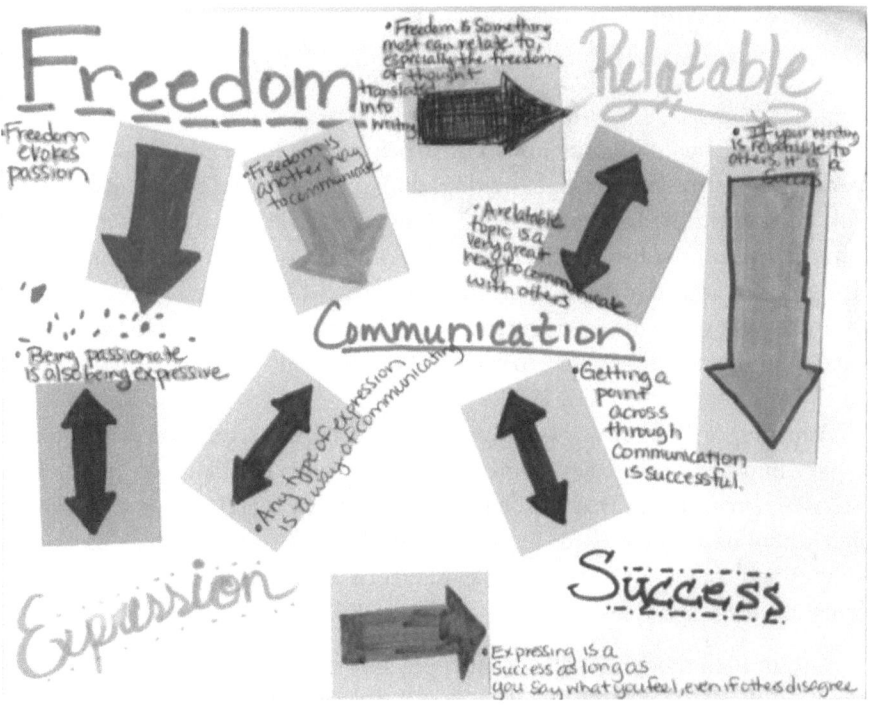

Figure 14.1. Imani's First Visual Map

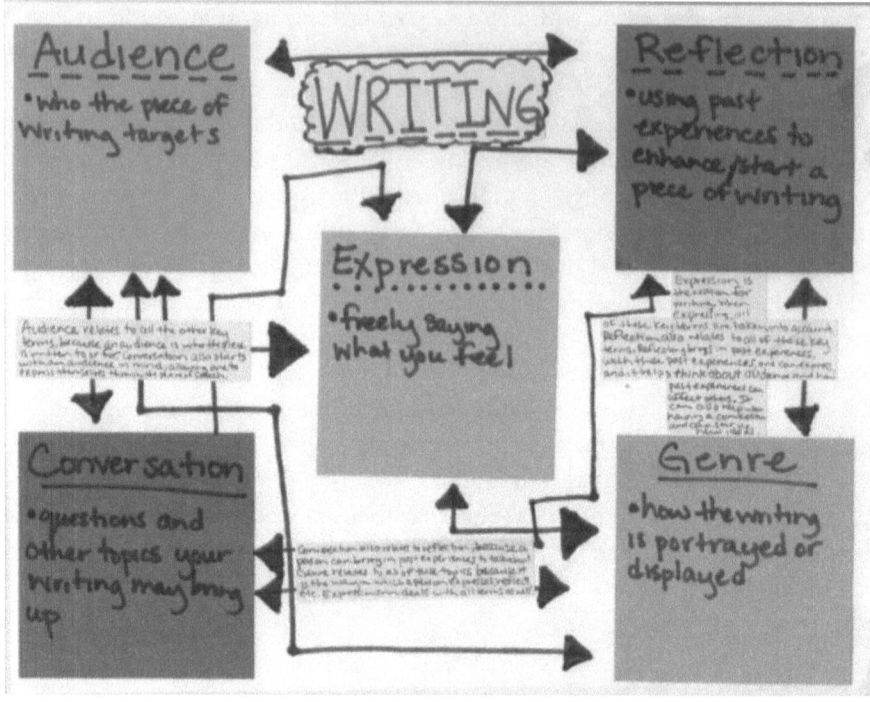

Figure 14.2. Imani's Second Visual Map

Rereading Imani's words now, I'm struck by her focus on perspective and sparking conversation through writing, and the resonance of her conception with Afrocentric rhetoric attentive to "language, style, discourse, perspective, community and suasion" (Carter-Tod, 2021). I'm also struck by the limitations of my earlier analysis, the lines of inquiry I missed by engaging Imani's dataset exclusively through an Aristotelian model, and what comes into view when expanding this "traditional rhetorical triangle to a star" and reframing the data via IE concepts (Carter-Tod, 2021).

Attending to Imani's *work* as conceptualized by IE reveals potential lines of inquiry into her writing development that were previously invisible. In our first interview, Imani noted that she "had been helping" a friend who is a "senior in high school back home" with her writing for AP literature and dual-enrollment composition classes. Reflecting on the differences between the writing Imani was doing in college and the writing her friend was doing in high school, she explains:

> In high school, it's all about length and sounding good, but
> I think she is understanding that audiences are different.
> That's one thing that I talk to her about, that audiences are

different, and it's important for you to know what type of audience you're writing to. *And right now, of course, she knows that her purpose in writing is just to get done so she gets a good grade* [laughs], but I tell her to think about exactly what she wants you to know. So, with her taking dual enrollment and AP classes, of course she has different teachers. Her having to understand what teachers likes what, like figuring them out—I think that's helping her to think more about purpose.

As Imani describes how writing is conceptualized in high school, she acknowledges how formative the work of helping her friend has been for her own conception of writing: "I actually realized now that I've been helping her with her essays that *instead of me just writing about my personal work*, I feel like me actually helping her I feel like she's understanding what I'm trying to get her to understand, I guess, by using those terms, and her writing is improving as well." Juxtaposed with "me just writing about my personal work" like she had done in the 2000-level writing course, this process of "actually helping her" is generative not only for her friend, but for herself.

Reflecting on the writing from her spring semester songwriting course, Imani explained, "I've thought a lot about my audience being a group of people who have a lot of different opinions and I'm still working on how to write for that type of audience." Unlike writing for biology lab where she understood her audience as people in the same discourse community, Imani was "still working on" how to approach the more diverse audiences she wanted to reach through songwriting:

> [Y]ou have a lot of songs that are classics, like everyone knows the song. And what makes those lyrics touch a variety of different people? like people that wouldn't normally be on the same track, I guess? or same train of thought or whatever. I've kind of been looking into that kind of thing. Because there's a lot of different songs that everybody knows. You can play any word and it doesn't matter who you are, you're going to know what that song is. So that's what I'm trying to do . . . still trying to figure it out [laughs].

As Imani continued writing for her biology lab peers and professor and concurrently exploring ways of reaching diverse audiences through songwriting, she started thinking about writing strategies for turning her freewriting into song lyrics that would resonate with embodied listeners:

> I just kind of freewrite a lot, so I'm not really thinking about a different audience at the time. I'm really writing because I

265

need to get out stuff. And then later on I'm like, "okay well let me go back and reword this a little bit so it fits like a certain group of people that I want to fit." *I always try to make my writing connect with people*, I guess. That's one of my goals, but I do that *after* I already have written it to go back and see, and then if it's not something I *like* like, I usually take the pieces and just rewrite.

Interestingly, *community* and *perspective* are implicit in Imani's discussion of where and how she does her most generative freewriting:

Friday nights, they have Freestyle Friday, like outside in front of [the library] at like 9 o'clock at night. From like 9–12. And I'll go up there about 10 or so, and I just like the vibe, so I'll just go and they're playing music. And I'm just sitting and it'll all just flow. I just write. I don't write what they say, but I write my own thoughts and things.

For Imani, spoken word pieces performed on Freestyle Friday are like "experienced journaling," where "it's more like experience- and reality-driven. . . . Spoken word is kind of like a deep kind of writing, and so bringing in *reflection*, it actually lets you bring in *real life experience* and things that you've *actually been through,* or you've *heard* or *seen*. It actually makes your writing more visual for the audience." Here, Imani talks about writing as an epistemological act grounded in lived experience, a way of clarifying one's perspective and effectively communicating that perspective for embodied others, both those with whom one shares community and those whose different perspectives require cunning linguistic and suasive styles. I'm struck again by the knowledge that Imani and I could have co-created had my own conceptions of writing and rhetoric been as expansive and attentive to embodied knowledge and lived experience as Imani's were.

IMPLICATIONS AND APPLICATIONS FOR FUTURE LIFESPAN RESEARCH

The methodologies I have explored in this chapter—institutional ethnography, autoethnography, and Dippre's logic-in-use—share a focus on embodiment, material texts, and routine practices, offering concepts and tools to study individuated writers' co-production of social reality. These approaches foreground the generativity of disjunction, tension, and rupture for (researching) individual and institutional development and transformation, even as individuals' embodied experiences of misfitting within academe are disproportionately felt by marginalized students and faculty "who do not quite inhabit norms" (Ahmed, 2017, p. 115). The marginalizing moves that Maraj, Evans-Winters, Richardson, Carter-Tod, Pritchard, and Imani address are pervasive in our institutions, perpetuated through routine material practices that are contoured by disciplinary discourses and ruling relations, those "structures [that] are not visible or tangible unless you come up against them," much like individual trees not visible in the forest (Ahmed, 2017, p. 214). Even as a queer, neurodivergent, disabled white woman from a rural Southern working-class background who often misfits, I am white and grew up so steeped in white supremacy that I "learn[ed] not to see it" (Ahmed, 2017, p. 157). However, "once we can see the ruling relations, we can begin to interrogate and challenge them," but bringing those ruling relations into view requires methodologies keenly attuned to the intersections among embodiment, material texts, routine practices, social coordination, and institutional regimes (Taber, 2010, p. 20). And, as I have illustrated through autoethnographic snapshots of consequential moments in my becoming-researcher, keeping individuals *and* institutions in view can be difficult with a single method of inquiry.

I opened this chapter with my own positionality because starting elsewhere was getting me nowhere. Even though standpoint, embodiment, and lived experience are integral to IE, it was only through concurrent collaborative autoethnographic research that I found the footing to move forward. The story of how I came to the discipline is inseparable from my (then) unexamined trauma-related coping mechanisms, including the act of "splitting," or seeing something in absolute terms within a good/bad binary. I began my MA program intending to continue studying literature, as I had done as an undergraduate English major with a creative writing minor—two disciplines entangled with traumatic and *literally* bloody writing experiences that, nonetheless, had driven me to graduate study because, with some exceptions, the academic trauma felt endurable as long it took me physically and metaphorically away from the trauma of my childhood and teenage years. Once I became hooked into writing studies, I unknowingly positioned (my understanding of) it as *good* in opposition to the *bad* of literature and creative writing so that what began as skepticism about a discipline that seemed to eschew creativity quickly transformed into absolute certainty that teaching anything other than writing studies concepts in FYW was a disservice to students. Splitting disciplines in this way precluded the possibility of my experiencing the kind of productive tension that enabled Brown to recognize what was missing from WAW and *NWWK*.

Even as I compose this conclusion, I'm aware of how much I'm leaving out, of nuances that blur the clean splitting of disciplines, of moments that opened space for thinking and imagining otherwise, even if only briefly. Sitting with and attending to these moments of disjuncture, I find my way into the standpoint from which I can finally pursue institutional ethnographic research into writing development through the lifespan, my own becoming-researcher, and the disciplinary discourses and ruling relations contouring my teaching and research, guiding practices that, left unexamined, reproduced the marginalizing moves and disciplinary anti-Blackness that result in writers like Imani no longer enjoying writing for fear of exposing something so personally meaningful to criticism by those for whom non-normative writing is something to be corrected, improved, and standardized. If one goal of LWR is disrupting writing normativities by bringing into view not just development, but also *change*, *stasis*, and *decline*, we need methodologies like AE and IE that center positionality, magnify individuals' practices and activation of material texts, and map social coordination and ruling relations to counter marginalizing moves and reveal opportunities for change.

REFERENCES

Adler-Kassner, L. & Wardle, E. (Eds.). (2015). *Naming what we know: Threshold concepts for writing studies*. Utah State University Press.

Ahmed, S. (2012). *On being included: Racism and diversity in institutional life*. Duke University Press.

Ahmed, S. (2017). *Living a Feminist Life*. Duke University Press.

Ahmed, S. (2021). *Complaint!* Duke University Press.

Baker-Bell, A. (2020). *Linguistic justice: Black language, literacy, identity, and pedagogy*. National Council of Teachers of English/Routledge.

Bazerman, C., Applebee, A. N., Berninger, V. W., Brandt, D., Graham, S., Jeffery, J. V., Matsuda, P. K., Murphy, S., Rowe, D. W., Schleppegrell, M. & Wilcox, K. C. (Eds.). (2018). *The lifespan development of writing*. National Council of Teachers of English. https://wac.colostate.edu/books/ncte/lifespan-writing/.

Brown, T. (2020). What else do we know? Translingualism and the history of SRTOL as threshold concepts in our field. *College Composition and Communication*, *71*(4), 591–619. https://doi.org/10.58680/ccc202030726.

Carter, D. S. (2020). Neoliberalism in higher education and its effects on marginalized students. In A. Palko, S. Sapra & J. Wagman (Eds.), *Feminist responses to the neoliberalization of the university: From surviving to thriving* (pp. 19–30). Lexington Books.

Carter-Tod, S. (2021, Mar. 9). Rhetoric(s): A broader definition. *FEN Blog*. https://compstudiesjournal.com/2021/03/29/rhetorics-a-broader-definition/.

Chu, J. A. (2011). *Rebuilding shattered lives: Treating Complex PTSD and dissociative disorders* (2nd ed.). John Wiley & Sons, Inc.

Crozier, M. & Workman, E. (2022). Discourse-based interviews in institutional ethnography: Strategies for practice. *Composition Forum, 49*.

DeVault, M. L. (2019). Institutional ethnography: A mode of inquiry and a strategy for change. In A. Marvasti & A. J. Treviño (Eds.), *Researching Social Problems* (pp. 83–101). Routledge.

Dippre, R. J. (2019). *Talk, tools, and texts: A logic-in-use for studying lifespan literate action development.* The WAC Clearinghouse; University Press of Colorado. https://doi.org/10.37514/PRA-B.2019.0384.

Dippre, R. J. & Phillips, T. (2020). Introduction: Generating murmurations for an actionable coherence. In R. J. Dippre & T. Phillips (Eds.), *Approaches to lifespan writing research: Generating actionable coherence* (pp. 3–11). The WAC Clearinghouse; University Press of Colorado. https://doi.org/10.37514/PER-B.2020.1053.1.3.

Dolmage, J. (2017). *Academic ableism: Disability and higher education.* University of Michigan Press.

Evans-Winters, V. E. (2019). *Black feminism in qualitative inquiry: A mosaic for writing our daughter's body.* Routledge.

Fixsen, A., Ridge, D. & Porter, A. (2022). Arachne, self-care and 'power-nets' on women's self-development programmes. *Gender and Education, 34*: 1–17. https://doi.org/10.1080/09540253.2022.2078793.

Griffith, A. I. & Smith, D. E. (Eds.). (2014). *Under new public management: Institutional ethnographies of changing front-line work.* University of Toronto Press.

Jackson, R. L & Grutsch McKinney, J. (Eds.). (2021). *Self + Culture + Writing: Autoethnography for/as writing studies.* Utah State University Press.

Jubas, K. & Seidel, J. (2016). Knitting as a metaphor for work: An institutional autoethnography to surface tensions of visibility and invisibility in the neoliberal academy. *Journal of Contemporary Ethnography, 45*(1), 60–84. https://doi.org/10.1177/0891241614550200.

Klevan, T. & Grant, A. (2022). *An autoethnography of becoming a qualitative researcher: A dialogic view of academic development.* Routledge.

Korn, D. L. (2009). EMDR and the treatment of Complex PTSD: A review. *Journal of EMDR Practice and Research, 3*(4), 264–278.

Kynard, C. (2013). *Vernacular insurrections: Race, black protest, and the new century in composition-literacies studies.* SUNY Press.

Kynard, C. (2021). Troubling the boundaries" of Anti-Racism: The clarity of Black radical visions amid racial erasure. *WPA, 44*(3), 185–192.

LaFrance, M. (2019). *Institutional ethnography: A theory of practice for writing studies researchers.* Utah State University Press.

LaFrance, M. & Nicolas, M. (2012). Institutional ethnography as materialist framework for writing program research and the faculty-staff work standpoints project. *College Composition and Communication, 64*(1), 130–150.

Larrowe, R. & Workman, E. (2022). Why are you (still) here? Flippin' the script on madness and mentorship [Presentation]. Conference on College Composition and Communication. Virtual.

Lund, R. W. B. (2020). Exploring "whiteness" as ideology and work knowledge: Thinking with institutional ethnography. In R. W. B. Lund & A. C. E. Nilsen (Eds.), *Institutional ethnography in the Nordic region* (pp. 101–114). Routledge.

Maraj, L. M. (2021). You can't do that here: Black/feminist autoethnography and histories of intellectual exclusion. In R. L. Jackson & J. Grutsch McKinney (Eds.),

Self + Culture + Writing: Autoethnography for/as writing studies (p. 175–185). Utah State University Press.

Mateos, M. & Solé, I. (2012). Undergraduate students' conceptions and beliefs about academic writing. In M. Castelló & C. Donahue (Eds.), *University writing: Selves and texts in academic societies* (pp. 53–67). Emerald Group Publishing Limited.

Miley, M. (2018). Mapping boundedness and articulating interdependence between writing centers and writing programs. *Praxis: A Writing Center Journal, 16*(1), 75–87.

Price, M. (2011). *Mad at school: Rhetorics of mental disability and academic life*. University of Michigan Press.

Pritchard, E. D. (2016). *Fashioning lives: Black Queers and the politics of literacy*. Southern Illinois University Press.

Reiff, M. J. & Bawarshi, (2011). Tracing discursive resources: How students use prior genre knowledge to negotiate new writing contexts in first-year composition. *Written Communication, 28*(3), 312–337. https://doi.org/10.1177/0741088311410183.

Rice-Evans, J. & Stella, A. (2021). #Triggered: The invisible labor of traumatized doctoral students. *The Journal of Multimodal Rhetorics, 5*(1), 20–32. http://journalofmultimodalrhetorics.com/5-1-issue-rice-evans-and-stella.

Smith, D. E. (1999). *Writing the social: Critique, theory, and investigations*. University of Toronto Press.

Smith, D. E. (2005). *Institutional ethnography: A sociology for people*. The Gender Lens. AltaMira Press.

Smith, D. E. & Griffith, A. I. (2022). *Simply institutional ethnography: Creating a sociology for people*. University of Toronto Press.

Smith, D. E. & Turner, S. M. (2014). *Incorporating texts into institutional ethnographies*. University of Toronto Press.

Taber, N. (2010). Institutional ethnography, autoethnography, and narrative: An argument for incorporating multiple methodologies. *Qualitative Research, 10*(1), 5–25. https://doi.org/10.1177/1468794109348680.

Workman, E. (2020). Visualizing writing development: Mapping writers' conceptions of writing through the lifespan. In R. J. Dippre & T. Phillips (Eds.), *Approaches to lifespan writing research: Generating actionable coherence* (pp. 211–224). The WAC Clearinghouse; University Press of Colorado. https://doi.org/10.37514/PER-B.2020.1053.2.13.

Workman, E., Crozier, M. & Vandenberg, P. (2023). Writing standpoint(s): Institution, discourse, and method. In M. LaFrance & M. Nicolas (Eds.), *Institutional ethnography as writing studies practice* (pp. 81–96). The WAC Clearinghouse; University Press of Colorado. https://doi.org/10.37514/PER-B.2023.2029.2.01.

Yancey, K. B., Robertson, L. & Taczak, K. (2014). *Writing across contexts: Transfer, composition, and sites of writing*. Utah State University Press.

Zebroski, J. T. (2020). Writing as a matter of life and death: Writing through the transition between employment and retirement in the USA. In R. J. Dippre & T. Phillips (Eds.), *Approaches to lifespan writing research: Generating an actionable coherence* (pp. 143–157). The WAC Clearinghouse; University Press of Colorado. https://doi.org/10.37514/PER-B.2020.1053.2.09.

CHAPTER 15.

WAYFINDING: THE DEVELOPMENT OF AN APPROACH TO LIFESPAN WRITING

Karen Lunsford
University of California, Santa Barbara

Jonathan Alexander
University of California, Irvine

Carl Whithaus
University of California, Davis

The Wayfinding Project emerged for us as researchers as we encountered anecdotes and updates from our former students–young people who had graduated from the University of California and who went on to diverse, creative careers as well as on to rich, rewarding personal and civic lives. Frequently, because we had taught these young people in writing courses or writing-oriented courses, they would talk to us about their writing lives, describing the writing they had done and what they had learned about writing after graduation. We realized, like many in the field of lifespan writing studies, that these young people's writing development was ongoing—and far more complex than we had heretofore considered. In particular, we were struck by the extent to which these former students not only adapted pre-existing knowledge about writing, but also actively sought new ways of writing and, just as often, stumbled into whole new ways of conceptualizing what writing is, what it does, and what it can be used for. Increasingly, the models of writing development we had been working with previously did not seem to capture the complexity, or what we came to call the *serendipity*, of the writing experiences that these writers were sharing with us.

Two quick examples from our pilot study's focus group interviews might help explain what we were seeing. This study was approved by our campuses' IRBs, and all reports use pseudonyms for participants' names. One writer, Francine, a teacher, spoke at length about a variety of writing experiences in both her professional and personal life, and we were especially struck by her description of encountering other former classmates who arguably had been harassed by a teacher. In the era

DOI: https://doi.org/10.37514/PER-B.2024.2289.2.15

of #MeToo, she began collecting stories, set up a social media account to archive them, and moved toward writing up accounts that could be used by her school to make sure this teacher was not harming any other young women. We admired Francine's tenacity and ingenuity in conceiving of her writing as an opportunity to affect the lives of others, by bringing together her experiences as a student journalist and as a teacher, and by including the collection of other people's stories in that conception of writing. Another alum, Julissa, likewise spoke to us about a rich set of writing experiences. Almost as an afterthought, toward the end of the focus group interview in which she participated, she surprised us by talking about her creation of makeup videos and blog entries as a sideline. The videos she described struck us as complex and robust attempts to communicate about her makeup artistry, and we were particularly impressed by her account of how they provided access to another income stream as friends and viewers began to ask her to provide makeup services for special events. Julissa's success fed her interest in generating revenue through the gig economy. Such a venture seemed very much something that she "fell into," not something she had initially set out to do and not part of a larger or longer career trajectory. It was an opportunity that came about because she had been inspired by watching similar videos and because her talents became visible to an ever-widening circle of appreciative followers.

Francine and Julissa provide fascinating examples of how our alumni have been developing a wide array of writing and communication abilities to make their way in the world and, often, to change that world for the better. In both cases, and in most others that we have been collecting and analyzing, these alumni's stories about their writing are characterized for us by a sense of wayfinding, a quite literal "finding of one's way" through different possibilities. In our earliest conceptualization of wayfinding, we understood it as a potentially useful *metaphor* for the kind of roaming, searching, and even stumbling around that seemed to be among the main hallmarks of the narratives about post-graduate writing experiences we were hearing. Initially, then, wayfinding was a *description* of what we were seeing, but curiously it also described *our own* research process as we began collecting data, listening to participants, and developing themes from multiple focus groups. Could wayfinding be both a modality of composing *and* a methodology for analyzing writing development?

As we described in our first published article, *wayfinding* has been "a technical term for nearly 60 years in fields as disparate as urban planning, architecture, library and information science, computer programming, and health services" (Alexander, Lunsford & Whithaus, 2020, p. 121). In urban planning and architecture, for instance, wayfinding characterizes the kinds of environmental signposts that not only guide, but also cue people into possibilities as they navigate complex terrains and environments. We chose this technical term because it captures both intentional and serendipitous impulses. For example, a visitor navigating through the Louvre might follow the signage to artifacts deemed by prior museum patrons to be important destinations, such as the *Mona Lisa*. Upon seeing the long line in front of the painting, our visitor might choose to continue to follow the signage, but might also choose to seek an alternate path—whether a less traveled method of getting to the same place (say, by attending a private viewing), or a path to a less well known, but more personally relevant, destination altogether (say, by wandering through another wing of the museum to come upon an underappreciated masterpiece). All of these choices fall within the idea of "wayfinding." Moreover, a wayfinder often shares with others information about the path taken, again, sometimes deliberately (e.g., blogging about the experience) and sometimes incidentally (e.g., the route happens to be recorded by a phone's location system). This aspect of wayfinding–the accidental, the stumbling, the serendipitous–seemed to us a particularly compelling dimension of the concept, one that captured some of the accidental ways in which our alumni were talking about stumbling into whole new ways of writing, communicating, and thinking about to what uses they could put their writing and what new writing abilities they could develop. Indeed, as we argued in our first article, "[a]ll of these uses emphasize that, although cues may provide signposting for accepted ways of proceeding through these environments, individuals' own experiences are often 'messy,' inflected by additional environmental changes, happenstance, and individual agency" (p. 122).

Following in the footsteps of others thinking along comparable lines, such as Kevin Roozen and Joe Erickson (2017), we could easily have spent our time focused on deep descriptions and investigations of single authors or small sets of authors. Yet, given the seeming *consistency* of wayfinding characteristics that we were seeing in stories shared with us, we took inspiration from the work of Deborah Brandt (2001; 2014), wanting to track not only the ongoing development of literacy in American lives but what she more recently refers to as the "rise of writing," or the coming into dominance of writing as the key contemporary marker of literacy. Further, we were inspired by her attempts to track literacy development over multiple participants. A key element within the Wayfinding Project, and more generally within lifespan writing research, is this attention to how participants describe their own writing development. As a methodology, wayfinding offers participants opportunities to co-construct knowledge about their writing practices and its significance in their lives.

The remainder of this chapter outlines some of the key dimensions of wayfinding as we have refined it into a framework through which to approach and theorize writing development. While we began with wayfinding as a metaphor for understanding such development, we have come to appreciate the many ways in which wayfinding attunes our attention to how post-graduate writers come to understand their movement in and through a variety of communication contexts. In turn, wayfinding's emphasis on pathways, whether intentional or serendipitous, has become for us a methodology for tracking how writers orient themselves or become oriented in multifaceted writing contexts. So, to answer our earlier question, wayfinding works for us as both description of composing practices and methodology for analyzing them. Key to our understanding of wayfinding as a methodology is the emergence of *orientation* as a significant and necessary dimension, which we consider in the next section. Then, we turn to the kinds of research questions generated from the wayfinding framework and provide specific examples of survey questions that we will implement in the next iteration of the study. In the final section, we consider how wayfinding is situated within the larger ecology of lifespan writing research.

ORIENTATION AS KEY TO UNDERSTANDING HOW WRITERS DEVELOP ACROSS MULTIPLE CONTEXTS

As an approach for studying writing, wayfinding necessarily foregrounds the many contexts participants navigate, create, and respond to. In doing so, wayfinding as a methodology resonates with two core insights articulated by Bazerman et al.'s (2018) Lifespan Writing Development Group (LWDG). The first has to do with the nature of "context," and the second concerns the importance of "orientation" as a methodological consideration. One of the core insights that the LWDG has brought to the table is their insistence on developing a robust conceptualization of context(s) that includes how multi-layered contexts influence writers as well as how writers shape—and continuously reshape—the contexts they encounter. That insight drives wayfinding as a methodology.

Our focus group participants' own words have shown us not only this plurality of contexts but also the many active ways in which writers choose to align with, select or discard elements from, decline engagement with, and otherwise actively create those contexts. The participants in the Wayfinding Project focus groups acted as co-constructors of knowledge about writing by not only engaging in conversations with the researchers, but also with each other during the focus groups. Listening to their accounts of writing as an activity that cuts across contexts, while also being embedded within multiple contexts, helped shape the ways in which we conceptualize writing development as contextual and also directional. One way that we have come to understand how individuals both act upon and react to contexts is through the concept of *orientation*—which includes, but is not limited to, the range of environmental cues, signposts, personal motivations, and happy circumstances that writers use to make their choices.

Understanding *contexts* as plural and malleable means our methodology needs to account for writers' generative relationships across, through, and with the contexts they engage. Near the opening of *The Lifespan Development of Writing*, Charles Bazerman et al. (2018) insist on the need to "account[] for the individuality of trajectories that can lead to distinctive voices and expressions" as well as the "complexities and many dimensions" that make up different context(s) (p. 21). Bazerman et al. remind us that context, especially when thinking about writing development over time, is never singular. It is always nested within multiple experiences that writers have as they move across contexts, and often a writer may carry elements from one context to another. These are not only interpretations of different contexts, but also the creation of context through a writer's understanding of a situation in relationship to, or rather with reference to, previous situations. Ryan Dippre and Anna Smith (2020) capture some of the vitality around this conceptualization of context(s) in their chapter, "Always Already Relocalized: The Protean Nature of Context in Lifespan Writing Research." Dippre and Smith "take up the word *protean* to describe [their] vision of context because it highlights the highly variable character of context—the responsive flexibility that the so-called 'background' of our social actions has to those actions . . . [They] see protean as a useful word located in interesting corners of literacy and writing research to articulate the complex social worlds within which writers and readers of texts live, work, and build" (p. 28).

This conceptualization of contexts as protean resonates with our wayfinding approach to studying writing because of the ways in which our participants defined contexts and pushed us to think outside of—or really *across*—school, professional, personal, and civic contexts. The protean nature of these contexts emerged strongly when focus group participants in the initial three-year pilot study were asked (as part of a series of eight questions) to "describe for us a time or situation in which you have written something meaningful. What was it and what was your process?" While we originally included this question in an effort to help us replicate some of the work in Michele Eodice, Anne Geller, and Neal Lerner's *Meaningful Writing Project*, our participants' answers began to push us to consider how they were defining and/or asking questions about what writing contexts we were interested in. Participants often asked us to clarify whether we were limiting the question to writing done while they were in school. When we did not define a context for them, or when we insisted that context was whatever they wanted to discuss, they would move on to include examples such as an obituary for a dog, an unsuccessful cover letter, a Master's thesis, a post about a social issue that unexpectedly went viral on Reddit, a family memorial, and lesson plans for a course in French, among many others.

Responses to this question illustrated not only the wide range of contexts in which participants found writing to be meaningful, but also how their sense of what counts as meaningful changed when their understanding of the context changed. For example, Julissa responded that her most meaningful writing was the poetry she wrote as an undergraduate in a setting deliberately crafted to be separate from her schooling: "I think I would have to get into my space, into my cozy writing space in my dorm at my desk, have a nice notebook specifically for this kind of writing, it's not my school notebook." She went on to explain that she had in mind a particular piece of poetry, "because it was about my family and I ended up submitting it. It was the only thing I ever submitted. It was like a runner up for fifth place for some UC poetry thing but it was such a huge deal . . . to share something in this sort of way." In other words, although Julissa generally created a private, "cozy" environment separate from her schoolwork to engage in poetry, the most meaningful piece was about her family that, "put something personal into a form I felt confident enough to share and then any sort of small recognition in that way is that kind of validation like, 'Oh, okay. This is something.'" Julissa's comments resonate with Ryan Dippre and Anna Smith's (2020) assertion that writing contexts are protean, always partially formed and overlapping, complex ecologies, where "the responsive flexibility that the so-called 'background'" is reshaped and re-envisioned as participants recall it. Dippre and Smith's insight that writing plays a "reciprocal role in producing context" (p. 27) has encouraged us to allow participants to define their contexts. With that said, our participants' insistence on the importance of context should not be taken as a claim that contexts determined why a piece of writing was meaningful. Rather, participants often articulated how their own agency, how their own actions to produce a piece of writing, made that writing meaningful.

Considering how writers *orient* themselves and *are oriented* by different contexts becomes a particularly significant way in which we can analyze the moves writers make within protean contexts. We can return to the case of Julissa for an example of what such orientation looks like in participants' discussion of their post-graduate writing lives. Following up on her responses to the most meaningful writing she has done, Julissa explained that she "rarely" wrote poetry at the time we spoke with her, again attributing her writing response to the *environment* she now inhabits: "Yeah. It's funny how getting into the land and business of words really zapped any energy to write them. Maybe on the subway sometimes." As Julissa's responses articulate the conditions under which her poetry is "meaningful" to her, they also indicate the environmental *cues* she attends to in order to make that determination: her sense of the coziness of her dorm and the special notebook (cues: emotions, space, and materials); her focus on her family and the resulting reward of her private interest being validated by public attention (cues: topic and response); and her reflection on how making words her professional business has led her to indulge in poetry only in transit (cues: time, space, and materials). As we have been developing the idea of wayfinding, we have found ourselves becoming ever more alert to how participants describe and attend to these cues which *orient* their writing, as well as their sense of what writing is for and the roles it plays in their lives.

The Wayfinding Project is not the first group of lifespan writing researchers to take up the importance of "orientation." Anna Smith considers how methodological approaches that emphasize orientations to writing development "across," "through," and/or "with" may enable researchers to embrac[e] the complexity of writing" (p. 16). For Smith, "an across orientation assumes writing—its writers, artifacts, practices, etc.—are in constant motion (Kell, 2009), and that writing in one location and time is not tethered or isolated to that context; rather, writing is a widely distributed, highly complex phenomenon (Prior, 1998; Shipka, 2011)" (p. 18).

As a way of studying writing and writing development, an *across* orientation acknowledges contexts but it also acknowledges writers' agency and how that agency changes and shifts not only what different contexts mean but quite literally what different contexts *are*. Smith's emphasis on considering *through* as another key orientation for lifespan writing researchers draws on Lemke's (2000) notion of using different scales of time for considering writing development—as when, for instance, ideas drawn from or developed over many different contexts and through many different scenarios crystallize in writing in a particular moment (p. 20). Finally, Smith (2020) notes that a methodological orientation towards studying writing *with* participants "makes writing researchers privy to critical in vivo insights," "provides proximity to practice that cannot be otherwise articulated," and as Django Paris and Maisha T. Winn (2014) have argued, is "potentially a more humanizing orientation than researching about" (p. 22). These three approaches emphasize the importance of researchers considering how participants view writing within the contexts of their lives.

Smith's attention to orientation has been enlightening and inspiring for us, but her primary focus in her scholarship is on *researchers'* attitudes and approaches. Our particular innovation with wayfinding is to recognize how *participants'* descriptions and reflections emphasize orientation in their own writing lives. We are interested in orientation as not just a research disposition but as a *phenomenological experience* of post-collegiate writers. Indeed, as with Julissa, many of our participants describe their writing lives as a complex process of orienting themselves to ever-shifting terrains of communication, some with clearly marked signposts directing them to particular modalities and genres of writing and others with unexpected and sometimes serendipitous pathways forged in the process of making discoveries, imagining connections, and encountering new possibilities for rich forms of writing and communication.

Methodologically, wayfinding picks up on this multifaceted approach to orientation, and it relies upon, analyzes, and plays with all of the meanings of "orientation." After all, as researchers, we are interested in how participants orient themselves within their writing environments – whether alumni are deliberately choosing personal or professional goals according to signals they encounter in their environments, or actively crafting and re-arranging their environments to be more conducive to their goals and well-being, or accidentally falling by happenstance into activities or environments they find suitable. Moreover, we find ourselves reflecting on our own orientations towards the project and to environmental factors (such as responses from our own reviewers and readers; the technologies available to us; the regulations that constrain us) that cue us towards certain research processes and away from others. In the next section, we consider how our own research processes have oriented us toward certain questions we have begun asking our participants about their writing lives post-graduation.

WAYFINDING'S RESEARCH QUESTIONS

As we have completed our three-year pilot study, we have come to realize that the consistency of our observations about our alumni that we named through the metaphor of wayfinding caused us to shift our own research methods towards thinking about and eliciting possible dimensions of wayfinding. That dialectic between our observations and the metaphor has become embedded within the project, moving us toward wayfinding as a methodology: Specifically, wayfinding pays attention to both the unexpected encounters and the orienting pathways that participants follow as they develop as writers across time.

Recently, we have deliberately sought to operationalize the methodology of wayfinding through specific interview and survey methods that we will employ when, late in 2023, we launch the full study of alumni from our three UC campuses (i.e., all alumni 3–10 years from graduation). The focus group interviews from the pilot, as discussed in the examples above, have suggested several robust themes to pursue. We will reprise these themes in the future focus group questions, and we have chosen to focus specifically on the themes of orientation, intention/serendipity, and the gig economy in the survey. We hope to leverage the large numbers of alumni from the UC system to elicit survey data to paint the large-picture context for the study.

As an approach towards understanding both intentional and serendipitous writing development among not just individuals, but large populations of participants, wayfinding guides us towards these overarching research questions:

1. How do participants orient themselves towards, navigate within, and, most significantly, create the different contexts in which they write? In other words, as researchers, we prioritize participants' agency as they decide for themselves what they want their writing to do, when, and how. We seek to analyze how participants make these orienting decisions, and what they identify in their environments as important elements by which they orient their actions, their knowledges of writing, and their decisions about where to invest their time.

We operationalize this research interest by asking survey and interview questions regarding not just what they learned in one context versus another, but about their histories of writing of all types (professional, personal, self-sponsored, civic, social) and how they came to write them. In our analyses, we are attuned to the signposts they mention in their decisions (for example, choosing to pursue or abandon writing in response to other people's opinions) and to unexpected opportunities that present themselves through writing (for example, realizing that a new activist project resonates strongly with an already developed creative writing project).

In the survey we have developed after the pilot, we are seeking to elicit more information about how the different types of signposts our initial respondents mentioned affect alumni's career choices. We include a series of questions about such signposts in the revised survey. In the pilot, for example, our alumni mentioned that they often make choices about writing based on responses they receive from others. In this current survey, we tease out the impact of these responses, such as in this question about the impact of positive responses on how alumni do or do not select writing opportunities:

> Others' positive responses to my writing have led me [check all that apply]
> - To pursue a different professional opportunity I did not anticipate
> - To pursue a different volunteer opportunity I did not anticipate
> - To pursue a different hobby or personal interest I did not anticipate
> - To try new types (genres) of writing
> - To discover a new talent
> - To renew my determination to pursue a career pathway I had chosen

Such questions, we hope, will elicit more data about writers' agency in orienting themselves towards different post-graduate writing experiences.

2. In general, we are interested in how historical and economic contexts influence our participants' understandings of writing, but wayfinding as a

concept turns our attention to a more specific question: **How do participants respond to and orient themselves towards cultural moments of change?** We are especially interested in this question because it emphasizes the serendipitous side of wayfinding, particularly when navigating through uncharted territory. Based on our experiences with the pilot version of the Wayfinding Project, we have revised our survey and interview questions to explore three areas of cultural change:

a. The gig economy, with attention to the many stories of our alumni creating their own economic niches through writing

b. The exacerbated civic divides within many countries, with attention to how alumni orient themselves and their writing towards different socio-political positions, and with particular attention to participants whose socio-political contributions are less visible than, but no less significant than, those of self-identified activists

c. The continuous impact of new media developments, with attention to how alumni take up new platforms' affordances for composing, publishing, reception, and rebroadcasting, and how, in response, alumni alter their understandings of what writing is and what it does

To take up one example, the issue of the gig economy, we have found through the pilot study that participants often do not count gig jobs as something worth mentioning to us, just as they often do not consider many things they do as "writing." If we want to know more about gig work, then we need to ask participants explicitly about these issues.

Through questions such as these, we hope to learn more precisely how frequently our alumni are taking up gig work in the current economy, to what extent such jobs involve writing, and to what extent our respondents consider them as deliberate or serendipitous moves towards new writing opportunities.

3. What roles do non-curricular and non-professional writing play in orienting how participants develop their individual knowledges of writing? As an approach, wayfinding does not privilege one learning context—schooling—over others. That interest often overshadows attention to how personal, creative, activist, social, and other forms of writing that alumni deem "unofficial" shape their understandings of writing—and especially how, for individual respondents, the boundaries among these different domains of writing are wonderfully porous. Participants may, for example, orient themselves towards self-defined overarching goals or aims that diminish or even negate distinctions among different contexts, as when a historian describes writing a novel never intended for publication as one of the ways she develops better understandings of other cultures. Those better understandings might inform her professional research articles, but, in her account, writing a never-to-be-completed novel is not positioned as a preliminary exercise towards those articles, but an equally valued way of continuously thinking about the world. Likewise, as researchers, we are attending to the multiple "teachers" of writing that participants identify, which so far have been as varied as family members, distant colleagues, friends, anonymous respondents on social media, and audiences for stand-up comedy.

Drawing upon the pilot study, the current survey contains a series of questions that name non-curricular/non-professional contexts and agents. These questions seek to elicit data about how the participant has oriented their decisions about when, where, and why they write. Moreover, they seek information about whether these decisions led participants to discover new career or non-professional writing opportunities. For instance, we have one set of queries about how participants respond to the requests of family members. Other questions in this series seek to suss out the impact of writing for creative purposes, activist purposes, non-professional organizations or volunteer groups, and social media.

4. How do participants themselves perceive the histories and futures of their writing pathways (as more traditional? serendipitous?), and thus how do they orient their identities as writers around these perceptions? Wayfinding comprises both deliberate and serendipitous occurrences during a writer's life. As researchers, we have learned from the pilot study to be cautious to avoid assumptions about how a participant perceives a certain event or sequence of events. What we might interpret as a happy accident, a participant might see as intentional, and vice versa. Moreover, our alumni have different tolerances for recursivity, writing during times of ambiguity, and dealing with the unanticipated. The pilot data from the focus groups suggest that alumni may more or less smoothly integrate new goals into the stories of the writing lives that they present. To avoid imposing our own interpretations of the traditional and the serendipitous on the histories and futures of writing that alumni articulate, we have again decided to include explicit queries about their perceptions, such as the following:

> Which of the following best describes your career path so far? [check one]
>
> - Since earning my bachelor's degree, I have been following a career path with well-defined steps
> - Since earning my bachelor's degree, I have been following a career path with unanticipated turns

These explicit queries also include questions about how COVID-19 has impacted their professional and personal journeys. Again, we seek to document our respondents' perceptions of the challenges and opportunities that the pandemic has brought, and how respondents integrate these moments into their accounts of their writing lives.

5. What are the different epistemological, cultural, subcultural, and lingual knowledges about writing that our participants identify, and how do these factors orient alumni's writing development? Of course, this question covers quite a bit of territory, a landscape shared by many writing researchers. However, we are specifically watching for moments of choice in these accounts, times when alumni decide for themselves what they want their writing to do, when, and how—and what elements they name as orienting those choices. In many cases, those elements come from contexts beyond school or professional cultures. As mentioned earlier, one of the most productive questions we asked during the pilot was a variation of the central question from *The Meaningful Writing Project* (Eodice et al., 2017). In the current survey, we include the following pair of questions about meaningful writing:

> What is the most meaningful writing you have done (for whatever reason, in all aspects of your life)? Why is it the most meaningful for you?

We are also asking similar questions in our revised focus group interviews. Our adaptation from Eodice et al.'s version is to decouple the questions from an inquiry about a school curriculum. In fact, when participants during the pilot asked us whether we intended to restrict answers to their school years, we responded that they could, but they could also consider writing in extracurricular activities and in the years since graduation. We also encouraged them to use their own definition of "meaningful" and to explain how they defined it.

Wayfinding encourages researchers to ask questions about the roles that serendipity, creativity, and the unexpected play in shaping literate practices across time and in different environments. Wayfinding also analyzes participants' awareness of their own ongoing writing development through reflection on their experiences. That is, wayfinding implies that who you understand yourself to be as a writer shifts over time and across contexts. Wayfinding opens up a way for writers to describe those shifting writerly identities in ways that are nuanced and based on lived experience, projected plans and identities, and imagined, even aspirational futures.

WAYFINDING IN THE ECOLOGY OF LIFESPAN WRITING STUDIES

In sum, we contend that wayfinding offers researchers in lifespan writing studies a compelling metaphor and methodology for conceptualizing how writers navigate different writing environments over time. Emphasizing writers' agency, wayfinding tracks writers moving across multiple contexts, stitching together a variety of experiences with writing while also grappling with unexpected challenges and opportunities. Wayfinding offers lifespan writing studies a multidimensional and flexible approach to studying writers' experiences.

Our interest in alumni writing development has often been understood by reviewers and interlocutors as a form of transfer. After all, aren't we tracking the movement of writing knowledge across different domains? Indeed, we have learned much from our colleagues who undertake research in transfer. At the same time, we have come to see how the metaphor of transfer privileges the impact of curricula in a fairly linear direction. We offer wayfinding as a more writerly driven and holistic accounting of writers' experiences across protean contexts. For instance, one significant difference lies in how transfer studies often focus on the movement of abilities and knowledges from one curricular context to another, or from an authority-defined context *outward*. Wayfinding is much more invested in the agency of writers and the choices they have to make, sometimes improvisationally, as they move through and navigate different, sometimes unexpected contexts. Second, transfer studies generally emphasize more of a one-to-one model of context-to-context, whereas wayfinding tends to emphasize the exploratory. Certainly, transfer studies often acknowledge the "fuzziness" of transfer across contexts, but wayfinding tends to *prioritize* that fuzziness, attending as it does to ambiguity, serendipity, and the unexpected.

Another frequent comment in response to our work pertains to its potential applicability in the teaching of writing, specifically in the composition classroom. At this point in our research, however, our interest has been in generating knowledge about post-graduate writing experiences as a primary object of scholarly research. In time, with more data and analysis, our research might generate insights about how to shape the teaching of writing in ways that anticipate some of the directions and trajectories that our participants suggest are important to them. At this time, though, we cannot help but return to the prominence of the serendipitous in the stories that such participants bring to us, and so we cryptically suggest that a wayfinding-inspired composition pedagogy might try to make room for chance, the accidental, and the unexpected. Further, wayfinding has taught us that a curricular focus does not always make sufficient room to acknowledge, much less honor, epistemologies and experiences outside the standard, normalizing curriculum. For instance, Kate Seltzer (2022) adopts wayfinding to describe a Latinx bilingual student's metacommentary on her own experiences as someone labeled as a "struggling" student; far from "struggling," though, this student wrote poetry and shared her writing with others, actively pursuing the "seeking and navigating that so many writers engage in, particularly those . . . who stake out a writerly identity and practice that eschews the white gaze" (p. 17). Making room in our research for such experiences when they exceed formal and curricular domains is increasingly crucial if we are to understand the complex wayfinding of writers' lives as well as interrogate the racist assumptions and practices that are still a part of much educational activity.

Some readers of this volume might also wonder about similarities and differences between wayfinding and improvisation, a concept highlighted in the introduction to this volume; we do see overlaps between the terms. Phillips and Dippre (this volume) describe improvisation as an approach where the performer has deep knowledge of techniques through extended practice, and is therefore prepared to recombine or reconfigure or renew them in order to respond to new information, new collaborators, new challenges. Similarly, a wayfinder can follow signposted cues to accomplish established goals but can also respond to the serendipitous. Where they differ: wayfinding also implies identifying pathways for others to follow and retrace, laying down new signposts as new possibilities are discovered, developed, constructed. Many of our students and alumni mention being highly responsive to their families and communities, and they readily share how they achieve their goals. Improvisation implies living in the serendipitous.

As researchers, we certainly engaged in our share of improvisation. When we started the project, we drew upon our own previous research experiences, and we looked to established research projects to identify elements that might be used to discuss the writing lives of millennials. We asked the scholars behind the Revisualizing Composition Project (Moore et al., 2016) to share their research questions and survey platform with us, so that we could deliberately replicate some of the elements and eventually compare the responses of our participants with theirs. Likewise, we looked to the Pew Foundation for survey questions about media use that could be replicated in order to define our survey population, and to compare that population with the Pew Foundation's findings (which the Pew Foundation's copyright statement allows). Not least, we took up a question from the Meaningful Writing Project because it seemed to us to be especially insightful. In other words, there were elements in the research around us that we reconstituted into our own project. In that sense, we were improvisationists. We have responded to serendipitous opportunities, ranging from feedback at conferences to advice from our graduate student assistants to, especially, the generous and unexpected responses from our participants.

But we are also creating pathways—research orientations—for other researchers who are taking up the idea of wayfinding to explain the combination of traditional and serendipitous paths that they are noticing in their own participants. Such development is moving our project from its own form of improvisational wayfinding toward a methodology to understand the phenomenology of writing experiences.

Ultimately, we believe that wayfinding as a methodology has the possibility of illuminating different ways of understanding writing throughout the lifespan, not just in the years immediately following graduation from college. While our participants were most likely no more than thirty years of age, we anticipate that the activities of wayfinding—particularly orienting oneself toward writing tasks and experiencing serendipitous re-orientations toward such tasks, as well as encountering openings to new and unexpected ways of composing—are common to the experience of writing at numerous points in one's life. For instance, the writers described by Lauren Rosenberg (2015) in *The Desire for Literacy: Writing in The Lives of Adult Learners*, as well as Chris Anson's (2016) autoethnographic experience detailed in "The Pop Warner Chronicles: A Case Study in Contextual Adaptation and the Transfer of Writing Ability," can all usefully be described, understood, and theorized through wayfinding. With that said, we might underscore how the attention wayfinding brings to *serendipity* might be particularly useful for understanding and conceptualizing writing experiences of those who are working (professionally, personally, or civically) in contexts in which writing tools, technologies, and platforms are rapidly changing or developing. We look forward to seeing how wayfinding develops as a theoretical and conceptual tool useful for a range of lifespan writing studies.

For now, we have chosen to focus on the first decade post-graduation, a pivotal time in the development of writers as they are making the transition from curricular to professional, career, personal, civic, and other domains in which the need for effective and ever-changing forms of communication are met with unexpected desires, opportunities, and potentialities for using writing—to connect with others, to discover and explore new passions, to build worlds through words and other media. Julissa's exploration of video is an extension of her creativity, expanding her social circle, and possibly enhancing her ability to earn money. Francine marshals narrative to think through how she might effect positive change in an educational institution. These are examples of alumni discovering ways to change their worlds through writing. It may be that the primary orientation of wayfinding is toward hope—toward a belief in the ongoing potentiality of writing itself.

REFERENCES

Alexander, J., Lunsford, K. & Whithaus, C. (2020). Toward wayfinding: A metaphor for understanding writing experiences. *Written Communication, 37*(1), 104–131. https://doi.org/10.1177/0741088319882325.

Anson, C. M. (2016). The Pop Warner chronicles: A case study in contextual adaptation and the transfer of writing ability. *College Composition and Communication, 67*(4), 518–549. https://www.jstor.org/stable/44783545.

Bazerman, C., Applebee, A. N., Berninger, V. W., Brandt, D., Graham, S., Jeffery, J. B., Matsuda, P. K., Murphy, S., Rowe, D. W., Schleppegrell, M. & Wilcox, K. C. (2018). *The lifespan development of writing*. National Council of Teachers of English. https://wac.colostate.edu/books/ncte/lifespan-writing/.

Brandt, D. (2001). *Literacy in American lives*. Cambridge University Press.

Brandt, D. (2014). *The rise of writing: Redefining mass literacy*. Cambridge University Press.

Dippre, R. J. & Smith, A. (2020). Always already relocalized: The protean nature of context in lifespan writing research. In R. J. Dippre & T. Phillips (Eds.), *Approaches to lifespan writing research: Generating an actionable coherence* (pp. 27–38). The WAC Clearinghouse; University Press of Colorado. https://doi.org/10.37514/PER-B.2020.1053.

Eodice, M., Geller, A. E. & Lerner, N. (2017). *The meaningful writing project: Learning, teaching and writing in higher education*. Utah State University Press.

Kell, C. (2009). Literacy practices, text/s and meaning making across time and space. In M. Baynham & M. Prinsloo (Eds.), *The future of literacy studies* (pp. 75–99). Palgrave Macmillan.

Lemke, J. (2000). Across the scales of time: Artifacts, activities, and meanings in ecosocial systems. *Mind, Culture and Activity, 7*(4), 273–290. https://doi.org/10.1207/S15327884MCA0704_03.

Moore, J. L., Rosinski, P., Peeples, T., Pigg, S., Rife, M. C., Brunk-Chavez, B., Lackey, D., Rumsey, S. K., Tasaka, R., Curran, P. & Grabill, J. T. (2016). Revisualizing composition: How first-year writers use composing technologies. *Computers and Composition, 39*, 1–13. https://doi.org/10.1016/j.compcom.2015.11.001.

Paris, D. & Winn, M. T. (Eds.). (2014). *Humanizing research: Decolonizing qualitative inquiry with youth and communities*. Sage.

Prior, P. (1998). *Writing/disciplinarity: A sociohistoric account of literate activity in the academy*. Lawrence Erlbaum Associates.

Prior, P. & Smith, A. (2020). Writing across: Tracing transliteracies as becoming over time, space, and settings. *Learning, Culture, and Social Interaction, 24*. https://doi.org/10.1016/j.lcsi.2018.07.002.

Roozen, K. & Erickson, J. (2017). *Expanding literate landscapes: Persons, practices, and sociohistoric perspectives of disciplinary development*. The Computers and Composition Digital Press; Utah State University Press. http://ccdigitalpress.org/expanding/.

Rosenberg, L. (2015). *The desire for literacy: Writing in the lives of adult learners*. Conference on College Composition and Communication/National Council of Teachers of English.

Seltzer, K. (2022). 'A lot of students are already there': Repositioning language-minoritized students as 'writers in residence' in English classrooms. *Written Communication, 39*(1), 44–65. https://doi.org/10.1177/07410883211053787.

Shipka, J. (2011). *Toward a composition made whole*. University of Pittsburgh Press.

Smith, A. (2020). Across, through, and with: Ontological orientations for lifespan writing research. In R. J. Dippre & T. Phillips (Eds.), *Approaches to lifespan writing research: Generating an actionable coherence* (pp. 15–26). The WAC Clearinghouse; University Press of Colorado. https://doi.org/10.37514/PER-B.2020.1053.

CHAPTER 16.

HOW MIGHT WE MEASURE THAT? CONSIDERATIONS FROM QUANTITATIVE RESEARCH APPROACHES FOR LIFESPAN WRITING RESEARCH

Matthew Carl Zajic
Teachers College, Columbia University

Apryl Lynn Poch
University of Nebraska, Omaha

If you open almost any journal article or book chapter that involves writing, you will most likely find a sentence that describes writing as a complex phenomenon. The Lifespan Writing Development Group laid out numerous reasons why writing is a complex phenomenon in the context of lifespan writing research (Bazerman et al., 2018). Dippre and Phillips (2020) continued that conversation to show that the complexities involved in understanding writing from a lifespan perspective had only just begun to be figured out. While that complexity often falls to the constellation of activities and experiences that researchers and educators attribute to writing, we argue that the complexity just as much falls on trying to delineate meaningful approaches to study the act of writing through time and context as is reflected in the leading question for this future-oriented chapter: *How might quantitative approaches assist researchers trying to make sense of how writing develops and what experiences matter to writers across the lifespan?*

    Like the composition of the initial Lifespan Writing Development Group, we assume that lifespan writing researchers come from a variety of disciplines, hold different pedagogical and theoretical orientations, and have received advanced training in various (but not always similar) research methodologies. As highlighted in Bazerman et al. (2018), the cross talk across disciplines can be productive and challenging: "We swapped articles and papers, wrote research summaries, asked one another questions, traded citations, argued and quibbled at times, and developed lists of convergence points" (p. 13). We begin this chapter with this mindset by acknowledging the challenges at hand for writing researchers interested in understanding lifespan writing development. The field of writing research is at times multidisciplinary, interdisciplinary, and transdisciplinary, given the many fields and communities involved (Adler-Kassner & Wardle, 2016; Berninger et al., 2012; Morin et al., 2021). Across these overlapping disciplinary identities are researchers who bring different insights, research designs, and methodological toolkits to the problems at hand. Our aim is to offer some insights into quantitative approaches given our own disciplinary expertise.

In the previous lifespan writing collection, we overviewed some broad concepts about quantitative methodologies and methods, particularly about more advanced longitudinal techniques using structural equation modeling (Zajic & Poch, 2020). This chapter continues that conversation but is not the next sequential step. Instead, this chapter takes a different perspective to how lifespan writing researchers might conceptualize the ways quantitative research approaches may inform future lifespan writing research. We focus on three main issues. First, we contextualize quantitative research within the broader landscape of research designs, methodologies, and methods. Second, we focus on quantitative longitudinal research approaches, highlighting their utility for lifespan writing researchers. Third, we draw from the eight principles put forth by the Lifespan Writing Development Group (Bazerman et al., 2018) to consider how quantitative research approaches may help to address the nuances of studying writing across the lifespan. We aim to highlight the utility of quantitative research approaches as *part* of the toolkit available to lifespan writing researchers and foster conversations among researchers to employ such designs and methods in future research endeavors. Thus, we focus on the productive conversations available within such a diverse collective where we can recognize the challenges but foresee the possibilities.

QUANTITATIVE RESEARCH DESIGNS, METHODOLOGIES, AND METHODS: DEFINITIONS AND CONCEPTUAL FOUNDATIONS

Researchers interested in lifespan writing development employ different theoretical frameworks for research designs that use a variety of methods. In many ways, this mirrors the broader literacy research field (Mallette & Duke, 2021), as literacy researchers, like writing researchers, make up a diverse discipline. In two recent studies, Parsons et al. (2016, 2020) conducted a series of content analyses across literacy research journals to determine the types of topics being studied and the theoretical perspectives and methods employed by literacy researchers. (Literacy as defined here includes "reading, writing, language, communication, and more" [Parsons et al., 2020, p. 341].) In their analysis of 1,238 articles across nine journals, Parsons et al. (2016) found differences across journals among the research topics, adopted theoretical perspectives, research designs, and data sources; their main conclusions highlighted a fragmented research field. In their subsequent analysis of 4,305 articles published in 15 journals, Parsons et al. (2020) found similar differences with an additional factor being that approaches differed between research and practitioner journals. Important to our discussion, they highlight the need to diversify methods used in research articles, as diversity in approaches will enhance the knowledge base of the literacy research field (see Mallette & Duke, 2021).

As we look at the table of contents of this current edition and the two previous edited collections (Bazerman et al., 2018; Dippre & Phillips, 2020), we could make similar conclusions simply based off researcher representations. Parsons et al. (2020) drew on the framework of "thought collectives" and "thought styles" (Fleck, 1979) to contextualize how research communities exchange ideas within a field. Importantly, they highlighted the benefit raised by Fleck (1979) that having multiple thought collectives and styles strengthened a research field, given that it provides diversity in thought and perspective. This current edition clearly highlights the multitude of different thought collectives and styles present to the study of lifespan writing research, as diversity brings novel ideas, approaches, and analytical toolkits.

Thinking of quantitative traditions as a thought collective (though an oversimplification, given several different ways one might think about quantitative data), we first define what we mean by quantitative research traditions. Quantitative traditions are best understood within the broader context of *research approaches* ("plans and procedures for research that span the steps from broad assumptions to detailed methods of data collection, analysis, and interpretation"; Creswell & Creswell, 2018, p. 3). Research approaches encompass three areas that differ by research tradition: (a) philosophical assumptions, (b) research designs, and (c) research methods (including data collection, analysis, and interpretation).

PHILOSOPHICAL ASSUMPTIONS

Most often, quantitative research traditions are associated with postpositivist assumptions that value the identification of causal mechanisms that influence various outcomes, such as those specified in experimental studies (Creswell & Creswell, 2018). The focus tends to fall on testing the scientific method by drawing on relevant theories and collecting data (through careful observation and measurement techniques) to test said theories. While the former may not be as relevant to our current discussion, we see the latter as an important contribution to emerging lifespan writing theories (e.g., Bazerman et al., 2018). However, a fixation solely on causal explanatory approaches limits the assumptions held with quantitative approaches. In his philosophical examination of different quantitative research methods, Haig (2013) referenced causal modeling as just one approach, with other prominent approaches highlighting the flexibility of exploratory approaches (e.g., exploratory data analysis) innate to quantitative approaches. Although confirmatory, causal, and experimental approaches may first come to mind when considering the assumptions underlying quantitative approaches, a focus on those approaches limits the perspectives taken by quantitative researchers and the potential value of such methods to lifespan writing research.

Research Designs

Research designs set the context and specify the procedures required for enacting a research study. Selecting the appropriate research design can often be a challenging task (Vogt et al., 2012). Research designs may be experimental in nature, with two prominent designs being *true (or randomized) experiments* and *quasi-experiments* (Reichardt, 2019). *Nonexperimental designs* include correlational or observational designs (Kieffer, 2021), and *longitudinal designs* involve data collection over multiple time points. We discussed structural equation modeling designs in our previous chapter (Zajic & Poch, 2020), some of which involve longitudinal designs. Further, Creswell and Creswell (2018) highlight *survey research designs* as encompassing both nonexperimental and longitudinal designs.

Research Methods

Lastly, the methods inform the process of data collection, analysis, and interpretation (Creswell & Creswell, 2018). Though the assumptions and designs are important and critical to the overall research process, this third component is perhaps the most challenging for lifespan writing researchers given the complexity around what factors researchers should target when thinking about the lifespan (Bazerman, 2018; Graham, 2018). Even outside of writing research, this is no easy task (Vogt et al., 2014). Creswell and Creswell (2018) group quantitative research methods into five broad categories to unpack some of their nuances. First, *pre-determined* means the types of items on instruments or tools used for data collection are typically close-ended (e.g., Likert or other rating scales). Second, *instrument-based questions* means data are collected using reliable and valid (and fair; American Educational Research Association et al., 2014) assessment tools. Third, *performance data, attitudinal data, observational data, and census data* involve asking participants to engage in a task or share their thoughts and perspectives, observing participants engaging in activities, and examining broadly available secondary research data. Careful consideration should be made by the researcher when selecting the types of data to be collected and analyzed for a given study. *Statistical analysis* and *statistical interpretation* represent the analytical approaches researchers use to make sense of the data and to interpret statistical findings (Motulsky, 2017; Urdan, 2022). Statistical analysis and interpretation often seek to make inferences about a research sample in line with the underlying population of individuals they represent (see Zajic & Poch, 2020), though different ways of making those inferences exist. Readers are likely most familiar with *frequentist* approaches, which include steps to calculate and interpret *p-values* and *confidence intervals* in line with null hypothesis significance testing. However, other approaches, like *Bayesian* approaches, are also available that draw on different assumptions for both simple and complex analytical designs (e.g., Depaoli, 2021; Kaplan, 2014; Stanton, 2017).

So, readers might be asking, why spend time bothering ourselves with quantitative methods? Mallette and Duke (2021) lay out five core ideas in line with their literacy research methodologies handbook that echo the intention of the Lifespan Writing Development Group: (a) Many different research methodologies make valuable contributions to the study of literacy; (b) Different types of questions and claims require different types of research approaches; (c) Standards of quality exist for every type of research; (d) Synergy across research methodologies is not only possible but also powerful and advisable; and (e) Researchers must pursue synergistic collaborations across research methodologies (pp. 1–2). The charge set forth by the Lifespan Writing Development Group echoes these core ideas when we shift the focus from literacy research more broadly to lifespan writing development. As researchers, we need to bring our methodological expertise to the collaboration to foster new approaches and understandings. With that, we turn to considering more about what longitudinal approaches might mean for lifespan writing research.

LONGITUDINAL QUANTITATIVE RESEARCH DESIGNS AND METHODS: CONSIDERATIONS FOR LIFESPAN WRITING RESEARCHERS

Conceptualizing how longitudinal approaches fit into the development of lifespan writing research methodologies is a daunting task. Longitudinal designs, as mentioned previously, involve data collection over multiple time points to examine change over some specified time period (Hoffman, 2015). But longitudinal designs sit at the research design level; when we consider specific methods, several approaches exist that depend on the nature of the research questions. Our prior chapter discussed the nuances of different time sampling designs and how choices in the data collection and analysis may impact the selection of appropriate longitudinal research methods (Zajic & Poch, 2020). Here, instead, we discuss some of the considerations for longitudinal, quantitative approaches in line with Bazerman's comments regarding the noted value (or lack thereof) of existing longitudinal studies from psychology (Bazerman, 2018).

In closing the Lifespan Writing Development Group's edited book, Bazerman (2018) provided an exhaustive discussion into the many facets researchers might consider when trying to conceptualize what exactly a lifespan study of writing development might look like. The thorough aspirations put forth by Bazerman in the technical complexity that lifespan writing research will need to properly understand the nuances of writing will keep researchers busy for decades to come. We want to highlight some of the key issues Bazerman brings to light as ways for writing researchers to consider the utility of quantitatively driven lifespan approaches.

Bazerman (2018) reviews a wide array of studies from fields other than writing research to draw on how those fields have performed this work and what they have learned. Of interest here, Bazerman (2018) highlights that much of the existing work is quantitative in nature (focused mainly on statistical issues, modeling issues, and computational tools) and may hold little relevance to the issues at hand with lifespan writing development. More specifically, Bazerman (2018) states the following:

> Such studies can be useful in writing studies to see if there are patterns in family and social situations, schooling characteristics, and the amount of writing or use of writing that might predict later engagement with writing, or to uncover other patterns to be investigated by other means, but such studies do not seek out the meanings embodied in texts, writing strategies or repertoires, writing practices or processes, the quality or efficacy of the texts, complex processes and practices, or the orientations and meanings for the authors engaged in specific situations. So while some statistical measures may be of use for studying writing development, they would likely need to be used in conjunction with more qualitative, individualized studies (pp. 332–333).

We focus on three components of these takeaways: (a) What do longitudinal studies look at?; (b) What value are such designs to lifespan writing researchers?;

and (c) How do we conceptualize the quantitative component of mixed methods designs?

WHAT DO LONGITUDINAL STUDIES LOOK AT?

Bazerman (2018) raises an important concern regarding what a quantitative lens brings to longitudinal studies. As Bazerman (2018) also highlights, there are typically five broad objectives for conducting longitudinal research (Baltes & Nesselroade, 1979):

1. Direct identification of intraindividual change (i.e., examining change within an individual over time).
2. Direct identification of interindividual similarities or differences in intraindividual change (i.e., examining if change occurs between individuals in similar or different ways).
3. Analysis of interrelationships in behavioral change (i.e., examining how certain changes are associated with each other).
4. Analysis of causes or determinants of intraindividual change (i.e., examining what factors serve as the catalyst for changes within individuals over time).
5. Analysis of causes or determinants of interindividual similarities or differences in intraindividual change (i.e., examining why different individuals change in different ways over time).

These objectives are not specific to quantitative approaches alone (see Rowe, 2018 for a further application to a mixed design in early childhood), but they have long guided quantitative approaches that use a longitudinal design. Different research methods are often used in line with these objectives (see McArdle and Nesselroade, 2014 for detailed examples). Other approaches allow for flexibility to answer several questions depending on the type of model specified within a group of models, such as observed with growth curve modeling (Grimm et al., 2016). To breakdown longitudinal design and analysis further, we highlight Hoffman (2015) who took a non-mathematical approach to introduce the complicated nature of longitudinal design and analysis.

First, Hoffman (2015) discusses the building blocks of longitudinal designs, offering definitions and examples of terminology common to such designs. Rather than define every term possible, we highlight two important terms in line with our list of objectives: *between-person* vs. *within-person*. Between-person analysis focuses on the differences that occur between different individuals. Such analyses are often focused on models measuring one outcome for an individual, as we care only to look at how differences occur between different individuals. We could have hundreds upon thousands of individuals for whom we have data, but we might still have only one outcome for all those individuals. Oftentimes, between-person analyses are conducted solely using cross-sectional approaches, though between-person analysis still plays a role in longitudinal design. In contrast, within-person analyses focus on differences that occur within the same individual(s) over multiple occasions (i.e., repeated measurements). The focus turns not to how individuals differ from other individuals but to how individuals differ from themselves over multiple occasions. At its heart, longitudinal analysis is predominantly interested in within-person change over time, but researchers might be most interested in how individuals differ not only in relation to themselves (#1 from Baltes and Nesselroade, 1979), but also if people change in ways that are different from others (#2 from Baltes and Nesselroade, 1979). So, while we can think about between- and within-person analyses as distinct approaches, numerous longitudinal models incorporate both approaches to address research questions that deal with how individuals change within themselves as well as how individuals differ in that change compared to their peers.

Second, Hoffman (2015) focuses on one of the most important components needed for longitudinal research: time. If researchers were not interested in measuring the impact of time, then they would simply examine skills cross-sectionally. But there is not a single way of measuring or accounting for time in longitudinal research. Hoffman highlights a few different models that can be used to describe *within-person fluctuation* over time (i.e., how a skill varies within an individual), account for *fixed* and *random effects* around time (i.e., values that are constant for everyone in the model vs. values that are allowed to vary for each individual), and describe *within-person change* over time (i.e., accounting for trajectories of individual change and not solely fluctuation).

Third, Hoffman (2015) introduces the issue of predictors (i.e., variables that try to explain fluctuation or change over time). Such predictors can be considered time-invariant (i.e., they occur at a single time and do not vary across time) or time-varying (i.e., they can change across multiple time points). Nuances occur around how one might include both types of predictors into advanced models, and entire chapters are dedicated to the role that such predictors play in longitudinal models and models examining both within-person fluctuation and change.

Fourth, Hoffman (2015) provides a brief overview of more advanced applications that address many of the objectives outlined by Baltes and Nesselroade (1979). Did you know that researchers can account for time on a variety of different metrics within longitudinal research designs? And what if we have groups of individuals across multiple time points; can we account for not only individuals but also individuals nested within groups over time? Needless to say, we recommend Hoffman (2015) as an introductory text that highlights many of the capabilities possible when thinking about longitudinal data.

WHAT VALUE ARE SUCH DESIGNS TO LIFESPAN WRITING RESEARCHERS?

The earlier examples offered by Bazerman (2018) align with the aforementioned objectives, as the focus falls on the identification of predictors at one time point, while anticipating a later time point. However, quantitative methods might allow for more nuance than simply identifying familial or contextual characteristics tied to later writing engagement (or other broad patterns of relationships). As mentioned earlier, a prominent issue in quantitative research methods is defining the phenomena for further examination. And existing studies often employing the use of quantitative methods most often do not have writing researchers on those teams. We are not at all surprised by Bazerman's main critiques of the existing literature being focused on issues of model fitting and statistical significance because said models were most often conducted without the nuances of writing development in mind. The wealth of knowledge and expertise carried by the members of the Lifespan Writing Development Group may provide new issues at hand for quantitative methodologists to wrestle with, which in turn can help researchers produce higher quality research for the fields of writing and research methodology.

Furthermore, we would argue that some of Bazerman's examples may be analyzable from quantitative perspectives that would contribute to but not remove the need for rich qualitative inquiry. If writing strategies or repertoires were assessed via direct observation or self-report over an extended period, could quantitative methods be applicable then? If writing practices and processes were observed, documented, or tracked for extended periods, could quantitative methods offer a novel perspective to understanding within- and between-person fluctuation and change? (And could particular factors like context, purpose, and genre be added as important covariates or predictors to the models to help explain how such examples might covary with observed fluctuations and changes?) Could we apply person-centered methods (approaches seeking to understand the presence of unobserved variability at the person level rather than the variable level; Laursen & Hoff, 2006) to understand within-group variability such as how we think about ourselves as writers and to what extent we shift in our thinking over time? Could we apply dyadic data approaches (Kenny et al., 2020) that look to interrelationships between individuals and collaborators to expand our knowledge about how writers write together? Put more simply, quantitative methods may help provide a nuanced perspective to issues like those laid out here, but it will take quantitative researchers on the research team to offer such perspectives. If we want these approaches to be appropriate for the kinds of data we care about as lifespan writing researchers, then we need to foster these collaborations to help disentangle the complicated construct that lifespan writing researchers conceptualize as writing.

HOW DO WE CONCEPTUALIZE THE QUANTITATIVE COMPONENT OF MIXED-METHODS DESIGNS?

Collaboration is central to the future of lifespan writing research methodologies, both for quantitative and qualitative approaches. Bazerman's final point about the need to use quantitative approaches in conjunction with qualitative ones is extremely important to not only this complex area of research but also to leveraging the expertise we have across disciplines. The point echoes the broader landscape of literacy research methodologies (Mallette & Duke, 2021). We need both quantitative and qualitative researchers in the conversations around what writing skills should be valued and understood from a lifespan framework. We need mixed methods researchers as well to contribute to discussions in both small- and large-scale projects to foster rich datasets where analysis would be informed by both quantitative and qualitative methods. Such involvement of multiple perspectives speaks to both the point raised by Bazerman (2018), as well as what we argued for in Zajic and Poch (2020). When taking into consideration the multiple factors that impact writing from both sociocultural and cognitive perspectives (Graham, 2018), we need multidisciplinary research teams to bridge representation across methodological communities to conduct not only high-quality research, but also research that informs other methodologies. Mixed methods designs are not solely the merging of quantitative and qualitative research methodologies, however, as careful considerations must be made as to their own design and use of methods from conceptualization through interpretation (Creswell & Creswell, 2018; Onwuegbuzie & Mallette, 2021).

APPLYING QUANTITATIVE THINKING TO THE LIFESPAN WRITING PRINCIPLES

In this final section, we focus on the original eight principles offered by the Lifespan Writing Development Group (Bazerman et al., 2018) to offer some considerations for future quantitative inquiry in lifespan writing research. For each principle, we offer some broadly aligned connections to designs and analytical approaches.

Principle 1: Writing Can Develop across the Lifespan as Part of Changing Contexts

To define context, we have opted to replace the term with community to represent changes in writing communities (Graham, 2018). Changing communities may represent both intraindividual change in community (i.e., how a writer changes in their writing as a product of themselves changing communities) or interindividual similarities or differences in intraindividual change in communities (i.e., how different individuals change in different ways across a variety of writing communities over time). Some questions that come to mind when thinking about changing contexts is naturally how writers perceive the writing demands of the various communities they write in. Testing hypotheses about involvement in educational, social, and professional communities over time could be done through developing instruments that examine constructs like beliefs and attitudes in those spaces and that seek to examine observed change across contexts as well as heterogeneity observed at the person level. We might adopt macro-level perspectives to communities in general or conduct more micro-level examinations into the different sub-communities that make up larger communities (i.e., different classrooms or spaces within a school, different online social media outlets, and different teams or team members we converse with for different reasons).

Principle 2: Writing Development Is Complex Because Writing Is Complex

The assumed complexity is ideal for testing hypotheses and theories using approaches like multilevel modeling and structural equation modeling. Such approaches build from simpler univariate and multivariate approaches to posit the complex interrelationships between different skills (through observable skills and unobservable constructs) and that individuals may be clustered based on specific contexts or time points (see Heck et al., 2022). Though we spent more time in Zajic and Poch (2020) covering structural equation modeling than we did here, when we hear the word *complex*, we think of analytical tools that allow for specifying complex relationships between both observable skills and unobservable constructs. The complexity of writing might be tested within or between the levels of the writers(s)-within-community framework (Graham, 2018), or we might test the same set of variables across communities to see if communities demonstrate properties of invariance either between groups or between time periods (i.e., do the constructs of interest have the same meaning across groups of individuals or across periods within the same communities?). Part of the challenge here for quantitative approaches will be operationalizing how to measure writing beyond foundational writing skills. But this might be an opportunity for defining constructs of interest through cross-disciplinary collaboration to understand how constructs may differ in observed manifestations while still representing a similar underlying phenomenon.

Principle 3: Writing Development Is Variable; There Is No Single Path and No Single Endpoint

Fortunately for those interested in quantitative approaches, path models do not have a single path, either! (We do, however, need to specify a final-time point, as models would not be able to be estimated without one.) With no single path or endpoint, we immediately think about the flexibility offered by some approaches like growth curve modeling where time points may be flexible (i.e., the time elapsed between time points does not need to be in equal intervals) and paths may include multiple skills at once to capture both change overtime as well as relationships between change overtime (Grimm et al., 2016). However, we also think potentially of person-centered approaches like latent class analysis and latent profile analysis with the added longitudinal component being latent transition analysis. Briefly, such approaches use mixture modeling applications to uncover hidden homogeneous subgroups within a larger heterogeneous group (see Abarda et al., 2020; Finch & French, 2015; Heck et al., 2022; Ryoo et al., 2018). But what if we believe those individuals might transition between groups over some extended period? Latent transition analysis examines how (if at all) individuals transition between identified classes and profiles over time (along with considering invariance assumptions across time points). Such designs may be useful for making sense of the heterogeneity present among individuals regarding how writing changes across the lifespan. Discussed models also allow for examination into issues of moderation (i.e., an interaction between predictors whose influence may depend on each other) and mediation (i.e., where variables can be both predictors and outcomes to examine both direct and indirect effects on variables of interest).

Principle 4: Writers Develop in Relation to the Changing Social Needs, Opportunities, Resources, and Technologies of Their Time and Place

Taking into consideration the ways each of these areas shape individual experiences with writing activities and development requires clear delineation of their measurable features. For example, technologies might include various mediums (e.g., handwriting; typing on a keyboard vs. a tablet; and dictating into a phone, a tablet, or a computer). Even reflecting on the use of technologies over the last two decades in educational spaces and the state of the research on how technology impacts learning for children with and without disabilities lends itself to an entire field of research. What comes to mind is thinking about models that might consider major shifts in one's writing development, such as access to your first computer or demarcating points of entry and exit of different jobs as ways to delineate writing experiences in different professional contexts. Analytical tools like regression discontinuity (a quasi-experimental design that introduces a treatment effect by assigning a particular cut-off above or below when that treatment is assigned; Weiland et al., 2021) and survival models that place the focus of the analysis on the time from when an event occurs (Legrand, 2021) may be useful to investigate how time around a change may impact writing activities. Considering the types of data to be collected to capture the different communities where individuals engage in writing and offer opportunity for valuing the changing use of writing across development may be challenging to operationalize, though still potentially feasible given a group of multidisciplinary experts.

Principle 5: The Development of Writing Depends on the Development, Redirection, and Specialized Reconfiguring of General Functions, Processes, and Tools

Writers rely on more than their writing skills to engage with writing across their lifespan. Much of the group's recommendations in terms of functions, processes, and tools highlight the use of cognitive mechanisms delineated in the writer(s)-within-community framework (Graham, 2018). Understanding how general functions, processes, and tools shape written language development and expectations speak directly to the authors' interests in understanding how to support writers who are considered neurodivergent in the context of learning and developmental disabilities (Poch et al., 2020; Zajic & Brown, 2022), so we are excited by this principle for reasons other than quantitative methods! As we highlighted in Poch et al. (2020), lifespan writing researchers need to understand how functions, processes, and tools play out beyond the educational spaces for individuals with disabilities. Again, what comes to mind might be mixture models that take into consideration underlying heterogeneous profiles of how writers engage with writing daily and come to think about their own writing processes across time and context, and how writing shapes and shifts conceptions of the self.

Principle 6: Writing and Other Forms of Development Have a Reciprocal Relation and Mutual Supporting Relationships

At the heart of longitudinal models is the focus on covariance (i.e., how much two variables vary together). The reciprocal relationship between writing and other forms of development may be well suited to be understood using dyadic modeling, which was highlighted earlier as a way to understand the processes that unfold in dyads (Kenny et al., 2020). However, many other models are well suited to examine the covariance of interrelated skills over time, both in terms of autoregressive paths and in growth curve models (Grimm et al., 2016; Zajic & Poch, 2020). However, such skills may also be modeled by looking beyond just writing performance to thinking about ways of modeling the writing process across contexts or how writers engage with text over a prolonged period. Many applications come back to how (and if) a phenomenon of interest can be measured and studied quantitatively vs. qualitatively.

Principle 7: To Understand How Writing Develops Across the Lifespan, Educators Need to Recognize the Different Ways Language Resources Can be Used to Present Meaning in Written Text

Oral language skills play a critical role in written language development, especially in early development. However, the Lifespan Writing Development Group draws attention beyond the early years. A multitude of modeling approaches may be beneficial when hypothesizing the role that language plays across the lifespan. Examining oral and written language in multiple languages over time (again, perhaps bound by certain points in time, such as taking courses in a second or third language) allows for models that measure multiple processes simultaneously over time. The interrelationship between oral and written language may also vary by context, prompting for approaches that capitalize on variability present across contexts both between and within individuals. Bazerman et al. (2018) draw attention to the need to attend to micro-level textual features, such as looking at oral and written language in produced documents over time (and perhaps across contexts). Panel designs may be particularly useful, as they allow for modeling parallel processes occurring simultaneously over multiple time points.

Principle 8: Curriculum Plays a Significant Formative Role in Writing Development

Our schooling experiences impact how we use and think about writing throughout our lives. Schooling experiences vary across classrooms, districts, cities, states, and countries, leading to nested data that requires multi-level approaches. Careful considerations need to be made about the contextual spaces where writing occurs over the school-age years and how access to those resources may change or influence future thinking about writing post formal schooling. Models may attempt to show growth and change in growth in children in a single school system or across multiple school systems, potentially being able to account for variability in classroom experiences (or examining how experiences contribute to variability in outcomes, such as writing self-concept or self-efficacy). For quantitative approaches to be helpful, researchers need tools to document the writing spaces that occur across primary, secondary, and postsecondary educational contexts. These tools should be sensitive to the dynamic contexts across grade levels and school systems. Documenting the many ways children engage with written text across the grade levels is a welcome initial point to help think about the multitude of variables involved. Such efforts may lead to developing effective models that document both short- and long-term longitudinal growth (and how such growth might impact understanding writing in contexts outside of school).

CONCLUSION

We began this chapter focused on the complexity innate to writing development, and we hope you still see writing as a complex construct. However, we also hope you have come to understand a bit more about the nuances of quantitative approaches. Our initial discussion highlighted what quantitative researchers generally consider when conceptualizing a quantitative study. Our look into the longitudinal issues at play highlighted that if we want methodological tools that are applicable and useful to writing research, then writing researchers need to be involved in those cross-disciplinary collaborations. We highlighted that quantitative approaches may hold important implications for the continued study of the lifespan principles that underlie writing development. We do not expect everyone to become an expert in quantitative methods (we would argue we feel similar, given the breadth of methodological expertise that exists in the field), but we hope this chapter leaves you with an appreciation for what quantitative approaches might bring to lifespan writing development research.

Given this edited collection and the focus on methods, we end on a hopeful note. We have been encouraged by the rich discussions fostered by the researchers involved with the Lifespan Writing Development Group that have begun tackling disciplinary divides and issues that occur when bringing together writing researchers across disciplines. While sometimes difficult and uncomfortable, these conversations are an opportunity for learning more about different and diverse methodological and philosophical approaches and beliefs rather than opposing such approaches and beliefs because they do not align with one's own. We are excited by the rich role that methodology will play in the ongoing understanding of how writing develops across the lifespan, both in terms of quantitative approaches and designs that incorporate qualitative and mixed methods. However, we highlight a cautionary note raised by Creswell and Creswell (2018): We must focus on research questions and not solely our own personal experiences and existing research communities. We draw strength by bringing together diverse perspectives and disciplines interested in this complex phenomenon called writing. We need to leverage that strength for productive collaboration, whether that be exploring potential uses for quantitative approaches or for how different methodologies may help to understand the many unexplored questions. Forming collaborations will produce research questions that can be answered using the diverse methodological toolkits at our disposals. It is now on us as writing lifespan researchers to enact these methods and propose research designs that lay the foundation for understanding the complexity of writing development and the use of writing across the lifespan.

REFERENCES

Abarda, A., Dakkon, M., Azhari, M., Zaaloul, A. & Khabouze, M. (2020). Latent transition analysis (LTA): A method for identifying differences in longitudinal change among unobserved groups. *Procedia Computer Science, 170*, 1116–1121. https://doi.org/10.1016/j.procs.2020.03.059.

Adler-Kassner, L. & Wardle, E. (2016). *Naming what we know: Threshold concepts of writing studies*. University of Colorado Press.

American Educational Research Association, American Psychological Association & National Council on Measurement in Education. (2014). *Standards for educational and psychological testing*. American Educational Research Association.

Baltes, P. B. & Nesselroade, J. R. (1979). History and rationale of longitudinal research. In J. R. Nesselroade & P. B. Baltes (Eds.), *Longitudinal research in the study of behavior and development* (pp. 1–39). Academic Press.

Bazerman, C. (2018). Lifespan longitudinal studies of writing development: A heuristic for an impossible dream. In C. Bazerman, A. N. Applebee, V. W. Berninger, D. Brandt, S. Graham, J. Jeffery, P. K. Matsuda, S. Murphy, D. W. Rowe & M. Schleppegrell (Eds.), *The lifespan development of writing* (pp. 326–365). National Council of Teachers of English.

Bazerman, C., Applebee, A. N., Berninger, V. W., Brandt, D., Graham, S., Jeffery, J., Matsuda, P. K., Murphy, S., Rowe, D. W. & Schleppegrell, M. (2018). *The lifespan development of writing*. National Council of Teachers of English. https://wac.colostate.edu/books/ncte/lifespan-writing/.

Berninger, V. W., Rijlaarsdam, G. & Fayol, M. (2012). Mapping research questions about translation to methods, measures, and models. In M. Fayol, D. Alamargot & V. Berninger (Eds.), *Translation of thought to written text while composing: Advancing theory, knowledge, research methods, tools, and applications*. Psychology Press.

Creswell, J. W. & Creswell, J. D. (2018). *Research design: Qualitative, quantitative, and mixed methods approaches*. Sage.

Depaoli, S. (2021). *Bayesian structural equation modeling*. Guilford Press.

Dippre, R. J. & Phillips, T. (Eds.). (2020). *Approaches to lifespan writing research: Generating an actionable coherence*. The WAC Clearinghouse; University Press of Colorado. https://doi.org/10.37514/PER-B.2020.1053.

Finch, W. H. & French, B. F. (2015). *Latent variable modeling with R*. Routledge.

Fleck, L. (1979). *Genesis and development of a scientific fact*. University of Chicago Press.

Graham, S. (2018). A revised writer(s)-within-community model of writing. *Educational Psychologist, 53*(4), 258–279. https://doi.org/10/gjk2qk.

Grimm, K. J., Ram, N. & Estabrook, R. (2016). *Growth modeling: Structural equation and multilevel modeling approaches*. Guilford Press.

Haig, B. D. (2013). The philosophy of quantitative methods. In T. Little (Ed.), *The Oxford handbook of quantitative methods* (Vol. 1, pp. 7–31). Oxford University Press.

Heck, R. H., Thomas, S. L. & Tabata, L. N. (2022). *Multilevel and longitudinal modeling with IBM SPSS* (3rd ed.). Routledge. https://doi.org/10.4324/9780367824273.

Hoffman, L. (2015). *Longitudinal analysis: Modeling within-person fluctuation and change*. Routledge. https://doi.org/10.4324/9781315744094.

Kaplan, D. (2014). *Bayesian statistics for the social sciences*. Guilford Press.

Kenny, D. A., Kashy, D. A., Cook, W. L. & Simpson, J. A. (2020). *Dyadic data analysis*. Guilford Press.

Kieffer, M. J. (2021). Correlational designs and analyses. In M. H. Mallette & N. K. Duke (Eds.), *Literacy research methodologies* (pp. 62–80). Guilford Press.

Laursen, B. & Hoff, E. (2006). Person-centered and variable-centered approaches to longitudinal data. *Merrill-Palmer Quarterly, 52*(3), 377–389. https://doi.org/10/bpj2wj.

Legrand, C. (2021). *Advanced survival models*. Chapman and Hall/CRC. https://doi.org/10.1201/9780429054167.

Mallette, M. H. & Duke, N. K. (2021). *Literacy research methodologies*. Guilford Press.

McArdle, J. J. & Nesselroade, J. R. (2014). *Longitudinal data analysis using structural equation models*. American Psychological Association. https://doi.org/10.1037/14440-000.

Morin, J.-F., Olsson, C. & Özlem Atikcan, E. (2021). Interdisciplinarity: The interaction of different disciplines for understanding common problems. In *Research methods in the social sciences an A-Z of key concepts* (pp. 145–148). Oxford University Press.

Motulsky, H. (2017). *Intuitive biostatistics: A nonmathematical guide to statistical thinking (4th edition)*. Oxford University Press.

Onwuegbuzie, A. J. & Mallette, M. H. (2021). Mixed research approaches in literacy research. In M. H. Mallette & N. K. Duke (Eds.), *Literacy research methodologies* (pp. 264–290). Guilford Press.

Parsons, S. A., Gallagher, M. A., Leggett, A. B., Ives, S. T. & Lague, M. (2020). An analysis of 15 journals' literacy content, 2007–2016. *Journal of Literacy Research, 52*(3), 341–367. https://doi.org/10/gknzn6.

Parsons, S. A., Gallagher, M. A. & The George Mason University Content Analysis Team. (2016). A content analysis of nine literacy journals, 2009–2014. *Journal of Literacy Research*, *48*(4), 476–502. https://doi.org/10.1177/1086296X16680053.

Poch, A., Zajic, M. C. & Graham, S. (2020). Informing inquiry into writing across the lifespan from perspectives on students with learning disabilities or autism spectrum disorder. In R. J. Dippre & T. Phillips (Eds.), *Approaches to lifespan writing research: Generating an actionable coherence* (pp. 195–210). The WAC Clearinghouse; University Press of Colorado. https://doi.org/10.37514/PER-B.2020.1053.

Reichardt, C. S. (2019). *Quasi-experimentation: A guide to design and analysis*. Guilford Press.

Rowe, D. W. (2018). Writing development in early childhood. In C. Bazerman, A. N. Applebee, V. W. Berninger, D. Brandt, S. Graham, J. V. Jeffery, P. K. Matsuda, S. Murphy, D. W. Rowe & M. Schleppegrell (Eds.), *The lifespan development of writing* (pp. 55–110). National Council of Teachers of English.

Ryoo, J. H., Wang, C., Swearer, S. M., Hull, M. & Shi, D. (2018). Longitudinal model building using latent transition analysis: An example using school bullying data. *Frontiers in Psychology*, *9*. https://doi.org/10.3389/fpsyg.2018.00675.

Stanton, J. M. (2017). *Reasoning with data: An introduction to traditional and Bayesian statistics using R*. Guilford Press.

Urdan, T. C. (2022). *Statistics in plain English* (5th ed.). Routledge. https://doi.org/10.4324/9781003006459.

Vogt, W. P., Gardner, D. C. & Haeffele, L. M. (2012). *When to use what research design*. Guilford Press.

Vogt, W. P., Vogt, E. R., Gardner, D. C. & Haeffele, L. M. (2014). *Selecting the right analyses for your data: Quantitative, qualitative, and mixed methods*. The Guilford Press.

Weiland, C., Shapiro, A. & Lindsey, J. (2021). Identifying causal effects in literacy research: Randomized trials and regression discontinuity designs. In M. H. Mallette & N. K. Duke (Eds.), *Literacy research methodologies* (pp. 160–179). Guilford Press.

Zajic, M. C. & Brown, H. M. (2022). Measuring autistic writing skills: Combining perspectives from neurodiversity advocates, autism researchers, and writing theories. *Human Development*, *66*(2), 128–148. https://doi.org/10.1159/000524015.

Zajic, M. C. & Poch, A. (2020). Quantitative perspectives to the study of writing across the lifespan: A conceptual overview and focus on structural equation modeling. In R. J. Dippre & T. Phillips (Eds.), *Approaches to lifespan writing research: Generating an actionable coherence* (pp. 39–65). The WAC Clearinghouse; University Press of Colorado. https://doi.org/10.37514/PER-B.2020.1053.2.03.

CHAPTER 17.

BECOMING RESEARCHER-POETS: POETIC INQUIRY AS METHOD/OLOGY FOR WRITING (THROUGH THE LIFESPAN) RESEARCH

Sandra L. Tarabochia
University of Oklahoma

> To what extent does anxiety
> about research tools, uneasy
> awareness of potential misfit
> and misuse, indicate arrival
> at overwhelming, intimidating
> even frightening kinds of work?
>
> What are ethical obligations
> at these junctures, and how
> and why might [I] responsibly
> stay with such [a] project[t]
> even as [I] contend with [my] own
> uncertain movements?
>
> (Found poem created by author drawing from Restaino, 2019, p. 153)

This chapter is about the promise of poetic inquiry—a method of creating poetry with, from, or around qualitative data—for writing through the lifespan research. It is rooted in my experience with poetic inquiry as a form of what Jessica Restaino (2019) calls a "misfit tool," a way of engaging in research that calls for approaches other than those we've always taken. When I discovered poetic inquiry, I had been wrestling with mountains of data from an ongoing longitudinal research project studying the lived experiences of faculty writers. I'd spent my tenure sabbatical (re)reading methodology guides and pouring over prominent examples of grounded theory, narrative inquiry, portraiture and more. Nothing felt right. According to Restaino "the failure of our traditional tools to perform as we might expect" is "clear sign that we are working in dark, uncertain spaces, that we are doing work that stands to overwhelm us" in meaningful ways (2019, p. 151). In such instances, she urges:

> We must work
> in this space of 'misfit'.
> Indeed we must ourselves
> become misfits. Our humaneness
> problematizes not only our work
> but who we are
> in the work.
>
> (Found poem created by author drawing from Restaino, 2019, p. 85)

Poetic inquiry reoriented me to my work, compelled me to be more present, to embrace the space of "misfit," to *become* a misfit in order to make meaning differently as a researcher, writer, and human. My journey with poetic inquiry is ongoing, but what I've experienced so far has convinced me of the potential value of a poetic approach to researching writing through the lifespan. As I continue to feel my way forward, I hope to entice others to think along with me about what poetic inquiry might bring to our collaborative endeavor. In that spirit, this chapter offers an overview of poetic inquiry as I understand it, along with initial thoughts about how, why, and when it might inform the work of lifespan writing researchers.

"'Poetic inquiry' is the use of poetry crafted from research endeavors, either before a project analysis, as a project analysis, and/or poetry that is part of or that constitutes an entire research project" (Faulkner, 2017b, p. 210; qtd in Faulkner, 2020b, p. 14). "Merg[ing] the tenets of qualitative research with the craft and rules of traditional poetry" (Leavy, 2020, p. 85), poetic inquiry researchers might write poetry as a form of fieldnotes or memoing, or as a way to analyze data, represent findings, or as a vehicle for reflecting on embodied experiences as researchers and writers. For example, I wrote the following haiku on the chilly Monday morning after Halloween in 2021 as I struggled to make the most of the time I'd allotted to my project that day:

> Heavy, hooded blur
> fat coffee-drenched tongue, sluggish
> sloshy swallow: hope

Placing this poem alongside traditional academic writing in a journal article manuscript or pairing it with a poem like the following, crafted from lines of interviews with faculty about their writing lives for an article on resilience

(Tarabochia, 2021), embeds me, my embodied experience, in my research in ways that fundamentally change "findings" about the "essence" of faculty writing lives:

> Wake up hot, sweaty.
> Awful, like being smashed down,
> but with no way out.

Poetic inquiry offers writing through the lifespan researchers wholistic, humanistic ways of understanding writers and writing development (our own and others'), dimensions that are not always surfaced through quantitative or even traditional qualitative approaches. Because writing is such a complex, multidimensional activity (Bazerman et al. 2017, 2018) "caught up in all facets of our lives" (Dippre & Phillips, 2020, p. 3), tracing and representing the "rambling pathways" of writer development (qtd. in Dippre & Phillips, 2020, p. 3) can be a complicated, daunting endeavor. Providing a unique "porthole to . . . experience," poetic inquiry offers an artistic, embodied, relational way "to attend to all this complexity" (Leavy, 2020, p. 98; Dippre & Phillips, 2020, p. 4) and (re)center human elements in the study of writers and writer development. Poems have the potential to capture the rich nuances of writing lives, to reveal what researchers might never access otherwise. In the words of Laurel Richardson, foremother of poetic inquiry in sociology: "a part of humanity that may elude the social scientist reveals itself in poetry" (qtd. in Leavy, 2020, p. 98). Lifespan researchers grappling with the following questions might find poetic inquiry to be a promising approach:

- How do I make visible the "human" in human subjects research?
- How can I more fully honor the nuance of participants' lived experience?
- How do I stay accountable to those experiences traditional research tools are most likely to miss or flatten?
- How might I orient to my work not as an objective analyst, but as a "vulnerable observer" immersed in the process (Behar, 1997)?
- How do I acknowledge my entanglement with dominant ideologies and (re)orient to my work in the spirit of knowing, being, and doing differently?
- How can my research directly challenge and begin to transform structures and systems that privilege certain bodyminds over others?
- How can I venerate and draw forth my work from the rich historical roots of theories of the flesh, forged by women of color to theorize from physical realities and embodied experience?

- How can I center relationships (with scholars/ship, research participants, self and readers) as both the foundation and goal for my research and writing?

HISTORICAL ROOTS OF A "MISFIT TOOL"

An embodied literary form that conjures abstract, multivalent meaning, attends to silence, and evokes emotion, poetry uniquely articulates human experience that doesn't "fit" dominant ways of knowing, being, or doing. It surfaces partial, situated knowledge, honoring subjugated voices, decentering authority, and disrupting binaries such as mind/body, rational/emotional, and public/personal (Leavy, 2020). Methods of poetic transcription have roots in theories of the flesh, the move by feminists and women of color to theorize from physical realities "flesh and blood experiences" in ways that bridge seeming contradictions in experience and meaningfully complicate conditions of living (Moraga & Anzaldúa, 2015, p. 19; Faulkner 2020b, p. 64).

D. Soyini Madison (1993, 1994), for example, uses poetic transcription to honor, analyze, and represent storytelling performances emerging from/within Black oral traditions because in poetic form words are less "isolate[ed] from the movement, sound, and sensory body that give them substance" (1994, p. 46). In this spirit, Ohito and Nyachae (2018) use Black feminist poetry as form of feminist critical discourse analysis to surface new insights about "the complex lives, lived experiences, and knowledges of Black girls and women" (p. 839). Noting the importance of the theoretical and epistemological constructs in which poetry is created, they generate "list" poems from research artifacts in the stylistic lineage of Black feminist poets.

These roots foreground the value of poetic inquiry as a (misfit) tool for resisting structures and systems that constrain conditions of living for certain bodies more than others. "Poetry is political," proclaims Faulkner (2020b, p. 30); "re-presenting research participants in ways that honor their stories and voice, call for social change, and offer new insight provides researchers with a means for advocating" (p. 156). To illustrate, I share a poetic representation of transcript from my first interview with Sadie, a Black woman who was pre-tenure at the time of our conversation in 2016:

> When I became a faculty member, I experienced the real academy.
> Oh! You think I am an idiot, all of you people—rest of the world
> thinks I am a stupid idiot. Oh! Constant onslaughts undermining who
> I am anxious about my writing, fearful about whether I will make tenure
> elusive, traumatizing, so much at stake—Fight! Gear up! Exhausting.

Grew up poor, working class, rural south Louisiana.
Black women told me I was a smart little Black girl.
When the schools weren't serving me, I had Black women
in my life, everyday brilliance celebrated.

Born in [a Midwest metro], single mother worked all the time,
overcrowded schools; I just wasn't learning.

Second grade, white[2] teacher: I can't teach her, she can't read.
Aunt: It's your damn job to teach her to read.
Young Black woman's classroom: Within weeks I was reading.

The day my aunt realized, I sat in her chair, started reading.
She heard me, poked her head out the bathroom—
butt naked just remember—walked out—stark naked—
Whole family there, danced around the house "Hallelujah!
Thank you Jesus!" She did all this. Crazy! Wonderful.
Second grade, seven years old, my aunt danced
stark naked for me because . . . I'm about to cry . . .
I was reading.

Celebrations of everyday brilliance
left an indelible mark, affirmed
I was a smart little Black girl.

Community of Black women supported my type of intelligence,
recognize[d] the capacity to think well through everyday life.
[When] I internalize not-good-enoughness, this loud voice in my head:
White supremacist, capitalist, patriarchal institutions have been
trying to kill you. Examples across your life, historical pattern.
And that voice becomes louder, in my head.
The women in my past have given that voice
a megaphone.

Poetry can connect and agitate; respond to current events and conditions; challenge and exert power; and critique dominant structures toward "re-visioning of social, cultural and political worlds" (Faulkner & Cloud, 2019, p. viii; Hartnett, 2003; Reale, 2015a, 2015b; Burford, 2018). Lifespan researchers might use poetry to advocate for writers and to pursue transformation in policies,

---

2   Following Sadie's preference, rooted in Kimberlé Crenshaw's (1991) practice, I do not capitalize "white" because it does not refer to a specific cultural group.

procedures, programs, pedagogies, institutions and ideologies to enhance mutual becoming.

A CASE FOR POETIC INQUIRY IN WRITING (THROUGH THE LIFESPAN) RESEARCH

Researchers from across disciplines employ many forms of poetic inquiry to engage with qualitative data and various terms have been coined to describe nuanced approaches (Leavy, 2020; Prendergast, 2009). However, the intention to use poetry to "synthesize experience in a direct and affective way" (Prendergast, 2009, p. xxii), to "present human phenomena in a manner that preserves its *livedness*" (emphasis original, Furman et al., 2007, p. 302), and enact feminist commitments to bodies and bodily knowledge (Faulkner, 2018; Howard, Nash & Thompson, 2020) remains constant. Because writing through the lifespan researchers are writers ourselves, poetic inquiry can make visible our embodied presence in our research, how we impact and are impacted by it, and how we develop as writers and humans in response to dynamic forces, including our research with and for writers.

Despite the promise of poetic inquiry, few writing studies scholars publicly claim it as a research methodology. A noteworthy exception, writing through the lifespan researcher Collie Fulford (monograph in progress) composes poetry as a practice of close listening, a way to enact reciprocity, and an analytical process-product. She uses poetic inquiry as one approach among others for analyzing qualitative data from her study of the writing lives of adult students at an Historically Black University. Creating found poems from interview transcripts, Fulford says, "allows a level of intimacy with another person's way of expressing ideas," attending to "meaning, rhythm and syntax" in an attempt "to distill what is already there" (personal communication, Nov. 17, 2021). More than member checking, sharing poems with participants becomes an act of reciprocity and mutual vulnerability. "It's evidence I was listening," Fulford explains, "and I found their words both meaningful and *beautiful*. We don't talk about aesthetics or pleasure much in composition research," she continues, "yet there they are." Participants react with surprise and pleasure when they read their words in Fulford's poems, which is how she often feels when composing them. Fulford hasn't decided if she will publish research poems as a product for readers to see. As Faulkner (2020b) notes, not all research poetry needs to be featured in analysis or even published. "Harnessing the power of poetry" behind the scenes, so to speak, can be a valuable way "to center creativity in the research process" (p. 155), and a good place to start for writing researchers looking to integrate poetic inquiry into their research and writing.

Like Fulford, I discovered the challenges and affordances of poetic inquiry slowly through fits and starts, in surprising moments of immersion and delight, and I continue to grope my way forward. Based on my experience, I urge lifespan writing researchers to take a playful approach; read widely—poetry as well as poetic inquiry scholarship—follow your intuition and try out the techniques and approaches that beckon you. In this section, I share ways I've experimented with poetic inquiry and describe the analytic, reflexive and relational affordances. Through an extended example, I model how lifespan writing researchers might imagine ways to incorporate poetic methods into longitudinal studies. My hope is that doing so generates more ideas about how those new to poetic inquiry might begin.

In my ongoing longitudinal study with 25 faculty writers from several universities, various institutional positions, and across disciplines, I've experimented with various forms of poetic inquiry to analyze and represent data, converse with published literature, consider feedback from journal reviewers and reflect on my own subjectivities in this work. I've used erasure poems, also called critical or counter poems (Lahman, Richard & Teman, 2019), to embrace "the imaginative power of redaction" (Runyan, 2021, p. 134; Kleon, 2010), to discover meaning in scholarship, fieldnotes, artifacts, or interview transcripts and to resist dominant structures and discourses (Lahman, Teman & Richard, 2019; Faulkner 2020a). A page from Jessica Restaino's (2019) book *Surrender: Feminist Rhetoric and Ethics in Love and Illness* became a source text with which to grapple with poetic inquiry as a form of methodological surrender in my research with faculty writers. The resulting poem and visual art has been a touchstone for me as I follow where this project leads.

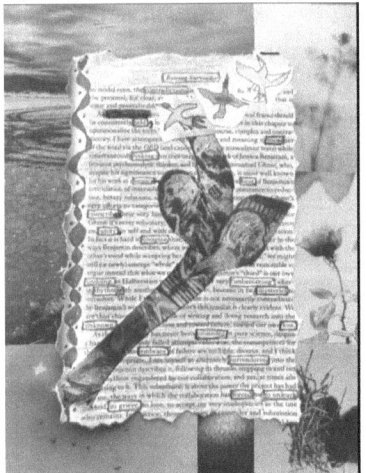

"Rooting Surrender"

Contradictions held
root-linking, music-bent
reinscribed unity, imagine
undoing, "unbecoming" rhythmic
mysteries unknown loss
grounded embrace: surrendering
forced to unlearn
to grieve

Figure 17.1. Erasure

A related approach, concrete poetry, takes physical shape on the page to reinforce content (Leavy, 2020; Meyer, 2017). I crafted a concrete poem from my first interview with Julie, a participant in my study, to represent what she was telling me about the shifting role of writing in her life as she transitioned from a graduate student to a faculty member.

"Letting Life Be"

```
r . . . u . . . n the risk of writing
in an b t a t world
       a s r c
   p      u
   a      n
W r i t i n g is part of it.
   a      v
   l      e
   l      r
   e      s
   l      e
When I was younger I could do everything somehow
find the energy and make it happen.
Not anymore.
```

At the heart of my article, "From Resilience to Resistance: Repurposing Faculty Writers' Survival Strategies," is a composite poem made of lines of transcript from interviews with 21 research participants conducted in Spring 2018 to explore the role of resilience in the lives of faculty writers (Tarabochia, 2021). The versatility of composite found poems for surfacing similarities and differences among individuals and groups within a set of research participants make it ideal for studying a phenomena like lifespan writing. For more examples see Commeyras and Montsi (2000) and Teman (2010).

In addition to using found poetry to represent data, I generate poems as a form of reflexive practice. My *Peitho* article (2021) includes an "I am from" poem (Janesick, 2016), in which I reflect on my researcher subjectivity and my orientation to this work as a faculty writer researching faculty writers.

> I am from straight, cisgender, slim, able-bodied, whiteness,
> from educated, English speaking, property owning, middle class
>   citizenship
> from married mother, neuro typical, (mostly) mentally stable womanhood.

> I am from "follow the rules," "confess your sins" and "hard work pays off."
> Good girl, good student, good choices.
> I am from check the details, put in the time,
> butt in seat, and "do you get up?"
> I am from crying
> at my desk, late, bone deep frustration
> on the stairs, baby asleep, what if I can't finish
> in the kitchen, across the island, no more to give.
> Awake, drenched, heaving, pounding
> heart burning.

In the same article, I use a series of poems, one self-generated, one found poem from scholarly literature, and one found poem, inspired by Adam Rosenblatt (2020), crafted from anonymous peer-review reports I received during the journal submission process, to examine my experience as a poet-researcher arguing for vulnerability as a strategy of resilience for faculty writers. I put a found poem composed from personal correspondence in conversation with another found poem from reviewer feedback to address concerns about the ethical dimensions of poetic inquiry raised during the review process. I used the haiku form to reflect on poetic inquiry as a methodological approach and on my stake in the project.

> Read their words, struggle.
> Visceral connection
> seeing myself there.

> Find the story
> each word amplifying the next
> reverberating.

> Heart drops. Stomach pounds.
> Cut pieces[3] strike a ~~chord~~ nerve.
> Here we are, exposed.
> Objective research,
> evidence: "the data shows."
> But the poet? Naked.

---

3 My gratitude to Jessica Restaino for her work on "cut pieces" in her book *Surrender: Feminist Rhetoric and Ethics in Love and Illness* and her virtual public talk "Surrender as Method, Subject, and Experience: Doing the Work that Undoes Us" on November 10, 2020 as part of Syracuse Symposium's year-long series on "Futures."

> Is it them or me?
> We (e)merge to discover
> a shared thread—the light.
> (Revised from version published in *Peitho*, 2021)

Currently, I am experimenting with "tandem found poetry" (Burdick, 2011) crafted from interviews conducted over six years with one faculty writer, to consider how interpersonal relationships impact academic writing lives and writer development over time. The faculty writer, Julie, and I each write found poems using her annual interviews as source texts. Our poems capture physical, mental, psychological, emotional, and embodied dimensions of the experience of writing through life events including professional and personal milestones, aging, health, social justice work, and abuse. We meet regularly to share our poems and reflect on how they speak to each other, shed new light on original transcripts, and generate insights about our ongoing development as writers, and in my case, a writing researcher. Engaging in the tandem found poetry process with Julie constitutes an artistic way of "continuing writing partnerships," a methodology Lauren Rosenberg (2020) argues has potential for lifespan studies. A creative way to engage with research participants, tandem found poetry offers lifespan researchers another tool for "undercutting a one-way knowledge-making tradition that privileges the researcher's findings . . . as final" and "challeng[ing] the conventions of research [by] foreground[ing] the insights of participants as they continue to reflect on and analyze their experiences" (p. 99). Writing and sharing poems with Julie has "reopened the research," fruitfully challenging our assumptions about writer development and "the researcher-researched" relationship (Rosenberg, 2020, p. 98).

I also create poetry clusters, series of poems around a particular theme, as "a powerful way of expressing a range of subtle nuances about a topic while simultaneously producing a more general overview" (Butler-Kisber & Stewart, 2009, p. 4). For example, I am creating a poetry cluster called "Writing Like a Mother" in which faculty writers reflect on academic writing and motherhood (see p. 315).

Poetic inquiry may also offer longitudinal lifespan researchers ways to attend to the nonlinearity of (writer) development. I will play out one extended example involving I-poems, a type of poem generated from qualitative data, usually individual interviews, in which the words of study participants are poetically rendered to "highlight the complex position of the narrated subject" over time (Koelsch, 2015, p. 98).

Originally introduced by Elizabeth Debold and elaborated by Lorie E. Koelsch (2015), I-poems are associated with research conducted using Carol Gilligan's Listening Guide (2015; Brown & Gilligan, 1992; Gilligan, Spencer, Weinberg & Bertsch, 2006).

"How to Make a Tenure Case"	Excerpt from "Every Time My Writing"
Stand there answering	I should have written today; I didn't.
bullshit questions feel	I feel guilty but I was running
the breast milk drip	errands, folding laundry, all these things . . .
down get back	Last night, not a pair of underwear in sight.
to the baby run	go to the laundry room, the basket, search.
home and wait—	In the very bottom, I found one pair. So . . .
lactating still	I feel bad. I did not write today.
bleeding—	There were other things
for the results.	to keep our family running.
(Victoria, Spring 2019)	(Elizabeth S., Spring 2021)

The Listening Guide method involves four rounds of "listening" to data to tease out various voices; I-poems are crafted during the second round of listening for the "I voice," which "locates the participants' sense of agency and self throughout the text" (p. 98). The researcher identifies each instance of "I" and extracts it from the interview text along with associated verb and additional words needed to create a meaningful phrase (Koelsch, 2015, p. 98). Listed down the page, the "I" phrases become a poem that surfaces the participant's (shifting, conflicting) sense of self. I-poems invite researchers and readers to "look beyond what can be externalized and quantified and listen to the many ways in which the self speaks" (Koelsch, 2015, p. 104). I can imagine constructing I-poems with interviews from faculty writers in my study as a way to, "defy singular interpretation," "invite the reader/listener to engage and grapple with the material," and "spea[k] to the aspects of experience that cannot be measured through operationalization" (p. 104). I hope this extended example, along with explanations of ways I've incorporated poetic inquiry into my work with faculty writers so far, inspires lifespan researchers to explore possibilities through playful experimentation and innovation.

WRITING GOOD (ENOUGH) POETRY: EVALUATING RESEARCH POEMS AND RESEARCHER-POETS

Concerns about how poetic inquiry should be employed and evaluated, and by whom, are frequently voiced by critics, researchers, and poets. Poetic inquiry has been "the subject of premature dismissal by some and intense scrutiny by others, perhaps in part due to misconceptions that it's easy or lacks rigor" (Leavy, 2020, p. 103). My experience corroborates Leavy's (2020) contention that "use of poetry in research increases rigor in the interpretation and writing process; it does not diminish it" (p. 103). As Sullivan (2004) explains, "engagement with craft slows us down, brings us into a new kind of attention to the data before us" (p. 35). Deciding how to enact poetic techniques requires researchers to attend to "subtle relations among elements" discovering nuances "not initially perceived, precisely because they are subtle, elusive, encoded" (p. 35). Nevertheless, ongoing debates over rigor and merit fuel the reluctance of many would-be researcher-poets exacerbating feelings of doubt like the ones expressed in my poem "Bedtime Ruminations," written one fall evening after ruminating about my worthiness as a poetic inquirer while snuggling my son to sleep.

"Bedtime Ruminations"

And if I'm not
a poet . . .
And if I fail . . .
to materialize, concretize,
crystalize, constellate?
What then?
Will it have been worth it?

Questions like these are vital: What "counts" as a successful poem in the context of poetic inquiry? What credentials, experiences and expertise are required to write "good" research poems? Some arts-based researchers (Piirto, 2002, 2009; Prendergast, 2009) advocate for clear standards for arts-based research, including research poems, out of "respect for the domain" and "in defense of quality and qualifications of the artists and their arts" (Piirto, 2009, p. 97). Others, (Bochner, 2000; Clough, 2000) worry that obsession with criteria, ultimately rooted in human values, choices, and often irreconcilable differences, can have a normalizing effect and derail researchers working with "alternative methods" from realizing the full potential of their approaches. Criteria can become a means of "contain[ing] our desire for freedom and experience, a way of limiting our own possibilities and stifling our creative energy" (Bochner, 2000, p. 267). Given that experimental forms are usually linked to resistant politics and social and cultural criticism, the conventionalizing effect of criteria can easily "serve a conservative and destructive function" (Bochner, 2000, p. 269; Clough, 2000).

At the same time, careful consideration of criteria has the potential to sharpen practice, enhance craft, and strengthen the power of a poetic approach. In that vein, I am compelled by efforts to discern quality of poetic inquiry and worthiness of poetic inquirers based on the *goals* for incorporating experimental writing into qualitative research, goals rooted at least in part in a feminist research agenda committed to "ethical and deep relationships between researchers and participants . . . engender[ing] change and mak[ing] participant lives better, and . . . social justice and equity for all" (Butler-Kisber, 2010, p. 97; Richardson, 2000). Bochner (2000), Dark (2009), and Leavy (2020) focus on audience response as another important measure: Does the research poem offer a moving story felt in the body not just in the head, invite connection, *feel* truthful, enact ethical self-consciousness that "provides a space for the listener's becoming," and inspire action (Leavy, 2020, p. 103; Bochner, 2000, p. 270–1)?

I am persuaded by arguments for "good enough" poetry as/in qualitative research (Lahman, Richard & Teman, 2019) with the caveat that researchers should develop the capacity to recognize "occasions" for research poetry (Sullivan, 2009), commit to revision, and hone poetic craft (Faulkner, 2020b). One way to "intensely concentrate on poetics" (p. 104) is for researchers to articulate *ars poetica*, beliefs about the art of poetry, and *ars criteria,* beliefs about what we want our poetic inquiry to do and be (p. 103). Faulkner (2020b) shares her *ars poetica* in the form of persona poems written from the perspective of beloved poets, through reflective prose, as diastic poetry (a found poetry technique similar to acrostic) and as found poems crafted from poets' published reflections on craft. Inspired by Faulkner's (2007; 2016; 2017a) iterative documentation of her evolving *ars poetica/criteria*, here is a recent record of my own, written eight weeks into a marathon training program when I was enthralled by the relationship between running and writing and their roles in my creative endeavors:

> Dear Sandy, running is poetry. So you are a poet.
> Poetry is breath, muscle, skin and bone-deep aliveness
> attunement, attention to crisp sheets of bleeding ink.
> Tensile tendons snapping out lip-smacking rhythms, punctuated by
> iambic slap, slap, slap of feet, meter by meter on dark concrete
> expansive lungs, root-like capillaries spider-cracking their way
> up, out, and down. Buzzy adrenaline induced ache
> fist pumping heart attacks the hill, the line, the syllabic beat
> Patience. Runner, poet. You are.

Despite skepticism about whether researcher-poets can be reliable critics of their own work, I agree with Faulkner (2020b) that in specifying the goals of a particular work, a researcher's *ars poetica* can constitute valuable criteria for judging the extent to which the project has achieved those objectives (p.142).

TRIANGLES, CRYSTALS AND CONSTELLATIONS: SHIFTING PERCEPTIONS OF WRITING/WRITERS THROUGH POETIC INQUIRY

Conversations about criteria make clear that poetry as an arts-based research practice should not be "judged according to positivist or traditional qualitative 'interpretive' standards" (Leavy, 2020, p. 102). Still, issues of validity are critical and must be addressed. As an alternative to triangulation, the use of multiple data sources (interviews, field notes and artifacts, for example) to validate findings, Richardson (1997, p. 92; Richardson & St. Pierre, 2005, p. 963) offers crystallization, an approach that does not assume a fixed point or object to triangulate, but rather strives to "pain[t] a picture with words through the rigorous use of language so that the meaning is clear and can be confirmed by multiple readers" (Leavy, 2020, p. 104). Crystallization highlights the need for criteria that honors the potential of poetic inquiry. Because poems are simultaneously abstract and concrete, spiritual and embodied, particular and universal, poetry moves us "from plane geometry to light theory, where light can be both waves and particles" (Richardson & St. Pierre, 2005, p. 963). This refractive capacity draws me to poetic inquiry as a way to perceive multidimensional phenomena such as writing and writer development.

Composing poems with data from his study of tutors in an alternative learning organization in Auckland City, New Zealand, Adrian Schoone (2020) creates constellations rather than crystals. "Drawing imaginary lines connecting the shining parts" (p. 40), constellations do not seek to "pull together" meaning, but to honor the gaps, the beautiful dark spaces between fragments of found poetry, each becoming a universe unto itself. Keeping the dark space throws into relief the self-generated light of the stars. The difference is between striving for multidimensional understanding (crystallization) and "radical specificity" (constellation) that "moves beyond detail per se to engage the exigence, fluidity, and particularity of living" (Sotirin, 2010, p. 4) while simultaneously "acknowledge[ing] the uncertainties and ambiguities . . . the spirit and the inexhaustibility of knowledge" (Schoone, 2020, p. 40).

Rooted in "Indigenous values of individuated creation and collaborative, interdependent communality" (Martineau, 2015, p. 30) the practice of constellating does not strive to substantiate objective analysis, but honors a "multiplicity of orientations" in order to "visibilize a web of relations" (Powell et al., 2014). The goal is not to triangulate but to "encircle" (Wilson, 2008, p. 38). The meaning lives "in what cannot be communicated rather than in the reassurances of comprehensibility and transparency because it is in this way that we can begin to think differently about what we know and what we might become" (Sotirin, 2010, p. 8). Honoring resonance with the *mauri* (the Māori life source), Schoone (2020) explains that poetic constellations are re/formed and re/imagined from reader to reader and moment to moment, "yielding alternative essences and understandings," keeping the "the research breathing and therefore 'alive'" (p. 40).

Poetry inquiry offers lifespan researchers a way to constellate the essences of writers (including ourselves). It invites readers to connect and reconnect the "shining parts" to make new meanings and generate new understandings that shift relationally, perpetually revealing insights undiscoverable through any other means. Poetic inquiry has the potential to disrupt the understandings we've developed about writing, writers, and writer development based on generalities and recognizable experiences, and to animate "'what cannot be represented' as a different take, a different conception, a different affect" (Sotirin, 2010, p. 10). For example, poetic inquiry might offer new possibilities for studying writer identity negotiation, a key theme identified by the Writing through the Lifespan Collaboration because poetry "defies singular definitions and explanations . . . mirrors the slipperiness of identity, the difficulty of capturing the shifting nature of how we are and want to be and resonates more fully with the way identity is created, maintained, and altered through our narratives and interactions" (qtd. in Leavy, 2020, p. 100; see also Faulkner, 2006). Lifespan writing researchers might use poetic inquiry to put into conversation the "essential" experiences of writers in different moments in their life-long and life-wide trajectories (Prior & Smith, 2020; Smith, 2020).

Rooted in relationality, how might poetic inquiry "draw the writing researcher nearer to the contours of writing development by enabling intimate perspectives on writers' lifespans" (Smith, 2020, p. 18)? How might "poem-stars" representing lived experiences of "non-writers"—the illiterate, the neuroqueer, those who compose in nontraditional ways—reshape familiar constellations or make visible new galaxies in ways that explode what we thought we knew about (writer) development? In the spirit of Naftzinger's (2020) argument for "writer-informed" approaches to lifespan writing research, how might poetic inquiry change where we search for "shining parts" and understand the "beautiful dark spaces" perhaps looking to visual artists, musicians, dancers, novelists, chefs, gardeners, architects and others who live and move artistically in the world to shape the questions we ask about "everyday" composers and what we hope comes of those questions?

In short, poetic inquiry stands to bolster the critical dimension of lifespan writing research. By "open[ing] unfamiliar connections and relations that move both beyond and against familiar storylines, emotional verities, and the all-too-recognizable critiques of cultural-political constraints" (Sotirin, 2010, p. 12), poetic inquiry can achieve "radical specificity" (magnify the stars) and open an ambiguity of meaning (craft various constellations) in ways that are resonant and accessible without privileging shared experience and understanding over difference. Striving for relational accountability (Wilson, 2008) in this way is crucial for lifespan writing researchers. If "writing is a process of the world's becoming" (qtd. in Cooper, 2019, p. 5), lifespan writing researchers are enmeshed—or entangled to reference posthumanist philosophy—in an "inescapably ethical practice, what Barad calls a worldly ethics" that is "about responsibility and accountability for the lively relationalities of becoming of which we are a part" (p. 6). I offer poetic inquiry as a method/ology for (lifespan) writing research that strives to fulfill such a crucial responsibility by acknowledging that writing is not just about understanding but about being (p. 4). In doing so, poetic inquiry has the potential to meaningfully disrupt generalizable understandings and attend more fully to the unique complexities of writing research; taking an artistic, wholistic, critically reflexive approach to the study of writer (and human) development across the lifespan, poetic inquiry can reorient lifespan writing researchers to our work and to the ways we shape and are shaped by our research with, for, and *as* writers.

REFERENCES

Bazerman, C. (2018). Lifespan longitudinal studies of writing development: A heuristic for an impossible dream. In C. Bazerman, A. N. Applebee, V. W. Berninger, D. Brandt, S. Graham, J. V. Jeffery, P. K. Matsuda, S. Murphy, D. W. Rowe, M. Schleppegrell & K. C. Wilcox (Eds.), *The lifespan development of writing* (pp. 326–365). National Council of Teachers of English.

Bazerman, C., Applebee, A.N., Berninger, V.W., Brandt, D., Graham, S., Jeffrey, J.V., Matsuda, P.K., Murphy, S., Rowe, D. W., Schleppegrell, M. & Wilcox, K.C. (2017). Taking the long view on writing development. *Research in the Teaching of English*, *51*(3), 351–360. https://www.jstor.org/stable/44821267.

Behar, R. (1997). *The vulnerable observer: Anthropology that breaks your heart*. Beacon Press.

Bochner, A.P. (2000). Criteria against ourselves. *Qualitative Inquiry*, *6*(2), 266–272. https://doi.org/10.1177/107780040000600209.

Brown, L.M. & Gilligan, C. (1992). *Meeting at the crossroads*. Harvard UP. https://doi.org/10.4159/harvard.9780674731837.

Burdick, M. (2011). Researcher and teacher-participant found poetry: Collaboration in poetic transcription. [Special Issue]. *Arts & Learning Research Journal*, *12*(1.10). http://www.ijea.org/v12si1/

Burford, J. (2018). Sketching possibilities: Poetry and politically-engaged academic practice. *Art/Research International: A Transdisciplinary Journal*, *3*(1), 229–246. https://doi.org/10.18432/ari29261.

Butler-Kisber, L. (2010). Qualitative inquiry: Thematic, narrative and arts-informed perspectives. Sage. https://doi.org/10.4135/9781526435408.

Butler-Kisber, L. & Stewart, M. (2009). The use of poetry clusters in poetic inquiry. In M. Prendergast, C. Leggo and P. Sameshima (Eds.), *Poetic inquiry: Vibrant voices in the social sciences* (pp. 3–12). Sense Publishers. https://doi.org/10.1163/9789087909512_002.

Clough, P. T. (2000). Comments on setting criteria for experimental writing. *Qualitative Inquiry, 6*(2), 278–291. https://doi.org/10.1177/107780040000600211.

Commeyras, M. & Montsi, M. (2000). What if I woke up as the other sex? Batswana youth perspectives on gender. *Gender and Education, 12*(3), 327–346. https://doi.org/10.1080/713668303.

Cooper, M.M. (2019). *The animal who writes: A posthumanist composition*. University of Pittsburgh Press. https://doi.org/10.2307/j.ctvcb5dnf.

Crenshaw, K. (1991). Mapping the margins: Intersectionality, identity politics, and violence against women of color. *Stanford Law Review, 43*(6), 1241–1299. https://doi.org/10.2307/1229039.

Dark, K. (2009). Examining praise from the audience: What does it mean to be a "successful" poet-researcher?" In M. Prendergast, C. Leggo and P. Sameshima (Eds.), *Poetic inquiry: Vibrant voices in the social sciences* (pp. 171–186). Sense Publishers. https://doi.org/10.1163/9789087909512_016.

Dippre, R. J. & Phillips, T. (Eds.). (2020). *Approaches to lifespan writing research: Generating an actionable coherence*. The WAC Clearinghouse; University Press of Colorado. https://doi.org/10.37514/PER-B.2020.1053.

Faulkner, S. L. (2020a). Nine Months. *S/tick. 4*(4), 4. https://theautoethnographer.com/collage-and-erasure-poems-baby/.

Faulker, S. L. (2020b). *Poetic inquiry: Craft, method and practice*. 2nd ed. Series Developing Qualitative Inquiry. Routledge. https://doi.org/10.4324/9781351044233.

Faulker, S. L. (2018). *Real women run: Running as feminist embodiment*. Routledge. https://doi.org/10.4324/9781315437859.

Faulker, S. L. (2017a). Faulkner writes a fmiddle-aged Ars Poetica. In L. Butler-Kisber, J. J. Guinney Yallop, M. Stewart & S. Wiebe (Eds.), *Poetic inquiries of reflection and renewal* (pp. 147–152). MacIntyre Purcell Publishing Inc.

Faulker, S. L. (2017b). Poetic inquiry: Poetry as/in/for social research. In P. Leavy (Ed.), *The handbook of arts-based research* (pp. 208–230). Guilford Press.

Faulker, S. L. (2016). The art of criteria: Ars criteria as demonstration of vigor in poetic inquiry. *Qualitative Inquiry, 22*(8), 662–665. https://doi.org/10.1177/1077800416634739.

Faulker, S. L. (2007). Concern with craft: Using ars poetica as criteria for reading research poetry. *Qualitative Inquiry, 13*(2), 218–234. https://doi.org/10.1177/1077800406295636.

Faulker, S. L. (2006). Reconstruction: LGBTQ and Jewish. *International and Intercultural Communication Annual, 29*, 95–120.

Faulker, S. L. & Cloud, A. (Eds.). (2019). *Poetic inquiry as social justice and political response*. Vernon Press.

Furman, R., Langer, C.L., Davis, C. S., Gallardo, H.P. & Kularni, S. (2007). Expressive, research and reflective poetry as qualitative inquiry: A study of adolescent

identity. *Qualitative Research, 7*(3), 301–315. https://doi.org/10.1177/1468794107078511.
Gilligan, C. (2015). Introduction: The listening guide method of psychological inquiry. *Qualitative Psychology, 2*(1), 69–77. https://doi.org/10.1037/qup0000023.
Gilligan, C., Spencer, R., Weinberg, M. K. & Bertsch, T. (2006). On the listening guide: A voice-centered relational method. In S. N. Hesse-Biber & P. Leavy (Eds.), *Emergent methods in social research* (pp. 253–271). Sage. https://doi.org/10.4135/9781412984034.n12.
Hartnett, S. J. (2003). *Incarceration nation: Investigative prison poems of hope and terror.* AltaMira.
Howard, J., Nash, K. & Thompson, C. (2020). Motherscholaring: A collective poetic autoethnographic inquiry. *International Journal of Qualitative Studies in Education,36*(4). https://doi.org/10.1080/09518398.2020.1852486.
Janesick, V. J. (2016). *"Stretching" exercises for qualitative researchers.* (4th edition). Sage. https://doi.org/10.4135/9781071878637.
Kleon, A. (2010). *Newspaper blackout.* Harper Collins.
Koelsch, L. E. (2015). I poems: Evoking self. *Qualitative Psychology, 2*(1), 96–107. https://doi.org/10.1037/qup0000021.
Lahman, M.K., Richard, V.M. & Teman, E. D. (2019). Ish: How to write poemish (research) poetry. *Qualitative Inquiry, 25*(2), 215–227. https://doi.org/10.1177/1077800417750182.
Lahman, M. K. E., Teman, E. D. & Richard, V. M. (2019). IRB as poetry. *Qualitative Inquiry, 25*(2), 200–214. https://doi.org/10.1177/1077800417744580.
Leavy, P. (2020). *Method meets art: Arts-based research practice.* (3rd edition). Guilford Press.
Madison, Soyini D. (1994). Story, history, and performance: Interpreting oral history through Black performance traditions. *Black Sacred Music, 8*(2), 43–63. https://doi.org/10.1215/10439455-8.2.43.
Madison, Soyini, D. (1993). "That was my occupation": Oral narrative, performance, and Black feminist thought. *Text and Performance Quarterly, 13*(3), 213–232. https://doi.org/10.1215/10439455-8.2.43.
Martineau, J. (2015). *Creative combat: Indigenous art, resurgence, and decolonization.* (Unpublished doctoral dissertation). University of Victoria, British Columbia.
Meyer, M. (2017). Concrete research poetry: A visual representation of metaphor. *Art/Research International: A Transdisciplinary Journal, 2*(1), 32–57. https://doi.org/10.18432/R2KS6F.
Moraga, C. & Anzaldúa, G. (Eds.). (2015). *This bridge called my back: Writings by radical women of color.* SUNY.
Naftzinger, J. (2020). A definition of everyday writing: Methods for a writer-informed approach to lifespan writing. In R. J. Dippre & T. Phillips (Eds.), *Approaches to lifespan writing research: Generating an actionable coherence* (pp. 81–95). The WAC Clearinghouse; University Press of Colorado. https://doi.org/10.37514/PER-B.2020.1053.
Ohito, E. O. & Nyachae, T. M. (2018). Poetically poking at language and power: Using Black feminist poetry to conduct rigorous feminist critical discourse analysis.

Qualitative Inquiry, 25(9–10), pp. 839–850. https://doi.org/10.1177/1077800418786303.

Piirto, J. (2009). The question of quality and qualifications: Writing inferior poems as qualitative research. In M. Prendergast, C. Leggo and P. Sameshima (Eds.), *Poetic inquiry: Vibrant voices in the social sciences* (pp. 83–99). Sense Publishers. https://doi.org/10.1163/9789087909512_009.

Piirto, J. (2002). The question of quality and qualifications: Writing inferior poems as qualitative research. *International Journal of Qualitative Studies in Education, 15*(4), 431–445. https://doi.org/10.1080/09518390210145507.

Powell, et al. (2014). Our story begins here: Constelling cultural rhetorics. *Enculturation*, 18, http://enculturation.net/our-story-begins-here.

Prendergast, M. (2009). Introduction: The phenomena of poetry in research: 'Poem is What?' poetic inquiry in qualitative social science research. In M. Prendergast, C. Leggo and P. Sameshima (Eds.), *Poetic inquiry: Vibrant voices in the social sciences* (pp. xix–xlii). Sense Publishers. https://doi.org/10.1163/9789087909512.

Prior, P. & Smith, A. (2020). Editorial: Writing across: Tracing transliteracies as becoming over time, space, and settings. *Learning, Culture, and Social Interaction, 24*. https://doi.org/10.1016/j.lcsi.2018.07.002.

Reale, M. (2015a). Can I call this place home? Poetic representations of a border crossing by sea. *Cultural Studies ↔ Critical Methodologies, 15*(1), 30–31. https://doi.org/10.1177/1532708613516432.

Reale, M. (2015b). How do you think I feel?: Poetic representation of African and Syrian refugees in a Sicilian refugee camp in wake of the Lampedusan tragedy. *Cultural Studies ↔ Critical Methodologies, 15*(3), 167–168. https://doi.org/10.1177/1532708614562882.

Restaino, J. (2019). *Surrender: Feminist rhetoric and ethics in love and illness.* Southern Illinois University Press.

Richardson, L. (1997). *Fields of play: Constructing an academic life.* Rutgers University Press.

Richardson, L. (2000). Evaluating ethnography. *Qualitative Inquiry, 6*(2), 253–255. https://doi.org/10.1177/107780040000600207.

Richardson, L. & St. Pierre, E. (2005). Writing: A method of inquiry. In N.K. Denzin & Y.S. Lincoln, (Eds.), *The Sage handbook of qualitative research.* (3rd edition). (pp. 959–978). Sage.

Rosenberg, L. (2020). A definition of everyday writing: Methods for a writer-informed approach to lifespan writing. In R. J. Dippre & T. Phillips (Eds.), *Approaches to lifespan writing research: Generating an actionable coherence* (pp. 97–110). The WAC Clearinghouse; University Press of Colorado. https://doi.org/10.37514/PER-B.2020.1053.2.06.

Rosenblatt, A. (forthcoming). Neglected cemeteries as places of human rights.

Runyan, T. (2021). *How to write a form poem: A guided tour of 10 fabulous forms.* T.S. Poetry Press.

Schoone, A. (2020). *Constellations of alternative education tutors: A poetic inquiry.* Springer Nature. https://doi.org/10.1007/978-3-030-35495-4.

Smith, A. (2020). Across, through and with: Ontological orientations for lifespan writing research. In R. J. Dippre & T. Phillips (Eds.), *Approaches to lifespan writing research: Generating an actionable coherence* (pp. 15–26). The WAC Clearinghouse; University Press of Colorado. https://doi.org/10.37514/PER-B.2020.1053.

Sotirin, P. (2010). Autoethnographic mother-writing: Advocating radical specificity. *Journal of Research Practice*, 6(1), 1–15.

Sullivan, A. M. (2009). On poetic occasion in inquiry: Concreteness, voice, ambiguity, tension, and associative logic. In M. Prendergast, C. Leggo & P. Sameshima (Eds.), *Poetic inquiry: Vibrant voices in the social sciences* (pp. 111–126). Sense/Brill. https://doi.org/10.1163/9789087909512_011.

Sullivan, A. M. (2004). Poetry as research: Development of poetic craft & the relations of craft and utility. *Journal of Critical Inquiry into Curriculum and Instruction*, 5(2), 34–37. https://doi.org/10.1163/9789087909512_011.

Tarabochia, S. L. (2021). From resilience to resistance: Repurposing faculty writers' survival strategies. *Peitho*, 23(3). https://cfshrc.org/article/from-resilience-to-resistance-repurposing-faculty-writers-survival-strategies/.

Teman, E. D. (2010). Now, he's not alive. *Qualitative Inquiry*, 16, 611–611. https://doi.org/10.1177/1077800410374036.

Wilson, S. (2008). *Research as ceremony: Indigenous research methods*. Fernwood Publishing.

CHAPTER 18.

APPROACHING LIFESPAN WRITING RESEARCH FROM INDIGENOUS, DECOLONIAL PERSPECTIVES

Bhushan Aryal
Delaware State University

This chapter provides introductory guidance for those who intend to research writing development by combining a LWR methodology with Indigenous, decolonial research methodologies. One of the objectives of this chapter is to make a call to expand the scope of the vision and mission of Writing Through the Lifespan Collaboration (WTLC) beyond western university perspectives so that writing can be understood broadly, historically, and culturally outside of the confines of the western hegemonic practices. As the contributors of this volume and WTLC participants have expressed at various forums, there is an interest in the collaboration being expansive in its approaches and participation; this chapter tries to argue for one way of doing so. For that purpose, the chapter first provides a short summary of Indigenous, decolonial research perspectives and then discusses how and to what extent Indigenous perspectives can be blended with lifespan research methodologies for a productive research project. The chapter also includes a short bibliography on Indigenous decolonial theories and research methodologies.

This chapter argues that LWR methodologies and Indigenous, decolonial research methodologies can be combined productively because both research orientations focus on contextualization and emphasize the inclusion of nontraditional pathways of literacy development. As the other chapters in this collection and previous LWR show, one of the main objectives of the WTLC has been to understand how writing develops within and beyond standard academic environments. The Collaboration emphasizes the importance of radical contextualization, longitudinal frameworks, and an openness to varied ways through which individuals learn to write and adapt their existing writing knowledge and abilities into the realms of life for which the skills were not originally intended. The Collaboration aims to capture the fullness of literacy development to demystify how humans learn to write and communicate at various points of their lives. Since the majority of the WTLC members are writing researchers and professors, one key objective behind the demystification of writing development is pedagogical. There is a wish: if a single deep grammar or a formula of how people learn to write were to be found, teaching writing could be so predictable and scientific. Such a formula does not exist yet and most likely will never be found. So, from the Collaboration's perspective, at least studying as many instances of literacy development as possible is important for shedding light on the question of how people learn and change as writers. Indigenous and decolonial researchers are likely find these WTLC orientations reflective of their own interests. However, Indigenous and decolonial researchers are particularly interested in how university research has historically been part of the colonizing process. Many of us in the Collaboration thus argue that researchers should take a more intentional, decolonizing approach in order to serve social justice and decolonizing purposes.

WHAT IS AN INDIGENOUS DECOLONIAL PERSPECTIVE?

An Indigenous decolonial perspective is a widely diverse, interdisciplinary lens that deconstructs western intellectual, cultural, and institutional practices. This perspective views western writing and research practices as instruments of colonialization and demonstrates how those practices have been responsible in the physical and symbolic violence against Indigenous peoples. So, resisting the colonial physical onslaught and exposing the discursive formations that justify colonization remains at the core of Indigenous movements. Along with this resisting angle, this perspective also aims to bring forth and recover Indigenous histories, epistemologies, and ways of being. The purpose is to create a decolonized political, cultural, and intellectual condition for Indigenous Peoples so that Indigenous communities, tribes and nations can regain their sovereignty.

As can be assumed from the statements above, the state of indigeneity automatically assumes the presence of the colonizing other, and thus Indigenous political, cultural, and artistic response is often crafted in response to that presence. A bitter truth reigns through Indigenous movements:

> Once absorbed into the 'chronopolitics' of the secular west, colonized space cannot reclaim autonomy and seclusion; once dragged out of their precolonial state, the indigenes of peripheries have to deal with the knowledge of the outside world, irrespective of their wishes and inclinations (Miyoshi, 1998, p. 730).

Undoubtedly, Indigenous sovereignty aspirations may point towards what Dipesh Chakrabarty (2008) calls "provincializing Europe," meaning putting the dominant western thoughts into its own place in order to imagine different forms of political and cultural sovereignties (p. 3–27) for Indigenous nations. Such imagination is difficult to achieve because of the absence of either the mythical precolonial golden past or the completely noncolonial autonomous present for Indigenous communities. So, most attempts are at crafting sovereignty at the intersection of this in-betweenness, the degree of which itself is different for an Indigenous community depending on its particular historical context.

Thus, the aspiration for sovereignty and political and cultural independence binds Indigenous nations and communities globally. Resistance, survival, and thriving are some of the common themes guiding Indigenous communities worldwide. Whether *Janajatis*—which itself is an umbrella term for many Indigenous communities in Nepal—or Native American tribes in the United States, they can identify with each other in their struggle against colonial encroachment and their quest for sovereignty. But what they exactly advocate for and how they mobilize their cultural and political capital may differ from one community to another, depending on their own cultural history, the state of colonization, and their relative power with the colonizer. For instance, within *Janajatis* of Nepal, they may unite their efforts together against the exclusionary Bahun-Chetri-led Nepali state for their common good, particularly for ethnic recognition, cultural preservation, and sovereignty. What *Tharus* aspire for, and how they think of their relationship with the land, differ from that of *Limbus*. Depending on their needs, what counts as literacy or an effective rhetorical move also may differ. Thus, since even how Indigenous communities define sovereignty may differ, when we think about the global Indigenous perspective, it has to be understood in their pluralistic forms.

For those researching writing from Indigenous perspectives, an understanding of this in-betweenness and hybridity is as important as recognizing the particularity of a community in question. For that, grounding the research project in theories and approaches coming from those communities can help researchers to see literacy practices from the vantage point of those communities better. So, there is no single Indigenous theory or approach, but a variety that originates depending on an Indigenous community's unique historical and cultural context. For instance, while the term "Native American" in itself encompasses a huge spectrum of tribes, heritages, and histories, theorist Gerald Vizenor's (1994) notion of survivance has proven to be productive to interpret artifacts and practices for many Native American scholars in writing and rhetorical studies (Vizenor, 1994; Powell, 2002; Stromberg, 2006). Survivance, as Vizenor theorizes, is a complex term that incorporates a range of existential, political, and cultural positions which together may look contradictory but define the condition of many Native Americans. As John D. Miles (2011) unpacks the term, "survivance is the active presence of Native people in public discourse and the practice of actively resisting dominant representations" of themselves (p. 40). Dominant representations undermine Native

American agency, often presenting them as vanished or vanishing tribes, either through existential attrition or through assimilation. Vizenor contradicts this characterization by highlighting how Native Americans have managed to survive, and even thrive, while undergoing massive colonial occupation and displacement. As Miles writes, "survivance offers rhetoricians one conceptual framework for understanding how agency emerges in Native texts that are produced in relation to, and yet apart from and against, dominant discourse" (2011, p. 41). Rhetorical and literacy acts of survivance, such as storytelling by Natives, try to enact an agency that is directed to the colonizing power as much as it is the product of the rhetor's own unique cultural and historical resources.

For literacy development researchers combining lifespan writing and Indigenous decolonial perspectives, one of the ways to ensure the better representation of Indigenous perspective is to use conceptual models, such as Vizenor's (1994) survivance, from within the community they are researching to sufficiently interpret the data. The inclusion of a context-specific theoretical model will demonstrate the nature and purpose of literacy as practiced in a specific historical context. Since those theoretical models are often developed from the perspective of the Indigenous communities, the application of the models may not only reveal the inner dynamics and purposes of the literacies but may also serve the interest of the communities. For instance, literacy practices in Native American communities can often be in response to what Vizenor terms as "manifest manners." Manifest manners, as Vizenor defines, are falsified/constructed characters said to be possessed by Native Americans. These fictional manners are constructed by generations of mainstream white writers, and the constructed manners have become so powerful over time that they pass as the "knowledge" from which even Native Americans themselves may be forced to learn about themselves. That learning would make the Indigenous people "manifest" the manners as constructed (and asked by) this network of narratives. Vizenor develops the notion of "survivance" to counter the "manifest manners," stating how native experience is marked with complexity that transcends the resistance-assimilation binary, and how Native Americans survive and work for sovereignty by using their own cultural resources as well as by appropriating the colonizers' tools. For a lifespan writing researcher trying to include an Indigenous angle in their methodologies, using context-specific concepts such as "survivance" and "manifest manners" in the case of many Native American tribes could better explain why certain kinds of literacies develop and for what purposes those literacies are used.

Often, such literacies may not resemble the writing the way it is understood at university settings. For instance, the practice of storytelling in Native American culture is a form of literacy that requires sophisticated rhetorical maneuvers such as retaining, revising, and re-contextualizing narratives to be deployed for various purposes including resistance, survival, and thriving and often those stories have not been "written" in the western sense of the term, or whatever has been written and circulated in the mainstream context maybe a version and a partial representation of the stories in action. And, again, as the concept of survivance captures, the quest should not be in finding the single grand story or an essence of a narrative but should be aimed for the versions of it as Native rhetors adopt and adapt stories to survive and thrive in protean historical trajectories. So, if the inquiry were to be focused on storytelling literacy, one could ask how one person or a group learns to receive, retain, and modify stories, and to what end those stories are used. As it is now widely accepted, literacy, or writing for that matter, is not a disinterested aesthetic phenomenon; it is a tool for survival and growth. While common human biological properties may be at the roots of the human ability to develop literacy, its exact nature, ways of acquisition, and use depend on contexts. In this regard, conceptual frameworks from specific communities would help to define what counts as writing as well as to find the purpose for which the writing is used. Researchers focused on contextualization of literacy research must acknowledge the "protean nature of context" because the purpose itself goes through transformation with the passage of time and space difference (Dippre & Smith, 2020, p. 27). A community in question may have a set of identifying traits that generally define its being, but those traits themselves undergo transformation over time. Recognizing the defining community characters along with the transformational history of the community is equally significant to understand an individual's lifespan writing development as well as the community in which the individual develops their writing. Such recognition underscores the dynamic nature of a community, something colonizing narratives often disregard about Indigenous communities.

POSTCOLONIAL DISCOURSE AND INDIGENOUS APPROACHES

Understanding an Indigenous context can be further clarified if we distinguish it from the context of the mainstream postcolonial discourse, such as the ones theorized by Edward Said and Homi K. Bhabha. Certainly, Indigenous movements may embody many of the radical lines within mainstream postcolonial discourse and may use some of the theoretical perspectives developed in that discourse, but Indigenous perspectives consider themselves distinct in the sense that they view many postcolonial nation-states (such as India) and their ideological apparatus as implicated within the western colonial and imperial structure. For instance, many tribal communities in India, which from the mainstream postcolonial perspective is a postcolonial nation state that gained its independence after its long struggle with British empire, conceive the Indian nation-state as the continuation of colonial occupation, sometimes even more ruthless in its encroachment into tribal lands compared to its European predecessor. From tribal Indigenous angles, the Indian nation-state demands resistance even in the post-independence context because the fundamental structure of domination and colonization still reigns over them, although the faces ruling over them might have changed. Within the context of countries like Nepal, which was never technically colonized by a western power, the Indigenous communities would point out how the state power has been monopolized by the upper-class Hindu majority while undermining Indigenous cultural, linguistic practices, and sovereignties. It is in these various contexts and connections that global Indigenous movements have intensified their efforts in the last few decades that have achieved recognition in many fronts, but there is a long way for them to find full sovereignty.

Thus, doing research from an Indigenous perspective asks for ethics, social justice, and the historicization of the notion of research because research in itself has been a part of modernity and its various political and cultural institutions. In her widely used book, *Decolonizing Methodologies: Research and Indigenous Peoples,* Linda Tuhiwai Smith (2012) argues that decolonizing research methodologies are "concerned not so much with the actual technique of selecting a method but much more with the context in which research problems are conceptualized and designed, and with the implications of research for its participants and their communities" (p. ix). Historicizing the practice of research itself, Smith highlights how "research as a set of ideas, practices and privileges . . . [have been] embedded in imperial expansionism and colonization and [have been] institutionalized in academic disciplines, schools, curricula, universities and power" (p. x). In Smith's theorization, Indigenous research "attempts to do something more than deconstructing Western scholarship" (p. 3). She presents a number of questions that Indigenous researchers should consider: "Whose research is it? Who owns it? Whose interest does it serve? Who will benefit from it? Who has designed its questions and framed its scope? Who will carry it out? Who will write it up? How will its results be disseminated?" (p. 10). These questions are critical when designing writing research from a lifespan perspective as well. For instance, when a lifespan writing researcher creates the writing development biography of a person or of a group of people or of a community, the narrative can be plotted differently depending on the researcher's project interests. What in that narrative receives accentuation and foregrounding is often the function of the researcher's choice, which determines the meaning of the produced text, and in turn, that meaning may lead to certain understanding or may call for certain actions. Meanings are to some extent always manufactured, and whose interest the produced meanings serve should be of major concern for a researcher connecting lifespan and Indigenous methodologies. Disinterested objectivity alone may not always serve the social justice imperative.

In another synthesizing study of Indigenous research methodologies, Alexandra S. Drawson and her coauthors (2017) identify three characteristics: first, researchers require "a contextual reflection, in that researchers must situate themselves and the Indigenous Peoples with who they are collaborating in the research process" (14). Secondly, they should include "Indigenous Peoples in the research process in a way that is respectful and reciprocal as well as decolonizing and preserves self-determination," (14). And thirdly, the research should have a "prioritization of Indigenous ways of knowing" (14). Embedded in these characteristics is the idea that research should not be merely about a disinterested quest of knowledge as often conceptualized in western modernity; it must consider its impacts in how it is done and whose interests it would serve. Since the privilege of formal research usually emerges within the non-Indigenous institutions, such as universities and governmental organizations, such consideration demands a radical openness on the part of non-Indigenous researchers to embrace and recognize nontraditional ways of knowing.

Thus, when we consider which methodologies would work for Indigenous, decolonial research, it is so far not a question of compatibility of the exact methods and methodologies such as ethnography, phenomenology, narrative inquiry, and others, but the intentions and awareness engrained in the researcher as well as methodologies. What counts is whether the research supports the decolonizing efforts or becomes another tool of further oppression. Thinking from a LWR perspective, when researchers conceive and execute projects, whether they are longitudinal studies that encompass a long period, or short studies focusing on a particular life moment of their research subject, the attention should be placed on the power dynamics and the implications of their studies. They should ask how the research subject gained the literacy development and how the literacy was used. They should interpret the data from a social-justice perspective to tilt their findings towards the decolonial side.

HOW DO YOU DEFINE WRITING AND LITERACY FROM AN INDIGENOUS PERSPECTIVE?

One of the major aspects of lifespan writing research using Indigenous decolonial methodologies should be to think about the notion of writing itself. When we think about writing from western, academic institutional settings, we privilege alphabetic and some other forms of multimodal literacies. When we think of the place of communication in many Indigenous contexts, we may have to expand the parameters of how we conceptualize writing. For instance, a researcher may plan to study a seventeenth-century Native American leader's writing development in the context when the leader's tribe did not have a "formal" writing script. Undoubtedly, the leader must have developed sophisticated literacy skills in order to lead their constituents. Limiting the definition of writing or literacy within western dominant models would not allow researchers to recognize and appreciate the literacy practices of the leader. The researcher would learn more about the leader's literacy development by incorporating the forms of literacies (and the communicative symbols) that can be vastly different from western literacy practices. This is critical because what is prized as literacy and writing in one historical and cultural setting can be vastly different from another and acknowledging and foregrounding those differences is at the core of Indigenous decolonial perspective. Such a move is significant from an Indigenous perspective because it recognizes Indigenous literacy practices as what they are and also helps to decolonize the Indigenous literacy history from western hegemonic conventions.

Thus, developing a decolonial writing research project begins with an acknowledgement that many Indigenous communities live with a different set of worldviews of their own, and do not want to come within the influence of western political, educational, and economic structures which are so hegemonic in the twenty-first century global context that it is difficult for almost any reader of this chapter to break through its sphere and to recognize the worldview outside of its frame. Nation-states, universities, legal and business forms, and many other western institutional and cultural paraphernalia have structured our minds so deeply that recognizing value in other forms of seeing may be difficult. It is in this context that postcolonial theorist Dipesh Chakrabarty (2008) presents the ideas of "provincializing Europe." Europe, as he defines it, is not a geographical location but has become the intellectual and cultural structure that has gradually gripped the imagination of much of the world for the last few centuries, and it has become difficult to think of alternative worldviews because of its hegemonic dominance. Since how we define literacy, writing, and research are also often the part of this structure, an Indigenous, decolonial research demands researchers being mindful of these structures as the intellectual location that constrains their work and be ready to "provincialize" Europe so as to recognize alternative forms of literacies that an Indigenous writing project may display.

This call for expanding the definition of literacy certainly is a part of lifespan writing collaborators' aims as well. For instance, Charles Bazerman (2020) has indicated the need of having to go beyond standard institutionalized versions of literacy when discussing the ideal of studying the totality of an individual's writing development over their lifetime. He writes, "our idealized model [of an individual's writing pathways] might come from whatever school curriculum we were familiar with or might reflect individualistic rebellion against school values and practices" (Bazerman, 2020, p. xi). Highlighting how researchers may be implicated within the conventional notion of writing, he further writes, "wherever our ideas about development come from, they likely would be allied with our beliefs about knowing what writing is and what counts as a skilled writer" (Bazerman, 2020, p. xi). Often literacy itself is defined in terms of formal education, on the basis of years someone has spent in the institutional school settings, and on the kinds of marketable and social communicative skills one has gained in the process. The absence of those years and skills is characterized as illiteracy. Bazerman's call to study the total story of a person's literacy development asks researchers to suspend common assumptions about literacy so that a diverse, full picture can emerge about how individuals from a wide range of historical and cultural contexts practice, value, and develop their literacies. This suspension of standard Euro-American versions of literacy is particularly critical in the research context of an ingenious person's literacy development.

Besides the suspension of standard definitions of literacy, researchers studying lifespan writing from decolonial perspectives should account for the fraught relationship between Indigenous communities and the western educational system if the research context demands that. Boarding schools and many other institutions opened for Indigenous children's education by Euro-American governments and missionaries have transformed literacy habits of many Indigenous individuals. The impact of those schools has not always been welcome news for many Native American tribes in the United States and First Nation communities in Canada. Many of them have interpreted western formal education as an assimilationist, colonizing weapon—as an intrusive encroachment into a person's cognitive developmental process, designed to alienate Indigenous persons from their native culture and identity so as to produce an "amenable Indian."

What this discussion leads us to is that many LWR projects from Indigenous perspectives may end up foregrounding literacy hybridity. Many Indigenous writers such as Leslie Marmon Silko combine literacies from multiple cultures and civilizations, and many of the Indigenous writers educated in western institutions channel their training for activist causes, to write back to the empire, while also using it to revive, rearticulate, and foreground their own Indigenous culture and identities. As Gayatri Chakravorty Spivak (1988) has argued in her widely anthologized "Can the Subaltern Speak?", a truly subaltern person or community completely free from western discursive hegemony may rarely be a subject of a university research project, let alone be someone with a voice or a literacy exhibition to be studied and analyzed, although such absence does not indicate the absence of literacies of such individuals in itself. The question should center around what colonial and Indigenous cultural and literacy systems shape the Indigenous writers to speak for, and what Indigenous and western philosophical and political ideas these writers draw upon to advance their own Indigenous and personal quests for sovereignty and self-determination.

DEVELOPING A RESEARCH PROJECT

One way to study lifespan writing from a decolonial perspective is to research the range of texts that the individual encountered, or found themselves in, and examine how that network of texts served as a catalyst in the research subject's writing development. There can be two trajectories of such research. One can focus on the transformations in the skill set of the individual, looking at language, stylistic, and rhetorical moves. While ideas and language forms are not exactly separable, another route of inquiry may focus on the ideas themselves, investigating what texts might have influenced the kind of thought the research subject is expressing. To understand such development, researchers can concentrate on the following questions: why could the writer write that particular piece of writing or compose a multimodal form of expression at that particular juncture in their life? What were the personal, contextual, and lifespan conditions that opened a space for the individual to generate the text?

While the study of the text itself is important, decolonial methodologies to lifespan writing should also go beyond the close-textual reading to understand and interpret the historical and personal context that conditioned, constrained, as well as enabled the composition, production, and dissemination of that particular piece of writing under investigation. And, besides the study of the person's writing development in terms of its kind, genre, and even stylistic sophistication, researchers should look for the rhetorical moves used for various purposes that may range from active resistance to communal glorification. For instance, Cherokee Nation's John Ridge's 26 February 1826 letter written to the book project of the Thomas Jefferson's Treasury Secretary Albert Gallatin can be an interesting project from this angle. In the letter, Ridge recounts the recent progress made by the Cherokees and claims that the Cherokees have become better than neighboring whites in terms of education, agriculture, and overall-civilization. He writes that Cherokees now "are farmers and herdsmen, which is their real character" (36). He continues, "there is not to my knowledge a solitary Cherokee to be found who depends upon the chase for subsistence" (36). He highlights the swiftness of the Cherokee progress: "And many a drunken, idle & good for nothing Indian has been converted from error & have become useful citizens" (41). This letter in its context was a complex and powerful rhetorical move. In the letter, Ridge emphasizes recent Cherokee "progress." He undermines the Cherokee past, particularly the pre-agricultural, hunting lifestyle, and presents that part as a drawback. Were these the true feelings of the writer, or were these the parts of a rhetorical performance intended to accomplish certain purpose? The Cherokee as a Nation and John Ridge as a person in that community were going through a difficult existential crisis. Ridge was looking into every avenue to address that crisis, and this letter was not an exception.

The questions from lifespan and Indigenous perspectives in that context would be to explore how and from where the writer developed writing and related literacy skills. One needed a certain skill-set to compose a letter like that. How did it become possible for a Cherokee whose tribe had just developed a written language in the last two decades to come up with such a letter? What of Cherokee oral tradition was transferred to the written culture of which this letter became part? Where did the letter composer develop the rhetorical skills embedded in this letter? Were the ideas and rhetorical moves injected in the letter generated within Ridge's tribe? To what extent did the Euro-American education that Ridge was part of play a role? What hybridity could be seen in terms of literacy? What aspects of the western education in Ridge's life were empowering? What of the western education did he have to un-learn and undermine in order to develop an Indigenous, decolonial writing?

LIFESPAN WRITING DEVELOPMENT RESEARCH FROM INDIGENOUS, DECOLONIAL PERSPECTIVES

In many ways, the LWR approach developed to date opens productively to a research project that takes Indigenous, decolonial perspectives into consideration. As should be obvious from the description above, both approaches share their orientation to context. Lifespan approaches to writing aim to understand the development of a writer in its possible totality. LWR also takes a longitudinal approach in its attempt to understand "how writing changes throughout the entire lifespan" (Dippre & Phillips, 2020, p. 3). As Bazerman argues, this is an idealistic aspiration, "a heuristic for an impossible dream," but it is something to strive for as literacy scholarship tries to demystify the acquisition and development of writing in a person's lifespan (Bazerman, 2018, p. 326).

One particular advantage of lifespan writing research approaches to an Indigenous writing development project is that it allows researchers to view a particular set of writing in a more comprehensive longitudinal perspective. Instead of capitalizing on some of the iconic texts and performances, the lifespan longitudinal perspective would instigate researchers to see a writer's development from a holistic, bigger frame as well as from micro-details of personal history to understand the generative forces conditioning a person's writerly development. As Anna Smith (2020) writes, "a power of lifespan studies is that not only are time and space points A and B within the scope of the research, but so too are points C, D, E, F, etc." (16). This is particularly important for Indigenous contexts because what counts as writing and literacy could be different compared to the western perspective, and LWR's longitudinal vision can capture that difference.

Yet, there are caveats that the researchers should be concerned about. In the course of charting out the objectives for LWR, Bazerman and his collaborators (2018) highlight Writing Studies' limited understanding of how students learn to write. For writing scholars, cracking the code—if there is any—would revolutionize the teaching of writing. From a LWR perspective, they first expect to "identify the kinds of challenges students in different situations and with different experiences and from different language backgrounds may be able to address productively and learn from" (Bazerman et al., 2018, p. 381). The main objective is to develop a theory of how people learn to write so that the knowledge can be used for instructional purposes, for which the LWR perspective tries to expand its horizon to incorporate the "radically longitudinal and radically contextual" study of a developing writer accounting for individual idiosyncrasies so that a pattern can be identified and articulated (Smith, 2020, p. 16). When we think from an Indigenous, decolonial perspective, there is no problem with the method and logic that tries to study writing development with a comprehensive approach. What could be problematic is the purpose of such research. Two simple questions should be: *For whose benefit will the knowledge created from the research be used? Will the research help Indigenous communities' quest for their sovereignty and freedom, or will the knowledge be further utilized to sharpen the colonizing process?*

CONCLUSION

The best way to conclude this essay would be going back to Bazerman and his collaborators (2018) when they tried to define the significance of LWR methodology. They write, "We still lack a coherent framework for understanding the complexities of writing development, curriculum design, and assessment over a lifetime. Because we lack an integrated framework, high-stakes decisions about curriculum, instruction, and assessment are often made in unsystematic ways that may fail to support the development they are intended to facilitate" (p. 21). In another study, Jonathan Alexander and Susan C. Jarratt's (2014) examination of the sources of student activism in college campuses found that college courses—including liberal arts and writing courses—have not contributed to activist orientations. In their article, the students who had previously participated in protests received their inspiration and moral imperative for their actions in their family histories and communities, not in the university curriculum. Both works suggest the insufficiency of what universities offer at present and point to the need of finding a better framework. From Indigenous, decolonial perspectives, the most critical aspect in Bazerman and his collaborators' (2018) statement would be the idea of the development that the new writing development framework could facilitate. While it is not the whole story, an activist mindset is what defines Indigenous, decolonial rhetorical activities, and since the dominant underlying approach to humanities education seems to be geared towards "fitting in" by producing graduates with skills and mental habits suitable for neo-liberal capitalist industries rather than questioning the status quo, a decolonial approach would ask for a larger, more social-justice oriented definition of writing development. The Indigenous activist orientation questions even the much-prized critical thinking methodology in terms of how it could itself sharpen the existing colonial and colonizing practices instead of questioning them and asks for how writing development frameworks should not be only about the stylistic and language sophistication that one gains through practice but should also be about the rhetorical modes and argumentation designed to interrogate hegemonic structures.

BRIEF BIBLIOGRAPHY ON INDIGENOUS RESEARCH METHODOLOGIES

Covach, M. E. (2010). *Indigenous methodologies: Characteristics, conversations, and contexts*. University of Toronto Press.

Drawson, A. S., Toombs, E. & Mushquash, C. J. (2017). Indigenous research methods: A systematic review. *The International Indigenous Policy Journal, 8*(2). https://doi.org/10.18584/iipj.2017.8.2.5.

Katanski, A. V. (2005). Learning to write "Indian": The boarding school experience and American Indian literature. University of Oklahoma Press.

Lambert, L. (2014). *Research for indigenous survival: Indigenous research methodologies in the behavioral sciences*. Salish Kootenai College Press.

Mertens, D. M., Cram, F. & Chilisa, B. (2013). *Indigenous pathways into social research: Voices of a new generation*. Routledge.

Na'puti, T. R. & Cruz, J. M. (2021). Mapping interventions: toward a decolonial and indigenous praxis across communication studies. *Communication, Culture & Critique, 15*(1), 1–20. https://doi.org/10.1093/ccc/tcab064.

Smith, L. T. (2012). *Decolonizing methodologies: Research and indigenous peoples*. Zed Books.

Strega, S. & Brown L. (2015). *Research as resistance: Revising critical, indigenous, and anti-oppressive approaches*. Canadian Scholars' Press.

Vizenor, G. (1994). *Manifest manners: Postindian warriors of survivance*. Wesleyan University Press.

Walter, M. & Andersen, C. (2013). *Indigenous statistics: A quantitative research methodology*. Routledge.

Wilson, S. (2008). *Research is ceremony: Indigenous research methods*. Fernwood Publishing.

Wieser, K. G. (2021). *American Indian and indigenous rhetorics: A digital annotated bibliography*. https://kimberlywieser.oucreate.com/americanindianandindigenousrhetbib/.

REFERENCES

Alexander, J. & Jarratt, S. C. (2014). Rhetorical education and student activism. *College English, 76*(6), 525–544.

Bazerman, C. (2020). Preface. In R. J. Dippre & T. Phillips (Eds.), *Approaches to lifespan writing research: Generating an actionable coherence* (pp. 27–38). The WAC Clearinghouse; University Press of Colorado. https://doi.org/10.37514/PER-B.2020.1053.1.1.

Bazerman, C., Applebee, A. N., Berninger, V. W., Brandt, D., Graham, S., Jeffery, J. V., Matsuda, P. K., Murphy, S., Rowe, D. W., Schleppegrell, M. & Wilcox, K. C. (Eds.). (2018). *The lifespan development of writing*. National Council of Teachers of English. https://wac.colostate.edu/books/ncte/lifespan-writing/.

Chakrabarty, D. (2008). *Provincializing Europe: Postcolonial thought and historical difference*—new edition. Princeton University Press.

Dippre, R. J. & Phillips, T. (Eds.). (2020). *Approaches to lifespan writing research: Generating an actionable coherence*. The WAC Clearinghouse; University Press of Colorado. https://doi.org/10.37514/PER-B.2020.1053.

Dippre, R. J. & Smith A. (2020). Always already relocalized: The protean nature of context in lifespan writing research. In R. J. Dippre & T. Phillips (Eds.), *Approaches to lifespan writing research: Generating an actionable coherence* (pp. 27–38). The WAC Clearinghouse; University Press of Colorado. https://doi.org/10.37514/PER-B.2020.1053.2.02.

Drawson, A. S., Toombs, E. & Mushquash, C. J. (2017). Indigenous research methods: A systemic review. *The International Indigenous Policy Journal, 8*(2). https://doi.org/10.18584/iipj.2017.8.2.5.

Miles, J. D. (2011). The Postindian rhetoric of Gerald Vizenor. *College Composition and Communication, 63*(1), 35–53.

Miyoshi, M. (1993). A borderless world? From colonialism to transnationalism and the decline of the nation-state. *Critical Inquiry, 19*(4), 726–751.

Powell, M. (2002). Rhetorics of survivance: How American Indians use writing. *College Composition and Communication, 53*(3), 396–434.

Ridge, J. (2005). Letter to Albert Gallatin: February 27, 1826. In T. Purdue & M. D. Green (Eds.), *The Cherokee removal: A brief history with documents* (pp. 35–44). Bedford/St. Martin's.

Smith, A. (2020). Across, through, and with: Ontological orientations for lifespan writing research. In R. J. Dippre & T. Phillips (Eds.), *Approaches to lifespan writing research: Generating an actionable coherence* (pp. 15–26). The WAC Clearinghouse; University Press of Colorado. https://doi.org/10.37514/PER-B.2020.1053.2.01.

Smith, L. T. (2012). *Decolonizing methodologies: Research and indigenous peoples*. Zed Books.

Spivak, G. C. (1988). Can the subaltern speak. In C. Nelson & L. Grossberg (Eds.), *Marxism and the interpretation of culture* (pp. 271–313). University of Illinois Press.

Stromberg, E. L. (2006). *American Indian rhetorics of survivance*. University of Pittsburgh Press.

Vizenor, G. (1994). *Manifest manners: Postindian warriors of survivance*. Wesleyan University Press.

CHAPTER 19.
MOTIVATING LIFESPAN WRITING RESEARCH TOWARD EDUCATION POLICY

Jeremy Levine
Wake Forest University

Writing studies scholars have long known that writers change along highly variable paths both across literacies (e.g., Lorimer Leonard 2013; Sarroub, 2005) and across time (e.g., Brandt, 1995; Carroll 2002). This work, along with the work of the lifespan writing collaboration, indicates that writing trajectories cannot be universalized. However, standards-based reform, the prevailing model of educational oversight in the United States, presumes that writers will grow only in one direction and only toward one goal of academic writing, broadly defined (Nordquist, 2017; Lin, 2014). Such a model seems like it cannot capture the complexity of a literate life, yet it dominates public education in the US.

Schools often position "development," "growth," or "progress" as the unassailable goal of education. Such an orientation renders modern standards-based reform legible (as you need a goal in order to have standards). As a result, standards-based reform is dependent on the growth model, even if that model neglects the foundational premise that writers shift in varied, unpredictable ways across time and space (Dippre and Phillips, 2020). I bring this disconnect to the attention of those interested in lifespan writing because curriculum is itself rhetorical. Schools can only offer a partial reading of teaching concepts, which are selected on ideological terms and reproduce society's understanding of the world; if a school teaches it, society might believe it (Giroux, 1981). As a result, it is this understanding of writing, not one that sees all of a writer's literacies as entangling across the lifespan, that is instilled in students. Yet, by intervening in policy conversations, we may be able to shift the popular definition of writing in the very long run.

How might these interventions happen? Bazerman et al. (2018) argue that two kinds of research are necessary for applying lifespan writing concepts to policy and curriculum: The first would identify the kinds of challenges that students with different experiences, languages, and contexts can address productively and learn from. The second would focus on the practices, challenges, and activities that can foster development over long periods. This chapter adds to this list by proposing a third strand of research: an understanding of how these two aforementioned strategies can become possible within existing frameworks for education such as standards, exams, and accountability. We must turn our research attention to the contexts around writers in schools to understand how state standards, zoning, class sizes, vouchers, teacher experience, district mandates, curriculum guides, pre-existing understandings of writing, and testing all do or do not create opportunities for teachers to cultivate a lifespan orientation in their classroom. Sometimes the effect on the student writer may not be immediately visible, but these contextual factors are what make (or would make) lifespan-writing-in-school possible—or not.

In pursuit of this goal, I argue here that the concept of writing embedded in the United States' education standards—and the tests used to measure them—is a result not only of unexamined assumptions about writers and their growth, but also by the very constraints and complexities of policymaking and school governance. As a result, this essay operates from an assumption of good faith regarding education policy.[1] While writing researchers often discuss what education policy misses, corrupts, or obscures about writing, hypercritical approaches to policy often overlook the legal, political, and organizational obligations of policy action—the need to ensure equity across races and income levels, the difficulty of bringing teachers and administrators up to speed as curricula change, the complexities of intergovernmental relations, and so on.

Lifespan writing researchers must work *with* these limitations rather than simply critique them, so that our work can become useable within a policy context. We can observe from a critical distance to understand the effects of policy at all conceptual levels (as is hopefully clear, this very paper is deeply indebted to those approaches), but must also understand policy's objectives and constraints when it is time to chart a path forward. Because these concerns are baked into the policy-making process at such a deep level, making connections between lifespan writing research and policy is fundamentally a methodological question: we cannot only ask how the results of our research can contribute to policy, but how our research can shift in focus and methodology to address policy at its core in both schools and government.

This essay focuses on education policy in the United States. While the policy landscapes of different nations will invariably lead to different intersections between writing research and policy, the United States offers a productive starting point for studying these intersections for a few reasons. Education in the United States is exceptionally decentralized, which creates many different simultaneous policy realities that writing researchers may encounter. Exploring how

---

1   This statement applies to broad, longstanding systems of education policy (e.g., standards), rather than the outright attacks on public schooling coming from the likes of Governors Ron DeSantis and Greg Abbott.

policy is taken up by these different localities and governing bodies can offer multiple productive understandings of the potential role of lifespan writing research in writing development. Education policy in the United States is also significant because the past seventy years has been defined by conversations, policies, and legal rulings around equity; starting this analysis with a country that has legal obligations to equity may keep connections between lifespan writing research and equity central as we transpose this analysis transnationally. Do note that the particularities of standards are often in flux in this country and they vary across the states. This text then focuses on the rationale of standards and testing in general, rather than the particulars of individual standards.

The foundational commitments of policymaking and writing pedagogy are each built on sound principals, even though the traditions, ways of knowledge-making, and above all stakeholders bring our work in different directions. I propose three themes for lifespan writing research's prospects for coming to terms with policy foundations:

- The decentralized nature of education policy, in which many actors have a say in what happens in the writing classroom
- The presumption of stepwise growth toward one writing goal that renders standards legible to these many stakeholders despite simplifying writing
- The concern for equity, which is a foundational concern for an education system that has such an unequal past and present

In the conclusion, I explore implications for lifespan writing research design, and offer perspective on motivating lifespan writing research broadly.

THEME ONE: WHAT IS POLICY, EXACTLY?

I begin with an exploration of the players involved in implementing education policy in the US, both to offer context on policy in general and to map the complexities of possible interventions. In the US, individual states set *content standards,* or goals that they want students to achieve at a certain age. The rationale behind this approach is to avoid state-mandated school actions (e.g., individual lessons or assignments); as long as the students can meet the standards (usually as measured by tests), the mode of getting there is left up to individual districts, schools, and teachers. This means that any investigation into the effects of education policy on student writing knowledge must connect the text of the standards to the system of educators who can influence writing pedagogy at the high school level. It is not enough to say "the standards say students must learn X, and so students will all do Y." Students may learn X by doing Q, R, or F, depending on many factors. This theme, which covers the complex relationship between policy and practice, addresses the many contingencies involved in implementing education standards as classroom practice. These contingencies pose some methodological challenges for tracking what standards have to do with student learning, while also creating avenues for implementing lifespan policies in classrooms in the short term. In this section, I will briefly illustrate this issue from four perspectives: a sense-making perspective, a school network perspective, a school context perspective, and a testing perspective. Then, I will address the implications for this diffused policy system for lifespan writing researchers.

The sense-making perspective concerns individual people—teachers, principals, superintendents, district curriculum personnel—and their understandings of standards. James Spillane (2009), in a study of nine Michigan school districts' implementation of state mathematics standards, uses "sense-making" to describe how these local district personnel interpret standards by relying on their own understandings of teaching concepts and their histories with standards (p. 62). For example, Sonny Naughton, responsible for the mathematics curriculum in his district, understood math instruction as teaching procedural knowledge (i.e., the implementation of stable formulae), rather than principled, conceptual instruction (the method favored by a new set of standards). Naughton did encourage the new curriculum's *activities*, like hands-on learning, but did not see these activities as in-service of a new way of understanding math because he himself understood math in a different way. Sense-making then involves a policy interacting with a teacher or district official's "mental script" (p. 78) for that content area, which may need to change to make room for new knowledge (see also Franzak, 2008; Tardy, 2011) or the leveraging of previous knowledge to implement policy on the teacher's terms (see Lin, 2014). In terms of writing, we might think about how many teachers could have divergent definitions of "argumentation" or "appropriate style," which may create many different versions of these concepts across the nation's classrooms. While this certainly poses a policy problem, it does create an opportunity for lifespan-related interventions, as teachers with lifespan-oriented definitions of writing may be able to implement those concepts while remaining within the boundaries of the standards.

Each of these mental scripts is a small part of a broader network of people through which standards are implemented, which means that we must also pay attention to the structure of school districts when considering standards implementation. This is the focus of the network perspective. Individual districts may implement a prescribed writing curriculum (e.g., McCarthey, 2008), leaving the teachers' interpretation of the state standards less relevant—they have been pre-interpreted. The network perspective also draws our attention to the line of communication between states, districts, and teachers. District policymakers do not only follow state guidance regarding changes to teaching practice; they may also consult the policies of other states, professional organizations, and private consultants (Spillane, 2009). Sometimes, working with multiple directives can lead to disjunctures between district and school understandings of which policy should be followed, which can lead to teachers relying on previous practices rather than adopting reform (Franzak, 2008). "The standards," then, change as they pass through the district and school.

Another filter through which policy moves from state or federal legislation to student desks is school context. Factors like funding, learner backgrounds, and size of school might affect how standards are implemented. Teachers also recognize the learning needs of their particular students, paying attention to their interest and abilities, in crafting literacy curricula (Murphy and Smith, 2018). Other school context factors determine the extent to which schools feel compelled to follow policy changes. Teachers in high-performing and low-performing schools may feel the effects of accountability differently, as schools under pressure may be more likely to do explicit test preparation (McCarthey, 2008). The pressure to raise test scores in these lower-performing schools can overshadow a teacher's beliefs about writing, as external pressures to avoid school closure or take-over become prioritized. The means through which policy is rendered as a classroom experience then has as much to do with the school's location—and as a consequence, its funding and its student body—as it does with teacher understandings or organizational capacity for meeting reforms. When considering what "the standards" say, then, we must also be aware of how the incentive system built around them will construct teacher agency and, by extension, writing activities unevenly.

We must also get specific when discussing "the tests" because the theories of writing found in writing standards are not always reflected in the tests used to measure them (Hillocks, 2002; Jacobson, 2015). By pressuring schools, tests can lead to a narrowing of curriculum, leading teachers who are nervous about low scores to teach only the material found on the test at the expense of other material, or to teach "shortcuts" that apply to the form of writing on the test but not other forms of writing (see Koretz, 2017; Gabor, 2018). We must also recognize that tests in all academic disciplines, not just English, may require writing and may therefore have the power to shape curriculum. It is then necessary for us to understand not only the content of the standards, but the content of the tests, if we are to hope for lifespan writing research to have any effect on K-12 schooling.

Policy's differential nature certainly provokes limitations: one cannot simply change the standards and expect everything else to follow. These varied influences on classroom activities also open up an opportunity for lifespan writing researchers. At the end of the day, it is classroom action and writing experiences that matters to students, not the text of the standards that they will probably never read. This means that our lifespan writing research can be directed toward cultivating lifespan orientations at the classroom, school, and district level. Teachers and lifespan writing researchers can work together to figure out ways to meet standards through a lifespan orientation, thereby sheltering the school from sanction in the short term while still cultivating this long-term understanding of writing in students. This approach does not address the larger system itself and relies only on the goodwill of individual teachers, which does not lead to long-term change (Elmore, 2004). It does mean, though, that short-term progress can be made in classrooms while we look toward long-term progress at the level of the accountability system. We could also hope that making changes at the local level could lead to revised expectations at the national level.

Effective inroads at the national level would involve expanding the scope of the research inquiry beyond the texts of standards, or even beyond the experiences of students, and toward the teachers, administrators, and tests in their worlds. Ethnographies of writers that explore institutional context are one place to start, as are smaller-scale studies of the lifespan orientations of educators and the accountability measures they face. With the results of studies like these, lifespan writing researchers can work with schools to identify the ways that a lifespan orientation can be built in the modern accountability context. Such research can also build knowledge about how policy is implemented, which is a critical step in understanding how policy can be re-imagined from a lifespan perspective.

THEME TWO: UNIDIRECTIONAL GROWTH

With the landscape of policy implementation established, it is important to cover what the dominant policy paradigm expects a writing curriculum to look like, so that lifespan writing researchers can understand how their work may be interpreted. Education reform often holds up "college and career readiness" as its goal, and to get students to this threshold, the Common Core State Standards were written with "anchor standards" in mind. These are a set of competencies that students are expected to meet by the time they finish compulsory schooling—and backward-mapped to the earlier grades (Loveless, 2021, p. 70). Writers are then expected to embark on "stair-stepped, closed developmental trajectories" (Nordquist, 2017, p. 9) as they progress toward these goals. For this second theme, I will discuss how lifespan writing researchers can work within this unidirectional growth framework by discussing the reasons for resisting this model of writing development in the first place, then proposing how individual schools and teachers can approach alternative models of development, closing with a proposal for a research agenda that can address this question in the long run.

There are (at least) two problems with the unidirectional growth vision. The first is a consequentialist argument: a concept of unidirectional growth assumes only one set of writing goals is worthwhile, while research underscores that students build connections to writing when given the chance to set their own goals (Eodice et al., 2017) and can become alienated from writing when goals are determined for them by teachers and administration (Beaufort, 2008; McCarty, 2019). Assuming growth toward one set of writing goals also means uncritically absorbing students into "school literacy," which often presumes a standard academic English, leaving students who speak any other language (or variant) to catch up to the dominant form of literacy on their own (Matsuda, 2006). As a result, orienting writing pedagogy around unidirectional growth toward "college and career readiness" can become a gateway for the erasing of non-dominant Englishes from classrooms and alienating of students from interest in writing.

The second reason to move away from unidirectional growth is that it is not in-step with modern research on writing development. Lifespan writing researchers are interested in growth but recognize that there is more to writing across the lifespan than all-growth-all-the-time. Lifespan writing research is interested in development as much as it is interested in "*change*, in *stasis*, even in *decline* in one's abilities. In short, we want to understand what happens in people's writing lives and why, regardless of whether what happens could be understood as "development" or not. (Dippre and Phillips, 2020a, p. 7). All changes (or lack of change) in writing are subject to inquiry. We must then explore how lifespan writing research can be activated to challenge this assumption of unidirectional growth.

One method is to use the structure of schools to our advantage. By teaching particular genres, techniques, settings, and concepts of writing, schools inevitably filter down the number of text types that are considered academic. When policies pressure schools to teach specific types of writing, the funnel gets smaller. For example, time spent practicing and testing handwritten argumentative essays is time not spent making infographics on a computer or poetry with sidewalk chalk, leaving those genres to live somewhere other than the academic and the legitimate. By contrast, lifespan writing research understands all of these forms of writing—and other forms of expression other than writing—as being part of a person's literate life. As a result, lifespan writing research seek to "[cut] loose from our moorings of normalization into the great varieties of experience, the great varieties of trajectories that look so different" (Bazerman, 2020, p. xii). This commitment is foundational to lifespan writing research, but schools normalize concepts whether we like it or not. As a result, we might wonder that if normalization is an inherent property of writing in school, can we *normalize the lifespan?*

Such a project would involve re-imagining our classrooms and, later, our policy, to place writing's lack of center at its center. This does mean that lifespan writing research focused on classrooms and the education system would need to make one concession—that we do, in fact, need to normalize something—but could do so on the terms of lifespan writing research. Smith (2020) suggests that lifespan writing researchers take up an "across" orientation that understands writing in one location and time [as] not tethered or isolated to that context; rather, writing is a "widely distributed, highly complex phenomenon" (p. 18). We may wonder whether it would be possible to normalize the "across" orientation in classrooms. In doing so, we can see that even as lifespan writing researchers hope to break loose from normalization in our *research* (and we should continue to do so), these changing circumstances for writing can be at the center of our *teaching*.

This would involve focusing on writing's capacity to enable a writer's experimentation and negotiation of new social roles (Carroll, 2002; Montes and Tusting, this volume). Thinking of writing as a consistent re-making of always-shifting roles gives writing an indispensable role in an educational journey. Writing is a way to make these new roles happen, to linger and reflect on them. If a classroom can place this re-identification at its center, then writing will always have a job tied to fluctuation, thereby rendering unidirectionality inert.

Normalizing lifespan writing is an example of how we must respond to the contexts and concerns of policymaking while maintaining our theoretical commitments to lifespan writing. Schools normalize. Shying away from this function will allow alternative definitions of writing to take center stage, but by strategically normalizing lifespan writing concepts in the lives of students, a lifespan orientation can become indispensable while lifespan-oriented pedagogy and research work with—not against—the basic architecture of schooling.

To be fair, this proposal may, yet again, address the problem of unidirectional growth only at the classroom level, and not at the level of policy. If one of the fundamental reasons for studying policy is to understand what helps or prohibits classroom teachers in teaching writing from a lifespan perspective, then "put all of the responsibility on the teachers to normalize the lifespan" is just not good enough. I propose that addressing this problem of unidirectional growth from a policy standpoint begins not with persuading legislators and standard writers that unidirectional growth is wrong, but to start laying out alternatives.

To do so, I close this theme by exploring where learning expectations come from in the first place. Herbert Kliebard (2002) argues that learning expectations for students originate in the nineteenth century practice of dividing students up into groups by ability, and later by age. Only once this system of classification was in place was a logic of expectations able to be mapped onto the student experience. Acknowledging this relationship between age and standards aids our analysis in two ways: One, knowing that the concept of stepwise growth is tied to the grade classification system, a premise of the American school system so foundational that it is taken for granted, means that we must work within these constraints for the time being (attempts to reform age divisions in the past have fallen victim to a few issues, namely that it is highly convenient for school management; see Tyack and Cuban, 1995). Second, knowing that the age classification system did *need to be invented* underscores the basic fact that it is not inevitable. If we imagine an education system without classification by grade, and thereby no assumption of clear, stepwise growth, we can envision a system that allows for progress, stasis, horizontal movement, and decline as all part of the lifespan itself. Considering writing research from outside the perspective of grades and age, instead focusing on activities, social roles, or processes of knowledge-making, may help untether our research from the expectations of grading. From that point, new orientations to writing and growth that can facilitate a challenge to unidirectional growth at a policy level may emerge.

THEME THREE: EVIDENCE AND EQUITY

While breaking up students by age *facilitates* presumptions of progress in the school system, there is more keeping the growth narrative intact. In this section, I argue that a constitutional obligation to educational equity is at the very bottom of the modern testing and standards system, and that pursuing a lifespan-oriented writing curriculum at the level of state or federal education policy would require an understanding of equity. As I will illustrate, valid concerns over equity leads to a presumption that writing must be decontextualized to be measured. Alternative definitions of equity stand on rickety persuasive ground because the U.S. Department of Education defines "evidence" rather narrowly. Overall, this section argues that it is important to engage with these concerns over evidence and equity rather than rejecting them because they are methodologically inconvenient.

Let's start with why there is a system of tests and standards in the first place. Many histories of standard-based reform in the United States invoke economic anxieties as a major rationale for implementing standard-based education reform (often via *A Nation at Risk,* see Loveless, 2021; Addison & McGee, 2015). These economic anxieties drive many of the assumptions of linear, stepwise growth toward one writing goal, but there is more going on.

McDermott (2011) argues that "in public education, equity has been the main justification for the move to judge performance" and to centralize policy (p. 3; see also Schneider and Saultz, 2020). This evolving definition of equity and centralizing of the education system stems from desegregation; the *Brown v. Board of Education* decision made the federal government responsible for enforcing civil rights in schools, thereby giving it a larger role in a previously decentralized and stratified system. The definition of equity used to enforce those rights evolved; *Brown v. Board of Education* started with an understanding of equity as access to the same schools, which evolved in later years to equal *funding*, to the concept that a truly equal education means equal *outcomes* (McDermott, 2011; see also Briffault, 2009). Standard-based reform offered a way to ensure this version of equity: if we test the students, we can see where they are underachieving and see where resources are needed. This is how we know about the achievement gap between white and Asian students and Black and Latino students (Koretz, 2017), which has mobilized so much productive work among education activists, teachers, and policymakers.

I do not mean to claim here that ensuring equity through testing works. As Koretz (2017) argues, "testing simply can't carry the weight that has been piled on it" (p. 15) and contributes to a bureaucracy that objectifies students of color and leads to drop-outs as schools under pressure fudge the numbers (Johnson, 2009). Instead, I hope to name an important problem for lifespan writing research: if we take the differences between various reading and writing tasks as a given (which we should) and understand that all writers will have different paths and purposes for writing (which they will), then how can we start thinking about equity? Our work revels in difference; could such difference-focused work be used to justify an argument two educations are equitable? "Equitable" does not mean "the same," but making substantive interventions into the field of education policy—where our data would be able to meaningfully challenge assumptions about how writers change—would require a definition of equity. Until lifespan writing can offer such a definition, the education system will continue to rely on the incompleteness of tests.

This is a massive challenge because the current equity-based system seeks to quantify and decontextualize student writing via standardized testing in order to facilitate comparison. Bazerman et al. (2018) argue that the complexities of lifespan writing, which incorporate formal qualities of writing along with values, understandings of technology, confidence, writing strategies, and other non-textual facets of writing cannot be observed by merely reading a student's writing. One would need to get to know the student, their context, and their history before being able to make judgments about how that writer is changing, through multiple methods of inquiry (Bazerman et al., 2018). By only relying on what is on the page, the decisions we make based on test scores come from an incomplete picture. Even if a student is in a lifespan-oriented curriculum, the current accountability system is not built to give the school credit for such an approach. Schools under pressure from the accountability system then have no reason to adopt a lifespan orientation, as a lifespan orientation's benefits are not visible on an exam.

Proposing changes to the dimensions of writing prioritized by the accountability system would dredge up another problem for lifespan writing researchers:

In the US, content standards are built around a research consensus that samples a limited range of methodologies, rather than the wide range of research methodologies that lifespan writing researchers endorse across this volume. It turns out that the difference is not arbitrary; lifespan writing researchers value the kind of research that can account for the contextual factors that are disregarded by the current system.

In 1997, Congress convened the National Reading Panel (NRP) to assess the body of research on teaching children to read, setting the stage for the evidence base used to develop content standards for both *No Child Left Behind* and the *Common Core State Standards* (Calfee, 2013). The "scientific" evidence base agreed upon by the NRP emphasized direct-instruction and mechanical reading pedagogy which led to measurable outcomes that could be held up as evidence that given policies were working (Young & Potter, 2017). The Department of Education established a hierarchy of research studies, considering randomly controlled experiments as most trustworthy and subordinating many of the methodologies that lifespan writing researchers use to account for the social dimensions of reading and writing like case studies, ethnographies, and observation (Ellis, 2013; Compton-Lilly & Stewart, 2013). This emphasis on randomly controlled experiments now extends beyond the NRP to the What Works Clearinghouse, an online resource sponsored by the Department of Education that hosts research and recommends learning interventions only if they are grounded in single-intervention, randomly controlled experiments (What Works Clearinghouse, 2020). The definition of "works," then, is quite narrow; if educators are accustomed to this definition of "proper" research, then those of us who work in the complexities of non-controlled experiments must actively seek ways to change this narrative.

How did randomly controlled experiments come to monopolize the Department of Education's definition of good educational practice? One reason is the make-up of the NRP itself; the vast majority of its members conceived of reading as a basic skill to be taught through direct instruction as opposed to whole-language approaches, a binary that characterized the "reading wars" of the 1990s (Calfee, 2013). Another reason is an understanding of the field of education as "subject to fads and . . . incapable of the cumulative progress that follows from the application of the scientific method" (U.S. Department of Education, quoted in Ellis 2013, p. 80). Lifespan writing researchers, who of course traffic in context-rich readings of writers, must understand these rationales. For lifespan writing research to be applicable to education policy, it would need to challenge these research paradigms or a find a way to enter them. Doing so intentionally would involve considerations of our research design—what do randomly-controlled experiments contribute, and how can lifespan writing research designs make intentional decisions around our research questions to demonstrate our contribution?

The scientism governing standard writing, funding awards, and the What Works Clearinghouse is partially rooted in a desire for replicability (Kerrigan & Johnson, 2018). Lifespan writing research should take seriously calls for replicability in composition studies (see Haswell, 2005; Anson, 2008). Lifespan writing researchers could set their sights on, say, *approximate replication,* which involves repeating studies while changing a few non-critical variables to suit the researcher's context, or *conceptual replication,* the process of testing previously uncovered results with new methods (Raucci 2021). Because replication seeks not to simply validate research but to contextualize and extend findings, it is a promising avenue for a collaborative research project like writing across the lifespan, which can work further toward cohesion through replication. Essentially, we can have replication without "essentializing phenomena in pursuit of the unnecessary requirement of generalizability as a standard of validity, ultimately weakening the research and its implications for understanding policy and its outcomes" (Kerrigan & Johnson, 2018, 291).

Replication is possible through both qualitative and quantitative research, and through many different research designs. A sustained, robust research body that substantiates claims about lifespan writing can be persuasive in higher education circles, local school governance, and professional development settings. This does not, though, mean that the positivist assumptions at the national or even state level will make space for studies that account for the complex contexts of teaching and learning (and interpretation of research results), regardless of whether such studies are replications or original. Instead, lifespan writing research ought to align itself with critical approaches to education research methodologies that continue to challenge the dominant paradigms posited by the U.S. Department of Education from the bottom up.

One way to do so is to rely on context-oriented, ground-up research methods connected to the outcomes that are often central to policymaking. We could foreground the multiplicity of reading and writing practices happening at a given site and how they make contributions to more "countable" metrics. For example, students transitioning to college may have to revise their notetaking practices to keep track of course material (Harklau, 2001). Notetaking, while not thought of as "academic writing" in many senses, is a vital literacy practice that could have connections to issues that concern policymakers, like grades and retention. Lifespan writing researchers can maintain its focus on a multiplicity of writing practices by drawing connections between them and traditional academic outcomes.

CONCLUSION

To make substantial contributions to the field of education policy, lifespan writing research must respond to the foundational concerns of that field: public education involves a complex network of actors with individual concepts of writing; it trends toward assumed progress in defined competencies; it must be equitable. To make productive interventions, we need an understanding of teacher and policymaker concepts of lifespan writing, a disruption of unidirectional growth that is functional within the school system, and a lifespan-oriented definition of equity.

While this essay is primarily concerned with writing research in the US, answers to these questions from many national contexts are necessary to chart a path forward. In order to address the challenges in this country, we need to both remain constantly aware of the limitations that act on policy actors and teachers and be able to understand possibilities for pedagogy and policy that are untethered from the current system in the United States. Similarly, other countries with different policy systems (e.g., a system that is more centralized, or a system that has less of a legal focus on equity) may benefit from seeing ongoing work in the US in order to see beyond their immediate contexts. Comparative efforts (e.g., Jeffery et al., 2019) can shed further light on how the challenges for applying lifespan writing research to policy concerns vary by national context and values—and how sometimes, they are facts of wrangling something as complex as lifespan writing research into policy.

Applications of lifespan writing research to education policy must take place at the level of research design. While studies of writers crossing contexts should remain a cornerstone of lifespan writing research, the aforementioned issues may require comparative studies of writers, institutional ethnographies, policy readings, and case studies of teachers. While these projects are already taking place in both composition studies and education policy studies, only by designing from a lifespan perspective can we ensure that they will generate the findings needed to move the lifespan project forward. For example, we might ask questions like: if two students with different literacy histories interact with the same state-mandated writing exam, what are the different understandings of writing that they might bring to, and learn from, it? Or: What concepts of writing progress do secondary school instructors have and how do their goals differ from or echo the understandings of unidirectional growth posited by the standards? How do these understandings then differ across contexts?

When thinking about motivating lifespan writing research in general (i.e., not specifically toward education policy), we must consider motivation as a dialectic. In the conclusion to their earlier volume on lifespan writing research, Dippre and Phillips (2020b) name both *building points of convergence* and *motivating the research* as two sequential steps required to apply lifespan writing research. Moving toward points of convergence refers to identifying assumptions and findings from seemingly divergent studies and articulating the finer agreements between them while motivating refers to orienting lifespan writing research to common points of interest. That chapter emphasizes the importance of identifying and operationalizing the shared research objects and understandings identified as points of convergence and detail the complexity of such work when research topics and methods might be so different. Indeed, patiently working through this complexity is necessary work for anyone hoping to apply lifespan writing research. However, a third step of recognizing the effects of the field we study on our research agenda is also necessary.

REFERENCES

Addison, J. & McGee, S. J. (2015). To the core: College composition classrooms in the age of accountability, standardized testing, and common core state standards. *Rhetoric Review*, *34*(2), 200–218. https://doi.org/10.1080/07350198.2015.1008921.

Anson, C. M. (2008). The intelligent design of writing programs: Reliance on belief or a future of evidence. *Writing Program Administration*, *32*(1–2), 11–37.

Bazerman, C. (2020). Preface. In R. J. Dippre & T. Phillips (Eds.), *Approaches to lifespan writing research: Generating an actionable coherence* (pp. xi-xiii). The WAC Clearinghouse; University Press of Colorado. https://doi.org/10.37514/PER-B.2020.1053.1.1.

Bazerman, C., Applebee, A., Berninger, V., Brandt, D., Graham, S., Jeffery, J., Matsuda, P. Murphy, S., Rowe, D., Schleppegrell, M. & Campbell Wilcox, K. C. (2018). The challenges of understanding developmental trajectories and of designing developmentally appropriate policy, curricula, instruction, and assessments. In C. Bazerman, A. N. Applebee, V. W. Berninger, D. Brandt, S. Graham, J. V. Jeffery, P. K. Matsuda, S. Murphy, D. W. Rowe, M. Schleppegrell & K. C. Wilcox (Eds.), *The lifespan development of writing* (pp. 369–381). National Council of Teachers of English.

Beaufort, A. (2008). *College writing and beyond: A new framework for university writing instruction*. Utah State University Press.

Brandt, D. (1995). Accumulating literacy: Writing and learning to write in the twentieth century. *College English*, *57*(6), 649–668. https://doi.org/10.2307/378570.

Briffault, R. (2007). Adding adequacy to equity. In M. R. West & P. E. Peterson (Eds.), *School money trials: The legal pursuit of educational adequacy* (pp. 25–54). Brookings Institution Press.

Calfee, R. (2013). Knowledge, evidence, and faith: How the federal government used science to take over public schools. In K. S. Goodman, R. C. Calfee & Y. M. Goodman (Eds.), *Whose knowledge counts in government literacy policies?: Why expertise matters* (pp. 1–18). Routledge. https://doi.org/10.4324/9780203796849.

Carroll, L. A. (2002). *Rehearsing new roles: How college students develop as writers*. Southern Illinois University Press.

Compton-Lilly, C. & Stewart K. (2013). "Common" and "core" and the diversity of students' lives and experiences. In P. Shannon (Ed.), *Closer readings of the Common Core* (pp. 62–70). Heinemann.

Dippre, R. J. & Phillips, T. (2020a). Conclusion as prolegomena: From points of convergence to murmurations across sites, researchers, and methods. In R. J. Dippre

& T. Phillips (Eds.), *Approaches to lifespan writing research: Generating an actionable coherence* (pp. 247–254). The WAC Clearinghouse; University Press of Colorado. https://doi.org/10.37514/PER-B.2020.1053.3.1.

Dippre, R. J. & Phillips, T. (2020b). Introduction: Generating murmurations for an actionable coherence. In R. J. Dippre & T. Phillips (Eds.), *Approaches to lifespan writing research: Generating an actionable coherence* (pp. 3–11). The WAC Clearinghouse; University Press of Colorado. https://doi.org/10.37514/PER-B.2020.1053.1.3.

Ellis, S. (2013). Whose knowledge counts, for whom, and in what circumstances? In K. S. Goodman, R. C. Calfee & Y. M. Goodman (Eds.), *Whose knowledge counts in government literacy policies?: Why expertise matters* (pp. 79–93). Routledge. https://doi.org/10.4324/9780203796849.

Elmore, R. (2004). *School reform from the inside out: Policy, practice, and performance.* Harvard Education Press.

Eodice, M., Geller, A. E. & Lerner, N. (2017). *The meaningful writing project: Learning, teaching, and writing in higher education.* Utah State University Press.

Franzak, J. K. (2008). On the margins in a high-performing high school: Policy and the struggling reader. *Research in the Teaching of English, 42*(4), 466–505. https://doi.org/10.58680/rte20086504.

Gabor, A. (2018). *After the education wars: How smart schools upend the business of reform.* The New Press.

Giroux, H. A. (1984). *Ideology, culture, and the process of schooling.* Temple University Press.

Harklau, L. (2001). From high school to college: Student perspectives on literacy practices. *Journal of Literacy Research, 33*(1), 33–70. http://doi.org/10.1080/10862960109548102.

Haswell, R. H. (2005). NCTE/CCCC's recent war on scholarship. *Written Communication, 22*(2), 198–223. http://doi.org/10.1177/0741088305275367.

Hillocks, G. (2002). *The testing trap: How state writing assessments control learning.* Teachers College Press.

Jacobson, B. (2015). Teaching and learning in an "audit culture": A critical genre analysis of Common Core implementation. *Journal of Writing Assessment, 8*(1).

Jeffery, J. V., Elf, N., Skar, G. B. & Wilcox, K. C. (2018). Writing development and education standards in cross-national perspective. *Writing & Pedagogy, 10*(3), 333–370.

Johnson, A. W. (2009). *Objectifying measures.* Temple University Press.

Kerrigan, M. R. & Johnson, A. T. (2019). Qualitative approaches to policy research in education: Contesting the evidence-based, neoliberal regime. *American Behavioral Scientist, 63*(3), 287–295. http://doi.org/10.1177/0002764218819693.

Kliebard, H. M. (2002). *Changing course: American curriculum reform in the 20th century.* Teachers College Press.

Koretz, D. (2017). *The testing charade.* University of Chicago Press.

Lin, C. C. (2014). Storytelling as academic discourse: Bridging the cultural-linguistic divide in the era of the Common Core. *Journal of Basic Writing, 33*(1), 52–73.

Lorimer Leonard, R. (2013). Traveling literacies: Multilingual writing on the move. *Research in the Teaching of English, 48*(1), 13–39. https://www.jstor.org/stable/24398645.

Loveless, T. (2021). *Between the statehouse and the schoolhouse: Understanding the failure of the Common Core*. Harvard Education Press.

Matsuda, P. K. (2006). The myth of linguistic homogeneity in U.S. college composition. *College English, 68*(6), 637–651. https://doi.org/10.2307/25472180.

McCarthey, S. J. (2008). The impact of No Child Left Behind on teachers' writing instruction. *Written Communication, 25*(4), 462–505. https://doi.org/10.1177/0741088308322554.

McCarty, R. (2019). Complicating the relationship between disciplinary expertise and writing development. In A. R. Gere (Ed.), *Developing writers in higher education: A longitudinal study* (pp. 113–130). University of Michigan Press.

McDermott, K. A. (2011). *High-stakes reform: The politics of educational accountability*. Georgetown University Press.

Murphy, S. & Smith, M. A. (2018). The faraway stick cannot kill the nearby snake. In C. Bazerman, A. N. Applebee, V. W. Berninger, D. Brandt, S. Graham, J. V. Jeffery, P. K. Matsuda, S. Murphy, D. W. Rowe, M. Schleppegrell & K. C. Wilcox (Eds.), *The lifespan development of writing* (pp. 210–243). National Council of Teachers of English.

Nordquist, B. (2017). *Literacy and mobility: Complexity, uncertainty, and agency at the nexus of high school and college*. Routledge.

Raucci, J. (2021). A replication agenda for composition studies. *College Composition and Communication, 72*(3), 440–461. https://doi.org/10.58680/ccc202131162.

Schneider, J. & Saultz, A. (2020). Authority and control: The tension at the heart of standards-based accountability. *Harvard Educational Review, 90*(3), 419–445. https://doi.org/10.17763/1943-5045-90.3.419.

Sarroub, L. (2005). *All American Yemeni girls: Being Muslim in a public school*. University of Pennsylvania Press.

Spillane, J. P. (2009). *Standards deviation: How schools misunderstand education policy*. Harvard University Press.

Tardy, C. M. (2011). Enacting and transforming local language policies. *College Composition and Communication, 62*(4), 634–661.

Tyack, D. B. & Cuban, L. (1995). *Tinkering toward utopia: A century of public school reform*. Harvard University Press.

What Works Clearinghouse. (2020). What works clearinghouse standards handbook, version 4.1. Washington, DC: U.S. Department of Education, Institute of Education Sciences, National Center for Education Evaluation and Regional Assistance.

Young, J. & Potter, C. (2017). Reading about reading: Addressing the challenges of college readers through an understanding of the politics of P-12 literacy. In A. Horning, D. Gollnitz & C. Haller (Eds.), *What is college reading?* (pp. 117–135). The WAC Clearinghouse; University Press of Colorado. https://doi.org/10.37514/ATD-B.2017.0001.2.06.

CHAPTER 20.

A GRADUATE SCHOOL "DROP-OUT"—AFTER SCHOOL

Suellynn Duffey
University of Missouri, St. Louis

When Kim Rankin, whom you'll meet in this chapter, wryly described herself as a graduate school drop-out, her quip relied on our society's sense that dropping out signifies failure. Implicitly, she called up our nation's problematic sense that growth and change are methodical and linear, planned and predictable. In contrast to the stigma around dropping out, Pegeen Reichert Powell (2014) argues against retention as a measure of students' academic success. She urges us to honor the reasons why students do and frame both school and dropping out as part of a whole—as the "long run" of students' learning, a run "better envisioned as a series of short sprints in a variety of directions, interspersed with long slow rambles and even extended periods on the bench" when students drop out (p. 111). Powell's insights about academic lifespans and Kim's literacy life itself challenge the cultural measure of growth and success. Kim's path, like so many others', is characterized by starts, stops, and tangential explorations; enriched within multiple contexts; and influenced by all of life's vicissitudes, elements significant in studies of lifespan writing and literacy that many investigative methods miss by isolating small parts from the whole.

Much of this chapter focuses on the recent stages of Kim's long run through literacy—on literacies emplaced within the mid-life context of co-parenting an adopted child born with considerable impairments that constrain both his physical health and literacy life. Kim and her family's commitment to social justice through an evangelical Christian lens led them to adopt this particular baby. This part of Kim's literacy lifespan, as well as the whole, includes desperate sprints, agonizing rambles, changes in direction, and the fierce learning of new literacies that concerns for this child's health have led her towards, ones motivated in ways similar to Jonathan Alexander's (2018) learning how to be a gay man. Alexander writes that "[w]e seek out different kinds of literacies, different ways of being literate in the world. And that seeking out often arises out of deeply felt needs to connect with others, to nourish affinities and form alliances that can, in some cases, be life saving" (p. 531). Kim has, for many years of her life if not all of them, developed and used literacies out of "deeply felt needs to

. . . nourish affinities and form alliances." Recent versions of it have been unmistakably "life-saving" as breathing emergencies have threatened her child's life.

Both Powell's insights and Kim's lifespan itself offer perspectives different from steady, linear growth. In Kim's case, dropping out is simultaneously dropping in because she dropped out of graduate school as her baby's health required her to enter new literacy worlds around the complex medical issues he suffered from, the swath of medical specialties he required care from, and the community services (and absence of them) that the baby needed. Her dropping out and dropping in speaks to a lifespan *ecology* of changing, flourishing literacies linked with withdrawals from institutional settings, an ecology within which family, community, religion, and social justice circumstances circulate and play powerful roles. Kim did indeed drop out of graduate school, but her literacy lifespan is anything but the failure that the term "drop out" calls up. She may have left her formal graduate school life unfinished, but her writing and literacy lives multiplied, and through them, she developed new, expert literacies closely tied to her family and community needs.

Kim's literacy life shows us the influence of one's family and community life on literacy, a perspective we easily consider with young learners. But our scholarship needs to explore this perspective in relation to older learners as well. For this and other reasons, Kim's literary lifespan makes it an especially important inclusion in this book. It speaks to the importance in lifespan methodologies this volume addresses and, especially, illustrates how any single episode in the lifespan of literacy might lead researchers to seriously misconstrue the whole, similar to the ways that Compton-Lilly (this volume) resists tidy conclusions about her participants' literacy and remains tentative in her analysis subject to further experiences. While it is unrealistic to imagine that a full lifespan of literacy can be examined only at the end of one's life, it is also clear that truncating a literacy's lifespan risks missing important components of our writing lives. As the editors of the book explain, "The way [this chapter follows] the complex literate action of . . . [Kim] across lifeworlds, events, histories, and long swaths of time highlights . . . not just where various methodologies fall short, but the richly literate lives that focusing on particular parts of the lifespan (or particular segments of life-wide writing) may miss." This chapter follows Kim's complex literacy life after the adoption of a special needs baby, but it builds on some of her earliest childhood literacy practices in which patterns were laid that she replicates here, in mid-life.

METHODS AND METHODOLOGY: HOW I HAVE LEARNED ABOUT KIM'S LITERACY ACROSS HER LIFESPAN

Because no single method or methodology nor a combination of empirical investigative techniques would have uncovered all that we learn about Kim's literacy life, this section suggests and the book editors acknowledge what might be lost by an overemphasis on methodology as a guarantor of scholarly excellence. To understand Kim's lifespan of literacy is impossible without understanding how deeply and complexly it is embedded within family, community, religious, and social justice contexts; institutional acceptance and rejection of non-traditional literate practices; and accepted methods of credentialing professionals. Through Kim's literacy life, she has become expert at improvisation—the heart of scholarly methodologies that Phillips and Dippre identify in their introduction—and in this way she herself *embodies* another central research methodology *in her lived experience*, another hint of what might be lost with exclusive emphasis on methodological purity.

At stake for lifespan writing research and its reciprocal impact on all literacy research is what writing studies has been learning for decades—that community, family, and socio-cultural lives and their diversity impact student learning and literacy behavior.

This chapter thus engages narrative to explain how I've encountered the range of Kim's lifespan literacy, but I should note a bit of background on this method. Storying and/or scholarly advice from one individual's perspective had prominent roles in mid- and late twentieth century scholarship. Then, the discipline called for something else, for evidence, empirical and often measurable evidence. Currently, *storying* and *counterstorying* are again becoming accepted methodological tools (Burrows, 2020; Maraj, 2020; Martinez, 2020) and for good reason. They counteract western epistemological dichotomies (logic/emotion, mind/body); they enable relationality as a principle of scholarship, a principle that feminist, Indigenous, and minority scholarship value; and they build on the intimacy that Jessica Restaino (2019) has identified as a component missing from much of our literacy scholarship. *Storying* and its power need to be better understood, as Amy E. Robillard and D. Shane Combs called for in *How Stories Teach Us: Composition, Life Writing, and Blended Scholarship* (2019).

For my *storying* here, I've garnered information from nine different sources: 1) Kim's writing in graduate classes she took from me and 2) our participation in a three-year long informal writing/study/focus group that arose out of those classes. I convened the group when it became clear that several students wanted more time to explore their literacy and the writing of their literacy histories. Toward the end of that group's meetings, 3) four of us created a panel for the Conference on College Composition and Communication about our literacy learning, and so we were collaborators if not co-authors.

After three years, 4) the group continued to meet socially now and then, and Kim and I kept in touch, especially when 5) either of us was involved in a writing project that required the other's eyes. For me, that was when 6) Kim wrote a mini-chapter for my book on place and literacy. For Kim, it was when 7) she was creating a keynote address for a conference on augmentative and alternative communication (about which you'll soon read more) and when 8) she was creating a family cookbook as a special gift. 9) Informal coffee klatches and Easter dinners have also figured into our "data-gathering," but of course that phraseology mischaracterizes the nature of those meetings.

To some extent, our work for this project uses writer-informed methods, but the inquiry we followed here is more free-flowing than even that method articulates (Naftzinger, 2020). Our interaction over these years has moved recursively and non-linearly, something that characterizes certain kinds of lifespan writing research, as Collie Fulford & Lauren Rosenberg and Catherine Compton-Lilly discuss elsewhere in this volume. When an initial project finishes, the participants stay in touch as a result of the relationships established, and other projects emerge. Serendipity also plays a major role in this kind of scholarly inquiry.

STORYING: DROPPING OUT

When I first met Kim, she had completed her undergrad degree and begun graduate studies. At this point, it would appear she was erasing her first drop-out status since she had returned to college after long years away—that she was now first-string instead of on the bench. Her public reason for returning was that it was "her turn" now that most of her children were out of the house. She also imagined that she would teach in a community college and thus needed the credential, a goal that changed considerably when overwhelming family needs caused her to drop out of graduate school.

Kim explains her first dropping out in a literacy history entitled "The Road to Reinvention." Her school life, from second grade through her young adult attempt at college, is where the traumas of her childhood focused their impact. For example, she changed schools and encountered drastically different curricula and methods that saw her as deficient and mislabeled her literacy abilities (as Mike Rose's [1989] were), but other trauma accosted her later, as well. After eleven years of public school and a bit of college, she dropped out at age twenty. To explain it, she writes "I needed something college courses couldn't provide. Healing." And what provided that healing was in part a very specific kind of literacy learning embedded in the heat of deep, rich, multifaceted, interpersonal connections that she had experienced before second grade, as I'll explain below. Her early literacy scenes are the kind of experience she reinvented in her adult life through evangelical spirituality and the homeschooling she invented for five of her own children as well as those in a homeschool writing cooperative.

FAMILY LITERACY LEARNING

Before Kim's second grade, her father taught at a historically black college in the South. During the very early 1970s, when "our country was . . . boiling with racial issues," whites in the town "ostracized the new professors" and the "Ku Klux Klan was wreaking havoc in my parents' lives" (Kim, p. 1). Kim's father and one particular colleague often "would discuss school dynamics and strategize where to apply for work when the federal grant money dried up" (Kim, p. 2). She writes that she felt "a particular liking" for this colleague who "would pull me into his lap for a story" (p. 2) before the adult conversation began. "My father's co-workers seemed as permanent a fixture in the household as the wide oak baseboard. Many accepted me onto their lap when I arrived with book in hand. Books meant adults, who never played, would stop and spend time with me. I felt loved through books" (p. 2). This scene, I believe, becomes the prototype for much if not all of the literacy learning that Kim values and creates, for herself and others.

When Kim was six, her father worked another job that also engaged her in his teaching and learning community. As soon as the school bus dropped her off at home, she

> would head straight to my Dad's math classroom. . . . I entered without knocking. Crayons and a thick, hardback, blank book sat on the corner of my father's desk. Mine for the taking. Sprawled on the floor, I would draw and listen to him teach (Kim, p. 2).

Kim was not only part of her father's classroom, but also integrated in other of the school's activities and communities, especially the drama performances. As the much older students finished math class and headed for the dorms, Kim went with them to pick up Shakespeare scripts, and then they all headed to play practice. Besides rehearsing and performing Shakespeare, she experienced "immense freedom" (Kim, p. 3) to, for example, compare the campus's rattlesnake population to field guides,

> write notes to other faculty children on classroom chalkboards, . . . sit with students in the boarding school cafeteria doodling on their homework, . . . be loud in the school library, and . . . be ignorant that most first graders experienced reading and writing very differently. I was immersed in an academic community of high school students, staff, faculty, headmaster and families pursuing excellence together. There was no line of separation between my abilities and what we experienced collectively (Kim, p. 3–4).

Although Kim doesn't note it, I see these moments as ones in which her parents' trust gave her much freedom from their direct control and, concurrently, significant levels of independence and self-sponsored and communal literacy activities.

During this time and later on a summer vacation or two, Kim was again an independent learner and the literacies she learned were often and significantly developed with her father. During her first-grade year, Kim and her father "would spend hours flying about the Arizona mesas in a red and white rented Cessna 150. As co-pilot, my job was to read the laborious pre-flight checklist from his silver clipboard" (Kim, 3). She would announce "each maneuver importantly" and her father would respond with "check," the collaborative signal between pilots that the task was accomplished (Kim, p. 3). At age six, Kim couldn't fully decode all the technical, pre-flight language, but that didn't matter. Her father had the list memorized and helped her. In these ways, her father created a collaborative role for his daughter, one as important to the task at hand as his was.

He created a similar collaborative role for her years later, when they surveyed property in the Colorado mountains for local contractors who were developing an outdoor classroom. "The literacy practices I had loved as a small child, reading and writing alongside adults, would come alive again in the mountains" (Kim, p. 7) where she "was positioned at the survey pole end of the chain" and together they "recorded numbers and words in thick, black, hardbound books" (Kim, p. 7). Kim saw the two of them as "collaborating authors" (Kim, p. 7) as her father declared: "'Couldn't write this without you at the other end of the chain'" (Kim, p. 7). These practices of and contexts for literate behavior parallel those of the Old Order Amish family that Andrea Fishman (1990) records in "Becoming Literate: A Lesson from the Amish." In the Amish family, we see imperfect literacy accepted as full literacy with the support of family members who fill in the lacunae in younger member's literacy. We see collaboration across literacy tasks among family members rather than competition in family games, letter writing, singing, and more.

Because of family circumstances, Kim's schooling became traditionally institutional in the second grade and continued through the next many years. For much of the time, she complied with school patterns of learning, but in her adolescence, the man who had held the four-year old on his lap reconnected through letters in which he "wrote of the energy and enthusiasm for life he saw in me, of my deep love of books, and the cherished time we shared reading" (Kim, p. 8). Kim says this man's "brief reentry into my life empowered me to defy the people and situations that were holding me back" (Kim, p. 9) even though the road to defiance was long.

A TURNING POINT: DROPPING OUT AND STEPPING IN

One clear marker of this defiance as well as Kim's independence and self-sponsored literate practices is when she dropped out of college to tour the British Isles for six months alone, using money she had earned from summer jobs. When she left this country, she took a backpack, a journal, and a Bible, which she read from nightly—"a new habit for me," (p. 10), she says. It was in an Anglican church where "Jesus found me," (p. 10), and on this trip her life as an evangelical Christian began. Kim also wrote regularly in her composition book and kept meticulous records of where she visited, the money she spent, and the exchange rates for each transaction—the kind of recording she had learned with her father and will use again with her son's medical conditions.

She calls her solo trip to the British Isles a "turning point" and with it, "the role of literacy changed" (p. 11) as "reading and writing [became] an extension of daily living" (p. 10) instead of unrewarding, school-enforced chores. She

> searched . . . books for snippets of history connected to what I had seen each day. I filled the blank pages [of composition books] with reading notes. I was history teacher—assigning pages of reading and planning daily field trips. I was student—collecting facts. . . . Reading and writing helped me sort out my life (p. 10).

Her behavior then is a prototype of hers later as a homeschool teacher.

Evangelical Christianity became especially threaded through her life as she soon married and "assimilated [into] the church culture of my husband's youth" (p. 12), a culture in which "[p]arishioners lived out their convictions of biblical patriarchy through homeschooling" (Kim, p. 12) and which gave her an institutional, familial, and self-supported motive for homeschooling. Although she and her husband would eventually leave this church and its constraints, early on it gave Kim a way to "ignore the [serious] wounds of my past" (Kim, p. 12).

HOMESCHOOLING

In addition to the literacies of evangelical Christianity and the healing it offered, Kim developed new and different ones as her children arrived, and she began homeschooling them in 1993. Then, she says, homeschooling was not common practice, and so she felt compelled to secrecy about it in public settings. For example, in grocery store check-out lines with a child who *should* have been in school, she took efforts to disguise her homeschooling gig. Nonetheless, she was determined to school her own children, and during the following years, she taught five of them. As homeschool teacher, her literacy life included deep research into state standards and homeschooling curricula—a big business I was unaware of—but she had developed enough agency not to succumb to its totalizing. "When I couldn't find science and history materials that met my expectation for excellence, accuracy, and hands-on learning activities, I created my own" (Kim, p. 12). An example of her curricular innovation appeared in an offhand class comment she once made. On the way to her main point, she casually referred to a day when, to study carbon, she and her youngest child were roasting a marshmallow over the kitchen stove. This homey science seemed as normal to Kim as any high school laboratory would to most teenagers and science teachers. Through this phase of her literacy lifespan, Kim also wrote along with her children, partly as a way to test the value of what she was assigning and to keep her writing skills not only sharp, but also to improve them.

In this first, long phase of homeschooling, Kim delivered modified versions of each grade, K-12, five separate times, once for each child she schooled. By one calculation (13 years of instruction X 5 children), she had designed and delivered sixty-five year-long language learning classes before she completed her undergraduate degree. She had also delivered writing instruction for many more than her own children through the homeschool collective I mentioned above, one of the means homeschooling parents design to offer their children the benefit of expertise they themselves may not have.

By any measure, she was an experienced writing instructor, but experience does not necessarily mean expertise. One of the things she has said about entering graduate school is that she wanted to learn if, as a writing teacher, she'd "done it right." What I know about her now suggests that she developed a well-honed sense of what we would call best practices. As much as I have been frustrated in my career when a philosophy and/or a history Ph.D. has been hired to teach college writing—hired without any training in composition pedagogy—I see flaws not only in our field's hiring practices but also our credentializing ones.

A NEW HOME LIFE—AND THE LITERACIES IT CALLED FOR

Kim's self-named images—Kim the drop-out and Kim-who-is-not-a-writer (as she self-consciously claimed)—are images I want to connect with Kim the informal learner, Kim the self-taught instructor, Kim the mother, and several other images of Kim, some of which we've not yet met, images from myriad coalescing ecologies of talent and skill; from need, advocacy, and self-instruction; from immersion in medical communities, institutions, and insurance agencies; and from medical treatments and the intricacies of untreatable impairments.

Kim's immersion in all of these intersecting ecologies relates to the medically-complex, voiceless infant she and her husband adopted nine years ago as the last of their biological children was leaving home. On the first night the baby stayed with them, he nearly died when he stopped breathing. The home-duty nurse, enlisted as a safeguard for the parents and child, did not know how to treat him. Neither did the first responders who were called to the home. The household was in a crisis, and life-saving means were called for. Kim and her husband, who had had the *preliminary but minimal* training required by the foster child placement agencies, became the experts in handling the baby's external breathing apparatus (by unplugging a tracheotomy tube). The nurse was unable to help, and the EMS technicians had to rely on the newly educated parents to keep the baby alive as they ambulanced him to the hospital. He has lived nine years since then. Kim, as a literacy learner, has been crucial in his longevity.[1]

This dire emergency was only one in a very long string of life-threatening events in the family's life. But the story I want to tell is not one of harrowing human crises—even though Kim can tell too many of them. Instead, it is one that leads away from crises into teaching and learning and advocacy and community involvement and so much more I can't even say all the components: literacy learning that many in our country undergo when a loved one is quite ill.[2] It is a kind of learning and care that forced Kim to drop out of graduate school. Did this dropping out again signal she had failed, as this chapter's introduction might suggest? Clearly not.

A NON-CREDENTIALIZED TEACHER, AGAIN

In this learning scene, we see Kim once again evolve from a novice to an expert outside of institutionalized means of credentialing. Within the very first years of the baby's life, Kim transformed into a teacher for the local EMS squads. She and her husband had been the experts in the baby's first crisis in their family, and because she knew more than the squad about how to address a trach crisis, she saw a need and responded to it, both that night and for months and years

---

[1] Kim and her husband are a deeply interdependent team in parenting the child, but because he works outside the home, Kim has necessarily taken the primary role in inquiry and literacy learning. We glimpse her in this role when she conducts a swallow study on their son to help identify in meticulous detail the exact source of one of his problems. Because his physiological problems are so complex and rare, physicians, medical teams, and therapists often have little if any experience working with the exact physiological profile they confront in the child.

[2] Jessica Restaino's (2019) book *Surrender: Feminist rhetoric and ethics in love and illness* details the medical literacies she had to learn as her friend suffered through and died from cancer. Her need to learn is embedded in her very close friendship, the many languages (besides medical) that she and her friend needed, and the value that intimacy brings to scholarly endeavors.

afterward, as she and the family joined a pilot program that taught the local EMS squad to equip responders with the skills they needed to serve the community better. For example, every Sunday evening, when the baby's routine trach exchange happened, the EMS folks were at the baby's crib to watch and then eventually to assist in order to acquire the expertise themselves. She and the baby, who soon became a toddler, eventually visited local fire stations to further enhance the community interactions with the family, and photos of the baby and fire trucks dot the family photo albums.

Kim and her family developed other close ties with the emergency responders. For example, serious floods have, in the years of the boy's life, threatened the escape routes her family could take from home, and even though flood waters did not threaten their house, the boy frequently and unexpectedly needs emergency hospitalization, and for the family to be stranded in their hilltop home could threaten his life. In such cases, Kim has been in direct telephone contact with the EMS squads for detailed information on how fast floodwater was rising, how long it was safe to remain on their hilltop, and when an escape route would be blocked.

But as we've seen, the EMS people also depended on her, and this interdependency creates a web in which the lines of agency and expertise overlap and integrate recursively. As this interaction evolved, both Kim and the EMS people engaged in lifespan literacy expansion that affected one boy's life, one family's medical security, and the wider sociocultural spaces they all operated within.

RECURSIVE LITERACY LEARNING: KIM'S CO-PILOT AND SURVEY SKILLS, REPURPOSED

What comes next is an expansion of Kim's self-sponsored learning as the parent of a child with complex medical issues, as an informed literacy-educator, and as a mother invested in linguistic justice for her child. Even before the boy joined her home, Kim had begun to educate herself on how to treat the child's needs, and she has never stopped learning and researching. For example, for one long stretch of time, she kept meticulous logs (using approved methods of medical research) on his feeding schedules and the results of swallowing to identify the exact source of a leak in his breathing and swallowing apparatus. She colored his food intake with playdough, just as medical technicians would use other kinds of substances in a laboratory test, and through them, she pinpointed where the leak had to have been happening.

She has a notebook full of records (like her earlier co-pilot and survey record books) that could have complemented the medical and therapy communities' diagnoses and treatment plans. Her logs and their data, however, were ignored by therapists because they didn't fit into prescribed protocols for patient treatment, even though they provided evidence that documented exactly the eventual diagnosis and treatment the experts arrived at. Their new diagnosis and plan validated the accuracy of Kim's findings, but because she worked outside the accepted disciplinary parameters, her records were ignored and the child suffered months longer than he needed to.

MORE CHOICES

Even in the child's very early years, Kim's extensive interaction with physical, speech, and occupational therapists and her significant observational skills gave her repeated and irrefutable evidence that what a child can do in a natural setting is very different from how his performance stacks up against benchmark protocols that professionals use—to determine eligibility for continued therapy, for example. The stakes are high and yet valuable information is ignored. Again and again, the family's lived experiences have demonstrated that the goal of an independent life for the child would require constant advocacy for him and, especially, dedication to extending her son's capabilities far beyond what professional protocols imagine.

St. Louis, our home location, is rich in medical resources, and Kim's family availed itself of much that our location offers—a battery of physicians, therapies, social services, and more. Kim's research, self-instruction, and advocacy interwove repeatedly and continually as the baby became a child and his multiple, recurring ailments needed new assessments and treatment. After a few years, Kim, in consultation with the medical teams here, developed a nagging feeling that the boy's future health might be beyond the care that St. Louis offered.

The family was facing a crucial decision in the child's life about needed surgery. The available options to correct his throat's physiological design offered two choices: one would enable him to swallow and eat normally; the other might allow him to speak. But no surgery would allow him to do both. As the life-altering choice lingered in the offing, Kim did extensive research to uncover medical centers that might offer experience with the kind of care her son needed. She found a sliver of hope in Cincinnati, and after lengthy consideration, she contacted a Cincinnati physician, explained the boy's complex medical conditions and needs, and received an immediate email answer even though the physician's automatic response had indicated he was on leave—such was his interest in the child's case and his desire to help.

This immediate response, the expression of interest in and experience with related problems, and in-depth conferencing between the two cities sent the family to Ohio, where the surgery was ultimately performed and where the boy now makes regular visits. The surgery has reduced his frequent ailments and hospitalizations that resulted from how his complicated airways and limited immune system interacted with viruses in life-threatening ways. Kim had had to educate herself on the exact conditions of her son's airways and the terminologies multiple disciplines used as their practitioners treated him. Not a medical professional herself but an intelligent woman schooled in research methods and fiercely devoted to family advocacy, she necessarily worked outside disciplinary boundaries as she schooled herself and her husband in a route toward the best care for their son.

THE CHILD'S SCHOOLING AND LITERACY ADVOCACY

When the baby was a toddler and it would have been time for him to start speaking, Kim set herself to another kind of learning—how best to teach literacy to a voiceless child—and in the process she herself had to learn more new literacies. Through trial-and-error practices, informed by all Kim knows about language instruction, some learned in the university and much learned on her own, she investigated several electronic tools and training systems and settled on one that comes out of the American Speech-Language-Hearing Association and its Augmentative and Alternative Communication (AAC).

AAC is an electronic "speech generating device capable of holding 14,000 words," one she gave her child when he was twenty months old, much younger than when received wisdom begins this kind of training. The device is programable so she can align its language with both the literacy learning the child needs and the literacies that her family and religious communities are immersed in. Since the child is voiceless, he has to use it whenever he wants to speak, whenever signing won't suffice, and whenever a child's patience and drive push him to take the time to punch out electronic words. Imagine a young, rambunctious toddler now nine-year old who must always carry a computer in order to communicate—to his family when he's excited about a truck he sees, to indicate pain when he's fallen, or to pray in church. That image might hint at the myriad efforts Kim and her husband have undertaken to teach the tools of communicative literacy to him—including the addition of a shoulder strap (created by one of their older sons) that attaches the device to his body so it is always nearby while his hands are free.

Through her knowledge as a parent, an informed literacy-educator, and a mother invested in linguistic justice for her child, Kim soon knew experientially much more about how and why to use AAC than professionals whose interaction with their clients was severely circumscribed by time, insurance company protocols, institutional school settings, and widely held beliefs about the limits on literacy learning for children like Kim's son. What he needs also often differs from the primary communities AAC serves, and so Kim has been on her own to invent what works for the child and their family. She keeps records, arranges her family's days and activities to model words and concepts in the boy's curriculum, and keeps in touch with the AAC community in ways that again signal her self-sponsored learning and credentialing.

When she first explored best practices and tools for teaching literacy to her son and, more robustly, as she settled on an AAC device, she used social media postings that led her to create a blog, one that soon developed a considerable number of followers—parents whose children need augmented communication practices and devices, AAC professionals themselves, and others. As a result, her researched practice, well documented and described in her blog, has made professionals eager to learn from her, and so she has been invited to speak as an authority on AAC communication in regional conferences. University speech pathology programs now also use her work in their academic courses.

Kim, as a self-sponsored learner and independent scholar and teacher, occupies a somewhat unique position in community and professional life. In some ways, she offers much more robust and targeted instruction for her son than schools are able to offer in special education programs. She has acquired a degree of professionalization that makes her a sought-after resource in the AAC community, but she has done so without the sanctioned credentials that academia and the health communities require. She and her family, dependent on community resources, have become resources to a number of different communities.

KIM BECOMES A KEYNOTE SPEAKER AND WRITES A SPEECH

Kim, self-styled as a meager homeschool mom, has earned the respect of significant figures in the speech pathology arena that gives testimony to her extraordinary talents, intelligence, perseverance, and literacy learning proficiencies. How Kim rose to national attention as an AAC expert is a story with many chapters, one I can tell only in brief. The tension between institutionally sanctioned expertise and informally acquired expertise is poignantly and hauntingly evident in the following example of her writing process. Called to keynote for the first time, at an AAC regional conference, she began writing in early spring for a (pre-pandemic) October delivery date. How she prepared is the final topic of this chapter.

The conference, aimed at an audience of speech and language pathology practitioners, routinely designed the program to include a parent's view as evidence of what using AAC looks like in context—in the home and in a child's and family's life. That parent was Kim, who saw her charge as delivering the real-life, parent's view of using AAC. Following her sense of mission, she aimed to inspire the audience to attend follow-up break-out sessions on how to use the device and its affordances. Her process merits our attention.

Beginning in early spring, she set August first as the deadline for completing the presentation. Describing the process, she explained that she conceived of the speech as a story, so that's what she composed first—a story or composite of stories. Then she chose and inserted pictures. Her guiding principle for images was "What is the audience going to look at as I'm saying this?"

Then, she began memorizing the speech. She practiced and practiced delivering the written speech. She walked around her home, reading the speech silently and laying it down in her memory. By mid-September, she had fully memorized her keynote address and sought an audience, her adult, social worker daughter, who asked, as I did much later, why Kim had written it all out, why she hadn't created a PowerPoint. Kim says that it never occurred to her not to write it all out. She struggled with feeling stupid and took every measure to prevent that appearance.

She also was guided by 1) her desire to meet the organization's expectations; 2) a felt responsibility to bridge a homeschool/public school divide (given an audience with many public-school teachers and other professionals); 3) a desire to advocate for non-speaking people (to counter their unemployability); and 4) her fear of getting nervous (during the presentation) and making mistakes. Kim took extensive measures to meet the standards she set, ones that combined her own with external ones established by the context in which she would speak. Kim had two more test audiences, a friend to whom she delivered the address once and her husband, who listened twice.

Kim's official audience was speech and language pathology practitioners at an AAC regional conference sponsored by a consortium of school districts in Michigan. The program routinely includes a parent's view as evidence of AAC in context. Kim delivered her entire speech, going "off script" only twice—she made a point of telling me—once when she'd forgotten an important item and had to go back to retrieve it and once when the audience lovingly exclaimed at a sweet image of the child. Since then, she has delivered twelve talks on literacy and been paired as keynoter with Master Educator Karen Erickson, who does ground-breaking work as the Yoder Distinguished Professor in Allied Health Sciences and director of the Center for Literacy and Disability Studies at the University of North Carolina at Chapel Hill (https://www.med.unc.edu/ahs/clds/directory/karen-erickson/). Kim's work is also used in academic programs that prepare speech and language pathologists.

CONCLUDING THOUGHTS

A Facebook post[3] about Kim's current and past schooling hints at the ways in which lifespan writing research explores and illuminates the serendipity and weave of schooled literacy, literacy after school, and spiritual life. Kim posted an image of materials she had used in her second venture into college life (Figure 20.1)—her portfolio from the class in which she wrote the literacy history, Glenn and Ratcliffe's (2011) book on silence and listening, and articles from a disability studies class on teaching writing. Her comment on the image follows the figure.

Figure 20.1. Kim's Facebook Image

---

3   I share this Facebook post with Kim's permission.

> [S]ort[ing] through boxes this winter break, [and] this one contained things I read and wrote when I returned to college to finish my undergraduate degree and take some master level courses. If there was any doubt that brief piece of my life was deeply connected to what was before and what was to come, this should clear it up. Of course the mom of a non-speaking child read essays on silence and listening the year he was born and [still] with a foster family. You might see a stack of papers and books. I see God's hand in this box. (Facebook, 12/30/20).

Kim's brief interpretation of the materials she collected in this image emphasizes the ecologies within which Kim's lifespan of literacy has circulated. Her literacy cannot be understood separate from its existence both in school and outside of institutional schooling, in "deeply felt needs to connect with others, to nourish affinities and form alliances" (Alexander, 2018, p. 531), in her spiritual and religious life, and in her family, community, and professional circles. Jonathan Scott's (2022) recent *CCC* article, tying the newest neuroscience research to classroom curricula via transactional reading theory, is pertinent here. He argues and Kim's long lifespan writing demonstrates the significant role that lived experience plays in analytic literacy tasks—a simple point that Kim's writing and literacy life show us the complexity of, complexity that lifespan writing research enables us to learn about and that enriches our knowledge of writing itself. Kim and this volume offer us riches to be thankful for.

REFERENCES

Alexander, J. (2018). Editorial comment: Desiring literacy. *College Composition and Communication, 69*(3). 529–533.

Burrows, C. (2020). *Rhetorical crossover: The black presence in white culture*. University of Pittsburgh Press.

Fishman, A. R. (1990). Becoming literate: A lesson from the Amish. In A. A. Lunsford, H. Moglen & J. Slevin (Eds.), *The right to literacy*. (pp. 29–38). MLA.

Glenn, C. & Ratcliffe, K. (Eds.). (2011). *Silence and listening as rhetorical arts*. Southern Illinois University Press.

"Kim." (2012). The road to reinvention. Unpublished manuscript.

Maraj, L. (2020). *Black or right: Anti/racist campus rhetorics*. Utah State University Press.

Martinez, A. Y. (2020). *Counterstory: The rhetoric and writing of critical race theory*. Conference on College Composition and Communication of the National Council of Teachers of English.

Naftzinger, J. (2020). A definition of everyday writing: Methods for a writer-informed approach to lifespan writing. In R. J. Dippre & T. Phillips (Eds.), *Approaches to lifespan writing research: Generating an actionable coherence* (pp. 81–95). The WAC Clearinghouse; University Press of Colorado. https://doi.org/10.37514/PER-B.2020.1053.2.05.

Powell, P. R. (2014). *Retention and resistance: Writing instruction and students who leave.* Utah State University Press.

Restaino, J. (2019). *Surrender: Feminist rhetoric and ethics in love and illness.* Southern Illinois University Press.

Robillard, A. E. & D. S. Combs. (2019). *How stories teach us: Composition, life writing, and blended scholarship.* Peter Lang.

Rose, M. (1989). *Lives on the boundary: A moving account of the struggles and achievements of America's educationally underprepared.* Penguin.

Scott, J. (2022). Transaction theory rebooted: What neuroscience's research on reading means for composition. *College Composition and Communication, 73*(3). 526–561. https://doi.org/10.58680/ccc202231877.

CHAPTER 21.
RADICALITY IN THE SHORT TERM: GENERATING STRUCTURAL CHANGE

Ryan J. Dippre
University of Maine

Talinn Phillips
Ohio University

From its inception, lifespan writing research has worked to take a big-tent approach, inviting and encouraging researchers from multiple disciplines and with multiple methodological orientations to contribute knowledge. Bazerman's initial work and his formation of the Lifespan Writing Development group made clear that a research object as ambitious as LWR would require many hands and many forms of disciplinary and research expertise. As Bazerman asks in the penultimate chapter of *The Lifespan Development of Writing* (Bazerman et al., 2018), ". . .how can we understand the complexity of even one individual's idiosyncratic pathway to the mature competence that provides a confident, strong, and unique written presence within the individual's lifeworld?" (p. 327). In our first edited collection we also address this explicitly:

> how can we mobilize the various traditions, methods, and understandings of writing in these pages (and beyond) *together,* in ways that build on convergent themes, theories, methods, and stances but also take advantage of the divergences of each approach? (Dippre & Phillips, 2020, p. 247).

If there ever was a sense that LWR is a simple research problem to solve, the wide range of adaptations and improvisations represented in this volume are quite definitive. It's not just that a wide variety of knowledge bases and methodological approaches are essential for lifespan writing research: it's that even those may not be enough. The methodological improvisations that these authors have demonstrated suggest that even now, writing studies may lack the methodological infrastructure to support projects of the scope and duration required to understand writing through the lifespan. We are also very aware that there are other important, relevant research methodologies that aren't represented in this volume at all. Yet, from quantitative analysis to poetic inquiry, what *is* represented reveals nearly 20 different approaches to lifespan writing research which form several collective arguments about how lifespan writing research moves forward.

We have argued for some time that LWR is an inherently radical endeavor (Dippre & Phillips, 2023). Specifically, it is radically *longitudinal*, calling attention to the fact that LWR is "taking longitudinal research to its extreme by studying writing from cradle to grave and, where appropriate, across generations" (p. 156). But it is also radically *contextual*, attending to writing as "occurring with, in, and through the construction of context over time" by writers (p. 157). As this volume makes clear, lifespan writing research is pursuing timelines, contexts, methodologies, and even working with participants in radical ways that then differ from other approaches to researching writing, even when the same methodologies are being used. As Compton-Lilly's dissertation research morphed into a longitudinal, ongoing project, she developed new methods for data analysis that could account for those longer timescales. Her relationship to participants also changed significantly over time as young children became young adults who had new insights into their own literacy development and into the research project itself. Cain, Childers, and Ryan also make visible the ways that research projects shift course and develop improvisationally over time, necessitating new methodological approaches, while Fulford and Rosenberg as well as Workman show the power and transformation that come from revisiting a project. For Fulford and Rosenberg, revisiting participants led to important changes in those participants' roles as McGowan and Long transition into co-authors. For Workman, returning to data with hard-won new knowledge of both her self and methodology led to a revitalized project that does more to account for the entirety and complexities of participants' experiences.

This collection also highlights just how vital cultivating relationships with participants is to much of our research–and "cultivate" is a fairly inadequate term in this case. Duffey, Compton-Lilly, Workman, Fulford, and Rosenberg are all working with participants over multi-year and even decades-long spans. The knowledge that these researchers have helped to create is impossible without their participants' willing and ongoing participation. We have always known that keeping participants involved in our projects was key to lifespan writing research success, but these researchers' projects begin to make both the stakes and paths to more substantive, complex relationships with participants visible. As we see these valuable insights into writing lives that can only come with long periods of research, our larger, collective work to understand writing across the lifespan takes on greater importance. In addition, these researchers are beginning to show the rest of us how we might do it–how we might grow and deepen and mature our relationships with participants over time by "dwelling together" (Fulford & Rosenberg, this volume).

The radicality of the lifespan writing project also necessitates the kinds of methodological improvisation that spark across this volume. Many of the chapters here make clear that effective LWR is not choosing a methodology and clinging rigidly to it until the bitter end. The timescales and complexities of LWR will force change, adaptation, and improvisation. And again, we use *improvisation* not to mean half-assed, but, as several of the aforementioned contributors demonstrate, to represent the skilled, considered changes that talented researchers make as the contexts of their projects and their participants change. But while many of the authors in Part I focused on improvisations to established methodologies that have deep roots themselves, the authors in Part II take a broader look.

Part II offered an expansive perspective on methods, methodologies, theories, and approaches to LWR as researchers engage and develop new methodologies. Cain, Childers, and Ryan along with Workman address new imaginings of established methodologies, such as autoethnography and institutional ethnography, both of which have wide application to LWR. Zajic and Poch remind us of the power and unique affordances of quantitative methods in LWR, a collection of methods that are particularly salient given Levine's challenge to develop the kinds of research that policymakers will engage. Lunsford, Alexander, and Whithaus and Tarabochia suggest quite new methodologies that were developed in response to particular research goals, while Montes and Tusting and Cirio and Naftzinger ask us to reconsider and deepen the commonplace concepts in LWR of "transitions" and "memory." And again, many of these researchers reveal improvisation in action as methodologies shift in response to new contexts. Cain, Childers, and Ryan; Workman; Lunsford, Alexander, and Whithaus; and Tarabochia all demonstrate methods and methodologies evolving in quite surprising ways. Together, these authors establish new vistas from which future research can develop. These authors can help us improvise further in response to our research questions, our research sites, and the needs of the emerging research agenda that we call lifespan writing research.

LIFESPAN WRITING FUTURES

As we sit poised on the brink of our second decade in this absurd project called lifespan writing research, this collection—particularly the final chapters of Part II—challenges us to think about our future work in terms that aren't just methodologically and disciplinarily radical, but to also take a more explicit outward or even political focus. For all of our radicality, many chapters in Part II also point to an underlying conservatism in our collective work thus far. Aryal, Levine, Workman, Duffey, and Fulford and Rosenberg all challenge us to ask ourselves, *What are the larger policy implications of methodologies for our work?* And perhaps more pointedly, *Are the research and methodologies that we pursue positively impacting the material lives and emotional wellbeing of the writers and populations we research? What is the relationship between research and activism?* In the remainder of this concluding chapter, we consider these questions as both editors and as the co-chairs of the Writing Through the Lifespan Collaboration (http://lifespanwriting.org). We see the important issues raised in these final chapters as helping us to chart a course for the future of our collective work.

What are the larger policy implications of methodologies for our work?

To date, LWR has had little engagement with education and education policy. The original volume by the Lifespan Writing Development Group (Bazerman et al., 2018) thought through some policy problems in its formulation of guiding principles and offered a concluding chapter with suggested forms of development, variables, and dimensions of writing development that can guide education policy, as well as some starting points for lifespan writing researchers to begin engaging with education policy. Several years later, however, that branch of the lifespan writing research mission remains underdeveloped.

Levine's chapter offers a useful jump-start to this work. Levine notes the "unexamined assumptions about writers and their growth" (this volume) underpinning many school standards for writing, but also—and importantly—highlights that lifespan writing researchers need to attend carefully to the "legal, political, and organizational obligations of policy action" (this volume) that shapes school writing instruction. How might we attend to the legal, political, and organizational obligations of policy actions while, at the same time, advocating for the insights that our research is showing us—insights that may, in fact, challenge the nature and understandings of such obligations of policy action? What does such policy work look like for us as lifespan writing researchers?

As LWR moves into its second decade, we suggest that shaping education policy become a distinctive element of the work that we do. Some of our professional organizations already have major policy arms, including the National Council of Teachers of English and the National Writing Project. Joining with their existing policy work can help all involved in the policymaking around writing operate within a richer context of people's writing lives. For if legislators shared an understanding of transitions as rhizomatic (Montes & Tusting), how might that help them to abandon an obsession with unidirectional growth?

Or what might happen if policymakers entered the room not just with data from the latest standardized tests, but also with the writing trajectories of Gabby (Compton-Lilly), Adam, (Compton-Lilly), Chief and Gwen (Rosenberg, 2020; Fulford & Rosenberg), Adrienne (Fulford & Rosenberg), Kim (Duffey), and Don (Bowen, 2020)? The work of lifespan writing researchers has made clear that adults continue to develop new, successful literacy practices throughout adulthood and outside the context of formal schooling. Can seeing successful writing trajectories of older adults like Shirley and Kim lower the stakes (by which we mean the desire for unidirectional growth) within the K-12 system? Perhaps Chief's (Rosenberg, 2020) particular challenges with literacy learning and the poignant images of Compton-Lilly's students who are abused by notions of "educational rigor" might prod policymakers to see the consequences of narrow approaches to literacy development? Perhaps Kim, as Duffey suggests, might help us to reframe national conversations about schooling, completion, and "dropping out"? And perhaps composite narratives (Sanders et al.; DeFauw et al.) might be one way to scale up our individual research projects so that we could rigorously represent the experiences of more people more powerfully to legislators and policymakers.

But Levine's chapter also strongly suggests that making policymakers aware, for instance, of existing lifespan writing research will not be enough to generate structural change in national writing policy–that policymakers are predisposed to value particular kinds of methodological choices. Levine argues that if lifespan writing researchers want to see structural change, then we will have to give more attention to methodological design as we plan our studies–that we must design not just for ourselves, but also for our target audience. This would seem to call for the kind of methodological improvisation and innovation that many lifespan writing researchers have pioneered, perhaps by developing more mixed-methods, collaborative studies that use quantitative methods (Zajic & Poch) to generate the kinds of large data sets which are persuasive to policymakers but which are richly contextualized through, e.g., parallel case studies or focus groups. Jacques et al.'s comprehensive examination of longitudinal writing research helps to make the landscape of such collaborations more clear.

Are the Research and Methodologies That We Pursue Positively Impacting the Material Lives and Emotional Wellbeing of the Writers and Populations We Research?

Throughout this volume, we have seen deliberate care and attention taken to understand the lives of writers (see Duffey; Compton-Lilly; Fulford & Rosenberg; Aryal) as well as the lives of us as researchers (see Workman; Tarabochia).

These chapters help us to focus on both individuals and communities—in short, exactly who we're hoping to support in and through our research. Unlike the larger issues of policy that are traced in our first question, this question brings us to the level of the individual and the community. How might we explore the ways in which our research and methodologies are positively impacting the lives and emotional wellbeing of the writers and populations we're researching? As Aryal points out, these are important considerations for any researchers who seek to engage in decolonizing the processes of academic research and ensuring it benefits more than just researchers.

We can imagine exploring this question in several ways. First, we can think about—as Fulford and Rosenberg do—how we are positioning ourselves in relation to those we are studying/studying with. How we build that relationship, how that relationship shapes our research, and how it is articulated in the research we produce for publication are all important questions that several chapters in this volume can help us consider. Is there a way that we can build off of the language of Fulford and Rosenberg, the considerations identified by Aryal, the challenges set forth by Duffey, and Sanders et al.'s composite narratives to generate more shared language, policies, and approaches for working with and representing research participants in future lifespan-related work?

Second, we can imagine the consequences of publication for those we work with. How might participating in or being published about materially impact the lives of our research participants? How might we make the consequences of the research they participate in impactful beyond a gift card? How can we identify, document, and build on the positive impact that our work with people on their writing has on those people's lives? Fulford, Rosenberg, Long, and McGowan offer a powerful model for this. As Rosenberg's work continues to develop, she writes with McGowan about the events impacting McGowan's life and not only in service to Rosenberg's own project. Fulford and Long interpret data *together*, drawing on Long's particular knowledge. As these two projects continue to develop, we expect they will give other researchers additional insight into how co-authoring with former participants might be valued by the co-authors themselves.

Third, we can imagine the consequences of research on not just individuals, but the wider communities of language users that those individuals are part of. How might we be able to generate new insights that can be positively taken up by these communities—and, furthermore, how might we make sure that these positive take-ups can also benefit future research, making the work we do more generative for the future communities we work for and with?

Issues of race, racialization, and language resonate throughout this volume, most powerfully in the chapters by Compton-Lilly, Fulford and Rosenberg, Workman, Tarabochia, and Aryal. Additionally, the early work of the Lifespan

Writing Development Group (Bazerman et al., 2018) set the stage for a deliberate challenge to normative (and problematic) pathways of development in its statement of lifespan writing research principles. However, contemporary research on race and racism in writing, the teaching of writing, and policy/ies around writing remain under-addressed in our current conversations. Anti-racist research in writing studies has produced thoughtful challenges to the subtle ways in which writing, writing instruction, and writing assessment have been and remain racialized (e.g., Inoue, 2015) along with anti-racist methodological insights and approaches (e.g., Lockett, Ruiz, Sanchez & Carter, 2021; Aryal, this volume). How might lifespan writing researchers use these resources to question, unpack, and revise their methodological, theoretical, and philosophical assumptions about language and writing? What new methodologies may emerge? Furthermore, how might lifespan writing researchers invite anti-racist writing researchers into lifespan writing research projects?

Certainly, anti-racist, translingual, and de-colonial approaches are not the only ones that could benefit LWR: this radical research agenda has much growing to do and many more methods, methodologies, theories, and philosophies to explore in order to tackle the massive research object that is writing through the lifespan. Reading into, thinking about, and researching through such anti-racist approaches, however, can challenge lifespan writing researchers to explore new sites and methods, to question their assumptions, and, in the process, reach new vistas from which they can get a better glimpse of the complexity of writing through the lifespan.

WHAT IS THE RELATIONSHIP BETWEEN OUR RESEARCH AND ACTIVISM?

Since the inception of the Writing through the Lifespan Collaboration, our focus has been on research on building a body of work that we can use to better understand how writing works throughout the lifespan. We deliberately set aside activism, operating on the twin assumptions that (1) it's a little difficult to engage in activism through a lifespan lens if we don't yet know what we can see through that lens and (2) research can generate activism, or at least support current, ongoing activist efforts. Now that research is emerging on writing through the lifespan, and now that principles, methodologies, and lines of inquiry exist for us to pursue, we can begin to imagine the ways in which we might go about using LWR to both engage in new activism and further contribute to ongoing activist efforts.

Although the output of research on writing through the lifespan is still relatively small, there are sufficient findings we can point to so that we might begin that work. Bowen (2020) and Rosenberg (2015; 2020), for instance, help us to understand how we might understand the writing lives of older writers which could set the stage for engaging in activism to support older writers through university centers on aging or nonprofit activities. By drilling down into the material reality of literate acts through, for instance, Bowen's (2020) methodology of literacy tours, we can start to build understandings of the literate lives of older writers that can shape how these organizations advocate for them.

Activism based on LWR could also be used to support local efforts for literacy programs unrelated to schooling, such as reading and book groups, writing groups, and nonprofit literacy centers. Lifespan writing researchers can look from broader findings to specific applications that work for particular communities and bolster the visibility of those communities' literacy needs. We encourage lifespan writing researchers (and others, of course) to think about how such research could be used to productively engage with activist work.

LINES OF INQUIRY: BRINGING OUR THREADS TOGETHER

We find it difficult to conclude a volume that we have spent so much time imagining as a beginning: the beginning of a book series, new conversations about methodologies in lifespan writing research, renewed attention to a "big tent" vision for studying writing through the lifespan. The themes we traced in this chapter have provided us with some avenues for moving forward in the coming years. As the project of LWR moves forward, we can ask ourselves how these themes can intertwine. How might the lines of inquiry we pursue inform our engagement with educational policy? How might transformed understandings of the relationship between race and language also transform our research methods, sites, and conclusions? And how might we be able to draw on our policy work, our research, and our understandings of race and language to engage in more visible activism that benefits our co-researchers and research participants?

In the conclusion to our previous volume (Dippre & Phillips, 2020) and elsewhere (Dippre & Phillips, 2023) we suggested lines of inquiry as a way for researchers to come together to investigate writing through the lifespan in a coordinated manner. We suggested some potential lines of inquiry that might allow for the coordinated study of writing via different methodological and theoretical approaches at different points in the lifespan as a starting point:

- Agency
- Context
- Identity
- Semiosis

These lines of inquiry can serve as the starting point for developing shared research initiatives across methods, methodologies, theories, and research sites. This current volume offers a range of methodologies for studying writing through the lifespan, and that might productively be aligned and improvised by different researchers at different research sites to pursue, through funded research, these and other lines of inquiry.

Much like our suggested lines of inquiry, though, the methodologies present in this volume are just the tip of the iceberg: there are a range of approaches that this volume does not address and that can be valuable for lifespan writing researchers to pursue. Even the chapters of Part II, which offer a collection of "Ands," just begin to uncover the variety of options lifespan writing researchers can have at their disposal. We suggest, then, that lifespan writing researchers use the lines of inquiry presented in our earlier work, along with the methodologies presented here, not as the totality but as the start of assembling research teams, applying for grants, and conducting methodologically innovative and diverse studies of writing through the lifespan.

These lines of inquiry can also help us to think through the implications of our work in a broader context. How can we use productive methodological overlaps and divergences to help us critique, expand, and revise our approaches to studying writing through the lifespan? How might, say, agency look different to grounded theory (Dippre), or temporal discourse analysis (Compton-Lilly), and what might we learn about not just our approaches but our understanding of agency by bringing the two together? Furthermore, how might these understandings shape our relationships with our participants, as well as our engagement with larger communities of language users? As the Writing Through the Lifespan Collaboration nears its tenth anniversary, we hope that these lines of inquiry will provide us with powerful and thought-provoking paths forward for not just research, but also activism and education policy.

We close this text by returning to the title: *improvisations*. The deep, multi-disciplinary knowledge that gets coordinated through lines of inquiry allows us to improvise–meaningfully, rigorously, and radically–not just with our methods and methodologies, but with education policy, activism, and our engagement with the richly literate lives of the populations we work with. Among many other things, we hope that this book has encouraged researchers—especially novice researchers—to recognize that pursuing writing research throughout the lifespan is engaging, important work, while also making clear that rigorous improvisation is an important part of many research projects. The people we research change, as do their contexts. In many cases our methods must also change in response. Yet, as novice researchers, we often are afraid of making changes to our research methods, afraid of backlash from IRBs or dissertation committee members. We hope that our contributors have made clear that some level of improvisation is part of the work and that they have empowered you to advocate for the methods that will best suit your research aims and the people you study. *Yes, and. . . .*

REFERENCES

Bazerman, C. (2018). Lifespan longitudinal studies of writing development: A heuristic for an impossible dream. In C. Bazerman, A. N. Applebee, V. W. Berninger, D. Brandt, S. Graham, J. V. Jeffery, P. K. Matsuda, S. Murphy, D. W. Rowe, M. Schleppegrell & K. C. Wilcox (Eds.), *The lifespan development of writing* (pp. 326–365). National Council of Teachers of English.

Bowen, L. (2020). Literacy tours and material matters: Principles for studying the literate lives of older adults. In R. J. Dippre & T. Phillips (Eds.), Approaches to lifespan writing research: Generating an actionable coherence (pp. 111–125). The WAC Clearinghouse; University Press of Colorado. https://doi.org/10.37514/PER-B.2020.1053.2.07.

Dippre, R. J. & Phillips, T. (2023). Radically longitudinal, radically contextual: The lifespan as a focus for longitudinal writing research. In J. Fishman & A. K. Hea (Eds.), *Telling stories: Perspectives on longitudinal writing research.* (pp. 150–189). Utah State University Press.

Dippre, R. J. & Phillips, T. (Eds.). (2020). *Approaches to lifespan writing research: Generating an actionable coherence*. The WAC Clearinghouse; University Press of Colorado. https://doi.org/10.37514/PER-B.2020.1053.2.07.

Inoue, A. B. (2015). *Antiracist writing assessment ecologies: Teaching and assessing writing for a socially just future*. The WAC Clearinghouse; University Press of Colorado. https://doi.org/10.37514/PER-B.2015.0698.

Lockett, A., Ruiz, D., Sanchez, J. C. & Carter, C. (2021). Race, rhetoric, and research methods. The WAC Clearinghouse; University Press of Colorado. https://doi.org/10.37514/PER-B.2021.1206.

Rosenberg, L. (2015). *The desire for literacy: Writing in the lives of adult learners*. National Council of Teachers of English.

Rosenberg, L. (2020). Revisiting participants after publication: Continuing writing partnerships. In R. J. Dippre & T. Phillips (Eds.), *Approaches to lifespan writing research: Generating an actionable coherence* (pp. 97–110). The WAC Clearinghouse; University Press of Colorado. https://doi.org/10.37514/PER-B.2020.1053.2.06.

CONTRIBUTORS

Jonathan Alexander is Chancellor's Professor of English at the University of California, Irvine. He is the author, co-author, or co-editor of twenty-two books in the fields of rhetoric, writing studies, popular culture, and life writing.

Bhushan Aryal is Assistant Professor of English at Delaware State University where he directs the university's Composition and Speech Program. From western Nepal, his research interests converge at the intersection of composition curriculum at HBCUs, digital writing, WAC, South Asian/American rhetoric, and constitutional rhetoric.

Kathleen Shine Cain, retired English Department Chair and Writing Center Director from Merrimack College, also taught at St. Mary's University College in Belfast, Northern Ireland. Active in regional, national, and international conferences, she has published articles, reviews, and textbooks, and has won several teaching and professional awards.

Pamela B. Childers, Caldwell Chair of Composition Emerita from McCallie School, directed the Writing Center and the WAC program and also taught university graduate courses. Recipient of the IWCA Scholarship and Outstanding Service awards and Distinguished Fellow of AWAC, she has authored hundreds of essays, articles, columns, chapters, and four professional books.

Joe Cirio is Assistant Professor of writing and first-year studies and convenor for the WAC program at Stockton University in Galloway, NJ. He teaches courses on rhetorical memory, professional writing and design, and the rhetorical construction of difference. His research often focuses on the material impacts of vernacular writing practices.

Catherine Compton-Lilly is the John C. Hungerpiller Professor at the University of South Carolina. In a current study, she is exploring the longitudinal school experiences of children from immigrant families. She has authored several books and scholarly articles. Her interests include examining time as a contextual factor in children's lives.

Danielle L. DeFauw is Professor of Reading and Language Arts in the College of Education, Health, and Human Services at the University of Michigan–Dearborn. In 2020, she authored *Engaging Teachers, Students, and Families in K–6 Writing Instruction*. Her research interests focus on pedagogical content knowledge of writing.

Ryan J. Dippre is Associate Professor of English and Director of Composition at the University of Maine. He is the author of *Talk, Tools, and Texts* (WAC Clearinghouse) and co-editor of *Approaches to Lifespan Writing Research*. With

Talinn Phillips, he is co-chair of the Writing through the Lifespan Collaboration (www.lifespanwriting.org).

Sarah J. Donovan is Assistant Professor of Secondary English Education at Oklahoma State University. Her expertise lies in ethical curriculum, methods, and assessment in secondary English classrooms. Her research can be found in *English Journal* and *Research in the Teaching of English* among other books and journals in teacher education.

Suellynn Duffey chairs the Department of English at the University of Missouri, St. Louis. She has published on serendipity in women's professional lives, silence and listening, writing program administration, basic writing, and place. She came to LWR shortly pre-pandemic and finds its work and community among the most exciting in writing studies.

Collie Fulford is Associate Professor of English at the University at Buffalo. Her publications on writers and writing programs can be found in *Pedagogy*, *WPA: Writing Program Administration*, *Composition Studies*, and *Across the Disciplines*.

Teresa Jacques is a Ph.D. candidate at the Center for Psychology of the University of Porto where she earned an MS in psychology, specializing in clinical and health psychology. Her research interests include language, writing, cognition, and emotion. She has been a member of the European Literacy Network since 2016.

Jeremy Levine is Assistant Teaching Professor in the Writing Program at Wake Forest University. He teaches writing courses focused on the rules and politics of schooling. His research explores the intersections of writing development, education policy, and equity.

Adrienne Long holds a bachelor's degree in psychology from North Carolina Central University where she founded the Adult Learners Student Organization and served as its president.

Karen Lunsford is Associate Professor of Writing and Director of the Writing Program at the University of California, Santa Barbara. Her research areas include writing in the disciplines (WID), science communication, intellectual property, and research ethics.

Jonathan M. Marine is a Ph.D. candidate in Writing and Rhetoric at George Mason University. His research interests include content analysis, writing engagement, longitudinal writing development, the scholarship of James Moffett, and the rhetoric of graffiti. He holds an MA in Literature, a BS in English, and a BA in Psychology.

Gwen Porter McGowan is an avid writer, reader, and community activist. She is an advocate for disability justice and transportation for the elderly. Gwen has a leadership role in many civic and religious organizations. She is involved in ongoing work on her writing experiences with Lauren Rosenberg.

Soledad Montes is a researcher and editor who investigates writing across the curriculum, literacy as social practice, and writing in transitions. She is currently the editor for the Latin American Section of the WAC Clearinghouse International Exchanges book series and a doctoral researcher at the Department of Linguistics and English Language, Lancaster University, UK.

Joy Myers is Executive Director of James Madison University's Grow Your Own Initiatives. As a former classroom teacher, Joy is dedicated to teacher education. In addition to presenting at conferences, her research can be found in journals such as *Teaching Education Quarterly* and the *Journal of Teacher Education*.

Jeff Naftzinger is Assistant Professor of Rhetoric, Composition & Writing at Sacred Heart University in Fairfield, Connecticut. He teaches courses on digital writing and rhetoric, everyday writing, and first-year writing. His research focuses on illustrating everyday writing and supporting digital pedagogies.

Talinn Phillips is Professor of English at Ohio University in Athens, Ohio where she teaches graduate courses in Rhetoric and Composition and undergraduate writing courses. With Ryan Dippre, she is co-chair of the Writing Through the Lifespan Collaboration.

Apryl Lynn Poch is Assistant Professor in the Department of Special Education and Communication Disorders at the University of Nebraska at Omaha. Her work focuses on supporting the written expression needs of adolescents with learning disabilities, as well as students' and teachers' knowledge of and beliefs about writing.

Paul Rogers is Associate Professor of Writing Studies at the University of California, Santa Barbara. He is the former Director of the Northern Virginia Writing Project, a co-founder of the International Society for the Advancement of Writing Research, and a co-editor of eight collections of research on writing.

Lauren Rosenberg is Associate Professor of Rhetoric and Writing Studies at the University of Texas at El Paso. She is author of *The Desire for Literacy* and numerous other publications, including the co-authored (with Stephanie Kerschbaum) "Entanglements of Literacy Studies and Disability Studies," the recipient of the *College English* Ohmann award.

Leigh Ryan is Writing Center Director Emerita at the University of Maryland (UMD), where she directed the Writing Center and the Academic Writing Program. She served in leadership positions and received outstanding service awards from UMD and various writing center associations and has published and consulted nationally and internationally.

Jennifer Sanders is Professor of Literacy Education at Oklahoma State University. Her research explores K-12 writing pedagogies, writing teachers' professional learning, and inclusive representations in children's and YA literature.

Her publications include *They're All Writers!* (Sanders & Damron, 2017), and *Literacies, the Arts, and Multimodality* (Albers & Sanders, 2010).

Sandra L. Tarabochia is Associate Professor of English at the University of Oklahoma. Scholarship based on her longitudinal study of faculty writers can be found in *Writing & Pedagogy, Composition Forum, Composition Studies, Written Communication,* and *Peitho*. She is a founding co-editor of the open-access journal *Writers: Craft & Context*.

Karin Tusting is Professor in the Department of Linguistics and English Language, Lancaster University, UK. She researches literacies particularly in workplace contexts, using new literacy studies and linguistic ethnography. Recent publications include *Academics Writing* (Routledge, with McCulloch, Bhatt, Hamilton, and Barton) and *The Routledge Handbook of Linguistic Ethnography* (editor).

Carl Whithaus is Professor of Writing and Rhetoric at the University of California, Davis. His research areas include the impact of information technology on literacy practices, writing assessment, and writing in the sciences and engineering.

Erin Workman is Associate Professor of Writing, Rhetoric & Discourse and Director of First-Year Writing at DePaul University. She researches lifespan writing development using methodologies that center positionality and lived experience. Her work has appeared in *WAC Journal, College Composition and Communication, Composition Forum,* and *Approaches to Lifespan Writing Research*.

Matthew Carl Zajic is Assistant Professor of Intellectual Disability/Autism in the Health Studies and Applied Educational Psychology Department at Teachers College, Columbia University. His research aims to understand and support autistic individuals' writing development. He has published in various journals and is on the editorial board of *Journal of Educational Psychology*.

www.ingramcontent.com/pod-product-compliance
Lightning Source LLC
Chambersburg PA
CBHW060547080526
44585CB00013B/472